TREK

My Peace Pilgrimage in Search of a Kinder America

A Memoir by Rand Bishop

WEIGHTLESS CARGO PRESS

ALSO BY RAND BISHOP

My List: 24 Reflections on Life's Priorities
(McGraw Hill)

*Makin' Stuff Up: Secrets of Song-Craft and
Survival in the Music Biz*
(Weightless Cargo Press)

The Absolute Essentials of Songwriting Success
(Albert Music Publishing)

Grand Pop
(Eloquent Books)

TREK: My Peace Pilgrimage in Search of a Kinder America

Copyright © 2019 by Rand Bishop

For information: www.RandBishopTrek.com

---

*Identifiers: LCCN 2019905734 | ISBN 13 978-1-7330299-0-2
(paperback)*

*First Edition. Bishop, Norman Randolph, author/publisher
DBA Weightless Cargo Press [2019]*

*Editors, Carla Perry, Mike Kloeck
Cover and Book Design by Kristi Ryder*

For Sebra

In memory of
Lisa-Catherine Cohen
Kate Cunningham
Duane DeVries
and
Christine Grace

Foreword

☮ ☮ ☮

*T*REK is the vivid, compelling journal of Rand Bishop's 900-mile walk for peace. What pressed him to undertake this journey was his sense of a "climate of meanness" taking hold in our country, and his need to do something about it.

But what?

The answer that came surprised him: *Walk. Walk for peace.*

Rand happened upon the story of Peace Pilgrim, a middle-aged woman who walked the roads of North America for 28 years. She vowed, "I will walk until given shelter and fast until given food, remaining a wanderer until humankind has learned the way of peace." It was her story that spoke to him: Walk. Walk for peace. And he answered,

I can walk. I can play guitar. And, I can sing.
So, that's what I'll do.

The author's trek began in Thousand Oaks, California, on May 1, 2017. The plan was to walk north to the central coast of Oregon. With him, was his dog, Millie, and the "Pilgrimmobile" — a cart carrying his tent, bedroll, guitar, water, power bars, and a banner declaring: Peace Pilgrim 2017.

Rand and I became friends at a summer camp teaching non-violence to children. When he told me he was going on a 90-day walk for peace, I expressed my admiration for his courage and commitment. But what impressed me most was his approach. He was going "in search of a kinder America." He would listen to the people he met on the way, especially those whose opinions differed from his own. He would…

…make a genuine effort to locate a few square inches of common ground.

As I read **TREK**, I became mindful of the countless pilgrims throughout history who stepped out of their daily lives to encounter the mystery at the center of their lives. I thought of Hindus going to the Ganges River to bathe in its sacred waters, Buddhists sitting under the Bodhi tree, Jews standing at the "wailing" Wall in the Old City of Jerusalem, Christians walking to Santiago de Compostela or the healing shrine at Lourdes, and Muslims traveling to Mecca.

Rand Bishop is a well-known, Nashville singer-songwriter. He has the gifts — the heart, honesty, poetry, eye — to help us see what he sees. He made it easy for me to walk in his shoes.

In almost every campground, the first bustlings of awakeness are similar: kindling crackling in a newly lit fire, the spout of an empty teakettle bumping against the spigot of a water faucet, footsteps treading across dirt and gravel, coughs, yawns, clearing throats, and the low murmurings of conversation. It's early, just past 6AM…

Bishop describes: a furious driver who spit in his face on a deserted country road, a woman who stopped to tell him about having met and befriended Peace Pilgrim in the 1970's, and a homeless man behind a California mall on a hot summer afternoon who handed Rand a popsicle from his precious supply.

A Pilgrim's emotional journey is as dynamic and ever-changing as the path he travels.

There were days when Rand's toes bled, tent leaked, the wheel fell off the "Pilgrimmobile," and no one looked up when he offered to sing a song. Days when he doubted himself, doubted the worth of his walk, doubted he could step onto the road the next morning. But a pilgrimage is not about going from south to north, or east to west. It is about arriving at the ultimate destination — within.

> I'm doing it first and foremost to prove to myself I can do it, and to fully immerse myself in whatever happens...

One of my favorite moments in **TREK** is his recounting of a woman who hurried across the road and said, "Are you really a Peace Pilgrim? Nobody talks about peace anymore." Spontaneous words, but they express, I believe, the dismay so many of us feel. How did we, children of the 60's, become so accepting of war? How did our passion for peace become so tame?

I felt relief anytime our pilgrim left the hot city streets and crowded highways for the quiet coastal roads and ocean breezes. And I appreciated his description of those moments.

> There are degrees of quiet, not unlike shades of color.

In a single morning, the author encountered a cab driver from Afghanistan, another from Samoa, two welders from Korea and Fiji, a waitress from Mexico, and a motel owner from India. He found our nation diverse and alive. And he found, not always, but mostly, welcoming folks who offered directions or rides or hospitality. He found "a kinder America."

> The greatest fulfillment from trekking those 900 miles came from the extraordinary opportunity to connect with a thousand decent Americans... Those encounters rekindled my faith...in the innate goodness of humankind.

Rand's pilgrimage ended on a July afternoon at the Peace Village camp in Lincoln City, Oregon. Waiting on the campground was a circle of 50 children, in blue T-shirts with the logo: Teach Peace.

As he walked the last steps of his journey, the children welcomed him with a song he had written for them, "Powerful Enough."

I am powerful enough to make a choice
I will always listen to my inner voice

…I am powerful enough to stand up for peace and love
I am powerful enough to take a stand

Rand Bishop walked and found a kinder nation, and his own peace. Page by page, he brings us with him on the **TREK**. But be careful. Pilgrim stories have a way of speaking. You may hear: Walk. Walk for peace.

Charles P. Busch

Director, Fields of Peace
Eugene, Oregon, 2019

TREK

My Peace Pilgrimage in
Search of a Kinder America

Preface

✦ ✦ ✦

On April 24, 2017, accompanied by my intrepid beagle, Millie, I left the comforts of my modest-but-cozy, two-bedroom apartment in Newport, Oregon, and its panoramic view of the Pacific Ocean to drive to Los Angeles in a rented Nissan Versa hatchback. The following Monday morning, May 1st, to be exact, after returning the little import to the Enterprise office in Thousand Oaks, California, I attached my dog's leash to the belt of my belly bag with a carabiner and started walking home.

No one forced me to do this, a fact I found necessary to remind myself of frequently over the course of the ensuing three months. This wasn't some form of penance or atonement. I wasn't serving a 90-day sentence of pavement walking. I hadn't accepted a dare, nor was I attempting to win some capricious bet. Being, supposedly, of sound mind, I willingly made the choice to walk 900 miles, from Southern California to the Central Oregon Coast.

Why, one might reasonably wonder, would a 67-year-old, semi-retired writer/musician, with a history of chronic knee and foot problems, minimal camping experience, and nary a clue about long-distance hiking, decide to challenge himself in this way? In one iteration or another, this is a question with which I was confronted at least once, often several times a day over that remarkable spring and summer. Admittedly, my earliest responses were unprepared, vague at best, and sometimes even inarticulate — for good reason. Although the anxiety, the disillusionment, and the heart-sickness that led me to commit to this quest were painfully clear to me, exactly why I had settled on such an unlikely means of expressing my mounting frustration, and what I actually hoped to accomplish, were not quite so clear.

Understandably, my inability to provide adequate explanation for what seemed to certain worried friends and family members quixotic at best served to exacerbate their concerns. Several, in fact, felt no qualms about informing and/or reminding me at every opportunity exactly how ill-advised and risky they considered my plan. Still, with their well-meaning trepidations echoing in my head, and still without distinct justification for my impulse, I remained undeterred.

So, as I trekked northward, I found myself responding time after time to one version or another of… *Why are you doing this?* As they say, practice makes perfect. Thus, this repetitive query helped me solidify in my own mind precisely why I'd chosen to tackle such an arduous venture. The words naturally followed and, eventually, I had my 30-second "elevator speech" down pat.

It usually began something like this: "Well, last fall, after the election, I just felt like this country was getting so mean…" No matter how many times I said it — over the entire 90 days I spent traveling the roads of California and Oregon on foot — not a single person ever took issue with this statement. Every bicyclist, every camp host, every shopkeeper, every curious motorist, expressed some level of agreement, if not in words, with a telling glance, a wry grimace, and/or a tilted nod of the head. One young, hard-hatted laborer took a momentary break from his job restoring a historic bridge to grasp my hand in a vise-grip and work my forearm like a pump handle. "I totally support your cause, Brother!" he effused.

I would invariably postscript my spiel with some version of, "So, I'm just trying to encourage people to cool it with the blame game, stop all the name calling, and engage in civil, constructive dialogue." And, to that, most every person would demonstrate some form of sincere appreciation. Many, in fact, expressed admiration, and more than a few thanked me for spreading the peace. Some even went so far as to confess envy, wishing that they, too, could muster my level of pluck and stick-to-it-iveness. The most cynical response I ever got was, "Well, good luck with that!" And, even that sardonic quip didn't challenge the idea that we should strive to soften the tone in this nation, acknowledge one another, show some respect, do more listening, and make a genuine effort to locate a few square inches of common ground.

I knew this trek would be a test of stamina and will, that I would have to drill down deep to find heretofore untapped strength and resolve. Too, I expected to suffer some very real physical pain. At journey's end, I can check all those boxes. I also dared to envision myself as a sort of restorative force, inspiring people to shed their biases, helping them open their hearts and minds, and encouraging them to work together toward solving a plethora of shared, yet too-long-neglected problems. While, in some small part, my pilgrimage may have had a healing, perhaps even inspiring effect on others — whether for the moment, or for the longer run — at the end of the trail, the life most positively affected was that of the pilgrim himself.

The official, original stated intent of my 90-day peace pilgrimage was: *To inspire civil, constructive dialogue in this deeply divided nation.* However, I must admit to having another motive as well — a simpler, more personal motive, maybe even a somewhat selfish one. In this bitterly divisive and contentious period in our nation's history, amid an uncivil war of spiteful words and actions, I needed to know there were still nice people out there in the world. I was searching for a kinder America.

CHAPTER 1

The Fretting Hours

I couldn't sleep. That's pretty much how all this craziness started. Well, let me take that back. I could get to sleep, initially, without much problem — for three, maybe four hours. I just couldn't stay there. And, once I woke up, which happened nearly every night for several years, I was helpless to return to sleep.

On a normal night, this would usually take place between 3:30 and 5 AM. Mischievous fireflies of worry would flit past the invisible border between my subconscious and conscious mind. Soon, I'd be lying there wide-awake, my head plagued with addled, frenzied thoughts. This maddening conspiracy to cat burgle my slumber usually lasted about 90 minutes, until I could finally draw in and release a few consecutive, deep, cleansing breaths to soothe and quiet my angst, calm my heartbeat, and drift off again to catch another 40 winks. Eventually, I attached a name to these periods of anxious insomnia. I christened them *The Fretting Hours*.

So, what concerns could possibly have been so dire, so urgent, as to revisit my bedroom night after night, shake me awake, and get me tossing, turning, scratching, and fretting in the darkness? Well, I wasn't worrying about my often-iffy finances, or revisiting relationship regrets, nor was I agonizing over my aging parents' health issues. I wasn't obsessing over my children's circumstances, or my grandchildren's futures. Well, let me take that back. My kids and grandkids actually did figure into my chronic sleeplessness — but only indirectly.

The obsession that so rudely and so routinely robbed me of all those hours of rest was this: the hyper-partisan vitriol, the blaming, the name-calling that has been polluting the political atmosphere of this country for decades. Night after night, I puzzled… *How, in this toxic environment, could we ever address the many serious issues we face as a nation, let alone go about finding solutions?* Climate change, student debt, gun violence, mass incarceration, income inequality, institutional racism, homelessness, a crumbling infrastructure, gerrymandering, voter suppression. These were just a few of the ghosts haunting me in the middle of the night. If Congress didn't grow up, if they didn't stop their childish bickering and start doing some real problem solving, and fast, what quality of life would be left for my grandchildren?

I thought we'd hit rock bottom. But, *surprise*! Just when I assumed the prevailing tone in this country couldn't possibly get any more dissonant, along came a two-year primary- and election-campaign brawl that somehow managed to sink us even deeper into the muck. By polling day, November 2016, America had cranked the mean knob up to 11. Certainly, our republic has suffered through its periodic, historical growing pains. And yet, some way, somehow, we've always managed to weather the turmoil, all the while evolving into a beautiful-but-messy, multi-cultural gumbo. Now, however, we seemed to be devolving into an unkind, cowardly nation of lazy-headed blamers, whiners, and name-callers. It was breaking my heart. I couldn't just sit idly by while this country, *my* country, became something I no longer recognized.

But what could I possibly do about it? Sure, I could blog till my fingers fell off. But that would just make me one more deeply concerned American, hiding behind a laptop, typing and posting his observations and opinions and, ultimately, preaching to the choir. So, what other truly meaningful action could I take? Well, I said to myself… *I can walk. I can play the guitar. And, I can sing. So, that's what I'll do.* But, there are a lot of singer-songwriters out there with a message, seeking an audience. So, in order to get anybody's attention, in order to make a truly meaningful statement, the walking part had to be of significant length. I was going to have to make a substantial, impressive commitment, a real, personal sacrifice.

I began envisioning myself walking the entire length of High-way 101, a distance of more than 1,500 miles, with Millie, my nine-year-old beagle. This route, from Southern California, through Oregon and Washington, seemed symbolic. After the aforemen-tioned election debacle, a majority of us here in the Pacific States suddenly found ourselves completely out of step with much of the rest of the nation — so far out of step that, thanks to the antiquated Electoral College, our votes didn't figure in the national results. We sit perennially on the cutting edge of culture and technology. We headquarter six out of the top-10 market-cap companies. Still, our states had suddenly been ostracized, ripped from the U.S. map, and relegated to outlier status.

At first, I kept this scheme to myself. I knew, as soon as I actually told someone, it would become real, and I would actu-ally have to go through with it. After a few weeks of rumination, I realized, if I didn't let the feline out of the gunnysack, I would ultimately chicken out, which would leave me even more frus-trated and heartsick, still deeply disillusioned over the sorry state of the nation, unable to sleep, and flagellating myself for my own spinelessness. I can't remember who I told first. What I do recall is that I surprised myself by announcing my intent with absolute conviction. Saying it out loud for the second time, meant there was no turning back. The walk was on.

Folks would often ask how long this holy march would take. My guesstimation of 70-to-80 days was based on the now-laughable assumption that I am capable of walking 20 miles per day, seven days per week. Had I based this presumption on any research, or the most rudimentary knowledge about long-distance hiking, or even an accurate gauge of my typical walking speed? Absolutely not! Finally, for my own information, I bought a pedometer. *Ha!* At my pace, 20-mile days would be impossible. Twelve to 15 miles per day would be far more realistic. It didn't occur to me to bone up on the experiences of long-distance hiking experts and benefit from their advice. That's not my style. My inclination is to make a gut-level decision and go for it, without bothering to get all the details.

*EMBARKING UPON THIS trek would not be the first and only
impulsive, bullheaded, shoot-from-the-hip decision I've
made over the course of my lifetime. I've leapt at marriages,
relocated from one end of the continent to the other, and
taken a number of abrupt career U-turns — all based on
that same, primal, gut instinct. Some of these moves were
questionable at best. Do I harbor regrets? Well, let's just say
I prefer not to dwell on mistakes of the past.*

*"If you're around for a while, first of all, you're lucky as shit.
And, second of all, you're gonna have some regrets."*
— HOLLY HUNTER

As I began preparations for my walk, it was already occurring
to me that I might very possibly be — even now, at the supposedly
wizened age of 67 — about to add yet another entry, perhaps even
the final entry, to an already lengthy menu of dubious actions. These
reflections of self-doubt would revisit me daily over the course of
the next several months.

As obligations limited the amount of time I could dedicate
to this mission, the more-accurate information provided by my
new pedometer forced me to recalculate my mileage goals. There
was another factor as well. My move to Newport from Nashville,
almost five years earlier, was for the primary purpose of being
nearby and available to assist my aging parents. I needed to insure
they, as they approached 90 and 91, would have adequate supervision and support. Those factors, plus my desire to stick around
for my mother's 90th on April 10th, led me to set a departure date
of April 15, 2017, Tax Day — symbolic for obvious reasons. My
recalibrated, more realistic goal: to walk 1,000 miles, departing
from Thousand Oaks, California, and ending in Astoria, Oregon,
on the border of Washington State.

CHAPTER 2

A Walk Becomes a Pilgrimage

The next several months were consumed by preparation. I was still visited every night by those unrelenting fretting hours. However, the trepidations that got me flailing and vexing no longer concerned the troubled state of the nation. Instead, they obsessed over the endless details of my upcoming trek. How would I carry my guitar, camping equipment, clothing for every kind of weather, and dog food? What kind of tent, sleeping bag, and ground pad would be light and compact enough? What were the best shoes and arch supports for a hiker who suffers from metatarsalgia and arthritic big toes? What was the most nutritious, yet readily available dog food that could be purchased in smaller, tote-able amounts?

With Social Security as my only regular, reliable monthly source of income and my sporadic music royalties down to a trickle, how could I possibly afford to hit the road for three months and cover my travel expenses, while paying rent for a vacant apartment, auto and health insurance, and utilities at home? I'd never tried crowd-funding before. I recoil at the very concept of asking — i.e. begging — for money. However, several friends and acquaintances, including my brother Greg, had successfully funded creative projects this way. After some pride swallowing, I concluded that crowd-funding was worth a try. Maybe, I rationalized, friends and family would even welcome the opportunity to contribute to my quest.

Setting up the online solicitation page, creating the graphics, authoring the fund-raising pitch, and producing a promotional

YouTube video made for a truly comprehensive set of tasks. Every hour of every day was filled with intense, focused resolve, as the strategically chosen launch date for my crowd-source campaign approached. On January 19th, the day before Donald J. Trump was to place his hand on the *Holy Bible* to take the oath of office, I sent out a mass email encouraging recipients to click a link and make a contribution. The text of the email began…

> TOMORROW, BIGOTS MOVE into the West Wing and white nationalism officially becomes mainstream. The nation that once held a lamp at its gate for "the huddled masses yearning to breathe free" will instruct Lady Liberty to hoist a club in her fist and shout, "Don't even think about it!" The nation that put men on the moon will scoff at science and let short-term corporate profits determine what is or isn't fact. Women's reproductive choice, LGBTQ rights, religious liberty, and freedom of speech will be in serious jeopardy.

The strident, self-righteous tone of this opening salvo provides admission that I have not always been a practitioner of the kind of civility I now believe is absolutely essential if we ever hope to heal the division in this troubled nation. For years, I'd been losing sleep over the paralyzing gridlock in our government, and condemning our political leaders for perpetuating it. Looking back, it seems I was just as guilty of perpetrating "us-against-them-ism" as they were.

Still, financial contributions immediately began flowing in — from expected, as well as some very surprising sources. I was thrilled. Knowing that healthy feet would be essential to the success of my trek, my first investment was a pair of top-of-the-line, lifetime-guaranteed inserts from the Good Feet Store. At REI, a very helpful young sales associate fitted me — yes, actually *fitted* me — with a backpack. When I got home, I realized I had no clue how to pack the dang thing or even what I should put in it. Fortunately, several experienced outdoor enthusiasts had been generous enough to share their pack-stuffing techniques on YouTube.

I spent hours every day online reading customer reviews. Amazon shipments arrived daily: trekking poles, rain gators, a collapsible, fabric dog crate. My third-floor walk-up had become a regular stop on the UPS route, with deliveries to Apartment 13 giving the ultra-fit fellow in the brown shorts a supplemental aerobic workout. Every other day, I'd answer the door to find Mark the Mailman grimacing and gasping for breath. After handing me yet another package, he would gimp back down the steep stairs on aching knees and a strained hamstring.

On January 21st, the day after the Presidential inauguration, I was among 1,800 people who took to the Newport streets to express solidarity with the massive Women's March in Washington D.C. After the demonstration, I took my friend Charles Busch to lunch.

"So," Charles noted, grinning between bites of grilled cheese, "you're going on a pilgrimage." A retired Congregational minister, Charles is the visionary founder of Peace Village, an Oregon-based nonprofit dedicated to teaching grade-school-age children the skills of conflict resolution. The word "pilgrimage" seemed more than a bit pretentious. Still, out of respect for Charles, I refrained from saying so and kept listening.

"Are you familiar with Peace Pilgrim?" he asked. Admittedly, I wasn't. But Charles had piqued my interest. I would soon find out much about New Jersey woman, Mildred Lisette Newman, who, in 1953, set out to walk 10,000 miles for peace and kept walking for 28 years. After viewing a documentary film entitled, *An American Sage*, and listening to some of her lectures, this laudable, under-recognized American peace hero quickly became one of my primary inspirations and a worthy role model. My newfound admiration for Peace Pilgrim and her important and noble sacrifice gave me a fresh perspective. I began reconsidering the entire focus of my mission. Peace Pilgrim's philosophy was simple… *"Overcome evil with good, and falsehood with truth, and hatred with love."*

At first blush, this axiom might seem banal and more than a bit naïve. But somehow, without so much as a penny in her pocket, carrying nothing but the clothing on her back and a smile on her face, this woman walked on behalf of peace for nearly three decades and well over 30,000 miles, accepting only food, drink, and/or shelter when it was offered. If, at the completion of her sojourn, she was still able to look at the world through a Pollyanna prism, her credo, as unsophisticated as it may sound, must contain more than a wisp of merit.

Certainly, one might argue that it was a very different America, a less complex America, a safer America in 1953, when Peace Pilgrim took to its roads on foot. Still, at the outset of her quest, she was a single woman of 45, during an era when the fairer gender either stayed home to keep house and raise a brood, or took the only jobs available — as teachers, librarians, nurses, or secretaries. Meanwhile, Senator Joseph McCarthy and the House Committee on Un-American Activities were taking their un-American witch-hunt to unprecedented lows, the Cold War was heating up, the generation gap was widening, and we were witnessing the first evidences of environmental catastrophe.

As her walk continued through the wild and turbulent sixties, descendants of slaves struggled for civil rights, assassins' bullets slaughtered one leader after another, a youth revolution popped/snorted/smoked consciousness-expanding substances and embraced free love, and the U.S. got itself entangled in another foreign civil war. Peace Pilgrim marched on into the seventies through a nation fiercely divided over Vietnam, where struggles for women's lib and LGBT rights were met head-on by a formidable Christian-conservative backlash, scandal led to the humiliating resignation of one president, and gas shortages, inflation, high interest rates, and unemployment abbreviated the tenure of another.

By the time of Peace Pilgrim's death in 1981, at the age of 72, the world's two great superpowers were bolstering their nuclear arsenals at a frightening rate. Peace — i.e. the very survival of humanity — was totally dependent on the constant, bone-chilling awareness that, should either side dare to use even one of these weapons, the result would be mutual assured destruction. Still, having hiked cheerfully through these dissonant decades, Peace Pilgrim still maintained, "The way of peace is the way of love. Love is the greatest power on earth. It conquers all things."

With nations aiming warheads at one another and culture wars raging, Peace Pilgrim still believed that, through the power of love, mankind could achieve peace. Was she gazing out from the edges of America's byways through an invisible pair of peace-colored glasses? If so, where, I wondered, could I pick up some of those magical specs? Was she able to discern something in the human spirit that, even against a backdrop of unremitting discord, assured her that good could, and actually *would*, overcome evil, that truth — especially her rosy version of it — would ultimately prevail? If so, that was the spirit *I* longed to discover — especially now, at this tempestuous, combative crux in human history.

I was not born with the natural inclination to skip down the sunny side of the street. My mother's stoic, Finnish blood runs thick in my veins and, for my entire adulthood, I've wrestled with clinical depression. Approaching my forties and starving for spiritual connection, I was drawn to the study of metaphysics and self-awareness. True fulfillment, I learned, required training myself to stand vigilant over my own thoughts and words. Through a comprehensive daily practice of visualization and affirmation I slowly, over a period of years, transformed my innately dour, gloomy outlook into an attitude of gratitude and abundance. This new and improved mindset made an enormously positive difference in my life experience.

> *"If you realized how powerful your thoughts are,*
> *you would never think a negative thought."*
> — PEACE PILGRIM

However, all these decades later, an army of nagging worries had begun invading my head in the dark of night, to torment my thoughts and steal my slumber. No doubt, the once-impervious foundation of positivity I'd constructed had sprung a few leaks. Some substantial spiritual and mental maintenance would be required. It was becoming abundantly clear that, while finding the ideal tent and the perfect sleeping bag were important, if I ever hoped to walk in the footsteps of Peace Pilgrim, there were other, less-tangible, but equally important preparations begging my attention.

To ready myself for interaction with the unknown, I knew I'd best work on modifying my language, recalibrating my tone, practicing my listening skills, exercising my smile muscles, and honing my ability to exude some irresistible good vibes. I would need to be prepared to deal calmly and constructively with any potential eventuality — including and especially the possibility of being confronted by hostility. Learning how to pack a backpack turned out to be a piece of cake. No YouTube clip, however, could fully instruct me how to do spring cleaning in my headspace and re-pack my attitude with positivity.

Meanwhile, another unexpected, but very welcome phenomenon seized my attention. On January 21st, that fateful Saturday of the Women's March, more than two million people, in 161 cities around the world, rallied in solidarity. Even in such unlikely places as Utah, Nebraska, and Arkansas — states that contributed to the surprise election of the 45th president — thousands came out to oppose his proposed policies. Virtually overnight, a powerful new resistance movement sprang up, not just on the coasts, but across the nation.

Then, only a week into the new president's term, in dramatic reaction to his controversial executive order banning travel from a targeted list of Muslim-majority countries, protests across the U.S. multiplied. Observing this, I experienced a "Wow! I could-a had a V-8!" moment. *Perhaps we Pacific Coasters,* I allowed myself to ponder, *are not so isolated in our thinking after all.* And… *Maybe, just maybe, we're not even the smartest kids on the block!*

Certainly, we're far from the most courageous folks around. It's easy to express resistance when you're marching with your family, friends, and neighbors. It takes real guts to get out there and buck the preponderant political posture of your community. I know this from personal experience. During my 16-year stint in Nashville, I was a prolific progressive voice on the letters-to-the-editor page of *The Tennessean.* Every so often, I'd come home to find an extremely hostile note in my mailbox. The most memorable was a hand-scribbled missive that, after accusing me of sedition for my opposition to the U.S. invasion of Iraq, conveyed the following: "I only wish I could put a bullet between your traitorous eyes."

Trump's election had inspired people of conscience to step up — even out there in those conservative-majority states! This provided living evidence that America still remains a land of many and varied opinions, strong convictions, and high ideals. As it turns out, in spite of my prior assumptions, not every red-state address subscribes to ugly Americanism after all. Therefore, it stood to reason that I was bound to encounter a wide range of attitudes while trekking along the shoulder of Highway 101. If Arkansas harbors lefties, right-wingers must call California home, too. This realization didn't intimidate me. Instead, this *Ah-hah!* insight charged me with exhilaration. I began visualizing opportunities to interact with people of all stripes. I relished the idea of listening to concerns and opinions from every degree of the spectrum and finding out if and where the issues people care passionately about might coincide. I was becoming infused with an earnest desire to discover where people of opposing points of view might find common ground.

Thus, the purpose of the long walk I'd been contemplating and planning for months had evolved. My trek would not be a statement of defiance, nor would it be an effort to rally my fellow Pacific Coasters around one mindset of independence. It would be about listening to anyone's and everyone's concerns, with the hope of inspiring civil, constructive dialogue — especially between people with very different, even opposite mindsets. With this as my new goal, I produced a second YouTube video, entitled *Peace Pilgrim 2017*, in which I posed some questions I hoped to address on my journey, while articulating the re-calibrated purpose for what I now dubbed, thanks to Charles Busch's suggestion, a 90-day Pilgrimage.

> NOTE: I ADOPTED the label "Peace Pilgrim 2017" purely in honor of the one-and-only original Peace Pilgrim. I do not, in any way, equate my commitment and sacrifice with hers.

Ninety days cannot compare with 28 years. The distance I would ultimately travel on foot is but a tiny fraction of the more than 30,000 miles she covered with nothing but the clothes on her back and the shoes on her feet. I remain in awe of the virtue, courage, and fortitude demonstrated by Peace Pilgrim and her incalculable contribution to improving the human condition.

CHAPTER 3

It Takes a Village

"How can I possibly go now?" Warm, salty tears were running down my cheeks, into my ears, under my earlobes and onto the pillowcase. "I mean… it's impossible."

Sebra knew it was better to refrain from uttering an opinion. She intuited that what I needed was a listener. Or, perhaps, maybe I just needed to hear my own confused thoughts spoken out loud into the darkness. Her time to speak would come soon. And she would pick the perfect words, exactly what I needed to hear at such an emotionally charged moment.

For three solid months, every single waking hour of my every single day had been focused on one big thing: preparing to walk 1,000 miles with my dog. Now, my almost 90-year-old mother was lying in a hospital bed incapacitated. My already-90-year-old father was devastated, overwhelmed, consumed with fear, and pretending a stiff upper lip. And here I was, the self-appointed caregiver to my parents, planning to abandon them for three months. *To pick up and leave now, at this juncture? Absolutely not. That would be far too selfish.*

Still, if I cancelled my walk, I would have to return the funds from my crowd-source campaign. Not only had I signed an agreement with an Arizona couple to sublet my apartment from May until August, I'd already spent their rent deposit. I had two videos on YouTube. Radio and newspaper interviews, and a featured-presenter slot at the Unitarian Fellowship, had been lined up, as well as a house concert/fundraiser. My pilgrimage had been gaining momentum, taking on a life of its own. I was feeling the enormous weight of obligation — to myself and to the many friends who were supporting me — to go through with it. But, surely, under the circumstances, going through with it was out of the question.

Yes, I was shedding some very anguished tears. But, to be absolutely honest, I was also feeling a certain sense of relief. My mother's stroke handed me a gift-wrapped excuse to cancel, or at least postpone, this very formidable endeavor. It presented the perfect opportunity for my lady to put her arms around me, kiss the tear-streaked stubble on my cheek and say, "Everyone will understand." That's what I fully expected to hear from her. After all, she'd been forthright from the outset, telling me how much she dreaded being separated for such a long time. She'd grown reliant on our weekends together; those three-hour, hand-in-hand walks on the beach; slow dancing in the kitchen; the laughter, the intimacy, the passion; the delicious, peaceful solace of snuggling in the same bed.

It must have been so very tempting for her. *Just say the words, Babe, and you can avoid the dreaded, painful letting go. You won't have to share your man with all those yet-to-be-met strangers. Tell me it's okay to abandon my quest and you can keep me for yourself.* But Sebra was wise enough not to attempt to dissuade me from my commitment. Instead, she posed some practical questions and helped me see the situation from some alternative angles.

Did I absolutely have to be the only responsible person in this scenario? Should I be putting the entire weight of this medical crisis on my own shoulders? Who else could help? I'm a very, very fortunate man to have such an extraordinarily giving, empathetic, and pragmatic woman in my life. Sebra is all about solving problems, getting things done. Helping a friend — in this case, the man she loves — gather the scattered pieces of a seemingly unsolvable puzzle, then start reassembling them into a whole, new, unanticipated picture… this task was smack dab in the sweet center of my lady's wheelhouse.

Even though it had provided me a perfect escape hatch, I deeply resented the blood clot that had wrought havoc on the left occipital lobe of my mother's brain, permanently obliterating half the field of vision in her right eye, throwing her equilibrium off kilter, and gumming up her brain function. But Sebra's education and background as an occupational therapist proved invaluable. She knew the right questions to ask and what services to request in order to get the best treatment for Mom.

The biggest impediment to my mother's potential recovery turned out to be the man who has loved her faithfully and passionately since 1948. The mounting years have increased my father's egocentricity. More often than not, he is able to see events only as they affect him, either in the present, or as he recalls them from the past. He also seems less and less capable of muting his comments and opinions. When a nurse, a doctor, or a physician's assistant asked Mom a question, Dad would invariably butt in to answer on her behalf. This annoyance not only prevented the medical professionals from getting critical information directly from the patient, Dad's answers planted suggestions in Mother's addled head. As TV attorneys often declare in those courtroom scenes, "Objection, Your Honor! Counsel is leading the witness." Observing the body language and facial expressions of the hospital staff, it was easy to see how frustrating this was for them. So, my role was not only to advocate for Mom. I also needed to somehow prevent or deflect whatever potential damage my butt-in-ski father might unwittingly bring about.

As soon as space became available, Mom was to be moved to a rehab facility, where she would receive daily physical and occupational therapy for two, possibly three weeks. After that, she would begin receiving in-home therapy. Meanwhile, until she could be relocated, physical and occupational therapists would visit her here in the hospital. This plan seemed ideal. It would not only get Mom into rehabilitation right away — critical for her best chance of recovery — it would also provide time for me to line up the professional assistance my parents would require when she returned home.

So, I was able to catch my breath — until the next day, when I got a call from Dad: "They're releasing your mother to go home this afternoon! Isn't that fantastic?"

I was staggered, absolutely dumbfounded by what amounted to a complete reversal of the plan the doctors had shared with us only the previous day. Explanation for the abrupt turnaround: Mom had performed so well in her physical and occupational therapy sessions, the therapists simply couldn't check off enough boxes to justify sending her to the rehab facility. *Okay, yes, Dad.* I had to agree. *That* part *was* fantastic. The hospital needed her bed. So, without providing us any time to prepare, they were giving her the boot. That part was *not remotely* fantastic.

In truth, my mother wasn't at all ready to come home, neither was her home ready for her. Dad may have been thrilled that Mama Bird was returning to the nest. I got that. And, it was sweet. I was happy that Pop was happy. But, as usual, he wasn't considering what was best for Mom — or for me, for that matter. He was not thinking about what it entails to care for a woman on the cusp of 90, whose brain was only just beginning to compensate for the loss of some of its critical components. My mother was like a partially blind two-year-old with Downs Syndrome. Stubborn, willful, and completely unaware of her own limitations, she needed constant supervision to protect her from injuring herself. She would be unable to cook, clean house, do laundry, or even bathe herself. For me, the person who would have to take on chief-cook-and-bottle-washer duties, all this was a bit much to swallow.

As devastating as my mother's stroke was, it did precipitate some positive outcomes. Blessing number one: Dad rose to the occasion. This 90-year-old man, who had never done a load of laundry in his life, rolled up his sleeves and figured it out on his own. Without complaint, he has relished being the stalwart, dutiful husband to the stalwart, dutiful wife, doing everything he can to make up for all those years when she did all the thankless, dirty work, while raising five hellions, then returning to college, founding a school, taking on a late-life teaching career, spearheading quilting guilds in two cities, and helming a weekly charity dinner

for the homeless. In a lot of ways, my mother has been the real
Peace Pilgrim in my family. I have such pride and admiration for
how she has conducted her life. That my father has responded
to her affliction with such unconditional love and devotion has
both surprised and delighted me. I'm pretty sure the old man has
surprised himself, too. And that, Dad, most definitely *is fantastic!*

A blessing equally as fantastic, and surprising — and this truly
warms my heart — is hearing my stoic, fiercely independent mother
ask, "Could you get me a cup of tea?" Any attempt to do anything
for her pre-stroke, and you'd surely get an icy, "I can do it myself!"
And, the blessings don't stop there! Mom may have lost a big hunk
of her vision but — Hallelujah, glory be! — the old girl has filled
that blind spot with a newfound sense of humor.

Additional godsends: Aging Wisely with Helping Hands was
there to provide home assistance. Samaritan Health Care dispatched
physical, occupational, and speech therapists. And, thanks to pro-
visions of the Affordable Care Act, Medicaid picked up the entire
tab. Friends visited, bringing food, flowering plants, and puzzles
to stimulate Mom's mind. A refrigerated box appeared on the front
porch from my daughter Emily and son-in-law James in Glendale,
California. The pre-measured ingredients and easy recipes spoiled
us with gourmet meals for an entire week. And, with brother Jayson
coming for the months of June and July to stay with the folks, I
started to feel much better about getting back to the business of
preparing for my pilgrimage. So, in a belated answer to the well-cho-
sen questions Sebra broached as I lay tearfully in my bed on that
melancholy night, thankfully, I didn't have to put the entire weight
of my mother's medical crisis on my shoulders after all.

If not for these institutions and individuals rallying around us,
I would most certainly have had to cancel my mission. Instead, my
departure date had to be set back only two weeks. April 15th, Tax
Day, became May 1st, May Day — equally as symbolic. My 90-day
pilgrimage was back on the calendar — in *ink*! I was filled with
gratitude for the support of this extraordinary village, mixed with a
whole lot of apprehension about the adventure about to commence.

CHAPTER 4

Goodbyes and Reasonable Expectations

APRIL 23, 2017

This morning, my slumber's interruption was precipitated by an exhilarating, yet disconcerting realization that these are my final hours of repose in my comfy, queen-sized bed for quite some time. This afternoon, I will exit my third-floor apartment at the Eagles Nest, perched on a hill above Nye Village, in sight of the ever-roiling Pacific Ocean. I will not be returning to the place where I've resided contentedly for almost five years until the final week of July. One thing for certain: an adventure lies ahead. Mixed emotions? A simmering stew, in which excitement bubbles and bobs in a broth of consternation, seasoned by equal parts wonder and self-doubt.

When I decided to take on my pilgrimage, it was way out there in the fuzzy future. From that vantage point, I could easily see myself passing this self-administered trial with flying colors. Don't get me wrong, I was aware from the get-go that I would suffer a measure of physical pain and discomfort, experience more than a few pangs of fear, while putting myself in some very real danger. After all, any worthwhile endeavor comes with its own set of obstacles, and some very real potential for failure. Curiously, with my launch date only a week away, it's becoming more difficult to actually picture myself taking that looming first step, let alone the next, and the thousands upon thousands of steps it will take to walk 1,000 miles across two states. Only Heaven knows who and what I might encounter along the way.

More than a few folks have expressed their trepidations over my plans. "You're not a hiker," my martini-sipping, Sandbar pal Debbie reminded me on several occasions. "You're a singer. Why don't you just do a concert tour?"

"What kind of sacrifice would that be?" I would parry. "I can always do concerts. Walking a thousand miles. That makes a real statement."

My youngest daughter Glendyn can't seem to understand what I'm trying to prove with this harebrained scheme. Still, her greatest concern is not her father. It's Millie, the amount of wear and tear trotting on presumably hot, gravelly pavement might put on a pup's paws. My dear friend Charlie is convinced that I'm setting myself up as a punching bag, that I'll be the target of assaults, both physical and verbal, from the Red Meanies. My Love, the beautiful, always-supportive Sebra can't seem to fight off the persistent fear that I will come home a changed man, one who no longer needs or desires her.

My father, however, expresses the gravest apprehension. When he pictures me trekking along the highways of California and Oregon, he can't help but imagine every worst-case scenario. The most optimistic, upbeat man on Planet Earth, Dad is as frightened for my wellbeing as he would be if I were shipping off to some foreign battlefield. "I have no intention of being a martyr, Dad," I've attempted to reassure my overly vexed father. "I'm not too proud to accept rides through dangerous stretches of road." While offering him some relief, this respite from worry is only temporary. I'm 67. I've been making my own decisions for a half century. He's about to turn 91. Still, in this case, he's incapable of trusting his eldest son's judgment. Once a parent, always a parent.

☮ ☮ ☮ ☮ ☮

It's a fiberglass storage box, black, 40 inches in length, 18 inches wide, and 20 inches deep. After spending countless hours online searching for a trunk large enough to carry and cradle my smallest guitar, this one turned out to be my best choice. One blustery February afternoon, Millie and I returned from our daily constitutional on Nye Beach to find a corrugated shipping container large enough to hold a small coffin blocking our apartment door. After wedging the gargantuan package through the door and sliding it inside, I managed to free the box (the fiberglass one) from the box (the cardboard one). Imagine my relief when, by placing the gig bag of my little, parlor-shaped Seagull acoustic on a cattycorner angle, I was able to tuck it snugly inside the top of the trunk. And, underneath the guitar, there remained just enough space to stow camping gear, clothing, and shoes for rain or shine, compact discs to sell, and a week's supply of dog food.

The design concept that instantly transforms this storage box into a pushcart came to me during one of those many sleepless, pre-dawn "fretting hours." My vision was made real by Eagle's Nest building manager and all-around handyman, Jered Dippre. Two mid-sized bicycle wheels attach to the sides of the box and a pair of extra-large skateboard wheels are affixed to the front axle, making the cart lower up front and higher in the rear. It rolls at a wheelbarrow angle, with most of the box's weight supported by the larger, easy rolling bike wheels. As per my request, the bike wheels are removable as to allow the box to fit into a car trunk or a hatchback — if and when necessary.

I lift the weighty box up and into the hatch of my Prius, managing, in a few lunges, to slide it forward enough for the hatch door to close. I coax Millie into her collapsible, fabric dog crate. She whines and yelps as I zip the mesh door closed. Trusting that it won't be long before my going-on-10-year-old beagle feels safe and secure in her new home away from home, I make an attempt to calm her anxiety in dog-speak falsetto, "It's okay, Baby. It's okay." I shut the hatch, take a farewell gander at the Eagle's Nest, force a smile, shake my head, sigh audibly, slip behind the wheel, fasten my seatbelt, push the "power" button, and back the Prius out of its parking space.

Peace Pilgrim said, "A pilgrim not only walks prayerfully but as an opportunity to contact people." Following in my role model's footsteps, the script of my *Peace Pilgrim 2017* video concludes with a parting wish: "As I make my way, I hope you'll invite this pilgrim in… to your home, your church, a backyard, a park, wherever we can gather. Let's discuss our issues constructively, share our concerns, our ideas. Let's sing some songs together. Maybe we can help each other make sense of these crazy, challenging times we're living in."

As I spoke those words, I visualized myself, smiling ear-to-ear, pushing my cart past the city limit sign of one town or another to be greeted by well-wishers, maybe even by a local journalist, a still-photographer, and/or video cameras. I imagined pulling out my guitar in a public park, singing a few tunes, and a crowd gathering around me. After a Kumbaya sing-along, we'd have a profound, sincere, teary-eyed discussion, sharing our mutual concerns. Then, some nice folks would invite me to their house for dinner, show me to their guest room, hand me a fluffy, freshly laundered towel, and treat me to a nice, hot shower.

How was I expecting to make this imagined scenario manifest? How exactly did this anonymous, lone pilgrim plan to go about creating his greatest "opportunity to contact people?" Well, this vision wasn't entirely fantasy. I had put some real pieces in play to make it happen. First, I compiled a directory of all the Unitarian Universalist churches on and peripheral to my planned route, from the southernmost congregation to the northernmost. I then designed a four- by five-and-a-half-inch postcard and had it printed in bulk. On the card, alongside some artsy, personalized photos and graphics, I crammed in as much info as space would allow:

A 90-DAY PILGRIMAGE

SPRING–SUMMER, 2017 – Rand Bishop – Grammy-nominated songwriter/author/activist & Millie the beagle… walking Highway 101 to inspire Constructive Dialogue. Climate Change, Partisan Rancor, Income Inequality, Militarism, Congressional Gridlock, Gun Violence, Obstructionism, Nativism, Student

Debt, Xenophobia, Mass Incarceration, Crumbling Infra-
structure, Misogyny, Alternative Facts, Religious Intolerance,
Voter Suppression. *RESISTING WHAT WE CANNOT ACCEPT
IS NOT ENOUGH. IT'S EQUALLY IMPORTANT THAT WE ENVI-
SION THE WORLD WE TRULY WANT FOR OURSELVES AND
OUR CHILDREN...* Inclusivity, Clean Air & Water, Universal
Healthcare, Renewable Energy, Affordable College, a Living
Wage, Respect for Science, LGBTQ Rights, Reproductive Choice,
Human Dignity, Cooperation, Civility, TRUTH!

Then, to make my intention as clear as possible, I concluded
the postcard's text:

AVAILABLE FOR: Meetings, Gatherings, Brainstorming
Sessions, Visualizations, Meditations, House Concerts,
Music Jams.

GRATEFULLY ACCEPTING: Nourishment, Lodging,
Luggage Transport, Fellowship, Contributions.

In a three-prong strategy, I first emailed the UU churches,
then sent follow-up postcards via snail-mail. After getting a more
concrete idea of when I might be arriving in each particular community, I planned to call each church office.

I had also established relationships with music-biz vet Steve
Love's nascent Socially Driven Music and World Wide Musicians
United, the California-based not-for-profit dedicated to "... empow-
ering music artists everywhere to... work together to create a fairer
and more vibrant world." WWMU co-founder Daniel DeMento
was already busy compiling a list of people in his ever-widening
circle to hook me up with — particularly in the Bay Area, where
he and his wife had lived and worked for a number of years.

But, even with my UU connections, Steve Love, and Danny
DeMento, even with my donors and supporters, myriad friends,
family, and other business contacts, I reminded myself... If there's
one thing I discovered during my 45-year music-biz rollercoaster

ride, one stark reality I gleaned over 25 years of studying meta-physics and practicing self-awareness, one life lesson I've had to learn and re-learn over the course of my lifetime, it's this:

> IF YOUR POTENTIAL happiness depends upon exactly how you expect other human beings to behave, you will experience a great deal of disappointment in your life.

I knew it was of ultimate importance that I never allow myself to lose my awareness of the following:

> THE SUCCESS OF this adventure begins with the mindset, the attitude with which I take my first step, my next step, and each and every step thereafter, and continues with my willingness to fully embrace each and every experience along the way.

So, regardless of whether any of my reasonable expectations are realized — how I'm greeted or treated by the UUs, what actual energy Steve Love and Danny DeMento rally around me, whether or not, in the guise of Peace Pilgrim 2017, I am celebrated, ridiculed, or ignored — I must accept from the outset that whatever will be will be. I must set out on this quest determined to seize this once-in-a-lifetime opportunity with an open, loving, grateful heart. If I can let that heart lead the way, anything any other person does to affect or enhance my experience will be frosting on an already sweet slice of cake.

In this sense, each of the next 90 days will be no different from any other day of my life. The quality of my experience, its mundanity or its magic, its trial or its triumph, will not be determined so much by whatever happens. It will be more about how I choose to perceive whatever happens.

> *"I certainly am a happy person. Who can*
> *know God and not be joyous?"*
> — Peace Pilgrim, in her final interview, July 6, 1981

CHAPTER 5

Failure to Launch

MAY 1 · DAY ONE

So begins the adventure I've been preparing for these last five months, the leap into the unknown I've only imagined until this very moment. Today's plan: Load the rented Nissan Versa — box, wheels, dog crate, dog. Drive from Reseda to Thousand Oaks. Find a place to unload the car. Return the car to Enterprise. Start walking north along Thousand Oaks Boulevard parallel to Highway 101. First day's goal: A Motel 6, 13.1 miles north.

The fact that I need to find a place to unload the car, away from and out of sight of the vehicle-return lot, bears some explanation. Six days ago, at the Enterprise office in Hillsboro, Oregon, while scanning the auto-rental agreement, I came to a certain bit of language that sent blood rushing to my face. The contract's strict "no-pets" clause, had taken me completely by surprise. Of special concern was the warning that any infraction of this rule would result in a $250 penalty. I didn't much like the idea of being dishonest with the rental company but I had no time to make alternative travel plans. Besides, Millie would be traveling inside her collapsible crate anyway, thus wouldn't be shedding on the upholstery, drooling on the seats, or scratching up the interior, so I checked the box, indicating that I agreed to abide by the no-pets provision. In doing so, I realized that returning the vehicle would require some evasive maneuvering.

THIS SHOULD HAVE also been my first hint that, while traveling the highways and byways of America on foot comes

with its own inherent set of challenges, attempting this feat
with a dog complicates matters tenfold.

Keeping my eyes peeled for a safe place to temporarily stash my stuff and my dog, I'm pin-balling the Versa around a two-block-square as if I'm driving a bumper car at the county fair. By a process of elimination, I decide on a small, rectangular section of grass in front of a strip mall, a block south of the Enterprise office. After carabiner-ing Millie to the box, I stroke her ever-so-soft beagle ears and attempt to comfort her anxiety with an "I'll be right back, Baby." Then, hoping she doesn't start howling, I climb back into the Versa for the rental return.

It's hot, probably in the high eighties. I'm pleased that Millie is trotting alongside me, tethered to my belly bag, in her little black-rubber protective booties. The cart is rolling nicely. However, tennis-ball-sized knots are beginning to protrude from my shins — from bumping against the sharp, bottom edge of the fiber-glass box — and the swelling only increases the likelihood that yet more wickedly painful, shin-box collisions will take place.

I start scouting for a sporting goods store thinking, surely, there must be some kind of shin guard available to protect my legs from further injury — maybe like baseball catchers use, or perhaps the padded leg sleeves employed by soccer players. I find a Big 5 Sporting Goods, park the cart and the pup outside, and enter. I peruse the baseball section — mitts, bats, and balls, but no catcher's gear. In the soccer section, the only shin sleeves I can locate are youth sizes. I find a young sales associate and tell him what I'm looking for. Wordlessly, he points across the store toward the section I was just in. "I was just there," I inform him. "I couldn't find any adult sizes."

"Well, that's where they are," he says, shaking his head, as if he assumes my advanced age has rendered me imbecilic.

"Okay," I say, taking a deep breath. My shins are throbbing. I've left my anxious dog outside in the heat. Poor customer service is a huge pet peeve for me. "Would you mind showing me? Because I can't seem to find them." With evident umbrage, the young man lifts himself heavily from the floor, where he's been putting price tags on a rack of athletic socks. I follow him to the very display I had just been looking through.

"Hmmm," he says, after a quick perusal. "I guess we don't have 'em."

"You don't have what?" I inquire.

"Adult sizes." He then shrugs his shoulders, turns his back on me, and simply walks away. Exasperated, I watch this guy plop back down on the floor to resume pricing socks. Marching toward the exit in befuddled fury, I'm unable to restrain myself from letting the young associate know exactly how I feel about how well he's doing his (bleeping) job.

Now, *I'm* the bad guy. "Well, sir. You don't have to be rude," he declares, quickly scrambling back to his feet and pointing an accusing finger. "I don't have to take that kind of language from you or anyone else!"

⊕   ⊕   ⊕   ⊕   ⊕

As I push my cart northward along the sidewalk, with Millie the beagle prancing, panting by my side, giving me those occasional sidelong glances, I'm stewing: *Only two hours into a pilgrimage to inspire civil, constructive dialogue and I've already contributed to an extremely unpleasant, not to mention profane, total breakdown in communication. Ouch! F*%K!* I've just bumped a shin on the box again!

At a street corner, we're waiting on the curb for the walk signal. I'm grimacing and rubbing my shin. Millie seems concerned. She can tell her human is suffering. The signal changes. As I push the cart off the curb and onto the crosswalk, the left-side wheel seems to bend and wobble. The cart goes catawampus, with the tire rubbing against the side of the fiberglass box. On the far curb, I stop to check on the wheel. Thankfully, it looks like the threads that fasten the detachable wheel to the box have simply loosened on their own. I tighten the wheel and push on, already seriously concerned about the viability of my cart.

I see a sign for Dick's Sporting Goods. *Excellent!* Maybe Dick's has something to protect my suffering shins. Midway across the mall parking lot, the cart wheel begins to wobble severely, now scraping even harder against the fiberglass box. Then, it comes off completely. I take a closer look and my heart plummets like a brick dropped off the Empire State Building. The aluminum-alloy hardware where the wheel attaches to the box is completely mangled. Three hours into a 90-day trek, and this pilgrim is already grounded. Awkwardly, I manage to push the crippled cart to the broad sidewalk that circles the mall. I take a photo of the disintegrated wheel connection and text it to my brother Theo, with the message: *Well, this happened.*

Within 30 seconds, my jack-of-all-trades frère calls. His recommendation — rational as always — is that I contact the nearest bike shop to see if they can replace the damaged part. I Google "Bicycle shop near me" and dial the number of the closest one. I try to explain my particularly unique situation — a converted storage-box cart, removable bicycle wheels, etc. The bike mechanic suggests that I email him the photo. His diagnosis via return email: the damage is beyond repair. So, my concept to convert a storage box into a pushcart and the design Jered Dippre worked on for weeks has turned out to be a total bust. And I have no Plan B.

Meanwhile, my iPhone is informing me that it's out of storage. This issue further complicates matters as, over the course of my pilgrimage — if and when my trek gets back on course — I will need as much memory as possible in my phone to take photos and shoot video. My cart is broken down. My phone is out of storage. Black-and-blue mountain ranges are emerging on my shins. And, I'm hungry. I will address these four challenges one at a time, starting with the most pressing one, which just so happens to be the simplest one to solve. If I don't get my lunch on time, I don't do well. When my blood sugar is low, my spirits sink, I become irritable, and it's impossible for me to sort out my thoughts. I find a shady spot between one of the main mall entrances and the dining patio of one of its fancier restaurants. This will serve as my interim base camp, where I'll leave my crippled cart and panting dog.

The Oaks Shopping Center, Ventura County's largest mall, could be a county unto itself. Apparently, my base camp is located as far away from affordable eats as a frugal-by-necessity pilgrim can get. Clutching a tuna sandwich on flatbread, an iced green tea, some kettle chips, and a peanut butter cookie, I press the "up" button on the room-sized, glass elevator to the main mall level. The elevator doors slide open to reveal an all-American tableau: a family of five, standing like statues, all staring down robotically at hand-held devices. There they remain, stationary, evidently totally unaware that the car has reached the bottom level, that the sliding doors have opened, and that an extremely famished, impatient pilgrim is waiting for them to regain consciousness and simply make the minimal effort to take the few forward strides necessary to vacate the glass enclosure.

If one of these zombies doesn't look up in the next two seconds, I fear I'm either going to start to cry, or I'm going to hurl a barbed profanity in their direction at a disturbingly shrill decimal level. I've already had one regrettable encounter today — in the Big 5. It's taking every bit of restraint I can muster to stop myself from initiating a second. Zombie Mom's glassy eyes shift up momentarily from the screen in her hand. She murmurs an indiscernible, coded message to her zombie posse who, still focused on their devices, all shuffle forward, ever-so-slowly out of the rectangular space as one amorphous 10-footed glob — no apology, not even the slightest acknowledgment of my existence.

By now, the elevator doors are beginning to slide shut. I lunge to stop them, squeezing the disposable, fast-food to-go cup a little too tightly, dislodging its plastic lid. As I sidle into the car and the glass room begins to lift, ice tea drips down my hand and forearm. Through the clear elevator doors, I shoot a squinted glare at the Family of the Walking Dead, now lumbering away en masse, still completely unaware of anything other than the tech toys in their hands, ignoring one another and the world around them.

By the time I get back to Millie, a woman has provided her with a bowl of water and is attempting to get her to eat a bite of a Cinnabon. Millie will have none of it, and is obviously becoming irritated with the well-intentioned lady. When Millie sees me, she lets out a series of excited beagle howls, as she almost always does. The patrons of the adjacent dining patio appear alarmed — or maybe perturbed, I can't be sure. As I attempt to quiet my dog, Cinnabon Lady explains, "I thought he might be hungry."

"Thanks," I tell her, "but she only eats organic food." Surely, I appreciate Cinnabon Lady's good will. However, I don't appreciate anyone presuming to feed someone else's pet something that is so obviously unhealthy — and, not just for dogs, for humans as well.

☮   ☮   ☮   ☮   ☮

The Monarch Camping Chair takes its name from the butterfly-wing shape of the canvas that stretches over its collapsible, aluminum frame. Pop it out of its cozy, compact bag and the magnetic sections immediately attract one another. You pretty much can't mess up that part of the assembly. But stretching the canvas over the frame, and attaching it properly and securely invariably takes some trial and error. Once you've got the ingenious invention fully assembled, the real trial begins — actually sitting in a chair with only two legs. Getting situated in the monarch is a balancing act not dissimilar to climbing into a hammock. Overshoot your weight distribution and you're likely to tip over backwards. Undershoot, and your posterior hits the ground — hard! Much to the amusement of the snooty patio diners, on my first attempt to mount the monarch, I lean back too far, tip over and do a backward summersault. I can't help but share a chuckle with the amused kibitzers, as this maneuver must have looked very silly indeed. My second attempt is successful — Tah-*dah*! — inspiring some applause from my audience.

I'm pleased to discover there is an Apple Store here at The Oaks and, as luck would have it, not too far away from my base camp. With some food in my belly, I'm feeling more energized and optimistic. I enter the vast i-Beehive to be greeted by a smiling woman holding an iPad. "Do you have an appointment?" she asks. Of course, I don't. So, I put myself on the waiting list for the next appointment available. I'll receive a text message, she informs me, about 10 minutes before my personal Apple Genius will be available to assist me. This, I'm thinking, is perfect, as it will give me time to get to the sporting goods store to shop for shin guards. Dick's, however, turns out to be even further away than the food court — only in the opposite direction. By the time I reach the massive retail space, I swear I must have crossed back over the Los Angeles County line.

I'm standing in the checkout line when I get the text. My Apple Genius will be ready for me, not in 10 minutes as promised, but in five! The Dick's checkout process, unfortunately, is not nearly as expeditious as locating and selecting one's product. I get a second text. I'm on the verge of losing my Apple-store appointment. Panicked, I snatch up my purchase and do my impression of OJ Simpson racing through the airport in those old Hertz TV commercials. *Remember when Juice seemed so charming and sweet?*

Apple Genius A informs me that the storage issue in my iPhone is common, easily solvable one. When his simple process fails, he consults with an associate. Genius B's fix also proves inadequate.

Apparently, an Einstein level of genius will be required to solve my issue. I'm shown to a waiting area in the middle of the store. Here, a dozen or so customers are either perched on white-lacquered cubes of fabricated wood or balancing on Pilates balls. Under any circumstance, I resent the idea of a single, idle, wasted minute. Today, of all days, even a split second of unproductive time is especially stressful. And, right now, I'm concerned not only for how long my wait will be, I'm worried about the forlorn, abandoned beagle outside, surely longing impatiently for her human's return.

"Hi, I'm Tyler," sandy-haired, khaki-clad Genius C informs me with a relaxed, friendly smile. Of course, his name is Tyler. He's probably 22, 23 maybe. If it wasn't Tyler, it would be Josh, or Justin, or Cooper. "How are you doing today?" His calm, proficient demeanor indicates that experience has made him hyper aware just how nerve-wracking this kind of situation can be, especially for a "more-mature" customer like myself. The best and most reliable solution to a stubborn storage issue like this, Tyler quickly determines, is to reinstall the hard drive. "We'll have you out of here in about an hour," he promises.

It's after three. I am unprepared to futz away another hour of precious time. Without my iPhone, I can't text, check email, go on Facebook, or peruse *Huffington Post*. As I didn't bring a book or a magazine, I find myself kibitzing listening in on other customers' conversations. One fellow, at least 10 years my junior, is trying to squeeze another few last months out of a flip-phone that reached obsolescence 15 years ago. A young woman seems baffled as to why the laptop she dropped from tabletop to floor is no longer functioning properly. It's just the first afternoon of my first pilgrimage day and I've already recognized one universal concern, one shared dilemma, one common frustration: we've become far too dependent on these infernal computer machines — as individuals, as a society, as a nation. And, when they cease to meet our expectations, we tend to panic.

An hour has passed. Tyler, my friendly, competent, top-of-the-food-chain Apple Super Genius, has not been spotted in quite some time. *Oh, good!* There he is now, emerging from the exclusive inner sanctum of the secret laboratory where, I imagine, dozens of tech-geek surgeons in white lab coats and magnified headlamps are performing oh-so-delicate procedures. Surely, he's on his way to return my newly revitalized iPhone. But no, he stops to gab with an associate. Finally, I catch his eye and, even from 50 feet away, he can't help but recognize shades of extreme anxiety painted across my face. Of course, they're a little short-handed today, he explains. One guy's out sick. Another tech is getting married. Tyler's eyes are darting past, over, and around me, all over the room. It's clear he's uncomfortable having to apologize for a promise unfulfilled. He's looking for any excuse to beg off.

Instead, I cast the bait: "So, tell me about yourself, Tyler."

Suddenly, his body language changes and his focus shifts back to me. Evidently, I've touched on the young man's favorite subject.

Tyler, it seems, has loftier aspirations. This Apple Genius gig is merely a stepping stone, a means to an end. He is working on his Master's degree at Cal State Northridge, in engineering.

"If you don't mind me asking," I interject, "you being a young, obviously smart person and all, what are your greatest concerns?"

He seems momentarily confused. "About this country," I clarify, "about the world."

"Well, I guess," he says, "countries fighting."

"So, you mean war."

Yes, he confirms, war is his greatest concern.

"Okay. I'm with you on that. Totally. But, as an aspiring engineer," I ask, "do you worry about the environment?"

"Well," he says, "if you're talking about climate change…" Now, the young man is lighting up like the red-neon *Hot Now* sign at a Krispy Kreme store. I've hit on an issue about which he has formed strong opinions. And, oddly, he is not all that worried about rising temperatures and sea levels. In fact, he says, the solution to global warming might actually be baked right into the problem itself. As the polar ice caps melt, Tyler expounds, potent gasses are emitted into the atmosphere. Our challenge is to figure out an expedient means of capturing all that escaping vapor and extracting the hydrogen from it. Then, the entire planet's energy needs could be met, carbon free, for centuries to come! Here's a budding young engineer looking at solving a very daunting global crisis from an engineering perspective.

I'm encouraged, not just because this idea has provided a glimmer of light at the end of what looks like a dark, increasingly steamy and stormy tunnel, but also because this bright young man is so fired up about it. I'm equally encouraged when Tyler hands me my iPhone and informs me that re-installing the hard drive has retrieved 10 gigabytes of storage!

So far, I've dealt successfully with three of my four major challenges: lunch, shin guards, and iPhone storage. However, these issues have gobbled up the entire afternoon. The day is pretty much shot and the fourth challenge, my broken-down cart, remains unaddressed. I emerge from the mall to be greeted by a very agitated beagle. Who knows how many dog-adoring mall people have stopped to baby talk her, pet her, or try to get her to eat some disgusting goody? I need to get her away from this high-traffic area.

I decide to call it a day, locate the nearest pet-friendly motel, summon an Uber (SUV required to haul the box and the dog), and regroup in the morning. I'm standing on the curb arranging for a pick up, when Millie starts barking ferociously. I whip around to see her snout-to-nose with an adorable, little Asian girl. The father of the terrified, wailing child swiftly snatches her up and out of range of the perturbed beagle. The incensed Asian grandmother, 90 pounds of pure ire, is standing there glowering in my direction, laser darts shooting from her enraged eyes, as if she's initiating a stare down with Satan himself.

"I'm so sorry," I manage to utter. "Really. I'm really, really sorry." My repeated apologies receive no acknowledgement beyond the elderly woman's incessant glare of condemnation. Like that Family of the Living Dead, I've just allowed a hand-held device to disengage me from the real world. My lack of attention didn't merely hold up an elevator, however, *it endangered a child!* And, that makes *me* the zombie!

A phone rings. But it doesn't sound like mine. *Oh, right! My ringtone preference got wiped at the Apple Store.* It's Bro Theo. He has an idea about how to meet challenge number four and he's charged up about it. Theo and his family live in Orange County — Lake Forest to be exact — further south of the L.A. sprawl than I am currently north of it. Still, he's offering to drive 80 miles through the big-city tangle to fetch me, the pup, and the box, and haul us back to Orange County, so he can give his burgeoning brainchild the old college try. Everybody should have a brother like Theo. Seriously.

Now, a mall security guard approaches. "How are we doing today, sir?" inquires the stocky, dark-haired woman in uniform. She's about 30. Her smile is kind, but cautious. I explain that I'm on a pilgrimage and my cart has broken down. She seems genuinely interested. She's heard about people taking similar journeys. I inform her that I'm waiting for my brother, then mention that my dog hasn't been too happy with strangers approaching her. "I know," she says. "We got a call." With a lift of a finger, she asks me to hang on for a minute, swivels, and strolls back to the curb while speaking into her walkie-talkie.

"He's on some kind of pilgrimage. Waiting for his brother to pick him up."

I ask her if there might be a safe place where Millie and I could wait, away from foot traffic. She says we can stow ourselves directly across the darkening outdoor parking lot, next to the now-closed Firestone tire store. I thank the uniformed woman for her help. She wishes me good luck. Slowly, laboriously, I guide the wobbly cart across the blacktop. As soon as we make it to the tire store building, the wheel once again falls off the box — for the final time.

Some kind of peace pilgrimage this is. So far, on Day One, while walking for all of three hours, I've managed to suffer contusions on both shins, get into an expletive-spiced shouting match with a Big 5 sales associate, and bust a wheel off of my cart. My dog has terrified a little Asian girl, making me the devil in the disdainful eyes of the child's grandmother, and getting me busted by mall security. Now, I find myself propped up in my Monarch Chair, against the stucco wall of a locked-up Firestone tire store in the chilly darkness, choking down the remains of a soggy, unpleasantly fragrant Subway tuna wrap, and reading the opening paragraph of the Kindle edition of *Zen and the Art of Motorcycle Maintenance* over and over again on my iPhone.

Brother Theo's Prius cruises stealthily into the parking lot. The driver-side window rolls down. "So, how's it going, Man?" he chuckles, exuding that inimitable pink-cheeked smile.

CHAPTER 6

The Pilgrimmobile

My brother Theo is a loving, generous, multi-talented enthusiast. Something needs doing, he jumps right in there and gets 'er done with undaunted vigor and a jolly, positive attitude. Assessing a problem, looking at it from every angle, figuring out a solution, then tackling it, is what makes Theo tick. And, if it's somebody else's problem, he gives it even higher priority and laser focus than he would if it were his own.

MAY 2 · DAY TWO

It's shortly after 8 AM when I trundle down the hallway into the living room of my brother's house. Theo, and his middle son, Kelly, are gazing with evident self-satisfaction at the project they have somehow managed to pull off while I was sleeping: my black, fiberglass storage box tucked neatly into the metal frame of a Baby Trend jogging stroller, supported by its tricycle wheelbase. Theo had never laid eyes on the storage box. He had no way of knowing its exact size. Last night, on his way to fetch big brother, beagle, and box, three counties to the north, he'd purchased this particular used model dirt cheap from a fellow he arranged to meet in a Home Depot parking lot. Miraculously, with the seat and bonnet removed, this stroller's metal frame is of absolutely perfect width to accommodate the box, which is wedged tightly in between the frame rails at a downward angle, higher in the rear, near the push handle and lower over the single, smaller, swiveling front stroller wheel.

Theo looks at me with a smile that goes ear to ear, "Ready to try it out?"

In the bright morning sunlight, I'm guiding my new cart through the placid, suburban neighborhood where Theo and Cindy raised their three boys. "You've gotta be careful of curb cuts," my brother coaches me. I'm amazed and delighted that the stroller wheels roll so smoothly down the sidewalk with minimal effort. However, every time I get to a driveway where the sidewalk slants to one side, the stroller leans up onto two wheels and the whole thing threatens to topple over. "See, that's what I'm talking about," he points out. This issue will require keeping a vigilant eye on the road surface ahead, some strategic driving, and a pair of strong forearms. But, I'd choose this challenge over having my shins battered and bruised any day.

Today's plan: my brother will drive me back to Ventura County to pick up where, only yesterday, due to the almost immediate failure of my original cart design, I was forced to push the pause button on my nascent pilgrimage. However, before we hit the road, Theo wants to wait for a certain item to be delivered. It seems my ultra-generous sibling has ordered something he believes will prove essential to the success of my trek. According to UPS tracking, the package is in the truck and should arrive soon. "Soon," however, stretches through the remainder of the day and into the early evening. Finally, having abandoned hope that the delivery will get here tonight, we are loading Theo's Prius for the drive north when the truck shows up. The gift is as thoughtful as it is pragmatic: a portable solar panel, to keep my phone charged.

I love my brother. I really, *really* love my brother.

I'm on the phone with Sebra, describing Theo's clever, hybrid invention. Delighted that a solution has been found to my cart breakdown, one that incorporates an idea she actually suggested months ago, she laughs and declares, "So, now you've got a Pilgrimmobile!" I burst into spontaneous guffaws at the absolute brilliance of this. One of my lady's many talents is popping out with the perfect and most creative word at the perfect time. More often than not, it will come totally out of left field, in the form of some old-fashioned, linguistic anachronism. By concocting the perfect moniker for Theo's engineering feat, she's nailed it again! And, I can now lay claim to being the proud owner/operator of the world's first and only Pilgrimmobile.

MAY 3 · DAY THREE

The sun is blasting down and it's verging on the cusp of genuinely hot. Millie has always disliked direct sunlight. She's panting and straining at the leash, pulling toward every patch of shade she sees. It's also evident that the rubber booties, meant to protect her feet from the burning pavement, are distressing her. When I remove them, she nips at my fingers and whimpers in pain. So much for all that research and experimentation to find the ideal dog shoe.

We skirt along lengthy stretches of rural road, past acres of vacant, dusty fields, without a tree or a patch of shade in sight. With her booties off, Millie seems revitalized, enjoying the jaunt. She's prancing alongside the cart, ears flopping, tongue drooling, and lapping at every rare breeze. I stop on the shoulder of the road to give her a drink of water. Catching the scent of some furry creature, probably a gopher, Millie lunges, yanking at the leash attached to the belt of my belly bag. I instinctively grab onto the handle of the stroller for balance. The top-heavy Pilgrimmobile, however, has balance issues of its own and promptly topples over on its side. As it thuds to the ground, the storage box dislodges from the stroller frame and rolls over, landing upside down in the dirt and gravel.

Lifting the hefty storage box on my own and placing it just so into the stroller frame proves to be a challenge — especially for a man of a certain age on the gravelly edge of a highway with an eager beagle tethered to his waist. This trick requires setting my feet wide, directly under my shoulders, squatting, grasping the box by its handles on each end, and pushing upward with my legs in a first motion, then quickly bending my arms at the elbow to lift the box to my chest in a second effort. This motion is what I'm pretty sure weight lifters call a clean-and-jerk. Or, at least, these are the first two stages of the clean-and-jerk. I'm not about to finish the process by raising the whole thing above my head, for criminy sake. Once I've hoisted the storage box to chest level, I need to swing it up and over the stroller frame and lower it precisely, so it falls into place. As the box itself prevents me from seeing exactly where I'm dropping it, this exercise requires several tries. By the time I've successfully wedged the box into its nesting place, I'm flop sweating like Albert Brooks in *Broadcast News*. Still, I feel a genuine sense of accomplishment. At least now I know I'm capable of accomplishing this feat without assistance.

After what seems like an interminable stretch of nothing — it's amazing how much priceless, coastal California real estate remains undeveloped — we reach the junction of Highway One. Crossing the busy two-lane thoroughfare presents yet another challenge, one that demands timing, quickness and, if I do say so myself, more than a modicum of daring. Every California driver considers him- or herself the most important person on earth, and he or she is in a big hurry to get somewhere. I would yell out, "Pedestrians beware!" But my dog and I are the only foot travelers in sight. Evidently, no one else is foolhardy enough to walk the clogged, haphazard highways of California. In a brisk jog, we reach the ocean side of the highway safely. My heart is beating fast and furiously. Each inhalation comes quick and shallow. I feel a jolt of electric excitement. A broad, spontaneous smile widens across my face. There's the gleaming, blue Pacific stretching out to the western horizon. Adrenalized, exhilarated, I push my cart northward for what I expect to be approximately eight more miles to Ventura.

Ventura's marina is picturesque, idyllic if you will. Upscale hotels and restaurants hug the shoreline. Expensive vehicles steered by well-to-do folks pull in and out of parking lots. Families of means load and unload luggage into car trunks and from SUV hatches. Stylish couples stroll hand-in-hand down boardwalks into eateries. Suddenly, Paul McCartney sings from the right hip pocket of my cargo shorts... *When I get older, losing my hair, many years from now...*

The light-hearted English music-hall parody from the "Sergeant Pepper" album has been my ringtone of choice since... *Bingo! Exactly!* Since my sixty-fourth birthday. Nearly four years have screamed past. Every time Sir Paul croons from my pocket, I remind myself that I need to change that ringtone. But I never get around to it.

"Hello, this is Rand."

I've been reaching out to Reverend Dana Walsnop for weeks. Prior to becoming pastor of the Unitarian Universalist Church of Ventura, Reverend Dana spent several months as interim minister of my home congregation, the Central Oregon Coast UU Fellowship. I'm delighted to hear from her. After apologizing for not getting back to me sooner, she suggests that I meet her at the church facility. There's a choir practice this evening and she suggests that I might want to sit in. Of course, I'd love to. "After that," Reverend Dana says, adopting the hippie jargon of my youth, "you're welcome to crash at my place." Then, she adds, "Oh, and the couple that was interested in hosting your house concert?" *I knew nothing about this.* "Well, unfortunately, he had a heart attack and he's in the hospital."

"Oh, wow! That's awful," I respond. "Is there anything I can do? Visit, sing him some songs?"

"No," she informs me, "he's not ready for visitors yet." She wants to know where I am, so she can give me directions. I'm attempting to describe my location to her, when she interrupts... "Well, wherever you are, you can't be too far away. And, surely you have some sort of map thingy in your phone, right?" She further informs me that she'll be going out to dinner and will be back at the church by 7PM.

I'm about to learn two huge lessons, both of which are secretly encoded in a pair of presumptions only just now expressed by Reverend Dana. Firstly, yes, a few miles "can't be too far away" — if you happen to be driving a motorized vehicle. If you're on foot, however, you're singing an entirely different song altogether, at a much more languid tempo. And, if a person is not accustomed to using their legs and feet for transportation — and scant few Southern Californians are — they can't possibly have any perspective on what someone traveling by foot might envision upon hearing the words "Wherever you are, you can't be too far away."

The second lesson is this: if your map app tells you to turn around, *do it!* In other words, don't try to outthink a satellite guidance system. When I enter the address of The Ventura UU Church into the map app, the nice robot lady instructs me to reverse my direction and return to a road I recall passing at least 45 minutes ago. The screen indicates that my destination is on the other side (the east side) of Highway 101. I can see the elevated throughway from here. So, I'm thinking, *surely there must be another underpass closer than a mile and half back.* The idea of retracing my steps just doesn't sit right with me. So, I decide to keep moving ahead until I reach the next underpass — a very unfortunate miscalculation.

I trek on, another mile, and another, and yet another after that, all the while getting that much further away from my destination. I feel like an absolute dolt. But I can't turn back now. That would necessitate re-tracking those three miles to the marina area, then walking another 45 minutes just to get to the street the map app originally wanted to send me to. I'm encountering my first steep uphill grade, which goes on for at least a half a mile. The force of gravity doubles the weight of the cart and my steps are becoming more plodding and labored. I haven't eaten. My spirits are plunging along with my blood-sugar level. Breathless and fatigued, I'm approaching the peak of the hill. I see a gas station on the horizon. This is a hopeful sign. Maybe I've finally reached a freeway interchange. Thankfully, this intersection crosses over the 101. And, here's a family-style restaurant to provide a source of sustenance.

☮ ☮ ☮ ☮ ☮

It's 6:30 by the time Millie and I finally arrive at the UU Church of Ventura. By now, I've circumvented the entire city, stretching today's relatively easy 11-mile walk out into an 18-mile ordeal. As I park the Pilgrimmobile under the roof overhang next to the front entrance of a converted, ground-floor office space, my weary feet and legs are complaining. I feed Millie, stow her in her crate, then assemble my Monarch Chair, hoping to boot up my MacBook, sit back against the side of the building, elevate my aching tootsies, and do some journaling. I've just gotten situated when cars begin slipping into the parking lot one after another — choir members, I assume, arriving for this evening's rehearsal. I can't help but notice looks of obvious distrust as, prior to entering the building, most steer as clear of me as they can. Some, however, approach. "Can I help you with something?" a gentleman queries. I assure him that I'm fine.

"Are you waiting for someone?" a lady wants to know.

"Yes," I respond, summoning my friendliest smile, "I'm waiting for Dana."

"Oh, uh, huh. Reverend Dana? Is she expecting you?"

"Yes, she is. She's out to dinner. I'm meeting her here."

"Well," the lady feels the need to explain, "I'm only asking because we have a lot of homeless people who, you know…"

"No, no," I interrupt in an effort to let her off the hook. "I'm not homeless. I'm on a pilgrimage…" The woman seems to find this information more confounding than calming. "My name is Rand."

She introduces herself as Ruth. Meanwhile, another choir lady scoots past, casting suspicion in my direction out of the corners of her squinted eyes. Wow! Here I was, expecting to receive an open-armed greeting from this congregation. Instead, they seem to be putting me on trial, judging and convicting me at first glance for a crime that isn't even a crime. *Is this really a church*, I wonder, *or is it a country club?*

Reverend Dana arrives. We shake hands politely. She's all business, evidently in a bit of a rush. "You can put your dog in my office if you want," she suggests. "Does he get along with other dogs?"

"Most of the time," I answer, "but you never know about Millie."

I start packing my computer and folding my chair, making small talk on a get-to-know basis. But Dana can't dawdle. She has an appointment, a parishioner waiting on her.

Ten minutes later, I'm tip-toeing through Reverend Dana's office with Millie on the leash, trying my very best not to disturb the intimate, hushed counseling session now underway. Immediately, chaos ensues. Dana's dog and mine have no interest in sharing the same space, and Millie's piercing, crying-victim howl makes it perfectly clear that she is completely freaked out about it. I pull Millie back with a quick, sidelong apology and step out into the expansive space that serves as the church sanctuary. There, I join the choir practice just getting underway. I'm sitting on the edge of a riser petting Millie, huddling at my feet, trembling in evident trauma. The choir director hands me some sheet music. "What's your range?" she asks. "Tenor, baritone, bass?"

I tell her I can sing whatever she needs. "We're short on tenors," she says. *Okay then, tonight I'm a tenor.*

"We have a very special guest here this evening," she announces to the group. "Rand Bishop."

Like fourth graders welcoming the fire chief on career day, several of the choir members smile and speak their requisite "Hi, Rands" aloud. As I scan the faces of the choir, acknowledging each person, my eyes meet Ruth's. Clearly, she is embarrassed about our earlier encounter. "Rand is on a pilgrimage," the director continues. "Tell me, Rand, would it be appropriate to say that you're on a pilgrimage for peace?"

Unexpectedly, I find this query to be particularly puzzling. For a moment, I'm literally speechless. Every eye in the choir is focused in my direction.

Since I first conceived this mission five months ago, my actual purpose for taking it on has evolved. Now, on the third night of my 90-day pilgrimage, I'm being asked a simple question. I should have a clear, concise response on the tip of my tongue. Instead, I'm caught unprepared. "Well, yes," I answer, hesitantly. "I guess you could say that. I mean, peace is an important part of it." I stammer through some rambling, convoluted sentences and sentence fragments, eventually getting back to this: "But, I'm actually walking to inspire civil, constructive dialogue."

The exact wording of the choir director's query and my inept response to it has suddenly made me painfully aware that my muddled message is still in need of further refinement. If nothing else, I've got a branding problem. Who am I? What *exactly am I doing? Why have I chosen to take on this so-called pilgrimage?* How, I wonder, can I hope to inspire civil, constructive dialogue — or any kind of dialogue — if I'm unable to articulate my mission statement clearly, concisely, and convincingly?

So, would it would be appropriate to say that I'm on a pilgrimage for peace? Here's the truth: I've been on a mission of peace for 50 years, since I huddled as close as possible to the pavement on the campus of Oberlin College, clutching a dampened towel over my face to prevent swirling, blue-grey tear gas from scorching my eyes and invading my lungs. I was on a pilgrimage for peace later that spring in D.C. when I linked arms with my brothers and sisters and marched from the Capitol Mall to the Pentagon, singing "We Shall Overcome." I was on a pilgrimage for peace 20 years later, when I embraced the Beyond War Movement and the principle of non-violence, and two decades later, when I stood with those noble few, shivering in the frigid, torrential Nashville rain, and when I penned all those letters to the editor of *The Tennessean*, and summer-after-summer, while leading sing-alongs for the campers at Peace Village, and every time I've ever felt the inspiration to compose a song of peace and sing it for whomever would listen.

So, what, if anything sets this particular part of my pilgrimage for peace apart from the lifelong mission I began all those decades ago? Back then, working for peace was about putting an end to wars between nations. And, without question, that kind of big-picture peacemaking continues to be urgent and vital to the survival of humankind and to the planet we share. However, along the way, I came to the realization that I cannot create peace on a big-picture level unless I make peace with myself and seek to create peace in my every interaction. In other words, I discovered a profound truth resonating in that corny old sing-along… "Let there be peace on earth, and let it begin with me."

So, from that perspective, one might say that every time you or I engage in civil, constructive dialogue, every time we demonstrate genuine respect for one another, every time we make the conscious effort to listen to and empathize with one another, we are creating peace — or, at least we are giving peace a better chance.

So, yes, Ms. Choir Director, it would be totally accurate, spot-on in fact, to say that I am on a pilgrimage for peace. Thank you so much for asking. And, by the way, *let it begin with me!*

I lift my beer glass and reach across the table. Reverend Dana hoists her martini. We toast. I listen as she shares her own journey, how she found her calling as a minister, the life-threatening illness that sidelined her for a time, the stint she spent at my home church on the Oregon Coast, and how she landed here to tend to the Ventura flock.

Maybe it's the beer. Maybe it's the wear and tear an 18-mile trek under a blazing sun can put on an old fellow. But, here we are, chatting about the state of the disunion, when my most cynical alter ego blurts out something about how the new regime in Washington D.C. is determined to create a fascist state. Dana wants to know what I mean by "fascist." Corporatism, I tell her, where big companies and elite executives control all the money and power, as in Mussolini's Italy, mixed with an equally unhealthy dose of nativism and government-sanctioned racism, as perpetrated in Nazi Germany.

Dana proceeds to take a peace pilgrim to school. Regardless of my definition, she counsels me, it's counterproductive to be tossing around buzzwords like fascism or calling anyone fascists. For a whole lot of people, accusing the new president and his cronies of promoting such an extreme agenda would automatically put the brakes on the conversation and cut off all possibility for constructive communication. Thus, any chance of finding common ground and/or seeking solutions would be lost, simply because I made a reckless choice of words. *Point taken.* I feel a genuine desire to listen to people's concerns, discover where they coincide with mine, and discuss how we might go about finding solutions. From now on, as I trek northward, I'd best pick my language with more care.

Thank you, Reverend Dana, for your insight and for ministering to a traveling stranger. Oh, and thanks for the burrito, the beer, and the bed, too. And, before "crashing" for the night, I offer something in return. Ventura may not have provided me the opportunity to perform a full-scale house concert as I'd hoped, but this moment seems perfect to sing for an audience of one.

"Would it be okay," I ask, "if I played you a song?" What's a gracious host gonna say to that question? *No? Some other time?* Not on your life.

As I tune my little Seagull acoustic into "drop-D," I explain that our conversation has reminded me of one song in particular. Subject? The Living Example, the one who, more than two millennia ago, walked the Earth and set that nearly unattainable bar, a prophet perhaps but still, as we Unitarians believe, a human being after all.

When ya comin' back? What's takin' you so long?
Whatcha waitin' for? So much down here has gone wrong
When ya comin' back? What's takin' you so long?

Maybe you came and no one even noticed
You didn't look the same, did a little hocus pocus
Maybe you were black, yellow, brown, who can say
You could-a been a woman, trans, bi, or gay

The wages of sin is death, that's nice
Cause everyone's a sinner and everybody dies
If Jesus is comin', I don't mean to be crude
But I just can't wait to have a beer with the dude
So, when ya comin' back? What's takin' you so long?

— "COMIN' BACK" BY RAND BISHOP, © 2016
WEIGHTLESS CARGO MUSIC, BMI

CHAPTER 7

Moisture

I'm sitting at a picnic table in front of the small, beige, masonry shack called the Faria Beach Café. Ocean waves are crashing — literally *crashing* — only 60 feet away, against the massive boulders piled up strategically to protect this little pimple of California coastline from being nibbled away and swallowed by the relentless Pacific.

I'm not nibbling. I savor another large bite. I had no idea oatmeal could taste this good. I rise and walk to the counter. "What can I do for ya?" the friendly woman asks. My request is simple, just some more brown sugar for my oatmeal. "Your sandwich will be ready in just a few minutes."

"No hurry," I tell her, "I'll be saving it for later anyway."

The café was closed by the time Millie and I arrived here last evening, much to the consternation of my growling stomach. Added to that disappointment was an even greater one. The 42 sites at Faria Beach Park are first-come, first-serve. Forty-two other campers came first, which left a late-coming pilgrim and his tuckered pooch out of luck. I decided not to let no room at the inn prevent me from locating what looked like a perfectly fine spot to pitch my tent. And I was pretty darn proud of how I'd set up our makeshift campsite, too, this being the very first time I'd actually fully assembled my snug, one-person bivouac. Right next to the red bivy, I set up Millie's crate, then draped the blue-vinyl tarp over my cart and the dog crate, and anchored the corner grommets of the tarp to the ground via a web of bungee cords and tent stakes. The tarping was for the purpose of protecting the crate and the cart from moisture. This close to the beach, I knew it was likely to get damp overnight. I had no clue how damp it would actually get.

The poached spot I staked out was on the outside edge of the only plot of grass in the park, designated for campers to walk their dogs. As we weren't taking up much space, I felt relatively certain that other dog owners wouldn't take issue with our presence. However, it hadn't occurred to me that Millie might object to the frequent visits from other canines galumphing by to do their business. This led me to issue a number of self-conscious apologies for my pup's growling and barking, while chastising her for chronically rude behavior.

Shortly after sunset, after glomming down a feast comprised of trail mix and a Kind Bar, I coaxed Millie into her crate, crawled inside my bivy — crawling is literally the only way a person can do it — and started mummying myself in my ultra-lightweight REI sleeping bag. As I lay there, a medley of two thoughts played over and over in my busy brain: *What if a park ranger comes along and catches us camped out in this poached site?* And… *My, Lord, that ocean is LOUD!* Although my mind was still at work, my weary body was more than ready to call it a day. Finally, physical fatigue won the tug o' war and I fell into a deep, luxurious sleep.

☮   ☮   ☮   ☮   ☮

The noise was as sudden as it was deafening. Some violent force seemed to be shaking my tent with intense fury. My first half-conscious thought was that a gale had kicked up at sea. Right before hitting the sack, I'd noticed the west wind rapidly becoming colder, damper, and stronger. The park campground protrudes out into the ocean, surrounded on three sides by water. *Of course*, I assumed, *it's the wind.* Then, as abruptly as it had begun, the noise and the vibration stopped and waves pummeling boulders once again took over as the dominant ambient sound. Thirty seconds later, my tent began shaking again. The noise crescendoed to a roar, but only for a few seconds. Then, as before, it was suddenly quiet, except for surf hitting rocks. By the time this happened again, I was fully awake and beginning to discern a regular pattern: 30 seconds of placidity broken up by five seconds of sound and fury.

Aha! I figured it out. And my conclusion did not make me a happy camper. We were on a patch of grass. Grass requires regular watering, especially in arid Southern California. The monster attacking my tent every half minute was the heavy spray from the park's automatic sprinkler system. It was only 11:10PM. I shined a flashlight beam above my head. Droplets of moisture were beginning to collect inside the fabric at the pitch of my bivy. I spoke some choice words, scolding myself for what was turning out to be an obvious and possibly serious mistake — choosing this spot of all spots to set up camp. After a dozen five-second drenchings, the man-made monsoons stopped. Assuming we'd weathered the worst of it, I pulled my sleeping bag over my head and went back to sleep.

At about 5AM, the sprinkler system's power nozzle took another dozen circles around the yard. Once again, a rudely awakened pilgrim murmured some choice words. This salty language, however, was not so much directed at my own stupidity, but more at the ridiculousness of this situation, and at my own sopping helplessness to do anything about it.

Before dawn, I was re-awakened, first by human voices, followed by some banging and clanging of metal on metal and, finally, the roar of a massive V-8 engine. A couple was pulling their RV out from the concrete pad next door. At first, I was annoyed, as I invariably am when prematurely shaken out of my slumber. Then, it occurred to me that this now-vacated spot might be an ideal place to dry out my overly irrigated camping gear. By the time the sun was visible in the eastern sky, I had lugged my waterlogged load off the lawn. Under the morning's first rays, I stretched out my tent and the blue tarp across the concrete slab and the picnic table. After three hours of dabbing the saturated fabric with paper towels purloined from the restroom, I packed it all in the storage box.

"Sir," the friendly woman inside the Faria Beach Café calls out, "Your order is ready."

⊛   ⊛   ⊛   ⊛   ⊛

There is an extra benefit to trekking the left shoulder of Pacific
Coast Highway. Not only does it allow us to see and be seen by
oncoming vehicles, it puts us nearer to the ocean and provides us
a fabulous view of the beaches. I'm also discovering the benefit of
bracing myself, both physically and psychologically, for the passing
of an approaching motor vehicle, even as fleeting as that whizzing
by might be. First, one must be ready for the aural component of
the encounter. The noise begins with the whirring of tires on pavement and is quickly drowned out by engine roar, which, at times,
rivals Leo the MGM lion in Dolby Surround Sound accompanied
by Eddie Van Halen power-chords. Then, there's the moving air,
which invariably has substantial impact. Depending on the shape,
size, and speed of each, individual vehicle, these wind blasts can
approach what feels to a vulnerable foot traveler like hurricane
velocity.

It feels as though I'm tightrope walking on the border between
two very different worlds. To our right, the faces we see through the
windshields and side windows of passing vehicles tend to radiate
an outward warmth. When I smile, regardless of a traveler's age,
gender, or skin color, they usually smile back. We even receive
the occasional wave. The morning, it seems, is the time for exuding fresh energy and optimism. Everybody appears to be in good
spirits. I mean, really, here we all are traversing the picturesque
California coastline on a gorgeous spring day. *How does it get any
better than this?*

To our left, however, is an entirely different picture. For as far
as the eye can see, RVs, massive camper trailers, and buses hog the
$35-dollar-per-day parallel-parking spots along the beach-side of
the road. It's as if a parade came to a halt and simply gave up on
any chance of moving ahead. Still, nearly every single float in the
parade has its generator running. Many fly American, military,
and/or sports-team flags. Dozens of *God Bless America* banners
hang proudly on display. Beneath awnings of red, white, and blue,
folks kick back in lawn chairs, sipping coffee, chatting with one

another and gazing out across the ocean. A good number of these
sedentary citizens appear to be significantly overweight. The aroma
of bacon on the grill wafts through the air. But another smell far
is more pervasive: diesel exhaust. Fossil fuel guzzling, it seems,
goes hand in hand with flag waving. How, I wonder, did so overtly
wasting energy and polluting the atmosphere become synonymous
with patriotism?

Unlike the more affable motorists and passengers sweeping
past on our right, the RV people on our left avoid making eye
contact if at all possible. And, when I do happen to catch the
accidental glance, sneers outnumber return smiles by at least a
five-to-one margin. For some reason, to these people, my presence
is unpleasant, unsettling, enigmatic. It's as though they'd simply
prefer not to acknowledge this fellow with the gall to push a cart
along the outskirts of their temporary, serpentine village. Although
I do share some obvious traits with many of the faces *not* looking
back at me — being white, as I am, and of a certain age — I'm an
alien to their sub-culture. Maybe there's an unspoken, unwritten
code 'round these parts, one that implies that, should any one of
them ever break their vow of muteness by emitting an impulsive,
spontaneous "Howdy" or a "How's it goin'?" they'd be risking a
shunning or, worse yet, excommunication from this soot-bilging,
flag-flying, bacon-grilling, white, white, white city on wheels.

As pilgrim and pooch finally reach the northern end of the
stationary caravan, I turn back for a last gander at what must be a
peculiarly American phenomenon snaking southward along the
coast for a mile or more. I'm overcome with a sense of bemusement.
Here we are trekking through presumably progressive California,
the state that leads the nation in vehicle emission standards and
renewable energy. Californians are obsessed with health, fitness,
nutrition, alternative lifestyles, and spirituality. Here, brown-
skinned people now outnumber white, and the man the Electoral
College put in the White House was rejected — by *millions* of votes.
And yet, if I polled the citizens of RV Town, I bet the tally would
reveal that, by an overwhelming margin, these voters marked their
ballots for the candidate who personifies the antithesis of every-

thing this state outwardly represents.

So, here's a wild idea! Instead of the Unitarians, maybe I should be performing a house concert for the citizens of RV Town. Maybe I should be listening to *their* complaints, hoping to find an iota of mutual concern. I'm curious as to what common ground might look like between a peace pilgrim and these nomadic, fuel-squandering quasi-patriots. And, if I asked them to close their eyes and visualize the kind of future they want for their children and their grandchildren, I wonder what they'd see.

The dedicated bike lane parallel to a stretch of 101 called the Rincon Highway is not only an impressive piece of engineering, it also gives the un-motorized traveler a spectacular view of the ocean and the beaches below. Constructed as an arrow-straight, concrete trough suspended over the sea, this lengthy passageway is just wide enough for northbound and southbound bikes and/ or walkers, with a painted line between.

Way down the lane, in the far, far distance, I spy something I've not beheld for at least two days, and never outside of an urban setting. I can scarcely believe my eyes. But this is not a mirage. I actually detect the presence of humans approaching on foot — two of them! As the gap diminishes between us, I make out what I believe is a man, substantially thinner and taller than his female companion. The woman is clad in an orange tunic, not unlike those commonly worn by workers picking up trash by the roadside. As she comes closer, I notice that the orange-vested one is also wearing a broad, unaffected smile.

As a fellow pedestrian in Southern California is rarer than a unicorn, I'm not satisfied with shouting out a quick "hi" in passing. When I inquire where these fellow pilgrims hail from, I'm surprised by their answer. "Wow! Sonoma?" I exude. "That's impressive! So, then, how far have you walked?" The woman, who looks 60-something, tells me they've covered more than 500 miles so far, which, from my perspective, after having trekked little more than an insignificant 30, might as well be 10,000. I ask if there is some special purpose for their walk.

The woman turns around, revealing the lettering on the back of her orange tunic, which reads, *Pat's Walk.*

"My mother died of breast cancer," Pat explains. "I couldn't be there for her when she passed, so I'm walking in her honor to promote breast cancer awareness." It turns out Pat's tall, slender companion is not her husband, but her husband's best friend. And, a very devoted friend he is. Pat's spouse is physically incapable of walking any distance, let alone 500 miles. So, while the hobbled hubby travels by car, his pal has nobly stepped up to accompany Pat as chaperone and body guard.

"This is a little something about me and what I'm up to," I say, handing Pat one of my postcards.

As she scans the card, Tall/Slender Man continues the conversation. "How are your feet doing?" he queries.

I have to admit that my underpinnings are already growing tender, as I was certain they would. My passion for running in my younger adulthood, added to 25 years of playing pick-up basketball, did some real damage to these gunboats, resulting in chronic inflammation in my metatarsus and a pair of arthritic big toes. Sore feet can also be a side effect of ankylosing spondylitis, a rheumatic spinal condition I've battled since my late twenties.

"Don't worry," he says. "Just stick it out. Your feet will toughen up."

After promising to connect on Facebook and keep in touch, we part ways, Millie and I pointed northbound; Pat and her gallant chaperone heading south.

The composition of the photo turns out to be rather perfect: The scrumptious BLT, prepared especially for me this morning, with loving care, by that friendly, here-to-please lady at the Faria Beach Café is gripped in my left hand, poised for my next bite. There in the background, is the Pilgrimmobile, parked by the curb. I finish off my yummy mid-day repast, dispose of its wrapping, pay an encore visit to the wayside toilet, carabiner Millie's leash to the belt of my belly bag, unlock the parking brake on the cart and start pushing.

Something is not right. It's taking far more effort than usual to move the stroller forward. A quick perusal confirms my suspicions. The small front tricycle tire on the stroller is flat. And, not just a little bit light on H2O. The wheel rim is actually sitting on the pavement. The cart has been gliding along perfectly all morning. Now, after sitting here stationary for no more than a half hour — in direct, plain sight, mind you — the tube has somehow exhaled every single molecule of its air. This seems odd, not to mention frustrating.

I'm regretting that I didn't have the foresight to buy a new, more reliable bicycle pump. By the time I've got the chubby thing jammed between the narrow spokes, I'm still unable to re-inflate the tire. This predicament provokes a spontaneous diatribe peppered by some choice expletives. My profane rant not only disturbs Millie, but attracts askance looks from several other folks in the midst of taking a relaxing wayside break. Although these onlookers seem curious, none is concerned enough to inquire if they can be of assistance. Surely, I'm thinking, there must be a cyclist around equipped with a better pump. My scanning eyes locate a woman standing next to an open hatchback. Her bike is propped up on its kickstand and she's removing her helmet. *Bingo!* She shows me her pump. *Dang it!* It's even chubbier than mine. Not a chance this one could ever squeeze between those narrow spokes.

Okay, on to plan B. I'll need to detach the wheel from the stroller and take it to the nearest bike shop to get the tire repaired. *But, damn!* Detaching the wheel will require a certain tool I neglected to pack. So, I cruise the parking lot, knocking on car and truck windows. Inexplicably, no one seems to be in possession of a crescent wrench. At the far southern end of the lot, a pickup slips into a parking space. I stride those hundred yards to approach the attractive young couple inside. Surfers, I surmise, from the boards lying in their truck bed. He looks in his toolbox.

"Will these work?" he asks, holding up a pair of needle-nosers — not exactly what I'm looking for, but worth a try. I find a spot to stash the Pilgrimmobile over a small hill, partially hidden from the parking lot. There, I unbolt the wheel. I stand up, surprised to discover the young surfer couple hovering over me.

"Oh, here," I say, extending the borrowed tool. "Thanks a lot." I'm assuming they've come to make sure I didn't try to make off with their pliers. Actually, she's curious about this pilgrim with the beagle, pushing his cart up the coast of California. I give them my postcard and tell them a little bit about my quest. She identifies herself as Katy Mac from Malibu. She, too, has been deeply concerned about the level of animosity and meanness in this country. We chat for a few minutes, quickly discovering much in common. I'd truly love to get into more depth with these smart, considerate, young folks. But my ride has arrived and this little tire needs immediate professional attention before the bike shop closes.

The Uber driver is an intense young man of Middle-Eastern descent. He's driving his brother's car, he explains, a beautiful, new, black-on-black Infiniti sedan, its seats upholstered in gorgeous, finely tooled, ebony leather. "I don't usually allow dogs in my car," he says, nervously. "I don't want to strand you here. But, if your dog scratches my brother's leather seats, he's gonna kill me."

Not to worry, I tell him. As long as we put Millie's camping bed down on the seat before she gets in, there should be no problem. But, he's not listening. He's in too much of a rush. He throws open the rear door of the sedan, hoists my backpack off the ground and tosses it inside, sending it tumbling end over end across the back seat. This is Millie's cue to leap into the vehicle. The clicking and scraping of her nails on the slick leather seat is audible, as she spiders to find solid footing. I dive in after her to push her off the seat and onto the floor mat so I can lay the bed down to protect the upholstery. Millie, however, refuses to stay on the floor. She needs to see out of the window. Before I can slip the dog bed into place, she leaps back up onto the seat and loses her footing again, making matters even worse.

As the crow flies, we're only about two miles away from our destination, just south of downtown Carpenteria. I've attempted to make small talk with the anxious driver, who keeps glancing into the rear view with squinty-eyed, furrowed-browed suspicion that his worst damaged-upholstery fears have already been manifested. He pulls into the lot adjacent to the bike shop. Sure enough, the back seat has suffered substantial scratches. "What am I going to do about this?" he wails piteously. "My brother is gonna *kill* me!"

I'm attempting to calm the distraught fellow, suggesting that maybe we could make some kind of reasonable arrangement. Instead, he tells me to forget about it, slides in behind the wheel, gives his brother's car door a violent slam, and screeches off.

In the aftermath of this Uber drama, I am comforted by the serene, cerebral demeanor of the bike shop's Geppetto look-alike proprietor. In mere minutes, the pensive, white-haired, white-mustachioed gent has skillfully whipped a new, thistle-proof tube into the tire.

⊕ ⊕ ⊕ ⊕ ⊕

As we climb the slope of blacktop into the wayside, my shoulders are aching from toting my weighty backpack a full three and a half miles. Arriving back at the Pilgrimmobile, I'm relieved to discover that only one item has gone missing — a fancy water bottle scored at a REI garage sale.

I ONLY MENTION this theft because, ultimately, I would leave the Pilgrimmobile unattended by necessity on numerous occasions: outside markets, in parks, and along roadways. Miraculously, the REI water bottle was the one and only item that ever went missing — over the entire 90 days of my trek.

⊕ ⊕ ⊕ ⊕ ⊕

As pleased and relieved as I am to have reached the end of today's trek, I have yet more walking to do. I free my tender, unhappy feet from my New Balance trail joggers, slip into my Moskito flip-flops, and summon my final scrap of energy to go back out there in search of sustenance. According to the nice girl at the front desk of the Motel 6, there's a Lucky Market right up the road. Of course, "right up the road" means one thing to the driver of a motor vehicle and something else altogether to a person traveling by foot, especially at the completion of a 15-mile day.

I come upon a woman sitting in a wheelchair, in front of what, at first glance, looks to be an apartment building. She calls out to me. While I'm in no mood to engage in chitchat, I certainly don't want to be rude. She points toward a pathway paralleling the creek and begins telling me how lovely it is, how she likes to sit by the babbling water and think about things. I'm nodding my head, as if I understand the significance encoded somewhere in this sweet lady's manic, semi-incoherent rambling.

Her clothes are clean, her hair kempt. It doesn't appear that she is homeless. Probably just lonely, I guess. Whenever there's a pause in her speech, I respond with an *I see*, or a *Really? That's wonderful.* She's obviously delighted to have an ear to bend and will keep bending mine as long as I'll allow. After a few minutes, I tell her it's been nice to meet her but I really must be moving on. She smiles and says, "Okay, then. You take care."

As I resume my tender-footed shuffle toward the Lucky Market, she sends me a little melancholy wave. Thirty feet up the sidewalk, I come to the large, painted sign in the front lawn of the "apartment building." It reads, *Gran Vida Senior Living and Memory Care.* I stop and turn around. A young couple, tatted and pierced, are now standing on the sidewalk, nodding their heads. As the sweet wheelchair woman blathers on, they appear to be as baffled as I'd been only a minute earlier.

CHAPTER 8

Sweet 'n' Sour Cherries

MAY 6 · DAY SIX

Anyone listening from outside must think we're dismembering bodies in here. Surely, the sound of electric sawing, drilling, and sanding must be easily audible through the walls of this motel room in Carpenteria, California. My brother Theo and nephew Kelly drove up from Orange County first thing this morning to execute some final modifications on the stroller they so ingeniously adapted for my pilgrimage only four days ago. Theo's new-and-improved plan to thwart the top-heavy design's tipping tendency involves training wheels from a child's bicycle, which he and his son are installing to the left and right of the stroller's smaller, front tricycle wheel. They've just finished bolting a rectangular metal plate onto the front of the stroller frame to prevent the storage box from inadvertently sliding forward and out of its metal cradle.

As the requisite hardware wasn't tooled specifically for these exact purposes, some substantial doctoring is required to make the pieces fit. Every time a component needs another custom tuck or trim, showers of sparks shoot out across the bedspread, as the shrill, eardrum-piercing sound of a spinning saw blade cutting through metal slices the air. Clearly, my brother is taking a maniacal delight in this process. The expression on his face resembles that of Dr. Victor Frankenstein applying massive jolts of electricity to reanimate his monster's lifeless flesh. My traumatized dog, however, is taking no pleasure at all in the proceedings. I, too, am not exactly thrilled by the noise, the acrid smoke, and the dust.

Still, I'm ever so grateful for Theo's efforts to provide his big brother's pilgrimage with a means of transport that stands a chance of going the distance — or at least of getting me a good way up the road. After today, however, Theo informs me, I'm on my own. He won't be there to rescue me the next time I have a break down. There's only so far he's willing to go. And, as of this point, he's gone that far. I totally get that. I'd be selfish to expect anything more.

☮   ☮   ☮   ☮   ☮

Montecito is a charming, picturesque hamlet nestled into the California coastline, just five miles south of Santa Barbara. That the main street of this idyllic, fresh-scrubbed village bears a certain Disney-esque cuteness suggests that life here must be free from the hard and harsh realities most folks deal with on an everyday basis. This, to its upper-crust residents, I suspect, is the community's most appealing feature. Most everyone who resides here is white and, compared to any comparably sized American town, wealthy. So, I'm not a bit surprised when, as we push along the edge of East Valley Road, pilgrim and pup begin turning heads.

Thus far, today, we've been greeted with far more smiles than glares. I do find it interesting that, as a whole, men tend to be more openly friendly than women. If anyone is stand-off-ish, it's usually a person of the female gender. Perhaps my maleness makes me seem more threatening. Or, it could simply be that a cart-pushing pedestrian and his tri-colored beagle present an odd and unexpected sight.

Of course, as per usual, Millie receives a lot of attention. Her confident trot, that lop-sided grin, and her long, floppy ears swinging to and fro invariably prove irresistible. People laugh spontaneously when they see my dog. They always have. She's a cartoon come to life, as endearing as a creature can be.

I resist crossing a busy street on impulse. Doing so impedes my progress. A 15-minute detour means at least a half mile we have yet to cover. The afternoon is rapidly vanishing. We have a minimum of five more miles to go. However, in a gas station parking lot across the road, a banner advertises the first sweet cherries of the season. Immediately, involuntarily, my mouth begins to water. I think about popping one of those babies in my mouth, imagining its cool, tight, ultra-smooth skin, the way the juice bursts out when I bite into it. I can almost taste the tangy clash of sweet and sour bathing my tongue. In my mind, I'm sucking every morsel of meat from the pit, then blowing that hard, round, slimy rock through my lips, watching it arc through the air to bounce off the sidewalk into the shrubbery.

A full block past the cherry stand, we come to a crosswalk. Sometimes a pilgrim surrenders to his craving, even if it requires waiting for a considerate motorist to notice us and stop.

I park the Pilgrimmobile on the edge of the gas station lot and stroll across the blacktop to the farm stand. The cherry lady is a zaftig woman, short in stature, brown of skin. I'm wearing a big smile, looking forward to a little direct human interaction — my first since Theo and Kelly headed home several hours ago — and still anticipating the pleasure of that presumably delectable fresh fruit. As she informs me that her cherries are five dollars a box, I detect an implication in her voice. She doesn't believe I can afford the price. It's an icy tone, a condescending tone, a tone that seeks to convey a message: *So, just be on your way. I don't want people like you hanging around my stand, scaring off the real customers. It's bad for business.* She picks up a tiny, paper cup containing three cherries and extends it to me. "Here, you can have a sample." Once again, she's telling me to scram. *Take the freebies, fellah, and ease on down the road.*

"No, thanks," I say, "I'll take a box." She looks at me incredulously, as if she thinks I'm demanding a handout. "I want to buy a box of cherries," I clarify, handing her a five spot. I don't know if it's because she feels embarrassed by her previous assumption, or because she's simply unfriendly by nature. Maybe she's just having a bad day. As she hands me my purchase, she still refuses to smile or even thank me for my business. The cherries, however, don't disappoint. They are spectacular.

As we cross back to the other side of the road, I'm reminded of a famous movie scene…

"I'm *WALKIN' HEEAAAH!*" Dustin Hoffman shrieks, beating on the hood of a New York City taxi cab with his clenched fists. Hoffman's character, Ratso Rizzo, had just come inches from getting run down in a Manhattan crosswalk. Although 1969's *Midnight Cowboy* is a fictional narrative, similar scenes are played out every single day, in big cities and small towns, from coast to American coast.

Pushing a cart along the roads and highways of this country is a humbling, eye-opening experience. People make snap judgments. A second look might change a first impression. But second looks are few and far between and changes of mind even rarer. I'm beginning to understand why so many homeless people become spiteful, why they curse and make rude hand gestures when cars cut them off at crosswalks or driveways. They are people, too. Yet, we consciously disregard them, deliberately circumvent them, and almost always avoid making eye contact with them.

By allowing any contact at all, we risk feeling guilty for their plight. Acknowledging their presence might mean we'd have to take responsibility and actually do something about a situation that is, for us, simply unpleasant. For them, however, it's not merely unpleasant, nor is it a momentary inconvenience. It's a way of life. How dehumanizing must it be for a person to be treated day after day as though they don't exist? Before I began my trek, I could only imagine how this must feel. Now, I'm experiencing this brand of alienation firsthand.

A storm is on its way. The forecast calls for thunder, lightning, and heavy rain all across this part of the California Coast by tonight. I decide the best course of action is to head for the Unitarian Society of Santa Barbara. Surely, they wouldn't turn away a pilgrim on a mission of peace, especially with a storm a-brewin'.

Following Google Maps, the shortest route through southern Santa Barbara takes us uphill and down, on funky, rutted streets, underneath the freeway from the east side to the west. Then, only a few blocks later, we cross back under again, from west to east. I've always pictured Santa Barbara as classy and upscale, a place where only beautiful, fit, perennially tanned people live. My map app is revealing that this city also has some sordid secrets hidden away in the long, dark shadows under the elevated interstate highway.

I roll past a church where homeless folk — and not just bearded duffers in rags, but also teenagers, young men and women, mothers with children — line up for a charity dinner. A block down the street, a posse of the downtrodden congregate in a filthy, trash-littered park, trading gap-toothed smiles and crude, boisterous laughter. Just a few hours ago, I was feeling such empathy for the homeless and their daily plight. Now, I find myself quickening my step, hustling briskly through this blighted area. Being as vulnerable as I am, and toting so many valuable possessions, all I want to do right now is slip past these disadvantaged souls unnoticed.

☮ ☮ ☮ ☮ ☮

A caption on the USSB website reads, "Since 1876, the Unitarian Society has been a beacon of progressive religion in Santa Barbara." And, by the looks of this magnificent church building, that spiritual ray has beamed from this location for most, if not all, of that time. My UU congregation back home, of perhaps 30 regular attendees, meets in a rented space at the Visual Arts Center. The UUs of Santa Barbara gather for their Sunday services in a cathedral.

It's approaching 7:30PM. A newly married bride and her entourage are taking advantage of the last available blink of daylight to pose for their final post-wedding shots. As the giddy, be-frocked party exits the church courtyard, I ask them if they know if anyone is inside. They don't think so. The building is locked up. However, they've left the heavy, wrought-iron gate unlocked, which allows me to enter and peruse the grounds. The sky is growing darker, partially due to nightfall, but also from those ominous rain clouds blowing in swiftly from the west. The wind is beginning to swirl, bending and swaying the tall, decorative shrubbery that borders the cobblestoned space. Millie is tired. She needs to be fed. I, too, am weary and famished. With the wind whipping stronger and colder by the minute, we retreat into the corner of the tiled porch area, underneath the roof overhang. Here, we rest and take sustenance.

☮   ☮   ☮   ☮   ☮

It's dark, *very* dark. Even though the porch roof protects us from the deluge, every swirl of wind wafts another sheet of wetness in from the storm. I've blanketed myself in my sleeping bag with the blue tarp wrapped around to shield myself from the moisture and the plummeting temperature. Millie has curled herself into a ball in the furthest corner of her crate. Although the darkness prevents me from seeing her, I'm quite sure that my nervous girl is quivering in fear as tree branches whip against the side of the exterior stone walls of the church.

"Hello?"

Millie growls at the sound of a strange man's voice, then lets out her quick, "protecting-the-territory" bark. A flashlight beam appears in the courtyard. Against the glow of a distant streetlight, I can make out the silhouetted figure, flashlight in hand, approaching with caution.

Carlos, who works for the security company contracted by the church, is making his routine Saturday-night rounds. While restraining my extremely peeved, protective pooch, I scramble to explain myself. *I'm a Unitarian from Oregon. I'm on a pilgrimage.* So far, this is all on the up and up. Then, my story veers slightly off the rails of absolute truth. I imply that I'll be singing for tomorrow morning's service. I don't know why I'm telling him this. I've been hoping to get an invite to perform for the congregation. But, as no one has answered my emails, responded to my postcard, or returned my phone calls, I have no indication whatsoever that anyone here is even remotely interested in issuing such an invitation.

Still, this partially fabricated tale makes me sound credible enough that Carlos places a call to the church events manager.

There's a room upstairs, Carlos informs me, where guests stay. This is precisely the kind of information I was hoping to hear. His call, however, goes to voicemail. Carlos has more stops to make on his patrol. He says he'll be back later. I thank him profusely and apologize again for my aggressive pup. Carlos returns to his patrol car and drives off. I allow a huge exhalation of relief.

It's after 10 PM when the security guard returns. The first squall has passed. Frigid droplets slide from the shrubbery and splash onto the slickened tile. A damp, chilly haze hangs in the air. Carlos says his phone is malfunctioning, asks to use mine, taps in a number, then hands it back to me. "The guy's name is J.D.," he says.

Certainly, I tell the events manager, the church staff must be expecting me because I've emailed and mailed and called. J.D. seems genuinely surprised that I haven't heard back and that he hadn't been informed of my arrival. He then instructs Carlos to show me to a side building. There, Millie and I can get out of the weather and bed down. J.D. will be here first thing in the morning. I'll need to vacate the space by 8 AM because Sunday School teachers will be gathering there to prepare their morning's classes.

MAY 7 · DAY SEVEN

I hear the clicking of a key in the lock, immediately followed by the sound of the metal door pushing open. I peak out of my sleeping bag to see a shaft of morning light and a man entering from outside. I sit up and reach for my eye glasses.

"You must be J.D.," I assume out loud.

He flips the light switches, illuminating a large, rectangular space, designed to accommodate multiple uses. Last evening, an improv theater group convened here. In an hour, it will provide a staging ground for Sunday School teachers to ready their curriculum. At present, it's an indoor campground for a peace pilgrim and his beagle.

J.D. is an extremely nice, considerate man. He has a busy day ahead of him: two morning services, Sunday School, an all-congregation meeting, followed by a wedding this afternoon. Still, he's

finding the time and the patience to tend to the needs of a surprise
guest and his dog.

First things first. He immediately shows me to the nearest
restroom. Good thing, too, because my bladder is hovering at full
capacity. After I take Millie on a short walk so that she, too, can
find relief, I quickly stow my mini-camp back in the storage box,
and the events manager leads us to an unused classroom where,
he says, we're welcome to hang out. Or, if I'd prefer, coffee will be
served in the community room in advance of the 9:15 AM service.

As I sit here in this church pew, I'm thinking that the universe
couldn't have picked a more fortuitous Sunday for me to be in
attendance. The theme of today's Service is, of all subjects, white
supremacy — what it is, how to identify it, how to know if we are
guilty of it. The Reverend Lydia Thompson officiates the proceedings from the grand chancel. And, I mean GRAND! I haven't been
in a church this impressive since I was an 11-year-old altar boy at
St. John's Episcopal Cathedral in Spokane, Washington.

Prior to the service, as I sat in the community room sipping
tea and pecking at my computer, I took notice of a number of
individuals, all draped head-to-toe in white, shuffling through
looking suspiciously like members of a religious sect. Maybe, I
surmised, they were preparing for the rapture, or expecting an alien
space ship to scoop up the faithful and sweep them off to a distant
planet of pure, eternal bliss. But no, these were members of the
choir, dressed in the theme of the day — and a very fine ensemble,
indeed, all together and in several featured solo performances.

As the service concludes, I'm all abuzz from the message and
the music. I scoot over eagerly to introduce myself to Ken, the
choir director.

"Oh, yeah," he says, sifting through his memory bank. "Didn't
you send me something? A postcard maybe?"

I verify that, yes, I did send him a postcard about my 90-day
pilgrimage, with a personal, hand-written note about how I'd be

passing through soon and would love to contribute my talents to your service in any way at all. "In fact," I tell him, "I have a song I think would be perfect for today's theme. And, I'd be happy to stick around for the eleven o'clock service. You know, if…"

"Well," Ken cuts me off abruptly, "we plan these things a long, long time in advance."

I, too, was once music director for a small church. I tell him I understand completely.

"But, here's an idea," he suggests. "The congregation is having a meeting this afternoon at one. I'll be happy to introduce you to the group. You can tell everybody about your walk, sing a song, whatever. How does that sound?"

All right! Now we're getting somewhere. Someone who hears me sing might even want to host a spontaneous house concert. Bottom line, surely Millie and I will make some new friends. Surely someone will offer us a place to stay tonight.

Outside the vestibule, Reverend Lydia is shaking hands. After waiting my turn, I introduce myself, and hand her my postcard. Without giving it a glance, she folds the card in two and tucks it into a pocket. While she's friendly enough at first, she almost immediately begins looking over my shoulder, as if there is somebody behind me she would rather be talking to. Then, the preoccupied minister echoes the choir director, suggesting that the one o'clock meeting would be my best opportunity to introduce myself to the congregation and do some networking. "Please come," she calls out, as I stroll away, "I'll be happy to introduce you."

With tacit endorsement from the choir director and the pastor, this afternoon's event is looking very much like the type of gathering I've been hoping to get involved in from the get-go.

☮   ☮   ☮   ☮   ☮

I've just purchased the map published for cyclists, tracing every bike lane in Santa Barbara County. A young man strolls across the bike shop floor. Small, compact, wound-tight, giving off a friendly but slightly edgy energy, he's curious where I'm riding from and to. When I inform him that I'm not traveling on two wheels, but by two feet instead, my explanation of why I've taken on this trek piques the interest of his girlfriend. Attractive, blond, thirty or so, she sidles up, absorbing my spiel with evident interest. Their names, I soon find out, are Kent and Kimmie. Adorable.

"I think, regardless of our differences," I opine, "we can always find something we share in common."

"I know one thing we all have in common," Kimmie chimes in.

"What's that?" I ask, genuinely eager to hear what she has to say.

"Everybody has a birthday," she says.

I am floored by this statement, absolutely stunned! On the surface, the truth Kimmie has just articulated seems obvious, even mundane. Of course, everybody has a birthday. *Duh! Big deal!* What else is new? However, to me, this observation is truly insightful — particularly in this context. The way I see it, not only do these words contain depth and wisdom, this young woman has distilled a profound universal truth into the tidiest of packages. As a word guy, especially one who comes from a songwriting background, I have a great deal of admiration for succinct, clearly expressed language. More often than not, less is more. That being said, here are some more words to expound upon what Kimmie's seemingly simplistic, undeniably obvious, but totally profound, four-word aphorism means to me...

ON A CERTAIN day, at a precise hour, minute, and second, each and every person begins life as an innocent, vulnerable, and totally dependent being. We all take our first breath unaware of anything other than our need for mother's milk and the warmth, comfort, and safety we intuitively seek in her arms. We have not yet recognized the color of our skin. We are oblivious to our sexual orientation and uninterested in our gender identity. We don't care which God our parents worship, or whether they worship at all, what flag they wave, or what team they root for. We could care even less who received their votes in the last election or who they plan to vote for in the next. At that first moment of human life,

*nothing separates us from one another. We, in fact, have
everything in common. We all have a birthday.*

The one o'clock meeting is about to get underway. I locate J.D.
and ask him if he can unlock the classroom so I can stow the pup in
her crate and fetch my guitar. However, as the put-upon fellow is up
to his eyeballs trying to get a hand-held microphone to work, he's
unable to fulfill my request. As Millie and I pass Reverend Lydia's
office, the pastor is counseling one of her flock. After locating a
vacant chair, I scan the room-wide circle. Choir-director Ken is
nowhere to be seen.

Reverend Lydia's microphone shorts out. J.D. scrambles to
substitute the failing mic with a temporary fix while he changes
a battery pack. Then, he can't get the sound to work on the video.
Someone tries holding the mic up to the computer speaker. Unable
to hear, congregants complain. The video is abandoned, and the
discussion begins.

The question: How can the UU church promote racial harmony
when its membership is overwhelmingly white? Some parishioners
express pessimism, even fatalism over this quandary. This would
be an absolutely ideal moment for my custom arrangement of Bob
Marley's "One Love" medleyed with Curtis Mayfield's "People Get
Ready." One chorus, and I'd have the entire room singing along
in a glorious Kumbaya. A feeling of optimism would be restored
in no time. My guitar, however, remains locked away in a vacant
classroom.

The forum breaks up at 2:30. J.D. is anxious to get pilgrim
and pooch out of his hair so he can grab a hasty bite before the
arrival of this afternoon's wedding party. He's tapping his foot
impatiently. But I need a minute to bid Reverend Lydia farewell.
I'm disappointed, I must admit. Today has not matched what I'd
allowed myself to expect.

I understand. This meeting was never intended to be about me or my trek. I'm also fully aware that a minister's first obligation is to her own congregation. Lydia has conducted two services, squeezed in at least one counseling session, and facilitated a 90-minute forum on a fractious subject that was fraught with technical challenges. Certainly, she must be bleary-eyed and, like J.D., probably famished, as well. Something had to give. And, this afternoon, that something was the peace pilgrim from Oregon. And, bottom line, I won't be in town to attend next Sunday's service, or the next, nor will I be dropping a check in the velvet offering bag anytime soon. With a parting hug, Reverend Lydia wishes me safe passage.

Even though J.D. is starving. Even though he's been putting out one fire after another since early this morning. Even though his workday will stretch on through this afternoon and possibly into the evening, he makes absolutely sure that Millie and I are good to go. "Would you like a bottle of water?" he asks. I tell him that would be great. "Here," he says, "take two."

This, I'm thinking, *is a good and decent man with a very challenging job.*

CHAPTER 9

Into the Hinterlands

From Goleta to Buellton, a distance of 34 miles, there are no public services along Highway 101. Not a single gas station, convenience store, or motel. In a car, these miles whisk past in a brisk half-hour. With careful planning, a cyclist can breeze through this desolate stretch in less than a day. For a cart-pushing pilgrim and his pooch, this constitutes a three-day trek. Fortunately, for much of the initial 15-or-so miles, CalTrans has constructed dedicated bike lanes paralleling the freeway. Although I have no clue where we'll be sleeping tonight, or what I'll manage to scrounge up for an evening repast, at least the walk bringing us closer, step by step, to those unknowns will be a pleasant one. Well, that was what I was thinking, until Google Maps sent us on a very unnecessary and distressing side trip.

The map app routes cyclists onto the shoulder of 101 for the next several miles. At the same time, foot travelers are instructed to follow a two-lane road down to a beachside trail. The pavement of said road is rough, where tall eucalyptus trees alter sight lines and an invigorating aroma pervades the air. The lane climbs up, then plunges down, and down some more. While pushing the 90-pound Pilgrimmobile on an uphill grade requires strength and stamina, going downhill makes for a different, but equally challenging task. The stroller has no handbrakes, so I'm constantly pulling back on the handle to prevent the heavy cart from running away. I dare not allow myself to get up any momentum, for fear of losing control.

On the steepest downhill segments, I shorten my steps and slow to a deliberate, plodding pace, putting the sole of each foot down carefully and solidly to avoid slipping on gravel, or an unseen, slick spot. This puts considerable strain on the knees, wrists, and forearms. A downhill trek also jams toes into the tips of one's shoes.

We come to some posh-looking, residential buildings on the left, ocean-side of the road. The architecture is mission style and the grounds are impeccably landscaped with gently curving walking paths and garden plots planted with succulents and palm trees. A uniformed guard mans the security gate. He lifts the gate to wave a Lexus through, then lets a Mercedes pass. This, I'm concluding, must be some sort of private resort, so private that, if it has a name, I've yet to see signage that might let a passerby in on it. I guess, if you belong to this club, you know what it's called. If you don't know, then you don't belong here. And, that's exactly how this pilgrim is beginning to feel.

At the bottom of the incline, the road ends abruptly at a parking lot. The few modest vehicles parked here look as though they've run their odometers up to high digits. This lot must be for employees — the landscapers who keep the grounds just so, the housekeepers who change the sheets and towels, and that uniformed fellow lifting the gate for luxury cars. When we reach the far edge of the paved area, the beach-side walking path is clearly visible. On the other side of some rusted railroad tracks, the trail meanders its way up the coastline until it disappears into the afternoon mist. This view is so alluring, so picturesque, it looks as though taking Google's prescribed route would be like traipsing into the pages of a pastel-painted storybook. Fulfilling this fairytale jaunt, however, presents one obvious problem. Separating the pedestrian from that awe-inspiring pathway to Oz is a chain-link fence and a padlocked gate topped off by razor wire. The *No Trespassing* sign posted on the gate is an unnecessary redundancy.

Once again, I find myself having to do that thing I so dislike doing — covering ground I've already covered, in reverse. Pushing a 90-pound cart up an eight-degree grade on rough, rutted pavement is real labor. I feel like I'm lugging a huge, heavy wooden cross to my own execution. As if the climb weren't wearisome enough, every so often, a pricey luxury vehicle passes in the opposite direction. Drivers and passengers leer at me from within as if I'm some decrepit, dying rhinoceros at a safari park.

In the distance, I hear a voice. A single voice. A man's voice. An angry man's voice. The idea of encountering a raging maniac on a shadowy, two-lane road is unsettling — even more unsettling when I'm finally able to pick out a particularly disturbing sentence from his ongoing rant: "*If your lawyer is a nigger,*" he bellows, "*get rid of the motherfucker!*"

Around the corner struts the perturbed person himself, mid-to-late twenties, extremely tanned, with buzz-cut hair, clad in ragged, calf-length trousers, shirtless, and swinging a jacket in the air around his head like a lariat. Our eyes meet. He glowers. My heart, which is already pumping at maximum clip from the effort of pushing this cart up a steep incline, leaps into my throat. While I don't want to anticipate the worst, primal fear — for myself and for my dog — is all I feel. Then, the surly, scowling fellow simply stomps by. Thankfully, I'm able to restrain Millie from lunging, or even emitting a bark. Curiously, as he passes, the skinhead mutters a sheepish, "H'lo," as if he's even a bit embarrassed that his racist rant has been eavesdropped by a grandfatherly pilgrim and/or a friendly beagle.

I stop, bow my head, draw in a deep breath, and exhale a tremendous sigh. A smile spreads across my face. I choke back a spontaneous self-effacing guffaw for allowing myself to fall into such a panic. If he overheard, if he thought for a second that I was laughing at him, who knows what might happen? Shaking my head, I push forward, upward, and over the top of the next rise in the road.

There, but for fortune, I'm thinking. *There, but for fortune.*

Daylight is fading. Visibility issues make walking along the highway at dusk far too risky. We're tuckered out. One advantage of hiking through a remote region like this is there's a far better chance of finding an inconspicuous, relatively flat, dry spot to camp. We locate such a spot between a frontage road and the freeway. In the center of a circle of eucalyptus trees, hidden from sight by shrubbery, I allow Millie to wander off leash for the first time in days. As she sniffs around for furry creatures, I pitch my bivy. The night air is unusually warm. After feeding the dog, I rummage through my supply bag. A package of turkey jerky will have to do for my evening meal.

MAY 10 · DAY TEN

Few road shoulders are even close to level. Keeping a top-heavy cart with tricycle wheels going straight ahead on a surface that slants left or right demands fortitude and concentration. Add hills, up and down — both which slow forward progress in their own ways — and a pilgrim is in for a whole-body workout that rivals any elliptical machine or stair-climber in the gym.

Earlier today, a truck driver in a massive rig not only refused to surrender an inch of the freeway, he hugged the right white line and blew his horn as if to say, *"Get the (bleep) off of my freeway!"* Apparently, he was unaware that I was walking a segment of the interstate open to both bicycles *and* pedestrians — *because no alternative route exists!* Or, maybe the guy was just plain unaware. (I'm reticent to apply the adjective "ignorant," as I wouldn't want to leave the impression on these pages that I'm a judgmental person.)

However, let's not dwell on my more discouraging experiences. Because I am discovering that one, single, serendipitous, positive encounter can erase all the unpleasant ones in an instant. And, as I enjoy soaking in this gloriously satisfying hot tub, I'd like to take the opportunity to reflect back on four such gratifying, soul-nurturing interchanges, all of which took place during these last two days.

As inconsiderate, or oblivious, or downright mean as some motorists can be, cyclists, almost without exception, represent the shinier flipside of the coin. Where two-wheelers travel, signs along the highway read *Share the Road*. Most cyclists not only ride by that credo, they live by it as well. As pilgrim, his Pilgrimmobile, and a traipsing beagle can easily take up an entire bike lane, I squeeze as close to the outside edge of the lane as possible to give bikes maximum room to pass. And, as we are walking in the opposite direction of traffic, a cyclist can usually skirt around us in a flash. Still, though I have just as much right to the lane as they do, I always feel a pang of guilt when I spy bikes approaching. The riders, on the other hand, don't seem to mind us at all. Three out of four convey a smile, and more than a few toss a wave or flash us a V-fingered peace sign. Once in a while I'll catch a grimace. But that's usually when he or she is struggling up a long, steep grade. So, I certainly can't fault someone for forgetting to be friendly in the throes of a lung-burning, leg-throbbing hill climb, especially when, looking over his or her shoulder for cars, and then steering around us adds yet another, unwelcome challenge to an already exhaustive undertaking.

Occasionally, a cyclist will stop to chat, as did a very nice young man named Chris. Particularly handsome, dark-haired, several-days-unshaven, perhaps 35, he asked coyly, "What are *you* up to?"

I explained that my frustration over the toxic, antagonistic atmosphere in this country had inspired me to embark upon a pilgrimage.

"Me, too!" he responded. "I took off from Santa Cruz a few days ago because I really needed to get away from the Internet."

For me, using the satellite guidance system, emailing, searching for motels and campgrounds, and keeping my Facebook followers abreast of my progress make regular Internet access essential. Still, Chris and I seem to be suffering similar frustration. And, like me, he felt motivated to take off on his own marathon, coastal California excursion. We were traveling in opposite directions, but were both trying to get to the same place, a place of reassurance that, regardless of the level of animus in this troubled nation, when it comes down to the nitty gritty, in their hearts, people are decent, good, and kind. Then, Chris expressed those very qualities by informing me that he'd left a large bottle of purified aqua next to a shrine just up the road. "If you need water," he offered, "feel free to partake."

Highway 101 from Gaviota to Buellton begins with a sharp, uphill grade that goes on for several miles. As I didn't relish pushing my cart up this unforgiving stretch, I decided this might be an appropriate time to swallow my pilgrim pride and solicit help from a stranger. The idea was to get to a wayside near the base of the grade and, there, I'd approach people driving vehicles large enough to carry me, Millie, the box, and the stroller — preferably pickups or SUVs — hoping to procure a lift. I figured we wouldn't pose all that big of an inconvenience to a Good Samaritan. It would ostensibly be just a quick load-up, a nine-mile scoot up the road, and an even quicker drop off. A maximum 15 minutes of generosity from some kind someone would avoid my having to put in five hours of physical drudgery. For that possibility, I was willing to humble myself and do some cajoling. I discovered one big problem: there is no wayside at Gaviota. No wayside meant no parked vehicles. No parked vehicles meant no drivers to approach. No drivers to approach meant no reprieve from the long, steep grade between Gaviota and Buellton.

There I sat, leaning back against a concrete freeway abutment, resting up for the dreaded climb, when a pickup glided from the freeway ramp and drove past us — slowly. When the vehicle stopped smack dab in the middle of the road, I felt a sudden jolt of trepidation. *Perhaps*, I worried, *this pickup represents a looming threat.* My concern grew even greater when the truck hung a U-turn, pulled up next to me, and the driver rolled down his window. "You've come a long ways!" he said. Hearing his friendly tone immediately relieved my wary posture.

He was a compact fellow, 30 or so, with neat, longish, dark hair. A deep tan suggested that he spent a lot of time outdoors. "I saw you the other day, in Santa Barbara," the tanned man stated. Then, he pointed at the Pilgrimmobile with admiration. "You must be an engineer."

Aha! That's it! The ingenious re-purposing of my cart caught his eye. I explained that my brother was responsible for adapting the jogging stroller to carry the fiberglass storage box. The guy was totally into it, even wanting to know how many spare tire tubes

I carried. It was man-to-man conversation, like guy next-door neighbors standing in the driveway, comparing their riding mowers. When he heard the word pilgrimage, it automatically prompted him to inquire if my mission was affiliated with a church.

"Well, no," I admitted, "I'm doing this on my own. But I'm a Unitarian."

"Are you a Christian, then?" he inquired.

It probably would have been a whole lot easier to just say *Yes* and not complicate things. But, whether or not a person is a Christian doesn't seem like something one should fib about.

"Do you know anything about the Unitarians?" I asked. He didn't. "Unitarianism goes back to Thomas Jefferson," I explained, knowing this wasn't exactly true, but thinking making mention of one of the founding fathers might satisfy the tanned fellow's curiosity. I handed him my postcard and asked him his name, which was Henry. I introduced myself. We shook hands.

With a final, admiring gander at my cart, he said, "Stay safe. Lotsa crazies out there on the road."

I refrained from confessing that, only a few minutes ago, I had been genuinely worried that he might be one of those crazies.

As Henry drove off, I wondered how many other folks so far have noticed me trekking by, and how many of them would have liked to ask how many spare tubes I carried or if I was a Christian. I wondered if, in ways I'll never know, I was making a difference, even a tiny one, by planting soul-searching questions in the minds of people I'll never meet. Contemplating this possibility was my fuel as I pushed the cart up the ramp and onto the shoulder of Highway 101. Then, as I gazed up at the seemingly endless slope ahead, I wondered why I hadn't thought to ask that nice, tanned fellow named Henry for a lift to Buellton.

For three consecutive, laborious hours, I pushed the Pilgrim-mobile up that steep grade, struggling not only with the weight of my load, but to hold my wheels straight on the pitched shoulder, while restraining the dog from trotting over the white line and into oncoming traffic. With every step, it felt like gravity's relentless pull was increasing, that the stroller wheels were putting up greater resistance. At more and more frequent intervals, I felt the need to stop, rest, catch my breath, and give my pounding heart a moment to calm itself. During these brief respites, I would lean at a sharp angle, pressing my full body weight against the cart handle, fighting the unyielding force of gravity and its natural inclination to extract the cart from my grip to career back down the steep roadway.

To give myself encouragement, I began repeating an affirmation. "I am strong," I declared repeatedly to no one but myself. I became *The Little Engine That Could*, willing myself to find resolve where I wasn't sure resolve existed. I was both the boxer training for the long-awaited title fight and the crotchety old trainer egging the boxer on. Then, just when I was losing faith that my body was capable of pushing ahead for one more step, that semi-truck charged past like a massive, raging bull, hugging the white line, and blasting its air horn. The anger and resentment I felt at that moment gave me the charge of adrenaline I needed to keep pushing forward and upward, to show that rude, mean-spirited trucker that I deserve to share this highway, and prove to myself that my mantra, my repetitive declaration, "I am strong," was not just an empty, meaningless platitude, but a statement of actual truth.

When, at long last, we reached the top of the grade, the vista opened up in a panorama of breathtaking scope. To the northeast, the Santa Ynez Valley rolled out in pastel shades of green and brown all the way to the Los Padres National Forest. Blue sky stretched across the horizon, decked out in cotton-ball-white clouds. And, straight ahead, to the north, Highway 101 snaked into and over the foothills, uphill and down, only to disappear over the far horizon. Although I was feeling deep satisfaction at having met and conquered my biggest physical challenge so far, I knew more miles and more challenges lay ahead.

When a motorist is in urgent need of a restroom, or it's time to walk the dog, or he just needs a few minutes to un-drowse his eyes and stretch his legs, a freeway rest stop is a welcome sight. For a traveler afoot, however, both words, "rest" and "stop," are loaded with special meaning. I was sitting at a picnic table, fueling up on Kashi bars and an apple. A trucker exited the men's room. Wiping his damp hands on his trousers, he noticed me and approached. He said he'd seen me on the road earlier, while driving in the opposite direction on his way to deliver his load. Once again, this pilgrim had piqued a passing motorist's interest. And, upon a serendipitous second encounter of a more face-to-face kind, the motorist felt compelled to ask the pilgrim some questions.

First, he wanted to know if I had food for the dog. Not to worry, I told him. Well, it turned out that John (that's the trucker's name) was already out of questions. He was really interested in a fellow human willing to lend *him* an ear. One can only imagine how lonely it must get, watching the world go by through the windshield of a long-haul truck cab. Starting in Florida, John had motored north to North Carolina to pick up a load of glass windows. From there, he hauled his cargo 2,600 miles across the country, coast to coast, finally making his delivery to a California community college. Now, after all that, he was trucking an empty rig all the way back to Florida.

"Wow!" I expounded. "That far. To deliver windows!"

After wishing me good luck, John swiveled and lumbered towards his rig. Then, he stopped, turned back, and fished in his pocket. He pulled out some folded bills, selected a five, and handed it to me. It was as though he was compensating me for listening, offering reimbursement for a few minutes of my time. Although my pride tempted me to decline his generosity, instinct told me that my acceptance and my thanks would make him feel good about himself. So, I took the fin with a smile and expressed my gratitude. I guess all truckers are not rude and mean. Some, like John, are kind and giving. I very much like knowing that.

Approximately a mile from Buellton, two Highway Patrol cars pulled onto the shoulder. Even prior to taking step one of my pilgrimage, I suspected that encounters with law enforcement would be likely, probably inevitable. The officers in uniform might have passed as twins. Both were in their mid-to-late thirties, muscular, square-jawed, and stood about five-foot-nine, with hair shorn military-style. However, only one of them spoke. He addressed me in a friendly, respectful tone: "We've been getting calls about a man walking the freeway and almost getting hit."

"Couldn't be me," I told him. "I haven't even come close to getting hit."

"Well, we need to follow up on these things," he said. "You understand." He informed me that I wasn't breaking the law, that walking this part of the freeway was perfectly legal, as long as we stayed out of the lanes of traffic.

I expressed my appreciation for his concern, assuring him that I fully intended to remain as far away from speeding vehicles as possible. Satisfied, the officers were on their way. *A pair of nice, young men, just doing their job*, I remarked to myself.

We hadn't traveled an exceptionally impressive number of miles, only 12 or so, but every single one had been physically demanding. My feet were throbbing, my calves ached, and I hadn't showered in three days. As we trudged heavily up the incline, a Leprechaun-like figure scooted across the lane in front of us and plopped down on the guardrail. The man, probably in his sixties, was wearing a backpack. The corners of his laughing eyes were creased by a broad smile that revealed he had but three or four, very crooked teeth remaining in front. As we passed, I returned his smile with a cursory, "How's it goin'?" I was dying to check into the motel and get to our room. Then, I heard him mumble something about "something to eat." It suddenly occurred to me, this would be the perfect opportunity to pass John the trucker's charitable gesture forward. I stopped, dug my hand into my pocket and murmured, "Let's see what I have." But, when I turned around, the old snagglepuss was extending two greenbacks in my direction. He wasn't asking me for money. He was asking if *I* needed something to eat.

I protested, "No, no, please. I can't accept that." His face fell. He looked crushed. Then, I said, "No, really. You've touched my heart, but you keep your money."

At that, his Leprechaun smile returned and his eyes began

sparkling again. This grinning, toothless fellow told me he had walked from San Francisco, a distance of 300 miles, on his way to L.A. Originally from New York, he used to work in a Greenwich Village deli.

I suggested that he might have made me a sandwich at some point. And, if that were the case, I joked, he would have provided me with "something to eat" years ago. We laughed, wished one another peace, and Millie and I dragged ourselves the last hundred steps toward tonight's accommodations.

☮ ☮ ☮ ☮ ☮

At first, the Sideways Inn fell considerably short of making a pilgrim feel welcomed. The desk clerk, a large, aloof fellow, clad in a pretentious-looking, heavily starched, black Nehru jacket, informed me that I would be charged be a 50-dollar "pet-cleaning fee." If that charge weren't punitive enough, the establishment added an additional 100-dollar deposit to be refunded if and when the motel staff determined that Millie had not soiled or damaged the property. My protests, however, fell on unsympathetic ears. Those were the establishment's policies, the humorless, inflexible fellow informed me. But, when he showed me a map of the property, the bar, the pool, and — *Halleluiah!* — the hot tub, my complaints were forgotten. And, when Millie and I entered our room, I nearly swooned. It was so lovely.

☮ ☮ ☮ ☮ ☮

There I was, feeling like an absolute dolt, unable to figure out how to unlock the wrought-iron pool gate. "You just lift up on the thing there." The voice was coming from behind me. I turned around, surprised to see the previously snobbish desk clerk. "It's child proof," he explained.

As I managed to finally locate "the thing" to which he was referring, I remarked, "Looks like it's adult proof, too." With that, the large, dour man in the starched, black Nehru emitted a hardy guffaw. Guess he's not so humorless after all.

I just took a selfie of myself soaking in this luxurious hot tub and texted it to Sebra. Her return text remarks at how thin I look. I'm thinking she's just seeing an illusion caused by the distortion of the water. After this, I'm hitting the bar for vodka and grapefruit juice. Tonight, this pilgrim plans to live it up.

CHAPTER 10

Don't Disturb the Mountain Lions

MAY 11 · DAY ELEVEN

Although the shoulder of Highway 246 is relatively narrow, the two-lane road is straight and flat, so, the Pilgrimmobile almost drives itself. The weather is ideal, partly cloudy, temperature in the mid-seventies, minimal wind. Too, the landscape is gorgeous: agricultural fields, the occasional farmhouse, surrounded by round-topped hills shaped like breasts of giant women lying on their backs.

As per Google Maps instructions, Millie and I turn at the junction of Drum Canyon Road. Here, on the right side of the two-lane, virtually smack dab in the middle of nowhere, sits a winery tasting room. I push the cart up a hundred-yard hill, park it in the fine dirt next to the winery driveway, grab a plastic water bottle, and trundle down to the facility to take a look around.

The tasting room is situated in a converted barn. One entire side wall opens onto a patio furnished with umbrellaed tables, where, at present, no one sits. I peek inside. The place is beautifully appointed. Its walls are lined with stained-wood wine racks and, in the center of the vaulted interior stands a circular bar where I'm assuming a host serves wine lovers with samples of the vintner's pride. Right now, no host mans the bar. In fact, no one seems to be here at all. In an alcove off of the tasting area, I spy what I'm looking for: restrooms.

Upon emerging from the men's room, I'm greeted graciously by an attractive, slender, young woman, with long, straight, dark hair. I inform her that I was just getting some water for my dog.

She asks if I'm interested in tasting some wine. I thank her, but refuse, with the caveat that I no longer drink wine. I used to drink it — quite a lot of it, I confess — until the acid started causing severe pain in my stomach.

"Well, we wouldn't want that," Kirsten remarks. (I've noticed her official name tag.) She then suggests I might enjoy another kind of refreshment. In a forearm-sweeping, spokesmodel-ish gesture, she points my attention to several pitchers filled with chilled, cucumber-infused water.

I hadn't realized how parched I'd become. While I'm gulping down at least a half-dozen eight-ounce glasses, she informs me that the hike to Los Alamos is a beautiful one. However, at one point, Drum Canyon Road becomes, in her words, "very narrow and twisted." I'd be wise to take extra care and watch out for vehicles, as drivers aren't always as cautious as they should be.

I ask Kirsten if it's typical for this tasting room to be empty, if the winery actually attracts customers. "Oh, yeah, things pick up around five," she says, "when everybody gets off work." My next thought… *Perhaps an after-work glass or two of vino might factor into drivers' lack of caution as they negotiate "narrow and twisted" Drum Canyon Road.*

We wind our way past sweeping hillsides and parallel rows of grape vines. Neighboring fields lie plowed, but unplanted, butting up against yet more rounded hills and small, scattered groves of scrub oaks. The going is slow, arduous. Every time it looks as if we we're about to reach the summit, another even steeper section of rough, two-lane blacktop appears around the next bend. I feel the need to sit and rest on a regular basis. During one such respite, I'm sitting on a flat rock across the road from your typical, all-American, family farm. Millie lays on her travel bed, panting and looking up at me as if to ask, "This is it for the day, right?" I'd like to know how much more ground we've yet to cover but my iPhone is out of cell tower range.

I'm ready to move on. Millie, however, is not the least bit interested in taking her feet. Across the road, a four-wheeler rumbles down the farm driveway, kicking up a trail of dust. The passenger hops off to open the gate, while the driver pulls the little vehicle out onto the road.

"You all right?" one of them asks. Ginger-haired and freckled, I'm guessing these boys are in their late teens. The older one is working on his first beard. His name is Joe. Nick, Joe's younger, peach-cheeked sibling, is the chattier of the two. "You're exactly five miles from town," he informs me. "It's about a mile of pretty steep road, then it's all downhill from there."

"Well," I boast, "I pushed this cart up 101 from Gaviota Beach to the crest going into the Santa Ynez Valley. Three and a half hours. I figure I'm up for the task."

"There's some pretty good places to eat in town," Joe volunteers. These farm boys never call Los Alamos by name. To them, it's just "town."

☮   ☮   ☮   ☮   ☮

This is where the road gets "very narrow and twisted," as Kristen predicted. From here, our route is reduced to one lane. And, not only is this single lane steep and curvy, it's rough, and rutted, and far from level from one side to the other. As steep as each stretch is at the foot of this hill, each individual incline only seems to get more severe as we gain altitude. A six-degree grade increases to seven, then eight. As the slope of the road becomes more challenging, the pavement, too, gets rougher. Out of sheer exasperation, and more times than I care to admit, I spontaneously invoke the name of a certain carpenter/prophet who, *The Holy Bible* says, lived in a town called Galilee some 2,000 years ago. The road has become so steep that I can only push 20 yards or so at a time before I need to stop and catch my breath. Drivers in passing vehicles look askance at Sisyphus and his beagle grappling desperately against the force of gravity.

I've stopped to rest for maybe the 15th time. My chest is heaving, I'm gasping for air when pickup pulls up next to me. It's Nick, the younger of the two ginger-haired farm boys. "You're almost there," he encourages me. "Just around that corner there's a cattle guard. Then, in about three-hundred yards, you'll hit the top."

Just around the corner, it turns out, is more like just around three, maybe four corners, with yet another hill to climb between each. When the boy mentioned a cattle guard, I pictured parallel white lines painted on pavement. This cattle guard, a series of parallel pipes, each four or five inches apart, extends across the road above a rectangular pit, two feet deep. I pull the Pilgrimmobile backwards, ever-so-slowly, bumping its wheels over one pipe at a time. All the while, I'm trying to prevent a severely sprained or fractured ankle from one or both of my aching feet slipping off and between the slippery pipes. Thankfully, I don't have to carry a wiggling beagle across. Although I warn her to stay, somehow, on her own, Millie figures out how to tiptoe over the pipes without breaking a leg.

But, there's still climbing ahead, with more steep, rough, banked, hairpin curves. At long last, we come to place were the lane flattens out. But, this mountain is a tease. After another 200 feet of merciful flatness, we swing around a corner only to discover there is still more steep terrain for Sisyphus to push this boulder up. At this sight, I swear out loud for the umpteenth time. This profane outburst is far louder, begins with the letter "F," spelled in invisible capital letters, followed by numerous equally invisible, but audible exclamation marks! Meanwhile, my endurance gauge is dipping below "E" for "empty." I put my head down, start to push, repeating my mantra: "I am strong. I am strong." And, unbelievably, this affirmation speaks the absolute truth. I must indeed be strong. Because we've made it to the top. And the view from here is spectacular.

As I stand at the peak of Drum Canyon Road on weary, wobbly legs, gradually regaining my breath and gazing out across the beautiful Los Alamos Valley, a mini-van pulls up. The man at the wheel is small and boyish, but at least 40. He pushes a stained, ragged ball cap back on his forehead as he addresses me. "I think my boys talked to you earlier."

Correctly assuming that Joe and Nick are the boys to whom he refers, I respond with a compliment, one father to another. "Good kids."

"Yeah, they take after their mother," he cracks. The self-depre-cating dad's name is Jobie. As I shake his soiled, calloused hand, I ask Jobie if he knows a place nearby where we might camp safely. He tells me there's a park at the bottom of the road. That option, however, would require trekking two and half more miles down a grade as severe as the trip uphill had been.

I'm beat, I tell him, and so is my dog. I point to a relatively level area, just off the road, under a pair of scrub oaks and ask if that spot might work.

"If you're beat," he says, "that spot's as safe as any."

☮   ☮   ☮   ☮   ☮

Our campsite is blanketed with dry, thigh-high grass. By the time I finish stomping down the overgrowth, my socks and shoes are impaled with foxtails. And now, the mosquitoes are starting to swarm. Best to set up my bivy, I decide, before I get eaten alive. As the sun disappears, I cover up every square centimeter of exposed skin, except my mouth, nose, eyes, and fingertips, and plop down in my monarch chair to swat skeeters and eat.

This dinner is by far the worst yet. Main course: two hard-boiled eggs I purchased a couple of days ago at a gas-station quick-stop. Although I don't have even a dram of salt to give them flavor, the rubbery eggs are at least edible. However, the two saltine crack-ers, which must have been stored in a time capsule for centuries, are turning into unswallowable wads of glue in my mouth. And, this more-orange-than-orange mini-brick of "light cheddar" has a lot of nerve calling itself cheese. Who knows what ingredients are in this dreck? But I eat it anyway. These days, I'm burning Michael Phelps calories and I need every ounce of fuel I can get. Supper is redeemed when I remember that I'd saved half of a giant Lenny and Larry's chocolate chip cookie — absolutely divine!

The forecast calls for high winds tomorrow. I climb into the sack hoping that Day 12 doesn't start with pilgrim and pooch getting blown off the mountaintop.

MAY 12 · DAY TWELVE

Mercifully, the predicted wind has yet to manifest. It's perfectly calm and still, inside and outside my tent. Well, perhaps I should be more specific. It's perfectly calm and still when a set of tires isn't rumbling over the cattle guard 50 feet away. This happens with far more frequency than one might imagine, Drum Canyon Road being, as it is, an extremely remote single-lane of very rough, decaying pavement curling over the small, but unquestionably steep, mountain that divides two valleys. And, these periodic passings didn't just start in the pre-dawn twilight. They went on all night. Even while negotiating a rutted single lane, around hairpin turns, over the crest of a mini-mountain, in pitch darkness, drivers lead-footed accelerators. Thankfully, what I didn't hear was the head-on-collision I fretted might take place. What I did hear at one point in the dead of night, however, struck a certain measure of dread into my heart.

It was well after midnight when I was awakened for the sixth, seventh, maybe the eighth time — who's counting in the delirium of fitful, desperately needed sleep? — by wheels rumbling over the cattle guard. This time, however, the sounds of tires and engine didn't fade into the night. These wheels slowed their roll, pulled noisily onto gravel, and ground to a complete stop. After the engine switched off, I could make out two voices, both male, coming from within the vehicle. A door opened, followed by a second. Both slammed shut. After a few audible footsteps in gravel, the guy-to-guy conversation continued. A boisterous outburst of laughter provoked Millie to growl. I sent a shush from inside my tent to her in her crate.

My thoughts immediately went to what I had on hand to protect myself. Neither the small hammer or the cheap, Walmart camping knife were within reach. I strained my ears to hear what the men were saying, but was unable to discern anything. Every 30 seconds or so, one or both of them would emit a rowdy laugh and Millie would respond with a warning growl. I kept still, paralyzed, mummied in my sleeping bag.

What seemed like a slice of forever was actually only a few minutes until, once again, feet shuffled across gravel, vehicle doors opened and closed, conversation became muffled, the engine fired up, and the tires pulled from gravel onto pavement and began rolling away. As our night visitors descended the slope toward the Santa Ynez Valley side of the mountain, one sound remained: my own palpitating heart.

☮ ☮ ☮ ☮ ☮

Anyone who has indulged in a refreshing, chilled beverage on a hot, summer day — and what red-blooded American hasn't? — is familiar with the natural phenomenon of condensation. Whether it's iced tea, a margarita, or a frosty beer, droplets of water appear and collect on the outside of the vessel, when warm, humid air comes in contact with a colder surface causing moisture to convert from its gaseous state to liquid form. While I was in search of the ideal, small, lightweight tent for my pilgrimage, a number of reviews mentioned the issue of condensation. The cozier the interior space of any tent, the less opportunity the exhalations of a sleeping camper have to dissipate. Moist, warm, expelled breath fills the tent. The tent fabric is cool from the exterior temperature. Bingo, condensation! This problem was mentioned in several of the reviews about the tent I eventually selected. However, the compactness, simplicity, and portability of the bivouac design far outweighed any concern I might have had about a little moisture.

This morning, the entire interior surface of the tent fabric is dripping. By the time I wiggle and writhe into my clothes, I'm a very wet camper.

It's shortly after 6AM when I birth myself from the saturated tent into yet more dampness outside. This is what they commonly call a pea-soup fog. However, due to its pallor, I think potato or clam chowder would be make far more apt soup metaphors. The magnificent valley view that greeted us at the end of last evening's climb is now blanketed in waterlogged whiteness. Although the air is chilly and wet, I decide to break down camp in bare feet and flip-flops. Last night, it took me the best part of an hour to extract the foxtails from my socks and shoes. Even a few steps in this grass would surely undo all that meticulous surgery and make today's walk a much more-prickly one. After an hour of decamping, I slip on my socks and shoes, and we commence our trek down Drum Canyon Road into Los Alamos.

The road is as narrow, steep, rough, and curvy in its north-side descent as it was during yesterday afternoon's arduous push up the south bank. My toes are jamming into the ends of my shoes and my knees whimper with the impact of every step. I lock my grip on the stroller handle to keep the cart from running away or tipping over. Then, there's making sure the dog doesn't get hit by the sporadic vehicle bumping by. Every time I hear a car or a truck approaching, I use one hand to yank Millie away from the center of the single lane, while assigning the other hand the strenuous dual task of holding back against gravity's tug while guiding the stroller wheels.

Finally, at the mouth of the canyon for which this cruel road was named, we arrive at an expansive, beautifully landscaped park. Although the morning is still in its infancy, several joggers and dog walkers are up and around. A pilgrim invariably finds his soul nourished, exchanging a smile with another living, breathing human.

Over my lifetime, I've visited parks in dozens of states and several countries. I've seen warnings posted about poison oak, rattlesnakes, bears, even sharks. This very official-looking sign, however, is a new one on me:

MOUNTAIN LIONS ARE a natural part of our ecology and should not be disturbed.

What? Are you kidding me? My dog and I just slept outside in a wilderness area where huge, wild, predatory cats commonly roam free? My heart nearly stops. Believe me, I have absolutely no intention of ever, EVER, *EVER* disturbing a mountain lion! *But what if a mountain lion just so happens to decide to do some disturbing of his own? What then?* Let's just say a big, hungry cat catches a whiff of dog in the middle of the night and comes prowling around. And, let's just say Millie acts like a beagle and starts growling or barking or howling at the skulking feline. What would have happened then? Would my sweet, little, tri-colored Snoopy dog have suffered a horrible, terrifying, torturous death at the claws and jaws of a vicious, voracious carnivore? Would my Millie have ended up being some kitty-monster's midnight snack?

Oh, my God! Jobie, you told me that spot was "just as safe as any" for us to camp! Maybe you might have mentioned that thing about mountain lions being a *natural part of the ecology.* Then again, never mind. It's probably better that I hadn't known after all.

☮   ☮   ☮   ☮   ☮

I've noticed Millie favoring her left, front leg. As the day wears on and the miles mount up, her limp becomes more pronounced. Obviously, this concerns me. My concern is even greater today, as it's not yet mid-morning and she's already noticeably gimpy. We've just pushed onto the freeway when my phone rings…

I met Wendy Hunter in Nashville at the Center for Spiritual Living. I always found her delightful and charming, albeit exceptionally chatty, with her Snow-White voice, her rat-a-tat-tat cadence, and the quirky way she blinks her eyes and flutters her eyelashes as she speaks. Wendy, who is Canadian, was living in Nashville because she had married a fellow from Tennessee. The couple has since departed the States to live in Vancouver B.C. An adventurous, highly independent woman, Wendy returns to Tennessee every summer for an annual camping excursion with a church group. She always takes time on her yearly cross-continental drive, to visit friends and do some sight-seeing along the way. After making one of the earliest donations to my pilgrimage crowd-source fund, Wendy suggested that, if the logistics worked out, we might rendezvous somewhere in California. She said she'd be most pleased to treat me to a motel room and a meal.

A bed with pillows and sheets, and a real, sit-down dinner sounds irresistible. And, anticipating being in the company of a delightful, generous, kindred spirit boosts my mood enormously. Where to meet is the challenge at hand. Millie and I have already trekked an extremely taxing distance today. With her sore leg and my tender feet, I'm skeptical we can cover the 16 miles to Santa Maria. Wendy comes up with what sounds like a very reasonable plan. She'll motor over from the San Joaquin Valley, check into a motel in Santa Maria, unload her car, then drive to wherever we are at that point and pick us up. In the meantime, we'll keep in touch via text message.

At about 3:30 in the afternoon, we locate an exit area that will provide adequate off-road space to disassemble the cart and load Wendy's car. We've been walking since 7 AM, bucking a bracing headwind for the last 10 miles. We're both fatigued. Surely, I'm thinking, by now Wendy must be no more than an hour away. Preparing to hunker down and wait, I set up the Monarch Chair and get Millie settled on her travel bed.

My phone dings — a text message. *Perfect, my benevolent hostess must be on her way from Santa Maria to fetch us.* Wendy's message, however, brings much less welcome news. After a late start due to a dead battery, she got stalled in a bottleneck caused by smoke from a wildfire. She doesn't expect to get to Santa Maria for another four and a half hours.

I have no other choice but to hoist myself onto unhappy feet, reassemble the monarch chair, suck up a deep breath, and hobble on northward.

☮ ☮ ☮ ☮ ☮

It's after 7:30, darkness is closing in, and spirals of frigid wind swirl around us like miniature tornadoes. We've been trekking along South Bradley Road since exiting the freeway. This morning, I woke up in a potato-soup fog at the crest of a canyon road more than 17 miles south of here. I've been pushing this cart against the wind for the best part of 12 consecutive hours, fueled by nothing but bagel chips and lousy lunchmeat purchased at a Los Alamos bodega. My feet are screaming and Millie's limp has gone from bad to severe.

The golden spires of the Orthodox Church of the Annunciation come into view. I'm making a decision: *this is as far as we go.* After feeding Millie, no coaxing is necessary to get her into her crate. She's happy to curl up in her bed and get out of the wind's unrelenting chill.

This will be the first time I've attempted to lift the box out of the stroller frame on my own. As it's wedged in very snugly between the metal rails, this presents a tricky task, especially for someone as exhausted, as hungry, and in as much foot pain as I am at this hour. But, once again, I surprise myself. After a few upward jerks, I manage to extricate the box, hoist it up and out, and set it down on the concrete. Everything is laid out on the sidewalk, ready to load into Wendy's car.

A ding from my iPhone. Wendy is still an hour away.

I don't recall the last time I dined at a Red Lobster. What I do know is this: It's 10PM on Friday night and this is the first real meal I've had since Tuesday. The lobster tacos and the Caesar salad are so scrumptious, I could die right here and now as a totally contented man. An equally wondrous revelation is the 20-ounce glass of 805 blond ale from the Firestone Walker brewery. I'm a very happy camper, especially since tonight, I won't be camping at all, thanks to the very generous Canadian woman across the table, babbling away in her Snow White tremolo, as she blinks her eyes, and flutters her eyelashes.

CHAPTER 11

An Unnecessary Detour

MAY 13 · DAY THIRTEEN

The gaunt, dark-haired man is gazing at my Oregon Drivers License with more interest than one would normally expect. A smile starts in his eyes and ripples across his Asian features. "Ah, Newpote!" he exudes, vigorously nodding his head, "I bin deah!" Even though Jim Liao has resided in these United States for decades, his fluent English still affects a thick Chinese lilt. Apparently, the address on my license has triggered a fond recollection of the Central Oregon coastal town where I live.

I find this information of cursory interest, but only in a normal, passing-conversation sort of way. I'm standing here at the front desk for one specific purpose: to extend my stay at the Santa Maria South Motel 6 for an additional night. Millie and I have walked for 12 consecutive days. We've trekked on dedicated bike lanes, urban sidewalks, freeway shoulders, rural two-lane highways, up and down steep grades, and on rough, twisted, remote, mountainous roads. Not only have we both earned a day of rest, I have laundry to do, errands to run, and critical supplies to secure. And Millie has an appointment this morning to have her ailing leg examined. Jim Liao, however, seems intent on keeping the chitchat going. It was about 10 years ago, the man behind the counter informs me. He traveled to Newport to check out a motel that was for sale. After taking a look, he decided against it. "Too cold in wintah," he says sternly, shaking his head for emphasis. "No beezness!"

One would think that the proprietor of a hectic hostelry would be the hurried one. Jim, evidently, has developed the enviable Zen skill of existing in the moment, of going with the flow. And, quite obviously, he's a people person. We continue bantering about how crazy and unpredictable the weather can be on the Oregon Coast.

"I give you room at same price as last night," Jim tells me. It's Saturday. Prices usually spike on weekends, 50% or more. He is not in any way obliged to do this. When my benefactor Wendy Hunter checked us in yesterday and told Jim about my pilgrimage, his first thought was that a 67-year-old man who would volunteer to walk the length of two states in 90 days must have a screw loose. However, now that he's met the pilgrim face-to-face, and especially now that he's discovered that the pilgrim is from "Newpote," he's reconsidering that initial snap-judgment.

Actually, I'm not so sure I concur with Jim's reassessment. Considering what I've experienced over the last several days, the danger and duress to which I've exposed myself, the thought has passed through my head more than once: *I very well might have a screw loose, and a few nuts and bolts as well.* I hand Jim a five-dollar bill for laundromat change. Cheerfully, he counts out 20 quarters. I ask him if he has laundry soap for sale. "I get you some," he says, and bustles into a supply closet. When I attempt to pay, he waves off my money. "No. Fo' you, Rand. Free."

☮   ☮   ☮   ☮   ☮

Wendy Hunter is, indeed, an angel. She has offered to extend her Santa Maria layover to chauffer me around to my various errands. First, the animal clinic, where Millie gets a prednisone injection and two prescriptions: a steroid pack and some doggy Advil. Fortunately, there is no detectible injury in her leg or shoulder. Unfortunately, her symptoms suggest arthritis. Add my multiple rheumatic issues to the beagle's, and we make a sad-sack pair of gimps. At Walmart, I pick up a nice, compact bicycle pump and spare, thorn-proof tubes for my stroller tires. After enjoying one of my very favorite guilty pleasures at Costco — a Polish Sausage drowned in onions, mustard, and ketchup, followed by a massive cup of frozen yogurt for desert — Wendy and I find ourselves with the remainder of the day free to do whatever.

For the previous seven months, every hour of every day has been about preparing for, then embarking upon this pilgrimage. Leisure time is an alien concept. I have no clue what to do with it. Relaxation is, however, an alluring proposition. Wendy suggests that we catch a movie. Seeing a film on a big screen, in a theater, the way God intended, while chowing down on popcorn sounds like Heaven. We choose a piece of laugh-out-loud, escapist fluff: Goldie Hawn and Amy Schumer in *Snatched*. Although its premise is borderline absurd, I find myself in simpatico with the characters, when they get lost in the Amazon jungle. Then, the guy posing as their guide falls off a cliff to his death, and they discover that the map he had been following was not a map after all, but really a restaurant menu. Google Maps, are you listening?

MAY 14 · DAY FOURTEEN

I'm in the motel lobby, pouring hot water over the tea bag in my travel cup. At the desk, Jim Liao is settling up the bill of a woman checking out. "That's Rand," he tells her, "He doesn't believe I bin to Newpote."

"Ha!" I say, with a smile. "You know that's not true, Jim." Through hard work, determination, smart choices, and a dollop of good fortune, this Chinese immigrant now owns and operates a thriving 108-room motel in Santa Maria, California. Jim Liao makes a positive difference every single day — if for no other reason than how he so generously shares his easy-going, good-hearted nature.

Here we are, two men from totally different backgrounds, motivated by different interests, and traveling very different life paths, looking one another in the eye and discovering we have so very much in common.

"Oh, oh, oh!" Jim says, "Heah iss my cahd." He presses his business card in my hand. "You send me text message so I have yo' numbah. Maybe I veesit you in Newpote."

"I'd like that very much," I say to my new friend, with total sincerity.

In the parking lot, Wendy and I take some selfies. After giving her a long hug and expressing effusive thanks for her generosity, I push the Pilgrimmobile around to the office to say goodbye to Jim. He comes running out.

"We need to take pickcha!" he demands giddily. Wendy snaps a shot of Jim Liao and this pilgrim, standing with our arms over each other's shoulders, beaming like two second-grade besties on the grammar-school playground. "Text me pickcha, Rand," says Jim.

I promise I will and allow the Pilgrimmobile to coast down the driveway to the sidewalk. I look back for a final over-the-shoulder wave and push on into Day 14.

☮   ☮   ☮   ☮   ☮

My camping chair is propped up against the peeling paint of this abandoned store, which is shielding Millie and me from a powerful, tenacious wind. Today is Mother's Day. I've just called mine to wish her the best. Due to her recent stroke, it's difficult enough to carry on a cohesive face-to-face conversation with Mom. Over the phone, the challenge is much greater. Of course, she could barely get a word in anyway. As usual, Dad dominated the call, butting in to speak on her behalf, raving about how great she's doing. My father, ever the optimist, the enthusiast, the cheerleader.

Suddenly, around the corner of the building cruises a black Cadillac Escalade. Clouds of dust are being swept away by the wind, as fast as the vehicle's tires can produce them. As the large SUV slows to a stop, I'm thinking this must be the property owner here to expel us. I start rehearsing in my head: *Yes, of course, I saw the No Trespassing signs. I'm so sorry. Certainly, we'll be on our way.*

The Escalade's passenger side window rolls down. The man looking out from the vehicle has the hooded eyes, the jowls, and the veiny, rosacea cheeks of a man who enjoys his cocktails. "Everything all right?" he asks. As I extract myself from my low-slung seat, I tell him we're fine, just a little bit off track.

"Where are you headed?" The woman behind the wheel is speaking. She is blond and quite beautiful. My answer, Guadalupe, prompts the veiny-cheeked fellow to confirm something I was already beginning to suspect. Since leaving the motel, we've actually been walking in the wrong direction, every single step taking us that much further away from our intended destination.

"That's Betteravia," he tells me, pointing to the strip of two-lane, "the road to Guadalupe." He turns to the woman. "It's what, Honey? Twelve? Thirteen miles?"

I want to scream! What he's saying couldn't be true because, according to Google Maps, Guadalupe was supposedly 11 miles from this morning's starting point. If we've been walking in the exact opposite direction for two hours, it must actually be more like 15 miles away! I thank the helpful couple profusely for caring enough to stop. I'm able to muffle my tantrum until the Caddy pulls out onto the highway. Then, I let loose with a string of self-flagellating profanities, kicking dirt, throwing whatever I can get my hands on, screaming at myself. A few minutes later, I'm pushing the cart back towards Santa Maria, muttering a stream of self-castigations for making such an unbelievably inexcusable error.

Here's what happened... The Motel 6 was on Main Street, which also happened to be the road to Guadalupe, a straight shot west, then a quick jog north, a flat — literally flat — 11 miles total. Compared to the distances we've been covering per day, 11 miles on level highway would have been a piece-a cake. However, I somehow made the assumption that the motel was on the south side of the street. So, in my mind, all we had to do was to turn left onto Main Street and keep walking. Double checking Google Maps seemed unnecessary. Doing that, I figured would only put an unnecessary drain on my iPhone battery. This simple, moronic miscalculation sent us walking east instead of west, and, when we came to a T in the road, south instead of north. That's when we came upon the abandoned store, sat down to call Mom, and received that critically important visit from the concerned, considerate couple in the black Escalade.

☮ ☮ ☮ ☮ ☮

The farms we passed yesterday were family-owned. Now, we're in factory-farm country — cultivation by corporation. Field after field, thousands of acres, are planted in neat, parallel rows of leafy vegetables. One field appears primed and ready to harvest. The crop in the next field has some growing to do. Giant farm machines traverse the fields like lawn mowers of the gods, sending massive dust clouds wafting over the road. I tie a kerchief around my neck and pull it over my mouth and nose to keep from inhaling the airborne particulates.

Although the pavement is narrow and the shoulder skimpy, gargantuan trucks bump and rattle along unimpeded at high speeds. Some haul freshly picked crops to be processed and packaged. Others head to distribution centers, stuffed with cellophane-wrapped, rubber-banded products. The occasional big-tired tractor pokes along on the outer edge of the road. Around here, a bike lane is more likely to serve as a tractor lane. Then, there are the cement trucks, grey under coats of dust, ominous in girth and weight and, filled or empty, sending fine, granular particles blowing into the atmosphere and random pebbles careening off of the blacktop.

The wind is ferocious, and getting stronger. The harder it blows — gusting at 30 miles-per-hour by now — the colder it gets. The sun hovers over the western horizon, its glare radiating less warmth with every passing minute.

☮ ☮ ☮ ☮ ☮

I know this kind young man's name is Arturo. I know he is kind because, even with the language barrier, I understand that he is offering us a ride to the next town. I understand this because, although I am embarrassingly deficient in Spanish, I have no trouble picking the word "Guadalupe" out of his rapid-fire speech, and his vocal inflection is punctuated by an audible question mark. I know his name because he has taken adhesive-backed, reflective letters, the kind a family might use to attach its surname to a mail-box, and spelled out "ARTURO" on his dashboard. Although he is already exuding a warm smile, when I call him by name, his entire face lights up. I'm attempting to explain to this kind young man named Arturo that, although I am moved by this demonstration of concern and his willingness to help, his tiny, two-door, sub-compact sedan lacks the capacity to accommodate my large, awkward load.

Immigration enforcement officers all over America — espe-cially here in California — are aggressively rounding up undocu-mented, brown-skinned folks. Why, I wonder, hadn't kind, smiling Arturo not simply scooted home to the safety of his home and family? Perhaps he has developed a false sense of security, living in a bubble, constantly surrounded by his own. In this part of California, Spanish is the language of the land and brown is its dominant skin color. The preponderance of businesses, even some of the corporate farms, bear names like Gonzalez, Garcia, and Rodriguez.

I hand Arturo my postcard and show him that the man pic-tured on it is me. He accepts it with the expression of someone who has just been given a surprise Christmas gift. Then, he says his first and only English words to me: "Thank you." As he drives away, I'm thinking, *No, Arturo. Thank* YOU! *You are a hero. God speed. May you stay safe and thrive in this country.*

The migrant laborers of my generation linked arms with Caesar Chavez to win recognition as human beings, each one equally valuable, productive, and worthy as any American. They instilled their children with a belief in the virtue of hard work. The fruits of this new generation's labor are evident. They don't just pick the crops now. They own the land. Time marches on. And the band in this parade ain't playin' Sousa. Its repertoire is mariachi or conjunto. And those who cling to the past and refuse to join the march forward will get left behind in the dust.

Meanwhile, dust is not our most pressing issue. *Dusk*, how-ever, *is*. Darkness is imminent. The wind is brutal, merciless. It's becoming urgent that we find somewhere to bed down for the night. A shuttered, sprawling food processing plant looks as if it's been plopped here on the Jolly Green Giant's Monopoly board. I park the Pilgrimmobile and go exploring, hoping this might provide a protected place to tuck ourselves away. The strongest gust of wind of the day whips in. I hear a faint crash. I turn around towards the road. The Pilgrimmobile has blown over and the storage box has rolled into a ditch. Exhausted, cold, and dispirited, I steady myself against the next blast of moving air, gather what's left of my strength, and hoist the box up and back into the stroller frame.

In the distance, I see what very well might be our last resort. There is one solitary tree on the entire landscape. It's one of those oaks that painters paint, directors put on film, or a company silhouettes for its logo. Hallmark puts trees like this on sentimental greeting cards. It's grand, and defiant, and iconic. With tornadic walls of wind at my back, I muscle the cart across the highway onto the rutted, two-lane stretch of Brown Road and toward the magnificent, lonesome oak.

A dirt driveway leads to and past the tree, elbowing onto a farm road. Down the unpaved lane, adjacent to a strawberry field the size of the battlefield at Gettysburg, is a line of porta-potties and temporary sheds. The sign posted clearly reads, *No Trespassing, Violators will be prosecuted to the fullest extent of the law.* I have no choice but to risk it.

The tree's 12-foot-wide trunk base and the natural mini-caverns created by its massive root structure will provide protection from the wind. Surely, at 200, possibly even 300 years old, this oak has stood up against gusts this strong and stronger since buckskin jackets and coonskin caps were in fashion. The plan is simple: after taking full advantage of the farm workers' porta-potties and scraping together what I have left for a meal, I'll stow the dog in her crate, prop my bed pad up against the oak, wrap myself in my sleeping bag, and rest until first light.

I'm cleaning up after my dinner, when the roar of multiple high-performance engines comes into earshot. Four expensive, shiny sports cars rocket past — a Porsche, followed by a Mustang, a Z car, then a Corvette. And to think that a half hour ago I was pushing my cart down the center line of that same road, staggering like a boxer who'd absorbed too many blows. How, I'm wondering, as they race their vehicles down a remote, country road in the final glimmers of twilight at 100 miles-per-hour, could that quartet of speed-demons have avoided a wobbly pilgrim and his spent beagle? I know we would have been helpless to leap clear of them.

Today is my late brother Bart's birthday. In October of 2010, the heart disease that had so unnecessarily gone undiagnosed smothered and snuffed out what had been, for just 56 years, a radiantly bright spark of life. Still, when he gets a hankering, I swear my brother sends his mischievous spirit out to play. I could have sworn I heard Bart's voice whispering over the great divide, urging me to stop here, to rest, refresh, and regroup.

According to the banner hanging outside this small, white, clapboard house, the Halcyon Store has been doing business since 1908. After getting Millie settled on her travel bed, I entered what appeared to be a hippie mercantile. Racks of hand-sewn or knitted clothing stood on display, alongside handcrafted furniture, knick-knacks, and art. A menu featured coffee, teas, and pastries. On a community bulletin board, flyers advertised upcoming entertainment, spiritual, and political events, next to business cards pinned there by massage therapists, pet sitters, and yoga instructors. A full-figured, blond woman in a flowing, cream-colored caftan sat next to a bay window, engaged in intense, hushed conversation with a man. "I'll be with you in a minute," she informed me. I found the cold drinks and selected a Yerba Tea.

On a bench outside the store, Millie at my feet, I sipped Yerba Mate, observing. A car, then a pickup, then another car, pulled up and parked. This Halcyon Store, I concluded, must be a very popular spot. Customers seemed extraordinarily friendly, pausing to inquire Millie's name, asking if they could pet her. When I reentered the building to recycle the can, the busty blond woman was behind the cash counter, conversing with a very tall, slender man. His grey beard was neatly trimmed and he wore a knit cap and pink-framed sunglasses. It had occurred to me that the proprietress of this sort of establishment might be interested, so, I slipped her my postcard. "Sorry to interrupt," I said. "I just wanted to let you know what I'm up to."

Looking at the card, she asked, "So, you're on a pilgrimage?"

This caught the attention of a pretty woman with long, straight, graying-blond hair, who queried the tall man in the pink-rimmed sunglasses, "What was the name of that Buddhist monk who did that?"

"Oh, yeah," he said, seeming to recollect something vaguely unspecific. Pink Sunglasses and Pretty Long-haired Woman, I surmised, were a couple. They introduced themselves as Bob and DeDe, then immediately started quizzing me about my trek: why I was walking, where I'd started, how far I'd walked so far, where I was headed, how long I thought it would take to get there. And, ultimately, the most important question of all...

"Where are you staying?" DeDe inquired.

Serendipity is a whimsical word for a seemingly random happenstance, a confluence of events that initially appear to take place by chance, but ultimately resound with unexpected significance. The word itself is as replete with mystery as the phenomenon it describes. Within these five, sonorous, playful syllables is embedded the implied questions, *What would have happened if...? What would have happened if not for...?* In this scenario, this is where serendipity turns on its turbocharger.

Only an hour earlier, I'd received a text from my friend in Newport: *My daughter is having family problems. She says it's not a good time for guests.* I'd been banking on our San Luis Obispo lodging, and very much looking forward to meeting the daughter of a friend and her family. And, as these arrangements had been made so far in advance, this news hit me unusually hard. Thus, I'd entered the Halcyon Store feeling a little bit downtrodden.

I informed DeDe that Millie and I have a motel reservation in Arroyo Grande for tonight, but that tomorrow night's San Luis Obispo plans fell through. "Well, that's where we live," DeDe responded without a second of hesitation. "You can stay with us." Her tone indicated that, as far as she was concerned, this was *fait accompli.*

So, here I am, on a Monday afternoon in May, in a hippie mercantile, a place I've never been in my life. Amazingly, a couple I met only a few minutes ago has just invited me to crash at their house. Let's apply those implied embedded questions to the current circumstance... *What would have happened if* I'd not received that text just an hour ago? Easy answer: I would have told DeDe that our local accommodations were all taken care of. Bob and DeDe would have wished me peace and love and I'd be on my merry way. *What would have happened if not for* my Brother Bart's matchmaking spirit whispering in my ear, urging me to stop here? Obviously, this meeting would never have taken place. As DeDe and I exchange contact info, I'm getting goosebumps.

"You know what? Bob produces events," DeDe informs me. "Honey," she suggests to her partner, "couldn't you send out an email to your contacts, you know, and put together a concert for Rand?" Bob assures me this is not only doable, but would be a piece of cake. He promises to book the community clubhouse and round up a nice, receptive audience for the pilgrim troubadour.

CHAPTER 12

Cyclists, Aliens, and Christians

MAY 16 · DAY SIXTEEN

An old barn and a single-story general store are the only signs of civilization visible from Highway 227. This anachronistic map blip is called Edna. Across the road from a winery tasting room, a still photographer focuses his telescopic lens on the two lanes behind us. A dozen or more folks congregate on the gravel shoulder, chatting excitedly. A temporary road sign indicates that traffic will be sent on a detour ahead. We trek another half mile, where a uniformed police officer is re-routing vehicles. Millie and I, however, are allowed to continue walking straight ahead. Intriguing. There doesn't seem to be anything that would prevent cars and trucks from passing through this stretch of road. Yet, the wheels of the Pilgrimmobile are the only ones allowed on it.

For 10 minutes, the only sounds are stroller wheels rolling across gravel and the trudge of my own sneakers. Then, a black-and-white CHP sedan appears over my shoulder and passes with its dome lights flashing, followed by a second, and yet a third. Two officers cruise by on motorcycles, shoulder-to-shoulder, one in each lane. Then another pair of police motorcycles pass, followed by an entire squadron of cops on bikes — 20, maybe more.

A second photographer stands on the opposite shoulder. Like the first, his telescopic lens is trained on the road over my shoulder. A third shutterbug teeters on tip toe, camera in one hand, shielding his eyes with the other, trying to catch sight of something down the highway behind us. An officer on a motorcycle pulls over and stops in our path 50 yards ahead. He stands, straddling his idling bike, his black-leather boots planted in the gravel, talking into the walky-talky attached to his shoulder.

When Millie and I reach the motorcycle officer, I inquire, "What's happening? It feels like I have a presidential motorcade."

"I'll bet it does," the young, mustachioed fellow cracks. "Ever hear of the Tour de France?" Of course, I have. "Well, this," he says, "is the Tour de California."

As Millie and I proceed northward, the gathering of spectators thickens along both sides of Highway 227. Still photographers, and now a few videographers, stand poised and ready. More motor-cyclists pass, these wearing tunics with *Marshall* on their backs, followed by another extended flotilla of police motorcycles. If anybody was ever looking for the perfect opportunity to get away with murder on the Interstate, this would be it. I can't imagine there could be even one more CHP officer available countywide to police the freeway.

The crowd begins to hoot and cheer. A small group of bicyclists fly past, all clad in bright cycling colors, their numbered, fabric bibs flapping in the self-made breeze. A pack of media vehicles keeps pace, hovering around them like remora fish around a shark. Another full minute passes before the peloton appears. Once again, the crowd cheers, applauds, and whistles. Some blow air horns. A hundred or more racers pedal furiously en masse like a swarm of brightly colored bees. This flock of racers is followed directly by a lengthy train of support vehicles — ambulances, vans carrying spare bikes, more media vehicles, a CHP van, a taco truck, more ambulances.

The militaristic show of force leading up to the event had gone on for an hour or more for a spectacle that raced by in a sum total of five minutes. Millie and I trek on as the now-quieted crowd disperses, presumably to slip into parked vehicles and head off to various somewheres.

Earlier this afternoon, I was nestled in the elbow of a placid, sloping, country road, gazing out over the Edna Valley, eating chips and a sandwich. Only a couple of hours later, I'm unexpectedly surrounded by an impressive demonstration of human cooperation: hundreds of people working together to actualize a highly choreo-graphed, weeklong, traveling circus. The dynamics of a pilgrimage on the roads of America can be extreme indeed. One moment, I'm the only human not traveling in a speeding vehicle. The next, I'm in the middle of a buzzing hive of human frenzy.

The motorists merging back onto 227 from their mandatory detours, however, don't appear to be even slightly amused by this afternoon's coincidence of events. Judging from their expressions, driver after driver is cursing his or her luck for picking this corridor at this hour to get from where they came from to where they were attempting to go. For the first time in 16 days, I detect pilgrim envy on faces behind those windshields. While they're all hopelessly stuck in a bottleneck, a man pushing a cart is free to move on down the road unimpeded. Millie and I may be moving at the pace of a tortoise. But at least we're making steady progress. Meanwhile, the frustrated hares drag forward in fits and starts, fuming — literally fuming, as vehicle exhaust bilges into the air and hovers around this traffic jam in a blue-grey haze.

"There you are!" DeDe exudes. "I'm so sorry. We've been trying to hook up this washer all day long." As DeDe gives me a quick hug, it all comes back to me. She and Bob (Pink Sunglasses) had been in Oceano yesterday to pick up a used washing machine — yet another critical piece in the confluence of seemingly unrelated happenings that led to our serendipitous connection.

The idea of living in a manufactured home park has never held any appeal for me. As I enter DeDe's place, my bias begins to evaporate. From inside, you'd never suspect that this is a pre-fabri-cated structure. Due to DeDe's aesthetic and her artistic sensibility, I could be standing in a cabin in the middle of a forest. Something simmering on the stove smells good. "I made a big pot of vegan lentil stew," DeDe says, setting a Kombucha down in front of me. "There's plenty. I hope you'll join us for dinner."

Bob arrives. I'm surprised to learn that, even though he and his lovely, long-haired lady have been in a committed relationship for seven years, he actually has his own place, just a skip-to-my-lou down the lane. So, to borrow a term coined by my Canadian documentarian friend Sharon Hyman, Bob and DeDe are not actually partners. More accurately, like Sebra and me, they are "apartners."

Over a bowl of DeDe's delectable legume concoction, I recount how Millie and I unexpectedly found ourselves caught up in the epicenter of a major bike race. While Bob seems to find this story of interest, he's acting a bit sheepish. The source of his uneasiness is revealed when he apologizes for flaking out on arranging the clubhouse concert he volunteered to throw together.

"Hey, it's okay," I tell him. "I was in the music business for forty-five years. I learned a long time ago not to count chickens." Translation: I've lived long enough to know that it's not wise to let my happiness depend on another person fulfilling a promise, even when that promise was made with pure, sincere intent. It's not Bob's fault if I'm disappointed. That's all on me.

We move on to other topics. I'm particularly interested to hear what Bob and DeDe might have on their minds these days, what they're concerned about. The repartee is lively and smart, as satisfying and nourishing as DeDe's stew. I'm eating it up. At this point, the shining face of youth appears, arriving fresh from play rehearsal. Quentin, I'm informed, is renting a room here while attending nearby Cal Poly. This bright, poised, impossibly handsome young man is the first aspiring thespian I've ever met who is not pursuing an acting career because the theatre is his passion, but solely to please his mother. Strangely, Quentin's mom was actually determined *not* to give birth to a doctor or lawyer. Her progeny, she decided, was fated for movie stardom. And, to predestine her baby boy's glittery future from day one, she named the infant after Quentin Tarantino. With hands destined to press wet cement on Hollywood Boulevard, Mama's future megastar grabs a bowl of stew, takes a seat and, with little or no context, high dives mouth-first into the conversation.

I'm more than eager to hear from a youthful perspective and

Quentin oozes affability and charm. However, it immediately becomes clear that this young man is completely over his head in this subject matter, and oblivious to boot. His remarks are as unabashed as they are uninformed. It's not simply that he's so off base with every opinion he espouses. Since he has little or no real life experience, I can easily forgive him for that. What riles me is that his words are delivered with such smugness and certainty. As we used to say back in high school, "This one's cruisin' for a bruisin.'" I'm hoping he has genuine talent to go with his swagger and finely chiseled visage.

"Well, here's what *I'm* really concerned about," Bob interrupts.

I'm relieved that an adult has re-taken the floor, rescuing me from further exposure to the naiveté of youth. Perhaps Bob has butted in out of consideration for the fidgeting pilgrim dinner guest. That theory is quickly disproved when Bob rockets the conversation into such far-out territory, I fear my head will start spinning.

"Here's what we *should* be talking about," he pontificates. "Mankind needs to acknowledge where our species came from." Bob's face is quickly becoming extremely animated and the pitch of his voice is modulating to a higher, more agitated tone. "I don't know why they keep it such a big secret," he continues. "But humans came from another galaxy. We were seeded on this planet!"

"Well, that makes perfect sense," I remark, half in jest. "After all, we *are* the only species on Earth that knowingly trashes its own environment."

Bob, however, is not jesting, not even halfway. He proceeds to give us all the details, naming the solar system and the planet our once-alien race came from, what the spaceships looked like, what kind of fuel they used, what year this happened, and precisely where our ancestors from another galaxy touched down. I'd like to keep an open mind. Still, I can't help but wonder how he can possibly speak with such absolutely certainty on this topic. And, even if there's a remote chance that what he's claiming is true, I find it difficult to see how, with so many urgent problems facing humanity, that acknowledging our alien roots could be the number one issue on Bob's, or anyone's, list.

Then, as suddenly as he broke into his aliens-seeded-the-planet spiel, Bob brings the conversation right back down to Earth: "I'm hungry for ice cream," he announces, grabbing his jacket and keys. "I'm going to the store."

I'm tuning up my guitar as DeDe serves up bowls of frozen coconut-milk confection. An audience of three humans and three dogs is my largest since I embarked upon this quest 16 days ago. Performing a short set for DeDe, Bob, and Quentin, plus a trio of snoring canines grounds me. This is my calling, my unique gift, to communicate to the world in the universal language of music. Whether it's one person, three people, hundreds, or thousands matters not.

Bob checks the time: just past 9:30. "The hot tub closes at ten," he informs me.

Well, then, concert's over. My body needs healing. To that end, Bob and I finish off the evening in ideal fashion, with an abbreviated, but very needed soak, while he fills me in on a little personal history. Bob was a magazine editor and publisher. He conducted major spiritual retreats and promoted multi-media events. Now, slipping into his late sixties, he makes ends meet by washing windows. I can't think of a more symbolic vocation. Bob has spent his entire life trying to help people see things more clearly. And, in a very literal sense, his life's work continues.

MAY 17 · DAY SEVENTEEN

"Here's what I'm really worried about," Bob announces. He hovers his lanky frame over the gargantuan road atlas on DeDe's dining-room table. "Right here." Bob traces a segment of Highway 101 with his long index finger.

"Not much there," I observe. For more than 50 miles, from Paso Robles to King City, there's not a single town on the map. This means no motels, no campgrounds, no grocery stores, nothing.

"I'm really worried about how you're planning to get through that leg," Bob says.

Fifty miles would take us a minimum of three days, more likely four. I've driven the grade north out of San Luis Obispo multiple times over the years. It's brutally steep and goes on for miles. I was already dreading that unholy climb. Now, Bob has made me aware that, on the far side of the mountain, we could look forward to trekking directly into a big, fat hunk of oblivion. This news is daunting, to say the least. However, as Scarlett O'Hara famously said, "I'll think about that tomorrow. Tomorrow is another day."

Today, Millie and I have other plans, 12 miles west, in Los Osos.

☮   ☮   ☮   ☮   ☮

How do I know I'm in a Christian household? Well, you don't have to be Hercule Poirot to pick up on these clues. Ladies and gentlemen of the jury, I give you exhibit "A," the centerpiece of the kitchen table: a *Bible*-study guide neatly stacked on a *Bible*. I feel an immediate uneasiness, wondering what I've gotten myself into. Silently, in my mind, I address my friend Marsha Stewart: *You said you wanted me to meet your brother, Marsha. But you didn't warn me that he was one of those!*

Sure enough, Brian Barnes is not the least bit hesitant to talk about his faith. Every other sentence is some sort of personal testimonial. Phrases like "Since I found Christ..." and "My Christianity has given me..." and "According to *The Bible*..." are woven into his conversation as casually as *gee* and *gosh* and *golly*. *This*, I keep reminding myself, *is just the way a man of Jesus talks.*

Brian's always-smiling, triangular visage maintains a constant countenance of bliss. As he testifies to his Lord and Savior with such ecstatic fervor, I can't help but recall the expression on a fellow musician's face, 35 years ago, when he told me that I couldn't possibly know the ultimate pleasure of shooting Heroin into my veins unless I actually shot Heroin into my veins. Don't get me wrong. I'm not attempting to equate Jesus with Heroin. I honestly have no way of knowing if Jesus and Heroin would even make a valid comparison.

Surprisingly enough, Brian's addiction to Jesus doesn't bother me — because he doesn't preach. Instead, Brian proclaims his faith by sharing his personal experience. If a person feels compelled to share his own story, I'm usually all ears. If, on the other hand, he feels the need to lecture me as to how I oughtta be livin' *my* life, that's another thing altogether, one I'm far less receptive to. It's obvious that Christianity has enriched this man's Earthbound years beyond measure. It's also abundantly evident that Brian is an exceptionally nice man with a keen, yet laid-back sense of humor.

We're taking a tour of the local sights, driving through a thick forest of eucalyptus trees. Back in the day, Brian confesses, decades before the hair on his dome went AWOL and the thicket of whiskers on his upper lip turned white, he was quite the partier, drinking and smoking pot. Then, he met a beautiful, virginal co-ed from the Midwest. Brian was smitten. Carol, too, was attracted to Brian. However, she made no bones about her intentions. Carol was determined to wed a Christian man. Non-Christians, she declared, need not apply. For a time, Brian struggled with this quandary. He attended church with Carol. Out of her sight, however, he kept the party going. Straddling this incompatible, double lifestyle eventually led to bouts of depression. Unhappy and confused, he knew he had to make a decision. He'd already given his heart to Carol. He suspected she wouldn't mind sharing it with Jesus. Of course, Carol was over the moon about Brian's proposal. And the three of them have made a happy, successful, love-faith triangle ever since.

My first thought was that Brian's initial, primary motivation for becoming born again was his desire to get naked with the woman he loved. That's an incentive I completely understand. After all, I was a young man once, too. When I actually meet Carol, however, I realize there'd been far more to the equation than lust. It immediately becomes clear that Carol Barnes is a beacon of light, a person who radiates pure love energy. Brian is a very fortunate man to have this woman in his life. He knew it then and he knows it now. And, from that sublime expression on his face, he's pretty happy about having Jesus around the house, too. Amen.

MAY 18 · DAY EIGHTEEN

Over pancakes, bacon, and scrambled eggs, Brian asks, "So, Rand, how often do you take zero days?" When I confess to having no clue what a zero day is, Brian seems simultaneously surprised and amused.

Long distance hikers, he informs me, provide themselves with periodic days of rest to allow their bodies to recover. These trail breaks are called "zero days." During a typical zero day, a hiker limits himself to two restorative, presumably pleasurable activities: relaxing and eating. From the start, I anticipated taking an occasional day off from walking. But, in my mind, that time would be dedicated to more pragmatic stuff like doing laundry, buying dog food, changing a stroller tire, or drying out my camping gear. I also felt it was important to remain time-flexible in case someone should invite me to stick around to do a house concert, visit a classroom, or make myself available for a media interview. Had I taken the time, had it even occurred to me to do even the slightest amount of research on long-distance hiking, I might well have inserted zero days into my itinerary.

Admittedly, I was looking forward to losing weight. I'd started out with some to spare. But burning a daily 5,000 calories or more has stripped 20 pounds from my frame in two and a half weeks. I need to be realistic. At this rate, by trek's end, should I survive, I'll be as emaciated as a prisoner of war. For my own health's sake, I need to follow the examples of those with real and extensive experience — eat more, eat better, and give this fatigued body the time it needs to recover. And, thanks to Brian, I now have a cool, legitimate-sounding tag for these self-imposed periods of passive self-restoration: *Zero Days*. So, why hesitate? Starting at zero makes perfect sense. And this scrumptious, fat-rich, high-caloric breakfast feast is getting my first official zero day off to an absolutely perfect start.

"This is what I'm talking about…" Brian is pointing to the road atlas on the kitchen table — right next to the *Bible*-study-guide-stacked-on-*Bible* centerpiece. His pointer finger follows along the identical stretch of roadway that Bob's same digit traced just 24 hours earlier: the 50 miles of Highway 101, from Paso Robles to King City. When one fellow takes the initiative to voice his concern, I'll take note. Another speaks up, unrelated, at a separate time, in a separate place, expressing the identical worry, a pilgrim had best perk up his ears. While I'm willing to make a sacrifice for my cause, I have no aspiration for martyrdom, nor do I have any desire to suffer any more hardship or danger than is absolutely necessary.

"Wait a minute, Bri," Carol says to her hubby, "we're driving to San Jose today. Couldn't we give Rand a ride to wherever he needs to go on the way?"

The entire horizon to the west glows in post-sunset orange. It's taken less than an hour for Brian and Carol to chauffer pilgrim and pooch past a desolate 50-mile stretch of desolation that would have taken us three, probably four days to traverse. At my prompting, Carol is sharing her most pressing personal concern. It's a pervasive issue that Carol sees in her every day interaction with students in the public-school system. "Unwed mothers," Carol shares, "babies having babies. That's what I worry about." *Now, here's a blast from the past,* I'm thinking, *a golden oldie.* Then, as the father of two daughters, I realize how grateful I am that neither Emily or Glendyn ever managed to "get themselves in trouble."

The fact that Carol's concern is nothing new doesn't make it any less important. Even in its most benign form, this syndrome is the source of emotional trauma, social stigma, and financial hardship for millions of Americans. In its most malicious manifestation, it contributes to a statistic that should make Lady Liberty hide her head in shame: this nation's extraordinarily high rate of incarceration and the disproportionate percentage of people of color populating our prison system. "Way too many kids are growing up in single-parent households," Carol elaborates. "Children need a mother and a father. I don't know why it's so easy for people to get divorced. Why don't they try harder to stay together and make it work?"

The teen pregnancy issue is one thing. First and foremost, I believe it's a failure in our educational system, stemming from our Puritanical reluctance to frankly and openly address a topic about which too many American's still harbor shame: sex and human reproduction. While divorce also results in far too many single-parent homes, this is really a separate issue altogether. And, in spite of what Carol may think, divorce is seldom "easy" — not practically, and especially not emotionally. I've gone through it three times, each split, regretfully, affecting a child. I'm not proud of this fact. Still, I know from personal experience that incompatibility can become insurmountable to the extent that no amount of "staying together to make it work" will heal the divide. Regardless of how amicable a couple may claim their split is, if kids are in the mix, divorce is like major surgery sans anesthetic.

However, in my first two divorces, involving small children, my exes and I took pains to work out shared custodial arrangements. Although it's never the "ideal" situation, rather than subjecting children to pervasive disharmony and unhappiness at home, shared custody can be the best way for offspring to spend quality time with each parent. And, in a case where abuse is taking place — verbal, physical, or sexual, against the child and/or a parent — there is no other choice than to totally remove the offending adult from the family environment. Yes, it's confusing for the children and they should receive professional counseling. But it's much better that they live in a more-peaceful, one-parent household than be exposed to the trauma of additional conflict and/or abuse.

I agree with Carol. There are far too many teenage pregnancies and far too many children growing up in single-parent environments. How single parents manage is beyond me. But, while kids are usually better served by the nurturing and tutelage of both parents, subjecting any child to constant conflict, abuse, or neglect is never the best solution. So, sometimes divorce is simply the least-worst scenario. When I suggest this to Carol, she's open enough to take a look at her pet issue from a different and broader perspective. It's too simplistic to presume, "Children need both a mother and a father." That presumption depends on who that mother and father are, how they treat one another, how they treat themselves, and how they go about parenting that child.

It's dark. We're standing in the parking lot of a Motel 6. After helping me lift my gear from the back of his truck. Brian slips something into the palm of my hand, a miniature book. I take a quick look at the cover.

"Just in case you want to know more," he says, smiling through that ever-present countenance of bliss.

I read the little tome's title out loud, in the form of the question it poses, "Who *is* Jesus?" Brian chuckles, gives me a warm hug, and climbs back behind the wheel. There are Christians, and there are people who call themselves Christians. The Brian Barnes I know is definitely the former, as is Carol, the woman who showed *him* who Jesus is.

CHAPTER 13

Just Like Everyone Else

MAY 19 · DAY NINETEEN

This town's name gets a song singing in my head… it was some-where near here, that the singer let her slip away. She was lookin' for that home, and he hopes she finds it. Still, he'd trade all his tomorrows for a single yesterday, to be holdin' that girl's body next to his.

By the time this stanza of "Me and Bobby McGee" rolls around, Kris Kristofferson's sonorous diary of two free-spirited hitchhikers has turned melancholic. And, as I walk Millie through the parking lot of this budget motel, that's exactly how this place feels. Salinas comes off like a town that never found what it was looking for and, if the folks around here had the chance, most of them would just as soon zoom back to a time before their hearts got broken and start over. The city even advertises its low opinion of itself on a massive Shell gas station sign looming 30 feet over the freeway. The "S" has fallen off, leaving the remaining letters to read, of all things, *hell*. From the motel desk clerk to the guy behind the counter at the liquor store, I've been met with dour, discontented faces. I've almost given up on trying to get a smile in return. But, finally, I encounter a friendly, positive person. And, *wow*! Is she ever friendly and positive!

In obedience to my new pledge to increase my daily calorie intake, I've just finished off a stack of very doughy pancakes, slath-ered in maple syrup, with a side of bacon. "Looks like it's warming up," the restaurant cashier says, as she counts out my change. "My

kids are gonna wanna play outside." She's maybe 30, thin, undeniably beautiful, with flawless brown skin. In this moment, her smile
radiates enough warmth to thaw every bit of frigidity I've felt so
far in this hapless town.

"Yeah," I agree. Her sociable spirit has taken me off guard. So
much so, it completely slips my mind that yesterday at this time, I
was 100 miles away in Los Osos. I actually have no clue what the
weather's been around these parts. "That wind," I remark. "Whoa!
It's been chilly."

"Well, we've gotta be grateful for every sunny day," she says,
her brown eyes twinkling. As I return to my booth and lay down
my tip, a spontaneous, involuntary smile spreads across my face.
At least for now, she's right. Looks like it *is* warming up.

☮ ☮ ☮ ☮ ☮

Unfortunately, the warming trend doesn't last. I'm sure parts
of Salinas must be lovely. However, there is little cheer in this
section of town, on our way to Highway 183. Litter lies rotting on
the sidewalks in front of decaying, shuttered-up commercial buildings. We're waiting for a crosswalk light to change when a fellow
pushes a bicycle up next to us. He's big, physically imposing, and
his wrinkle-creased face is carpeted in thick, grey beard. "How's it
goin'?" I ask him. This passing pleasantry doesn't typically inspire
such a detailed response…

"Well, it would be better if I could get away from this coastal
nightmare," he snarls. "Too expensive." Then, his complaint turns
even more bitter. "I *hate* living in Mexico!" I'm assuming this is a
metaphorical racial slur, aimed at the dominant Latino population
in this part of the state. "I was born in Manhattan," he mutters
as he pushes his bike across the street. "I guess I'll go back there."
I wonder if he'll find weather this inviting in the Big Apple, or
more-affordable prices for that matter. Certainly, Spanish won't be
the only non-English tongue he'll hear in Manhattan. And, after
hearing those candidly prejudiced remarks, I'm doubting he'll find
much consolation in that.

At another intersection, I meet up with another cart pusher. Although his rig has obviously been purloined from a grocery store parking lot, I'm thinking this might be an opportunity for a moment of solidarity, a fraternal connection, if you will. But when I attempt to make eye contact, the young, dark-haired man keeps his laser stare fixated on some invisible spot straight ahead. A crazed intensity in his gaze warns me to keep my distance. Instinct strongly urges that I immediately cross to the opposite side of the street.

We're heading down the sloping sidewalk under a highway overpass when the clatter of wobbling castors on cement begins reverberating off the concrete tunnel walls. I look across the way to see the intense young man, not pushing, but standing up over the rear wheels of his grocery cart, white-knuckling its handle, and careening down the opposite sidewalk at breakneck speed. His dark hair is blowing straight back and he grins in crazed delight, while whooping like a native warrior galloping bareback into battle. We've trucked a block down the road, when I hear a voice in the distance — shrill, female, extremely vexed. She shouts out a couple of sentences in protest. Then, there is quiet. A few seconds later, more shouting, followed by another brief respite.

On a steep hillside above us, in a grove of trees, I can make out a woman. She calls out abrasively, identifying herself as the source of the previous, antagonistic outbursts. I trace the direction of her gaze to the subject of her fury. There, beyond the four lanes of pavement, a grocery cart is lying on its side, its contents strewn this way and that. The crazed, young man who was riding it with such manic abandon sits on the ground rubbing a skinned-up leg with one hand and waving at the air with the other, as if to tell the unhappy woman in the trees that he is unaffected by her shrewish jibes. I have no idea what the relationship might be between these two people. I will venture to guess this is not one of their better days.

"You don't want that one." The woman's voice speaks in that graceful accent that blends proper-British with Hindi vowel sounds.

"It's not good."

I quickly set the pre-packaged sandwich back down in the refrigerated display as though it's radioactive.

"Over there. Some fresher ones."

I turn around. The petite, coffee-skinned woman is speaking to me from behind the Quick Stop cash counter, directing my attention toward another display near the middle of the convenience store. I follow her finger to an edible-looking tuna salad on wheat. After deciding that I might as well plan ahead and buy two while I'm here, I place my purchases down on the cash counter.

"I like your set up," the woman says. Her raven hair is pulled up tightly in a bun and she's wearing a red, coarse-cotton, traditional Indian-style dress adorned in tiny, round mirrors and ornate embroidery. *Set up?* I'm not quite sure what she means. "Your arrangement, your rig," she clarifies, "it's nice." Ah, she's talking about the Pilgrimmobile. "And, you're so *clean!*"

Now I understand completely. She must see every sort of vagrant and ne'er do well in this place. In her estimation, I'm different, a cut above. She means this as a compliment. "No," I correct her, summoning a smile, "I'm not homeless."

She smiles back, cocks her head to one side and nods, as if to say, *It's all right, you don't have to pretend.*

"No, really," I attempt to convince her. "I have an apartment."

Now, a hint of incredulity begins to crinkle at the corners of her dark-brown eyes.

"In Oregon," I continue. "I live on the Oregon coast. I have a great apartment with a fantastic view of the ocean."

She's finding this information inexplicable. Two and two is not adding up to four.

"Then why are you…" she stammers, nodding her head toward my cart and my dog in the parking lot, just outside the shop's front window, "you know…?"

I explain that I'm on a pilgrimage, walking for 90 days, hoping to inspire civil, constructive dialogue.

"So, you're doing this because you choose to?"

As I hear my own voice responding in the affirmative, I'm

almost beginning to make no sense to myself.

"Aren't you frightened," she wonders aloud, "out there on the highway?"

I confess, in all honesty that, yes, every once in a while, it can get a little bit dicey. But, most of the time, I assure her, I'm fine.

"So, then," she presumes, "you don't have a car, right?"

"No, I have a car," I tell her, "a Prius. It's parked in my girl-friend's driveway. In Oregon." By the expression on her face, I might as well have told this woman that I flew in from Egypt on a magic carpet and, from here, my plan is to swim to Japan. That a man who owns a perfectly good automobile has decided to walk from California to Oregon is just that fantastical to her. I hand her my postcard. "Here, this explains who I am and what I'm doing."

As she takes a moment to peruse the card, other customers are beginning to cue up behind me. Self-consciously, I toss a quick "I'm sorry" over my shoulder for the hold up. At last, it seems, this tangible, rectangular piece of printed card stock has convinced the curious proprietress that, as preposterous as my claim may sound, I'm actually telling the truth.

"But, don't you get frightened out there, you know, walking on the highway?" She's repeating the question, this time, not so much from skepticism, but from genuine concern. She extends the card in my direction, attempting to return it.

"Don't you want to keep it?" I ask, smiling. Somehow, my offering to let her have the card is the final proof she needs. If I can spare even one single postcard, leave it behind without a second thought, then I must indeed be a legitimate peace pilgrim. This is my *Princess and the Pea* test and I've passed.

She looks at the card again, shaking her head in disbelief — no longer out of distrust, but because she remains both bewildered and impressed that anyone would choose to do what I am doing. "I'm going to tell people about you," she says, through a smile of admiration.

On summer mornings between my Junior High School grades, I seldom slept in. Instead, after peeling myself out of bed in the pre-dawn darkness, my mother would drive me, sack-lunch in hand, to a certain street corner by the bowling alley. There, I'd climb into a dingy, dented school bus. Aboard that bus, I'd pick out a hard, bench seat next to an aging, unshaven black man from Portland's downtown skid row who smelled of cheap wine and rancid tobacco. Together, we'd take the bumpy ride to the strawberry fields of the Willamette Valley. There, from first light to mid-afternoon, we'd toil in adjacent rows, picking fruit. My yield was only a fraction of what adults, whose livelihoods depended solely upon this menial work, could gather in the course of any given hour. By the time we climbed back onto the bus for our return trip, my fingers would be dyed rust-red, my face and neck would be another shade browner from the mid-summer sun, and I would have five or six bucks in my pocket for my day's efforts. With some of the money I was able to save laboring in those fields, I bought my first acoustic guitar.

As Millie and I trek the shoulder of this rural highway, I can't help but notice how much things have changed since those long-ago summer days. There are no pubescent five-dollar-per-day dilettantes in these vast fields. When these workers have filled up yet another flat of freshly picked berries, they hoist their yield up over a shoulder like a waiter in a posh restaurant, then sprint between the rows, hustling to turn the full one in and get an empty in return. There are no idle moments out here. This is skilled, high-efficiency labor; serious, nose-to-grindstone stuff.

Further evidence of this crew's dedication and professionalism is seen parked at the edge of the fields. Back in the seventies, if a farm laborer even owned a car, it was a beater, a dented rattletrap, with a sad, sagging bumper, a cracked windshield, and a wire-coat-hanger antenna. Today's scene is remarkably different. SUVs and big-wheel, king-cab pickups surround the fields. On one hand, it's great to see tireless, diligent, deserving folks receiving a decent wage for their efforts. On the other, I find it unfortunate that they've indentured themselves to the banks that finance such extravagances and the oil companies they compensate daily to fuel those high-powered V-8 engines. I can't help but picture a couple driving home from a day's toil in the fields in a sparkling, brand-new Silverado to 14 family members from three generations, all crammed into one two-bedroom apartment. In Southern California, status comes from the vehicle one drives, even when it means making major sacrifices to put up the artifice of class. Succumbing to societal pressure, the farm worker of today is far too proud to be seen driving an old jalopy.

MAY 20 · DAY TWENTY

Castroville, a municipality of approximately 7,000 people, brags of being the Artichoke Capital of the World. Modernity seems to have skipped over this town. And, that appears to be to its most appealing quality. Aside from one Burger King, I see no other generic, corporate, brand-name evidence of so-called progress. The absence of a single Starbucks, Walgreens, and/or McDonalds is refreshing. The only food stores along the main street are cramped bodegas, and the eateries are authentically Mexican. And, unlike so many other historic towns, gentrification hasn't swept in to give the authentic, vintage architecture a plastic, Disney gloss. Castroville is real. Castroville is also very obviously poor.

An old friend has motored down the coast from Santa Cruz to treat me to a meal. Although this is prime breakfast hour on a Saturday and the "world famous" Big Artichoke Restaurant has the capacity to serve a hundred customers, he and I comprise exactly half of the establishment's current business. Frederick "Fritz" Torp was one of my three best friends in high school. He, Gary Reig, Tim Sadler, and I were all active in Jack Lee Powell's ambitious theatre-arts program at Lake Oswego High School. In sophomore year, Fritz portrayed King Henry II to my title-role turn in Jean Anouilh's *Beckett*. The following season, I was Biff, eldest son to Fritz's Willie Loman in *Death of a Salesman*. On weekends, when we weren't taking curtain calls, and when I wasn't gigging with my high school garage band, our guy-pal posse would cruise out to Fritz's family ranch to ride horses by day and practice our beer-swilling skills by night.

Post high school, I visited Fritz at Columbia University in New York City and attended a meeting of Students for a Democratic Society, as future-FBI-most-wanted Mark Rudd and other notorious revolutionaries strategized protests that would eventually explode into an historic occupation of campus buildings. Fritz and I marched arm-in-arm in the first anti-Vietnam War moratorium in Washington, D.C. then lived together as campus radicals in Seattle. We lost touch in 1977 and have had no contact since.

With decades to catch up on, there are a lot of "How's your…?" queries about family members, and "Have you heard anything from… ?" probes to find out if and/or when either of us has had any contact with him, her, or them. I find it particularly intriguing that when one of us asks the other a version of "Do you remember when…?" or "Remember the time…?" our recollections diverge so radically. What's even more curious is that a memory that seems so vivid and consequential to one of us barely rings a bell with the other.

Fritz admits that, although he has been deeply disturbed by the current political climate, he has made no effort to get involved. He votes. But that's pretty much it. This sounds out of character coming from one of the most informed and committed people I've ever known.

"One of our classmates recently posted on Facebook," I tell him, "that you had the highest IQ in our class."

"Well, I *was* on *Jeopardy*," he says.

As they say, you could knock me over with a feather. Either I never knew this factoid about my old friend, or it was one of those events momentous and memorable to him, while being less significant, therefore easily forgettable, to me. Now, I'm swelling with pride, just hearing about my pal's impressive accomplishment.

"I was runner up," he informs me, with a plaintive grin.

Up until now, I'd been confused as to why Fritz hadn't invited me to stay in his home as I passed through. Now, there is no need to explain. With a prodigal daughter returned to the nest and about to give birth to a first grandchild, it would be highly inadvisable to introduce added stress to the mix in the form of Dad's old high-school pal and his beagle — even for one night. However, as he very much wants to make a contribution to my pilgrimage, Fritz does have an invitation in mind. He offers to make a reservation and pay for Millie and me to stay in a nice hotel in Santa Cruz. I am both moved and profoundly grateful for my friend's generous gesture. And, I'm very much looking forward to having more time to get reacquainted when I get there.

☸   ☸   ☸   ☸   ☸

Today's destination is the campground at Sunset Beach State Park. One can't make a reservation less than 48 hours in advance. So, I'm gambling there will be a spot for us when we get there, which should be somewhere around 5 PM.

Highway 1 is bumper-to-bumper in both directions. It's an exceptionally lovely afternoon, and my beagle and I are receiving an unusual number of smiles, waves, and thumbs-up from passing drivers and passengers. I've come to the conclusion that, at any given moment in California, every thoroughfare is either a race, a parade, or a parking lot. It's hard to fathom how many folks in such an infinite number of vehicles are trying to get from place to place. Doesn't anyone ever actually get to where they're going? And, if so, how can there still be so many people in cars still trying to get someplace?

A small, light-blue compact pulls to the shoulder in front of us. As we draw closer, I notice a *Re-Store Habitat-for-Humanity* bumper sticker. We pull up next to the open passenger window and I'm greeted by a smiling, round, cherubic face. A closer gander reveals he's missing several front teeth. In the stubby fingers of his extended hand, he's holding a five-dollar bill.

This circumstance presents a momentary dilemma. Here is a friendly, generous fellow assuming he's doing a good deed for a homeless man and his dog. One look at his modest vehicle and his gap-toothed smile makes it obvious that he's not even remotely well-to-do. Certainly, he must have plenty of use for that five spot.

Do I explain that, no, I'm not homeless, that I'm on a 90-day pilgrimage? Wouldn't that risk throwing a wet blanket over his magnanimous gesture? So, as to not douse this man's feeling of good will, I accept his gift with a hearty, sincere thanks.

As he puts his car in gear, he looks at me through sincere, sympathetic eyes. "You're just like everyone else," he says.

As I trek on, I wonder if he'd still say that if he found out I'm traveling this way not by necessity, but by choice. Would he think I'm just like everyone else if he knew the real reason I'm pushing this cart along this roadway, that my purpose is to inspire my fellow Americans to be kind to one another, to encourage folks to take a break from the name-calling and seek some common ground? I would have loved to use this five-dollar bill to buy him a cup of coffee, to sit down, listen to his story, and share mine with him.

Quite honestly, at this moment, I don't feel "just like everyone else." Everyone else is riding in a motor vehicle, powered by fossil fuel. Everyone else is capable of traveling further in one minute than I can in half an hour. Of course, I understand what the cherubic highway angel was expressing — that, in my essential self, in my most fundamental humanity, I am just like everyone else.

Suddenly, I'm having an epiphany — realizing that there is another fundamental human truth, maybe even a deeper, more profound commonality encoded in his proclamation. It's at the very core of what I'm doing right now. It's why I'm placing one foot down in front of the other, why I'm putting myself out here at the whims of the unknown. Assuming a person has adequate air, water, nourishment, clothing, and shelter, this is the primary reason why anyone does anything at all. It is our greatest motivator, what every human being seeks — consciously or unconsciously — every hour of every day. We all desire, long for, need, more than anything else, to be acknowledged, to be accepted, to know that we matter. We live for *connection* — with other humans, with animals, with nature, with the universe, with God. Without connection, our existence is vapid, empty, meaningless, unfulfilled.

As a failure to connect can be a source of heartbreak and alienation, it's no wonder we bond naturally with those we perceive to be most like us. There is far less risk in associating with people who look like we do, who speak the same language, eat the same food, root for the same team, enjoy the same games, vote like we vote, sing the same hymns, and despise the same enemies. Being a member of a like-minded family, organization, or subculture provides comfort. It furnishes our lives with predictability, and tells us we're traveling the correct and accepted path. There is great solace in knowing that our ideas will remain unchallenged, that we'll never be forced to consider other points of view — except, of course, to ridicule them as idiotic, immoral, or insane.

Yes, "just like everyone else," I find succor and reassurance among people of like mind. But I'm out here seeking another kind of connection as well, one that lies beyond the borders of my comfort zone. I am open to experience — no, I am *eager* to experience — connection that will provide even greater fulfillment for everyone involved, because it *does* come with a certain risk of failure, and therefore might not be the least bit simple or easy to achieve.

☮   ☮   ☮   ☮   ☮

We've walked almost 14 miles. It's nearly 5 PM. And, although we're less than a half a mile from our destination, we can't get there from here — at least not the way the map app is telling us to go.

"Yeah," the guard at the bird sanctuary says, matter-of-factly. "Google Maps always sends hikers and bikes this way. You'll have to turn around and go back to San Andreas Road."

"But that's two miles in the wrong direction!" I protest. Thanks to Judas Maps, Millie and I have gone four miles out of our way, which will add two more hours onto today's trek. The soles of both of my feet are inflamed and every step is more painful than the one before.

It's 7 PM by the time we get to Sunset Beach. The only vacant site I can find is a nice one, with a flat tent area, a fire pit, and a picnic table. However, the orange traffic cone on the cement RV pad seems to indicate that it must be reserved. A man pulls up on a four-wheeler, shuts off the motor, dismounts and strides in my direction. "Good evening," he says, "Can I help you?"

"I assume this site is reserved," I answer. He tells me it is indeed reserved — for overflow. "Can I have it?" I'm way too worn out for chitchat. I need a quick yes or no. There's not much daylight left to set up camp.

"You look like you could use it," the man responds, a warm, compassionate smile spreading across his face. "If you've got thirty-five bucks in cash, it's yours." I reach into my belly bag and count what I have — thankfully, $36. I hand him 35 and pocket my one remaining bill. He identifies himself as Mark, the camp host. We visit amicably while I unlock the box to set up camp. Before leaving, Mark yanks a bundle of firewood off the back of the four-wheeler and heaves it next to my fire pit. "Here," he says. "No charge. Compliments of the friends of Santa Cruz."

CHAPTER 14

Vagabundo

MAY 21 · DAY TWENTY-ONE

I seem to hold up pretty well for the first 12 miles of the day. At that point, like clockwork, fatigue begins to set in. This weariness is not just physical. It's emotional, too. The pain in my feet, the relentless traffic noise, and the repetitiveness of walking and pushing, walking some more and pushing some more, combine to wear me down. I feel my spirits plummeting and, invariably, have to remind myself that this mission is one of my own choosing, that every step, every mile, and every day gets me closer to my goal. I don't always have the luxury of planning easily doable 12-mile distances. Oft times, getting from where a day's journey begins to its planned conclusion means pushing further than is comfortable. Seventeen miles is too far. But, I've done it before and I can do it again. And, at least I know that luxury awaits me at the end of the road, thanks to my generous pal, Fritz Torp.

☮ ☮ ☮ ☮ ☮

For the very first time since I began my trek, I'm being given a bit of the celebrity treatment. I have to admit, I'm enjoying the attention. "Are you the man doing the walk?" asks the young woman, unable to mask what, by all appearances, is genuine excitement. The vision behind the Hotel Solares lobby desk is not simply beautiful, she is a living, breathing work of art. Her slender, exposed arms are tatted in mesmerizing, flowering patterns of pastel ink, while several subtle shades of orange and rust are woven into her blond, shoulder-length hair. By her query, it's clear that my reputation has preceded me. Fritz, I'm assuming, was the hypester. Two young male desk clerks, both as pretty as their tatted female co-worker, and ever-so-gay, scoot over to catch a gander. All day long, this youthful trio must have been wondering what a pilgrim walking from Southern California to Oregon might actually look like. At last, at nearly 7 PM on a Sunday evening, here stands the object of their curious anticipation on two very sore feet. I'm hoping they're not disappointed.

A pair of hot tubs sit side by side, each teeming with boisterous, energetic students from the East Bay area. A lanky, bushy-haired lad by the name of Christopher seems unusually interested in my pilgrimage. He tells me he has already done quite a bit of long-distance hiking and looks forward to challenging himself in the future with more trials by foot. The Pacific Crest Trail is on his list. I'm encouraged to meet a young man with interests that expand beyond materialism and immediate self-gratification, particularly one who wields such excellent, respectful conversational skills.

Christopher and his friends are here on their senior-skip-day trip, which has already lasted through the weekend, and will extend over Monday night. When he informs me that this lark is actually sanctioned by the school's administration, I am struck by how times have changed. Tim Sadler and I must have invented senior skip day when, as our graduation approached 49 years ago, we took flight from campus for all of one Friday afternoon, drove from the burbs to downtown Portland where we holed away at a tiny diner, ate French fries, and studied for finals. Our absence from class was both unexcused and unsanctioned, resulting in a mandatory visit to the principal's office and a stern tongue-lashing.

MAY 22 · DAY TWENTY-TWO

If you're ever interested in observing an eclectic slice of American culture, look no further than the nearest laundromat. I took notice of this modern, glass-walled structure as Millie and I pushed past yesterday evening on the home stretch of our 17-mile trek. From the outside, the property appeared far cleaner and more inviting than most such establishments. And, upon stepping inside, I find myself impressed with row after row of gleaming, stainless steel, high-tech, industrial appliances. Certainly, an investor must fork out big bucks for top-of-the-line equipment. Still, I'm not sure a cycle demanding 22 quarters gets my underpants any cleaner than the buck-fifty wash-rinse-spin thrill ride they took at Jim Liao's no-frills Motel 6 laundry room in Santa Maria.

Posted high on the wall, directly over Dexter Stack Dryer #12 is a rectangular placard reading, in large, red, capital letters: ABSOLUTAMENTE NO VAGABUNDOS. That the owner of the enterprise has chosen to post this warning solely in Spanish says a lot. However, not being a purveyor of the language, I can't help but find the word "VAGABUNDOS" amusing. Surely, if anyone in this place at this moment qualifies as a genuine, certified vagabond, it's me.

It can't be easy for a mom to look after a kinetic toddler while she gets her fluffing and folding done. I'm sure the young lady just wants to keep her child occupied. However, perhaps a matchbox racer or a superhero action figure might be less disruptive to everyone else in the place, while also being considerably more age-appropriate. The boy couldn't be much more than two. Still, to keep her adorable little imp busy, Mommy has supplied him with a roll of exploding caps, the kind you throw down on the sidewalk to make a loud, abrasive *crack* sound. This kid, however, isn't outside on a sidewalk where the offending noise might dissipate into the atmosphere. He's inside a rectangular echo chamber that only serves to amplify it. And, at this moment, his mother isn't occupied with folding laundry. She's absorbed in flirtation with a tatted, pierced, stocking-capped stud.

Meanwhile, with every ear-piercing micro explosion, Millie's little doggy nerves are becoming more and more frayed. I'm not one who would normally offer unsolicited parenting advice. In this case, however, on behalf of my pup, I feel obliged to speak up. "Excuse me," I interrupt the young mom in mid-flirt, "but those caps, they're really bothering my dog." The expression on her face indicates that now *she's* the one who is bothered, and that, if a gentleman and his beagle find her son's racket intolerable, they always have the option of stepping outside — which is exactly what we do.

I'm sitting on the curb in the parking lot checking my iPhone. I notice that the cracking and popping has ceased. Either the mother has actually done the right thing or the kid ran out of ammunition. Anyway, here comes the toddler, meandering out the laundromat door, unattended, looking for some other mischief to occupy his bottomless well of undirected energy. I'm just about to get up and return the little lad to his neglectful mother, when she strolls out casually, grabs his hand and escorts him back inside.

As the young Patagonia Outlet associate rings up my purchase, he asks if I'm planning on going on a hike.

Ha! I most certainly am! In fact, I've been on a hike for 21 days, which means I have 69 more days to go. I hand him my postcard. He asks me where I'm headed next.

My answer: *Sunnyvale.*

"Whoa!" he says, "I hope you're not planning to walk on Highway 17!"

"Well," Fritz declares, emphatically, "You can't walk on Highway 17!"

My old friend and I are sitting in an upscale bar gazing out through floor-to-ceiling windows at a cinema-scopic view of the beach, the boardwalk, and the legendary Giant Dipper wooden rollercoaster in the distance. I'm totally relaxed, luxuriating in the liquid indulgence of vodka and lime on the rocks. Basically, Fritz forbids me from taking the only available route to tomorrow's destination, specifically the road commuters between Santa Cruz and the San Jose area have traversed for a half century. "It's one of the most dangerous highways in the country," he elaborates. "Just the other day, there was a fatal accident."

Once again, if one person volunteers to give me an unsolicited warning, I take note. If another person, totally independent of the first, sends up the exact same flare, I'd best pay close attention.

Back at the hotel, I consult my directory of Unitarian congregations. As I scan the list, I am encouraged to see there are two fellowships in this area. Surely, I'm thinking, someone in one of those church groups commutes the Highway 17 route. They'll come to my rescue. I call both numbers and leave voicemails:

"I'm a UU from Oregon on a peace pilgrimage. I'm hoping that someone with an SUV or a pickup might be willing to give me a ride to San Jose."

I'm packing my newly washed laundry when Fritz calls. If no other option presents itself, and if we can fit everything into his Honda Civic, he volunteers to motor us over the hazardous Highway 17 corridor.

"I take that route every morning to work, anyway," Fritz says. My old friend has been so very generous already, buying breakfast in Castroville, paying for our first night's stay at Hotel Solares, and picking up the tab for drinks and dinner tonight. But one last favor remains. He'll have to completely empty the trunk of his Civic because we're definitely going to need every square inch of cargo space. This, he tells me, is no problem. He'll pick us up at 5:45 AM.

MAY 23 · DAY TWENTY-THREE

This is Fritz's routine. He stops at this same Peet's Coffee in Sunnyvale every morning before teaching high school English. Although the timeframe and location remain identical, on this particular morning, the pattern diverges slightly from the norm. Because here and now, in this nearly vacant parking lot, he'll part ways with an old friend. Together, we unload the car. I promise to visualize a positive outcome for his family's upcoming big event — a smooth entrance into the world for his healthy grandchild, his daughter embracing motherhood, and maintaining her sobriety.

Fritz expresses gratitude that I took the initiative to reach out to him in the midst of my trek.

As I watch Fritz's Civic pull out of the parking lot, my heart feels warmed, expanded by this long overdue, yet somehow perfectly timed reunion. Once again, my soul has been nourished by that essential experience called connection. Merchants are arriving at this small strip mall to open up shop. Pilgrim, pooch, and cart are beginning to attract suspicious looks. After imbibing a large cup of yogurt and granola, I push the Pilgrimmobile on in search of new adventures.

CHAPTER 15
Bent Wheel, Mutinous Belly

MAY 24 · DAY TWENTY-FOUR

Here we are, in the sprawl of another megalopolis. As we set out upon another day's journey, I muse, reflecting back on the concern expressed by friends and family members about our plan to walk Highway 101. Yes, trekking on the shoulder of the freeway bombards the senses. And, certainly, some drivers have been overtly rude. However, not one single stretch of interstate has been as fraught with peril and anxiety as this. Crossing an overpass over an interstate highway requires periscopic, eyes-peeled vigilance. Keeping the Pilgrimmobile and dog on a sidewalk barely wide enough for one person, then traipsing across a freeway ramp, between bumper-to-bumper vehicles piloted by stressed drivers — all invariably distracted by some hand-held device, an unruly child, and/or cup of hot liquid, and intent on getting from here to there — makes for an adventure and a half. Thankfully, we survive yet another treacherous fording of the freeway river.

☮ ☮ ☮ ☮ ☮

Silicon Valley is an endless maze of industrial parks. Each company campus is massive. One three- or four-story building, the length of several city blocks, looks much like the one before. Seas of shiny vehicles are tucked in side-by-side like dominos across the expanse of football-field-sized parking lots. And, these companies are not superstar, top-market-cap enterprises. These are companies no one outside of Wall Street ever hears about. They sport generic-sounding monikers like SanDisk, and Flextronics, and Intersil. They don't make the computers; they manufacture devices that store the data. They develop the software and make the batteries more powerful. Curiously, every fourth or fifth 50,000-, 100,000-, 200,000-square-foot property is vacant, its parking lot devoid of vehicles, its grass gone crabby and shrubbery overgrown. Billboard-sized, commercial real-estate signs advertise Available for Sale or Lease. Still, with all this square footage uninhabited, there are more, even larger, industrial developments under construction.

Thousands upon thousands of acres that previously bore fruit, land that has provided natural habitat for creatures of the wild since long before the Ohlone nation converted to Christianity, are all being gobbled up by progress. Nature is still being crushed under concrete and blacktop. Gargantuan excavation machines and earth movers dig lake-sized foundations. Cranes, three-stories tall, swing steel beams through the air like toy Lincoln Logs. Cement mixers churn incessantly, regurgitating rivers of grey lava. All this, so our phones can keep getting smarter, so we can play Angry Bird on our lunch hours, and so our kids can indulge in Mindcraft.

Khaki clad, button-down tech employees walk to and from lunch in packs of threes and fours, young men palling with young men, and young women with young women, bantering and laughing among themselves. No one seems the slightest bit curious about the oddest pedestrian on the sidewalk, the cart-pushing pilgrim. The majority of these fresh faces are brown or yellow.

By the time we arrive at the Motel 6 in Fremont, it occurs to me that I haven't conversed with a single person all day. It's almost as though I've been floating through the busy-ness of it all in a bubble, observing like a spirit from another dimension. The motel rooms are situated around a common courtyard area. There, a group of Latinos have congregated, sitting on patio furniture around a brick barbecue grill. Something smells delicious.

"What are you cooking me for dinner?" I joke to the bulky fellow in the chef's apron.

He's poking at several whole chickens on the grill rack. Schmaltz drips onto the white-hot coals. "Tube steak," he replies. This rude quip invokes guffaws from his crew. "Wanna beer?" he asks me.

Thanks, but no thanks, I respond. I've just walked 13 miles, and I'm headed out to pick up supplies. I ask them if they need anything. They don't.

A slender, good-looking fellow, one of the youngest in the group, points to my legs, now baked dark brown from the sun. "Well, you sure got the calves for it," he jibes. "Now, what would make a man walk thirteen miles?"

I know I'm being made fun of. Still, I smile and respond sincerely: "I'm on a pilgrimage, walking from California to Oregon."

At this, the young man's attitude instantly transforms from mocking to reverence. He reaches out his hand. As my palm meets his, he says, "It's an honor to meet you sir."

MAY 25 · DAY TWENTY-FIVE

"If you want to make God laugh, tell him about your plans."

— WOODY ALLEN

With a little over seven miles to go, we were on pace to arrive in Hayward ahead of schedule, when the sidewalk got funky. The curb cuts became steeper, the concrete was severely cracked in spots and, with the street lined with parallel-parked vehicles, circumventing the disintegrating areas presented a challenge. Still, although the sledding was rougher than it had been in recent days, this was a stroll in the park compared to Drum Canyon Road. So, I thought nothing of it. I had no idea how severely weakened the stroller's hardware had become from nearly 300 miles of daily pounding, bumping, twisting, and jolting.

I swung the Pilgrimmobile out into the street to avoid a spot where tree roots had torn up the sidewalk. Then, when it looked like the concrete ahead had flattened out adequately, I guided the cart swiftly toward a driveway. Unfortunately, the slope of the curb cut didn't come flush with the road and, when I hit that spot, the front wheel jerked to an abrupt and total stop. I tried to push it over the bump but it wouldn't budge. The shock of the collision had crumpled the metal wheel mount. Dissembling and reassembling the entire cart twice, and repeated attempts to bend the metal back, went for naught. I tried to push ahead on the bent wheel, hoping I could make it at least the remaining seven miles to today's destination. We hadn't traveled even one block when a crack in the sidewalk finished the wheel mount off for good, leaving the metal hopelessly mangled and useless.

I texted a photo of the twisted hardware to Bro Theo. His response: *I'm surprised it lasted this long.*

Faced with the stark reality of this circumstance, my pulse began pounding in my ears, my cheeks heated up like a pair of steam radiators, and my throat closed. This time, no profane expressions exploded from my mouth. I could actually feel my leaden heart sinking in my chest. And, for a few minutes, I actually allowed a dark, soul-crushing thought to buzz inside my head: *I might have to abandon my trek altogether. This could be all she wrote.* Maybe here, on a cracked, East Bay sidewalk, my glorious pilgrimage was whimpering out in a final, premature, pitiful, insignificant sigh, heard by absolutely no one.

"Okay, Norman," I said to myself. "Take a deep breath. No need to leap to worst-case scenarios. There'll be plenty of time for that."

> WHEN I TALK to myself, I often address myself by my legal name, which is Norman Randolph Bishop. It's the rational, mature-adult me addressing the overwhelmed, immature-child me.

Some urgent pragmatics demanded my immediate attention. First, I had to get this box off of this sidewalk and get myself and my dog to a safe place. Then, and only then, could I get back to sussing out next options and looking at the bigger picture.

☮   ☮   ☮   ☮   ☮

After three strenuous trips, I've managed to drag the box, the crippled stroller, my backpack, grocery bags, the dog crate, and the solar charger two long blocks to the driveway of the Goodwill parking lot — without losing the dog. Thanks to a very nice police officer, I found out that local cab companies offer minivan service.

The cabbie is a large man in both height and girth. Thankfully, he is willing and eager to use his physical strength to help me with the heavy lifting. As we commence the seven-mile trip, he is extremely displeased to discover that, even at this early hour, he's merged the minivan into a very slow-rolling parade. And, while he is visibly and audibly agitated by what seems a very minor, totally temporary setback — especially as compared to the more-disastrous situation in which I find myself — I'm genuinely pleased that this molasses pace gives me time to strike up a conversation.

Mohammed immigrated from Afghanistan during the Russian incursion. He arrived in the States alone, at 19, having left his entire family — parents, brothers, and sisters — behind. Only once in 24 years has he returned to visit them. The three long, international flights are too expensive, somewhere in the neighborhood of $3,000. Having never actually met a person from the country where U.S. troops have been at war for 16 years, I'm curious. I ask what he thinks about American foreign policy in his homeland. At first, he opines, the struggle seemed righteous. The sides were clearly drawn. The Americans and their allies were the heroes, while the Taliban and Bin Laden's mob wore the black hats. Now, he says, too many factions are battling each other — not just us, but other countries, including Great Britain, and Russia. But the one enemy that unites them all is ISIS. "They kill everybody," he says. "It doesn't matter. Women, children. They don't care." Suicide bombings, too, are still commonplace. "Those guys come from Pakistan."

It occurs to me to ask about the state of women's rights in his homeland. Mohammed thinks women have a good deal of freedom now. But, he says, a Taliban leader just finagled his way into a high-ranking position in the government, so a change for the worse might be imminent. Interestingly, even after two and a half decades living in this country, Mohammed makes an effort to keep up with current events across the globe, in the land of his birth.

After the 25-minute ride, I hand Mohammed my debit card. He looks at it as if he's never seen such a thing before. It seems inexplicable that a taxi company in Silicon Valley would be incapable of accepting an electronic payment. With only 42 dollars in cash, I'm short. Mohammed says that will be good enough. I tell him how sorry I am that I can't give him a tip. He smiles and tells me not to worry about it, then lumbers his bulky frame to the minivan and pulls away.

Bro Theo emails me a sketch of a concept he thinks would both repair and strengthen the stroller's twisted wheel frame. A Google search locates a local welder, whose hopeful-sounding outgoing message puts the first smile on my face in hours. "Remember," the greeting says, "this is the place where dreams are designed." Sounds to me like serendipity is once again stirring the pot. I sprawl on the bed for the first afternoon nap I've taken in months. I'm awakened by Paul McCartney.

I inform the caller that I'm holed up at the Motel 6. "Oh, I know that place well," Lee the welder responds. "That's where I always stayed when my wife kicked me out of the house."

"Well, if you get kicked out tonight," I quip, "come on over. I've got an extra bed."

Lee appreciates the invitation. But, his marriage is on more solid ground these days, so he doesn't think that will be necessary. Instead, he asks me to text him a photo of the twisted stroller wheel and Theo's sketch. If the wheel mount can be repaired, he can get to it first thing in the morning.

MAY 26 · DAY TWENTY-SIX

I thought Mohammed, yesterday's cabbie, was a big guy. This Uber driver, a young man of Samoan heritage, with a name I make several attempts at pronouncing, but can't twist my tongue around, is a human mountain. "But, hey," he cracks, "if you think I'm big, you should see my little brother!" His younger sib entered University of Washington last fall on a football scholarship, topping the scale at more than 400 pounds. Numerous times over the course of my trek, I've wondered how large people — Charles Barkley for example — are even able to turn around in motel shower stalls, let alone get their heads under those low-slung shower heads. I ask this mountainous Uber driver how he or his 400-pound little brother can use the lavatory on a plane? "It's not easy," he admits. I count my blessings. There are distinct advantages, it seems, to being a smaller-than-average man.

I've asked my jocular driver what he thinks about the current political situation in this country. He clears his throat. "Trump," he says, pausing for moment to weigh his words with ultimate care. "I guess we'll just have to give him more time."

It's probably wise for an Uber driver to refrain from taking sides politically. You never know who might be riding in your car.

I'm sitting at a metal worktable on a hard, rusty, metal folding chair in back of an arched-roofed, corrugated metal structure that serves as a welding shop. There is dirt under my feet, and rust under my MacBook Pro. The periodic shriek of a metal saw drowns out festive, exuberant Mexican music, while arcs of sparks shoot across the dimly lit space. The jogging stroller is undergoing major surgery. Occasionally, I'm called in for consultation. Lee, his partner Manny, and I huddle to confer as to what exact angle the newly reinforced wheel frame should be set to provide maximum turning capacity. The welding tag team is attacking this challenge with absolute earnestness. This morning, a pilgrim's cart might as well be the lunar lander, with the amount of attention it's getting from these two soldering scientists.

Lee is an intense, muscular Korean-American with a shaved head. He looks me directly in the eyes, as if he's attempting to peer into my heart and soul. Manny, short, stocky, pock-marked and ruddy cheeked, hails from Fiji. He keeps his head down, focusing exclusively on the job at hand. The operation takes slightly less than two hours. The front stroller wheel frame looks like something out of a Mad Max movie, intimidating, steam-punk, and indestructible. I hand my debit card to Lee to settle the 165-dollar tab. He looks at it with sudden surprise in his eyes. "Your *name* is Bishop?" he queries.

"Yes, Rand Bishop," I reply.

"Oh," he says, with a note of semi-disappointment, "I thought you were a priest."

Evidently, when I identified myself on the phone and told Lee I was on a pilgrimage, he leapt to the conclusion that my mission was of a religious nature, and that I was a Bishop of the church. This might explain his penetrating, probing attempts to catch a glimpse into my soul. And, I can't help but wonder if he would have made himself so readily available to address my crisis had he known I was a mere layman who had chosen to walk for 90 days — not for the glory of God, but for other less-pious reasons.

Yesterday's cabbie was from Afghanistan. This morning's driver was Samoan. The two men who mended my broken cart were Korean and Fijian. My return Uber ride to the motel is piloted by an affable fellow named Kumal from India. The president claims, "There are a lot of bad hombres coming into this country." But, I've walked the highways of America for three and half weeks and I haven't run into a single one of the scoundrels the POTUS wants us to be afraid of. All the immigrants I've encountered so far, regardless of their skin color, ethnic origin, or religious faith, have been unthreatening, hard-working, law-abiding folks. Some of them sacrificed everything to come to this country. Like generation upon generation of courageous dreamers before them, these are the kind of people who built this great nation. They, however, can't make America great again. Because these are the people who make America great, already.

☮ ☮ ☮ ☮ ☮

The nausea sneaks up with the stealth of a Ninja and grabs my gut in a stranglehold. Of late, I've been reveling in the permission to gobble up as much of anything I crave anytime I feel the urge. Right now, however, I fear there's a very real possibility that, if I lift fork to mouth one more time, I'll heave up what scrambled eggs, bacon, hash browns, and waffles I've already packed away. When my very sweet waitress set my late breakfast down on the placemat in front of me, I was fully prepared to take my palate on a thrill ride to Gluttonville. Instead, with barely a third of it gone, I raise my hand in a wave of surrender. "What's the matter, Honey?" the waitress asks. "Something wrong? You didn't like your breakfast?"

"No, it was great," I lie. I can't be sure, but I suspect something I've just eaten might be making me sick. "I just need my check, please."

By the time I wobble into my room, I'm feeling so puny, I can barely sit up in a chair, let alone stand upright.

CHAPTER 16

Gut Check

Rio Vista, California, was never on my itinerary. But, as she often did 40-some years ago when she was my wife — my first and only wife at that juncture — Melanie has volunteered to nurse me back to health. James, Melanie's fourth husband — or fifth, if you count the guy she stuck with the longest, but never quite got around to making it legal — has valiantly acted the role of ambulance driver. This gallant, heroic gesture was made even more laudable by the unfortunate happenstance that today is Friday of Memorial Day weekend. So, what would normally have been an hour-long scoot stretched out into a tedious, two-and-a-half hour crawl.

My declining the vodka martini James just shook and poured for me, catches Melanie's attention. "Oh, dear," she says with alarm. "I hope you haven't got the nanovirus!" Always an excellent cook, Melanie spent the last hour preparing her specialty. But the very idea of eating anything at all seems revolting, especially something as rich as sauce-laden pasta with lobster tails. All I want to do is lay down and sleep.

MAY 27 · DAY TWENTY-SEVEN

I wake up from a fitful sleep with a revelation. I have not contracted the nanovirus — or any other virus for that matter. Due to irregular meals and an erratic diet, all-too-often including food my digestive system is not accustomed to, I am, I've figured out, suffering from a vicious one-two punch to the gut: acid reflux and severe gastritis. I don't come to this self-diagnosis out of the blue. Having dealt with both of these maladies — albeit on separate occasions — I am all-too familiar with these extremely un-peaceful, un-easy feelings. Melanie cheerfully agrees to take me on a quest to hunt down a cure.

Delta Pharmacy in the old village of Rio Vista is the kind of drug store/homey mercantile I recall from my childhood. Here, a helpful pharmacist actually emerges from behind the counter to help customers find the right off-the-shelf product to put 'em on the road to recuperation. My choice is a product that has been reliably soothing wrenched guts for nearly a half century: Tagamet.

Melanie, however, refuses to return me to my guest/recovery room until I've had the "Foster's Big Horn Experience." The opening line of this joke might be: *So, a pilgrim with a belly ache walks into a bar with his first ex-wife...* The punch line, however, is not even remotely funny.

In a room the length and width of two semi-trailers, from eye-level to the 15-foot ceiling, every square foot of wall space is adorned with the severed, stuffed, and mounted heads of wild animals, each having been tracked and gunned down in its native habitat, decapitated, and meticulously transformed into a ghastly, ghostly trophy. Bighorn sheep, wildcats, water buffalo, bison, maned lions, wild boar, rhinos, even an elephant. And, aside from that solitary, giant pachyderm, whose trunk and tusks extend out over the room from the far wall as if frozen in the midst of whipping up a rebellion on Noah's Ark, there is not just one of each species. There are, for example, four rhinoceros heads. Talk about *over*kill! Needless to say, the "Foster's Big Horn Experience." does nothing to calm my queasy stomach.

I am immeasurably relieved to escape from this dark corridor of horrors into the bright, spring, Delta air. Melanie and I peruse the wares at the modest farmer's market to the comforting strains of vintage blues and country played by a ragtag combo of aging pickers. I'm about to ask the band if they'd allow a pilgrim to sit in for a number or two, when the pungent aroma of fish on the grill turns my sour stomach. I need to lie down.

MAY 28 · DAY TWENTY-EIGHT

In 1915, fire destroyed the Chinese neighborhoods of Walnut Grove, California. As state law prohibited Chinese immigrants from owning property — a statute that was not declared unconstitutional until 1952 — the displaced workers approached landowner George Locke with the proposition of leasing a plot of land to build a new town.

By 1925, Locke's Main Street was lined with speakeasies, gambling halls, opium dens, and houses of prostitution. Today, a Sunday stroll down the town's wood-plank sidewalk makes for a vivid flashback to a bygone era. Although Main Street is freshly paved and lined with parallel-parked cars, pickups, and motorcycles, it has never been widened. The two-story, wood-framed gambling halls are now museums, reeking of mold and mildew. Sic Bo tables, dice, dominos, and cards are protected under Plexiglas, alongside plaques to fill visitors in on fun facts about Locke history.

Melanie, James, and I enter another, far less placid interior world. Originally built as a brothel, Al the Wop's Saloon is hopping with leather-vested, long-bearded bikers and their busty ladies. Alcohol is already being served up liberally and getting tossed down with holiday-weekend gusto.

Al Adami, the town's first non-Chinese business owner, was a character. When a patron dared to enter wearing a necktie, the saloonkeeper insisted on cutting it off with a pair of scissors before serving him a libation. Al stirred ladies' drinks with his fingers, put chewing gum on dollar bills and tossed them in the air, sticking them to the ceiling — during the Great Depression! Unlike the grotesque trophy kills at the Longhorn, the two handsome bucks displayed behind this bar are still putting their antlers to use. A variety of bras and panties dangle from those six-pointed racks. I can't help but wonder what kind of ring-toss games must get played around here on late weekend nights. One mounted trophy adds a hilarious finishing touch to his lingerie headpiece. Dangling from the buck's long, severed neck is the pointed end of one of the neckties Al the Wop scissored off more than 60 years ago.

But the most eye-opening moment of our Locke visit comes in the Boarding House Visitor Center. One of the first three structures erected in Locke in 1915 — alongside a saloon and a gambling parlor — the old boarding house testifies to the Spartan conditions under which an immigrant laborer of the 1920s lived. For pennies per night, guests got a five-by-eight-foot cell, a saggy cot, a bedside table, and a water bowl. The bathroom — shared by all tenants on the floor — was the size of a small closet and contained nothing more than a commode and a sink.

We take so much for granted in this nation. Yes, I've been known to throw a fit when the cable goes out. But there have been nights on this pilgrimage when I would have been grateful for the basic luxury of a roof over my head, a cot to lie on, and a pot to piss in — even a shared one down the hall.

MAY 29 · DAY TWENTY-NINE

As Melanie steers the Lexus SUV down the sloping residential street, I am suddenly overwhelmed with an unexpected sadness. Millie has been by my side, constantly, steadfastly, for 300 miles. But Melanie has convinced me to give the beagle a few more days off. My dog, on the cusp of 10, has lost considerable weight, has been limping on an arthritic shoulder and, if she could talk, would probably tell me that the pads of her paws are as bruised as my feet. And, if showing mercy to the tuckered pup wasn't already reason enough to consider making the next few days of my travels canine-free, online research indicates that getting from one side of the San Francisco Bay to the other with a dog and a pushcart is either illegal or logistically impossible. It's a last-minute decision. Still, as forlorn as I am at this moment, I know it's the right choice. And, as the pup drives away with the ex, I'm comforted, knowing that, in just three-days' time, pilgrim and pooch will be re-united once again to resume our adventure together.

Thanks to my new friend Daniel DeMento of World Wide Musicians United, I have beds to sleep in and a full itinerary for my three-day tour of the Bay Area. My first host, Michael, is a small, wiry, bushy haired Oakland resident of approximately 40. It immediate becomes clear that this guy is exceptionally intelligent and well-informed on a wide range of subjects, including the history of American pop music, rock, and jazz. We immediately leap head-first into intense conversation, primarily about records and the artists who make them.

Time flies. We're both hungry. It's Memorial Day. The next challenge is locating an open restaurant that is walkable. By choice, Michael does not own a car. Our options are even further limited by the fact that he is also vegan.

The hike is 20 minutes, up steep hills and down, on craggy, shattered sidewalks, and around fractured manhole covers. Soon, we've crossed an unmarked border where accelerated urban restoration is aggressively encroaching upon hard-scrabble, poverty-stricken, urban decay.

This unique, strip-mall eatery replicates a Philly Cheese Steak joint in every possible way — except for the cheese and the steak. It also appears to be extremely popular. Long, metal spatulas in hand, the white-aproned cooks flip fake meat on the stainless-steel grilling surface while firing glib jibes to the clientele waiting in line.

As Michael and I chow down, the subject of conversation segues from the safety of music into more perilous territory: politics. The Bay Area has long been a bastion of uncompromising, diehard liberalism. Not surprisingly, Michael sings in enthusiastic unison with the local choir. My heart, too, has always leaned hard left. And, admittedly, in the past, while raising my voice in condemnation of intolerance, I've been guilty of the very sin I so often railed against. I was being intolerant of anyone who didn't see things my way.

It baffles me how two presumably intelligent people, one here in Oakland — or, even more likely, Berkeley, California — and the other in, let's just say, Dallas, Texas, can be looking at the exact same world at the exact same moment and come up with two entirely different pictures of reality. Presumably, there is one absolute truth, one set of verifiable facts. It matters little if someone is incapable of seeing it, or if they deliberately pretend it doesn't exist, the truth itself doesn't go away. And, although two completely contradictory realities can't exist in the same space at the same time, that's exactly what seems to happen constantly in the bizarre Fantasyland of American politics. A man from the Bay Area and a man from Dallas both look out at the same landscape, leap to absolutely opposite conclusions, and call one another idiots for it. (To be clear, Michael never called anyone an idiot.)

☮ ☮ ☮ ☮ ☮

Clad in a wrinkled T-shirt and a pair of slouchy jeans, the shag-haired young man sips from a long-necked beer bottle. A roadie for Bay Area alt-rockers Violent Fems, Kyle rents the downstairs room in the Fortes abode. Presently, Kyle's better half and 18-month-old son are back in Georgia. The young man seems tortured by circumstance, caught between the work he loves and his inability to afford more suitable environs for his family. Making matters worse, he is recovering from a serious hand and arm injury that, for the time being, prohibits him from working at all.

Kyle says he envies me. He wishes he could do what I'm doing. To a wounded young man — physically and emotionally — 2,000 miles from his wife and child, going stir crazy in a rented basement, it must seem like a romantic notion to be fancy free to walk the highways on behalf of peace and brotherhood. To me, however, it seems an ironic notion that a young person with so much life to look forward to would envy an aging fellow with so much of his life already lived. Although he speaks softly, I can hear a silent scream of distress echoing in his words. I detect deep sorrow in his eyes.

Kyle's misfortune may be good fortune for me, however, as there's a good chance he'll be able to give pilgrim and pooch a lift over the bridge to Marin on Friday, on his way to a physical therapy appointment.

A malfunctioning wheel on the jogging stroller demands attention. As I trundle to the bike shop, a palpable vapor of desperation and hopelessness hovers in the atmosphere. This is the Oakland one thinks about when one thinks about Oakland. Disintegrating sidewalks pass dilapidated houses. Every other yard has a gnarly, ferocious guard dog leaping at a chain-link fence. People of color shuffle and meander up, down, and across the streets. My smile gets no response. All eye contact is avoided. Tiny, elderly, pinched-faced Asians sweep the walkways and sidewalks in front of their homes, fighting a never-ending battle with filth and grime. Commercial buildings are locked, shuttered, and befouled with spray-painted graffiti. The only shops open for business are a couple of laundromats and a bodega or two. Churches not boarded up are begging for paint.

At the Bikery, Mario, a slight man with intense eyes, addresses my stroller-wheel issue with the compassion and sincerity of a veterinarian examining a beloved dog with a lame paw. His professional diagnosis: the wheel needs rebuilding. Sounds serious. However, Mario assures me this is routine. He promises to have it done in an hour.

I decide to do some exploring. I've been to every corner of Manhattan, from Greenwich Village to Harlem. But nothing in New York City compares to the harsh, down-and-dirty urbanity of this half-mile walk to Fruitvale Station — the street people, the litter, the BART (Bay Area Transit) trains clattering on elevated rails, the shrieking brakes of city buses arriving at their stops, the blue-black clouds of air-born soot bilging from their tailpipes as they pull away.

IN THE EARLY morning of New Year's Day, 2009, a 22-year-old ex-convict named Oscar Grant III was starting to get his life back on track. Oscar had a job and a girlfriend. He was making good decisions and steering clear of bad influences. He finally had a real future to look forward to. Instead, a bullet in his back, fired at close range by a police officer, stole the young man's life and future.

It's been eight years since that young man bled out on a train platform. Now, the environs surrounding Fruitvale Station feature a farm stand with clean, fresh fruit and vegetables, a kiosk with cut flowers, several lovely restaurants, gourmet food stores, and coffee shops. After having only just trekked through such inhospitable, clamorous, urban squalor, I find myself exhaling a sigh of relief that I'm once again trekking a more welcoming landscape. And, as I savor a waffle cone of coffee ice cream, I can't help but think about Oscar Grant III, and feel a little pang of guilt about that.

CHAPTER 17

San Francisco Values

Michael lives in Oakland, but works in San Francisco. Carless by choice, he utilizes a ride-sharing program on most work mornings. Commuters cue up at designated places, where signatory drivers stop to pick up passengers for the Bay Bridge crossing. Riders pay one dollar as a contribution toward gas and tolls and, on the City-side, fan out to their individual destinations via public transportation. On an average day, it takes Michael approximately an hour to an hour and 15 minutes for his commute.

Dawna Knapp resides in San Francisco, but works in Berkeley in the East Bay. For Dawna, who does own a car, an average City-to-office commute takes — *get this!* — approximately an hour to an hour and 15 minutes. Dawna is a big lady. Not necessarily overweight, but tall and powerfully built. Her gregarious personality is as broad as her shoulders. You can't help but like Dawna from the get-go.

As Dawna motors me from Oakland to her San-Fran digs, she peppers me with questions about why I'm doing what I'm doing. Her habitual, automatic response to almost everything I say is, "Yeah, right?" But not in that sarcastic way this phrase is commonly used. Dawna's *Yeah, right?* comes in an inflection of total agreement that says, *Boy oh boy, Brother, you've just said a mouthful!* On the way, we stop at Trader Joe's. I leave the store feeling guilty that I've asked for a shopping bag. Dawna, who works at the Sierra Club, carries her purchases to the car in her arms.

That the Sierra Club is now headquartered in Berkeley is a tale unto itself. When Dawna first took her position there, the prestigious environmental society was still the pride of San Francisco, its home for well over a century. But, while there are invariably big winners in every economic boom, there are losers as well. The tech bubble has not only made San Francisco unaffordable for middle-class renters and first-time home buyers, it has made doing business unrealistic for iconic not-for-profits as well. When the time came for the Sierra Club to renew its lease, the landlords doubled the rent. So, a century-long San Francisco institution was forced to do the unthinkable — skedaddle across the Bay to less-pricey, more-accommodating Berkeley.

As we drive past vintage Victorian townhouses, many over a century old, I feel an enduring affection for a city that no longer exists. Inside these same bay windows, hippies passed joints, dropped acid, and jammed. They immersed themselves in each moment, soaking in life, one day at a time, sharing everything they had with anyone and everyone, even their bodies. Now, you'd have to be swimming in Scrooge McDuck cash to afford to live in one of these stately, antique structures.

Atop a knoll in the Presidio, surrounded by peace and quiet, Dawna Knapp lives in a converted military barrack. With a tidal marsh to the north, and trees at every other compass point, if I didn't know better, I wouldn't have the slightest clue that I was within the boundaries of teeming metropolitan sprawl, where every square centimeter is more valuable than a brick of gold. As she unlocks her front door, Dawna informs me that she has three roommates. No sleuthing is required to discern the dominant personality of the residents who inhabit this communal den. Backpacks, surfboards, paddleboards, and trekking poles lean against hallway walls. That Dawna's roomies are outdoorsy folks makes perfect sense. She is, after all, employed by the Sierra Club.

MAY 31 · DAY THIRTY-ONE

Oh, how the memories flood back! San Francisco memories…

Spring break, senior year, with Fritz Torp and Tim Sadler, perusing the head shops of North Beach, the aroma of sandalwood and patchouli wafting over the cobblestones. Jim Morrison screamed "Break on Through to the Other Side" from every record store hi-fi. We sat five feet away from the Matrix stage as a raspy-voiced wild woman named Janis Joplin swigged Southern Comfort and belted "Down on Me," backed by Big Brother and the Holding Company.

At the Fillmore, I walked right up to Jerry Garcia, shook his hand, and announced, "I'm in a band, too," as if I thought he'd be impressed. After The Who performed "Tommy" at Winterland, I tailed Peter Townsend to his hotel. I followed tatted, bandana-ed Ron "Pigpen" McKernan through the concourse of San Francisco International in his dark shades and biker leathers as he attracted stares of shock and disgust. Later that same day, I accompanied my girlfriend Becky to Planned Parenthood to procure birth-control pills.

The Wackers gigged at the Coach House and cut albums at Wally Heider Recording, produced by Gary Usher. Impish Jack Cassidy of the Airplane lurked in the studio hallway like a bridge troll, devilishly tempting passersby to join him in toking the wickedest dope on Planet Earth. There was that beautiful Chinese high-school girl named Daisy who had just begun her fatal flirtation with Heroin.

More recently, I gave my daughter Emily away to her betrothed, James Sudd, beneath the statuesque redwoods of Golden Gate Park and took my son Dustin and youngest daughter Glendyn on a cable car ride to Fisherman's Wharf.

This morning, when I toted my backpack and guitar onto this Muni bus, I was its sole passenger. Now, the bus is packed with every shade of skin and ethnic dress. The elderly sit next to middle schoolers. The athletically fit, lean and sneakered, stand to make room for the pregnant or the infirm. In spite of their evident differences, these passengers have one thing in common: they are all veterans of the Bay Area public transportation system. They climb aboard with confidence and ride for a while, engaged in their smart phones, or reading their newspapers — *yes, Bay Area residents still read print newspapers!* Then, with no more than a brief upward glance to get their bearings, they yank the cord and hop off. Me, I'm keeping a very nervous eye on the street signs. *I think this is my stop.*

I hoist my backpack and guitar, descend the stairs onto the sidewalk and into the clamor of the city. The bus pulls away. I check Google Maps. I'm still nine minutes away from the Balboa BART station — by bus. I got off too early. Disoriented and confused, I walk a few blocks in one direction, then back track, then turn around again. Finally, I find where I can catch the right bus. It sits by the curb, stationary. I wait — 10, 12, 15 minutes. More riders begin cuing up, some asking me if this is the #10 bus. I tell them I hope so. Finally, the youthful Chinese-American driver opens the door. As I fork over another two and a half bucks, I ask, "Which stop do I get off for the Balboa BART station?" His smile implies that I must be the dimmest bulb on the tree. And, that's exactly how I feel when he informs me that it's the very first stop.

The bus travels over a hill and around a curve, four blocks tops. "Balboa Station," the driver announces. The walk would have been a piece of cake. *Nine minutes by bus? Really, Google Maps?* I buy a 20-dollar BART pass and trundle down the stairs to the sub-strata platform. Which train, I ask a fellow, will take me to the 24th Street-Mission stop. He points to the opposite track. Up the stairs, down again on the opposite side. The train speeds in, stops, I step on, grab a spot, backpack on lap, guitar between knees. I dare not commit the mortal sin of taking up two seats. Another 10 minutes, and I'm emerging into the most glorious San Francisco day ever.

Under cotton-candy clouds drifting across a robin's-egg sky, caressed by a warm, balmy breeze, I walk the half mile up and over the hill to Café Fiore for a gratis lunch, courtesy of Danny DeMento.

☮   ☮   ☮   ☮   ☮

Not only is Nicholas Binion literally stepping out of my personal past, he looks as if he's walked right out of this city's past as well. A slight, petite man, with a grey ponytail, Nick's style statement authentically harkens back to the days when flowers had power, and San Franciscans wore them in their hair. The wrinkles around his eyes suggest he might have lived here when that history was made. But, I know better. Because, like me, in 1968, Nick was attending Oberlin College in Ohio.

"I can't remember when we last saw each other," Nick remarks.

We're looking across the table as if we're trying to see our 18-year-old college-freshman selves through 67-year-old eyes weakened by presbyopia. "I want to make a contribution to your walk," he says, fishing for some cash.

I know Nick can't afford this. He exchanges dog walking for his single-room digs. I attempt to decline his offer but he insists.

"I thought fifty was a good number, but what the heck." he says, looking at the three 20-dollar bills he's just pushed across the table. When I tell him I'd be happy to give him a 10 in change, he seems relieved.

Nick chatters away in a non-stop stream of consciousness, mentioning one name I vaguely remember from our mutual past, then rapidly ping-ponging to another. My remembrances of freshman year in faraway, flat, bleak Ohio, however, are spotty at best. And most of what I do recall is unpleasant. Mercifully, our collegiate recollections breeze by briskly and we move on to hit the highlights of the half-century since.

Nick's post-Oberlin life, it turns out, makes for a past as checkered as mine. So, sipping Chai tea and occasionally breaking nibbles off of an enormous peanut-butter cookie, I find myself mostly listening, rapt — for two hours. Particularly enthralling are my friend's stories about working with the notorious Jack Scott, whose groundbreaking philosophies revolutionized collegiate athletics and helped shatter the color barrier for both athletes and coaches. Ultimately, in spite of Scott's many notable accomplishments, he would be most remembered for harboring kidnapped heiress Patricia Hurst when she was on the run from the FBI.

Nick is working on his own memoir about his history with Scott. So, this story is best left to the man who lived it. Let's just say it's a tale well worth telling.

I love San Francisco. And, I love San Francisco for the exact same reasons so many — in particular, many who voted for our new president — berate this city with such disdain. Conservatives speak the words "San Francisco values" as if Bay Area culture represents everything that is un-American, everything that threatens the so-called "American way of life." Contrary to that twisted, parochial point of view, I happen to believe San Francisco values are the real, truly American values.

On these streets, inclusion and acceptance are seldom, if ever, in question. Skin color, ethnicity, gender, and sexual orientation are all secondary here. First and foremost, these are human beings simply going about everyday life. One man's skin is brown, his hair wrapped up in a turban. Another is white; he wears a cowboy hat. *So what?* Her face is blue-black; she feels comfortable in a sarong. Another woman's skin is yellow; she wears tight cigarette jeans and a graphic T-shirt. *What's the big deal?*

Some tend the shops. Some shop. San Franciscans interact as if they don't notice their obvious differences, because those differences are far less important than their interaction. *It's none of my business what you wear, what God you worship, who you love. I simply want to buy this yerba mate tea. And, yes, thank you. I will have a nice day. You, too.*

On these streets, one observes that evil bugaboo called multiculturalism at work, in real time. This is the looming threat that sends panic into the hearts of so many around this nation. It's what conservative commentators and evangelical preachers constantly warn us about. Here, they say, is the rapid, precipitous decline of civilization as we've known it, the dilution, the degradation of Western-European-rooted Christian America.

But, *look out!* San Francisco values are creep, creep, creeping over the purple mountains and across the fruited plains. *Heaven help us!* Pretty soon, we're going to have to start uncrossing our fingers when we sing, *Amerrrrica, Amerrrrica, God shed His grace on thee.* And crown thy good with what? *Brotherhood?* Oh, no! Really? Not that! *From sea to shining sea? Oh, Lord!* What if a man in a turban, or a woman in a sarong, or a homosexual, or one of those trans-pervs moves into my neighborhood? And, what if, when I meet him, her, it, I find myself actually liking them? And, what if their kids start playing with my kids? Because kids, well, they don't know any better. They haven't yet learned the proper values, the wholesome values, the righteous values. They have to be taught to judge and fear and despise another person, simply because that person is different.

But maybe our children have more to teach us in this regard than we have to teach them. Here's a delicious, wonderful thought: Maybe *every* child is actually *born* with — *Heaven help us!* — San Francisco values!

☮ ☮ ☮ ☮ ☮

Nora Shourd and I go back more than 25 years, to when our daughters became best friends as fifth graders. Through their Junior High school years, my daughter Emily, and Nora's daughter Sarah, were inseparable, and we often traded off weekends tending to each other's offspring.

As I mount the porch of this brightly painted Victorian, Nora introduces me to a half-dozen people in less than two minutes. One name sticks in my head: Bernard, a beautiful, longhaired blond boy of perhaps four or five exhibits a crafty, curious smile, and kinetic, pinball energy.

The cooperative living arrangement at the Cathaus has been carrying on successfully for nearly two decades. Eight people reside here at present; six adults and two children. Some, I'm told, have lived here for the entire duration. Nora, who moved in a year and a half ago, is the makeshift family's most recent adoptee, and its most senior citizen.

Jesse Palmer owns this magnificent house and has done all the renovation himself. In addition to his carpentry skills, Jesse is a lawyer, an activist, and the editor/publisher of a free, quarterly newspaper. Evidence that he hails originally from my home state is his Oregon Country Fair Security T-Shirt. Jesse seems completely unimpressed with me. He's bicycled cross country a number of times so, to him, a 90-day pilgrimage is just something someone does. "You're not going to change the world by doing that," he informs me.

I smile and respond, "I'm not trying to change the world."

Maybe my host is testing me. Surely, he's run across plenty of phonies, scoundrels, and blowhards in his lifetime. He's conditioned to keep his guard up. This is Jesse's encampment. He's the chief, the one with the ultimate responsibility of protecting the interests and safety of his tribe. And, I'll bet Jesse's natural skepticism is a big reason why the Cathous has survived as long as it has.

After dinner, Jesse takes me on a tour. First, we pass through the shared kitchen and the mud porch, down the creaking wooden stairs, past Nora's basement bedroom, to a space presently under construction. Bernard is just starting kindergarten, but the boy's mother plans to raise her son to maturity as a member of the Cathaus clan. So, Jesse has already erected a sturdy, two-by-four frame for the walls within which Bernard will ostensibly grow into manhood.

The backyard may not be impressive in size, but it has been put to maximum productivity. A fruit and vegetable garden yields a plethora of organics, while an elevated, wooden hot tub under the spreading umbrella of a primordial oak looks like something out of Neverland. I'm expecting Tinkerbell to flit out of its prickly leaves and spread fairy dust over our heads.

Back in the 30-by-20 living/dining room, I pull out my guitar and lyric book. Mothers have gone to put their young children down and Jesse has retreated to his upstairs law office. While this space would be ideal for a spontaneous house concert, I'm not gathering an audience. Nora slips out of the kitchen with cups of tea — one for me, another for herself — sits, shuts her eyes, and listens as I render a few selected tunes.

Nora seems content. She wants to live out her remaining days here as the elder matriarch of this cooperative family unit. Tomorrow, she informs me, she'll be spending the day volunteering for a charity that collects and distributes clothing for the homeless, work she finds enormously fulfilling. Sarah will be here for dinner tomorrow evening. If Jesse gives the go-ahead, Nora would like to invite me back. I'd like that very much.

JUNE 1 · DAY THIRTY-TWO

There are few passengers on the train. I'm paying close attention as to not miss my stop. However, I'm finding it difficult to understand the distorted announcements blasting through the P.A. system. "Is this Fruitvale?" I ask the nearest woman.

"No, Fruitvale's next," she says. Middle-aged, black, the lady has a kind smile.

"I'm from Oregon," I explain, implying that I'm a BART neophyte.

"I heard about those stabbings in Portland," she remarks. Smile gone, she's shaking her head, baffled by the inexplicability of it all. "And, for what?" she wonders aloud. "For hate?"

TWO DAYS AGO, on a Portland TriMet MAX train, a 35-year-old man named Jeremy Christian burst into a racist harangue directed at two girls. When a trio of men stepped in to protect the young ladies, Christian pulled out a knife and stabbed all three in the throat. Two of the men suffered fatal wounds. The attacker defended his violent actions by claiming that enemies of free speech deserve to die.

My fellow passenger works as a hospice nurse. Her husband, she informs me, is about to have major surgery. As the train slows to a stop, she and I both agree that, unlike the white supremacist who murdered two Good Samaritans in Portland, most people are indeed nice. As I'm trundling along the train platform to the stairs, she hustles to catch up with me. She wants to make sure I know where I'm going from here. This woman has her own stuff.

Her husband is about to have surgery. Yet, she's concerned about a stranger from Oregon. Yes, most people *are* nice.

When I locate the #62 bus, the driver is nowhere to be seen and the bus doors are closed. Another gentleman, black, wiry, shoulders stooped, wearing a baseball cap, and walking with a cane, asks me, "Is this the bus to Highland?" I'm not sure what Highland is. "Highland Hospital," he clarifies. It occurs to me that I could easily answer his question. A few pokes at my iPhone and I'm able to assure the man that, yes, this bus will take him to Highland. "I thought so," he says, with a self-congratulatory grin.

The bus driver arrives from his break, opens the door, and climbs aboard. I follow him up the stairs and extend my two dollars and 50 cents toward the cash kiosk. "No," the driver says, "just take a seat." A free bus ride. Excellent. He motions for the wiry black man to take a seat, too.

As the bus pulls away, I get nosy, asking the wiry black man if he's visiting someone at the hospital. No, he informs me, he has an appointment with a specialist. I wonder if he's always lived in the area. Well, yes, he recalls, except for those eight years in Sacramento. This is something, I observe, that he and I have in common. We've both returned to our roots — mine in Oregon, his here in Oakland. This provides me an opening to tell him about my pilgrimage. As he listens, it's almost as if decades are falling from his face. He can relate, he tells me. He was a truck driver. He's seen a big hunk of this country himself. He smiles and extends his hand across the aisle, "I'm Dennis," he says warmly. It's a good handshake.

I hand him my postcard. "This is what I'm up to."

Dennis takes off his sunglasses and squints at the card, attempting to focus on the print. "When I get to the hospital," he says, "I'm gonna read this more carefully." He tucks the card away and pats his pocket. I pull the cord to let the bus driver know the next stop is mine.

Even after three days of recuperation in Rio Vista, and then primarily traveling for these last two days via bus and train, my feet are still suffering. Several of my toenails have turned black, threatening to die and detach, and a blister has developed underneath the nail of my right pinky toe. If not for my sore feet, an urban mile to an athletic shoe store called Kicks would be an easy, pleasant afternoon stroll.

A young woman — I mean, not yet out of her middle teens — comes around the corner dressed in a tight-fitting, cleavage-revealing, pink, terry-cloth jump suit that barely conceals the vivacious curves of her nubile body. "Hello, sir," she flirts. I wonder if she's working the street. As I stride toward the shoe store, the pink-clad siren confirms my suspicion. A car stops. She leans into the passenger window. After a five-second negotiation, she swings open the door and slides into the passenger seat. The vehicle scoots around the next corner, where presumably she'll perform who knows what for a pre-agreed sum.

In 2009, Sarah Shourd, then 32 and teaching English to Iraqi war refugees in Damascus, Syria, invited my daughter and her husband on a hiking excursion in Iraqi Kurdistan, near the border of Iran. Thankfully, Emily and James declined Sarah's invite.

In July of that year, Sarah, her boyfriend Shane Bauer, and friend Joshua Fattal, were backpacking toward a popular tourist destination called the Ahmed Awa Waterfall, when they were taken into custody by Iranian border guards. Emily's junior-high-school best friend, the confident girl who, on so many occasions, chattered away unabashedly from the back seat of my car, was accused of spying for the United States. She would spend the next 14 months in solitary confinement at Iran's Evin House of Detention. Never put on trial, Sarah was ultimately released on humanitarian grounds. Bauer and Fattal, after being found guilty of illegal entry and espionage, received eight-year sentences. (A negotiated financial arrangement freed the young men in September of 2011.) Sarah, Shane, and Josh recall their ordeal in an excellent memoir entitled, *A Sliver of Light.*

Today, Sarah is a highly intelligent, extremely worldly woman. The word "worldly," in this context, takes on a double meaning, in that Sarah may have seen more of this world than any person I know. Something she says leads me to a profound realization: *The feeling I've been getting when I find connection with someone from an entirely different background is not unlike the exhilaration of falling in love.* Both experiences produce a similar rush of endorphins. But, when I connect with someone from another culture, I not only feel strong affection for that person, I actually like myself better as well — for letting down my defenses, opening up, and making my own, true, best self available for whatever happens to unfold naturally.

For me, it's a new and invigorating experience to relate to Sarah this way — not adult-to-child, as we were all those years ago, but peer-to-peer. For Sarah, however, this is probably not out of the ordinary. The bright, precocious child I recall, never doubted for second that she was on a peer level with adults.

JUNE 2 · DAY THIRTY-THREE

Before I depart, there is one remaining unchecked item on my Cathaus agenda. I unpack my guitar, tune up, climb the creaky back stairs, and knock on Jesse's office door. He's on the phone with a client. Jesse's law practice is all about advocating for the little guy, especially when the issue is fair housing. And, these days, with Bay Area real-estate greed at flood level, and vulnerable poor folks being forced to walk the plank every single day, you can bet there are plenty of drowning victims in desperate need of Jesse Palmer's legal life raft.

Yesterday, while riding a BART train, I missed my stop. I had been distracted by an impressive opinion piece in the latest issue of *Slingshot,* contributed by Jesse Palmer. Instead of taking the expected, rigid, "principled," uncompromising stance one might expect from a left-leaning Berkeley activist/journalist, Jesse advised his readers not to allow progressive dogma to stand in the way of hard-won, incremental, step-by-step progress. Reading Jesse's words filled me with a strong urge to share a certain song with the author of such a sage and grounded opinion.

I've been fortunate enough to accomplish a fair amount as a songwriter, creatively and commercially. My songs have been recorded and performed by legends. Some have been broadcasted countless times over radio and television, and featured in film soundtracks, while tallying multiple millions in sales. "Answering the Call" is relatively new. It's about staying the course, following a ray of hope, even when voices around us say, "Cut your losses, roll up your tent, and pack it in!" Unlike some of my more popular compositions, this song has been heard by only a handful of folks. Still, I'm as proud of this copyright as any I've ever created.

It is a true privilege to play this particular song for a fellow Earthbound traveler on a mission, a brother who lives to make a positive difference in this world, working tirelessly, persistently, every single day on behalf of justice. To share these meticulously chosen words with an erudite man of letters holds special meaning for this wandering troubadour.

Although I didn't know it at the time, I wrote "Answering the Call" for Jesse Palmer. Well, at least I must have written this one lyric line with him in mind...

Sometimes a slingshot is enough to slay the giant.

Starting tomorrow morning, beginning in San Rafael, I will continue northward for the remaining 58 days of my pilgrimage. From this point on, however, I will be trekking solo. Melanie has convinced me to retire Millie from the trip. My dog is rail thin, weary, and as hobbled as me. And, to be honest, I hadn't realized how complicated (not to mention, expensive) it would be to bring the dog along. This is better for those little paws — especially as summer arrives and the pavement begins to bake — while giving me much more flexibility in my daily journey.

It will definitely be lonesome, though, without my faithful pup to talk to and cuddle with. *Gonna miss ya, Mill Mill.* But Melanie and James will take good care of you. (Thank you, thank you, *thank you,* Mr. and Mrs. Weber, for taking that beagle girl in.) Surely, these next two months will pass quickly enough. And, at trail's end, pilgrim and pooch will be reunited once again.

CHAPTER 18

Popsicles and a Naked Woman

JUNE 3 · DAY THIRTY-FOUR

Today's trek begins with the challenge of steering the Pilgrimmobile along the half-mile of narrow, cracked, rutted sidewalk that provides the only northbound escape route from Motel Hades. Vehicles hug each other's tails on the frontage road a few feet away, screaming past, switching lanes erratically. Once again, some of the most trying, stress-filled walking stretches are not on freeways, as so many worried, but next to them, under them, and over them. After having the front stroller wheel rebuilt at the Bikery in Oakland, it rotated flawlessly. However, the stroller pulled severely to the left. So, I returned to the shop to ask Mario what could be done to cure what was clearly an unacceptable steering issue. His advice was to have the front wheel frame re-welded — this time, into a fixed, straight-forward position. With the steering mechanism now rigid, I find that even the slightest turn requires lifting the back wheels up off the pavement to redirect the cart. I'll need to learn a new set of cart-driving skills and develop a new set of muscles as I move ahead from here.

I'm pushing the Pilgrimmobile up a steep lane past block after block of well-tended, ranch-style, suburban homes. At the road's crest, I come upon a stationary cyclist straddling his bike, perspiring, and attempting to catch his breath. He's tall, with sloping shoulders, greying hair, and doesn't appear to be in tip-top health.

"You okay?" I ask.

"Yeah," he responds, still wheezing, "Just trying to figure out where I'm going from here."

Aren't we all? I quipped silently to myself.

"You walking?" His observation is couched in a question that requires no answer. "Good for you."

"Just trying to encourage people to be kind to one another."

"Well that's a good thing," he remarks, "'cause I can be an asshole!" Mark says he's been clean and sober for nine years. "But, still," he confesses, "I get so angry... in traffic, at drivers. I ask Jesus what to do. He tells me, 'Ride your bike.' It helps."

"Maybe rage is your new addiction," I offer.

Fortunately, he doesn't take offense at this rather presumptuous remark. Instead, he smiles, as if this is an idea he's already considered. He tells me he'd love to retire to Oregon someday. I suggest that he consider Newport.

☮   ☮   ☮   ☮   ☮

Tuckered after a 13-mile trek on a warm-verging-on-hot day, I park my cart behind a mall, drop my derriere onto a curb, and start Googling, hoping to find a nearby motel. I'm damning my here-one-second-gone-the-next cell signal, when a fellow cart-driver pushes his closet on wheels around a corner and parks it next to mine. "Nice rig," he remarks, admiring the Pilgrimmobile. He's a large man in his late-fifties, broad-shouldered, barrel-chested, with dark, cropped hair and a goatee. "Want a popsicle?" he offers. I'm hot and parched. That sounds fantastic.

"That's very kind of you," I respond, choosing raspberry over grape and banana. As I unwrap the icy confection, he informs me that it's sugar-free, which inclines me to inquire if he might be diabetic.

"Yeah," he says, "Got heart problems, too. Just trying to find a place to put my feet up. The cops. They know me. Worked here all my life. Raised my kids here. But they're running all the homeless out. They don't care."

We introduce ourselves and shake hands. His name is Peter. A woman with bushy, salt-and-pepper hair pulls up on a bicycle, followed by third character, male, on foot, wearing an over-sized Golden State Warriors T-shirt. The rootless trio compares notes on the lay of the land around town. Evidently, these three are a street team. They've got each other's backs. Peter offers both of his pals a popsicle, but neither take him up on it.

Meanwhile, I've managed to get a cell signal and find a motel room — nothing fancy, just an old Travel Lodge another mile up the pike. My mood boosted, I pull a five from my pocket and extend it to Peter. "That was a five-dollar popsicle," I tell him with a grateful smile. At first, he turns my offer down, then accepts it anyway.

"For that, you should get a second helping," joshes the fellow in the Warriors jersey. Peter extends the box of popsicles. I don't mind if I do. As I push my cart toward the mall parking lot, Warrior Fan calls out… "Hey," he teases, "have a peaceful pilgrimage!"

Chuckling, I toss a good evening over my shoulder, and trek on, invigorated by two sugar-free, raspberry popsicles given me by a homeless diabetic named Peter behind a mall in Novato, California.

☮　☮　☮　☮　☮

So, here's why there's a naked woman in my motel room…

I was toting a sack of supplies from Trader Joe's, eager to relieve my complaining feet and dig into a microwave burrito, when I heard a female voice shouting in a tone of semi-hysteria.

"Where did you *go*?" On a second-floor balcony of the Travel Lodge, a woman with brown, shagged, dripping-wet hair was glowering down at me as if I was guilty of some nameless sin. "I thought I was a good person," she wailed. "And you just *leave* me here? Is *that* how it is?"

Admittedly, over the course of my lifetime, some ladies have blamed me for their unhappiness. And, in a certain percentage of those cases, I was probably at least partially guilty as charged. However, being accused of something I didn't do and couldn't possibly have done by a woman I've never laid eyes on in my life was a first. Another factor made this experience that much more exceptional: the woman was as naked as Eve in the Garden, sans fig leaf.

I was waiting for the elevator when guess who came charging down the corridor toward me, snorting fire, still barefoot but, mercifully, her body now wrapped in a white bath towel. "Are you the guy I was just talking to?" she inquired.

Reluctantly, I confessed to be that guy.

"Where was I?" she demanded. This poor lass was so blotto, she couldn't remember which room she'd locked herself out of, the name of the dude who left her in it, or even what he looked like. I took another desperate jab at the elevator "Up" button.

My inner monologue... *When these sliding doors finally open, I should take my groceries, slip inside, ride to the third floor, and beat it for the safety of my room. (The slowest elevator in the state of California gave me time to do some re-thinking.) But wouldn't abandoning this woman make me equally guilty, perhaps even more guilty than the guy who stranded her in whatever room she found herself in earlier? What fate might befall her if I fail to help?*

"What if I could lend you something to wear?" I heard myself asking. And, that's why there is a naked woman in my room. Because, once inside, she immediately dropped the towel. Putting clothes on is not near as important as the half-full, plastic motel cup of Vodka and grapefruit juice she's spied on the TV stand.

"What's this?" she queries, coyly, stealing a swig. "Got any more?" My attempt to pry the cup from her unsteady hands sends the remainder of the sticky liquid squirting over the bedspread.

I notice the wound on the side of one of her calves — ugly, rust-brown, bloody in spots. A burn, she explains, through her Devil's-daughter grin, a meth accident.

"You know what I *really* want?" she abruptly announces. "A burrito! A *burrito* would be perfect right now."

I tell her I'll be happy to share my burrito with her — but only if she'll agree to put on some clothes. (Truthfully, I wouldn't be at all happy to share my burrito with her, or with anyone for that matter. A 15-mile trek makes a pilgrim hungry. I need calories. And, I certainly don't relish the idea of hoofing it back to the market on sore feet for more grub. I also wouldn't be remotely pleased about sacrificing my favorite yellow sweat shorts and V-neck T-shirt.)

When I toss her the shorts and T, she lets them drop to the floor. "Whose clothes are these?" she asks, gazing down at the garments with absolute befuddlement.

"They're mine," I explain. "I'm lending them to you. But you have to promise to return them."

Her impish grin instantly transforms into the squint-eyed glower of a *King Lear* witch. "These are *not* your clothes!" she hisses, grabbing a vinyl Trader Joe's supply bag from the bed. She proceeds to examine the contents of the sack and chuck each item violently against the wall.

"Please," I'm begging. "Stop disrespecting my property!"

"I don't disrespect people," she argues, as if by my implication, I'm the disrespectful one. "I'm a good person," she rails. "I'm a *woman of peace!*" By this point, she's emptying the second supply bag and hurling its contents. "Besides, this is not *your* stuff! It's *everybody's* stuff!"

Trying to maintain my cool in the midst of such turmoil, I retrieve the clothes from the floor. "Just put these on," I command. "Put these on! And leave! Okay?"

Her squinted eyes grow round and weepy. "So," she says, sorrowfully — at last, unsteadily slipping her badly burned leg into my favorite, yellow sweat shorts — "this is the way you want it, huh? You're gonna throw me out? That's what you're gonna do? Wow! How ya gonna feel when I'm in jail? Huh? That gonna make you happy?"

What would make me happy right now is to be rid of a certain erratic, unstable woman! That's what I want to say. But I restrain myself. With her private parts now covered, what takes place outside this motel room will no longer be my problem. I take her by the shoulders, swivel her around, and guide her gently down the narrow hallway. Surprisingly, she puts up no resistance.

Now, the inebriated, shag-haired young woman is standing outside the open door of my room, in my clothing, looking back at me with forlorn, disillusioned, victim eyes, her mouth agape, her hands and arms outstretched, as if to say... *How can you do this to me?*

I slam the door and exhale the enormous, tremulous sigh of a convict who has just made a harrowing escape from prison. After basking in calm solitude for no more than a few seconds, the trepidations return. *What*, I worry, *might happen to this deeply disturbed person, this wild woman who blasted into my world for a tortuous half-hour, causing such drama and disruption?*

I open the door and step outside. I survey the corridor in one direction, then the other. She is nowhere to be seen.

CHAPTER 19

In Certain Circles

Sunday drivers have a reputation for lollygagging. Not *these* Sunday drivers. Not *this* Sunday. A rural highway with very slender shoulders wouldn't be so bad, had several northbound freeway lanes not been closed due to road construction, which sent hundreds of impatient drivers scurrying onto San Antonio Road in hopes of circumventing the bottleneck. Evidently, these motorists assume they're still motoring on an interstate highway. They're maintaining freeway speed — or, at least what seems to be freeway speed, from the perspective of a poky pedestrian.

As I come to a bridge over a creek, the map app indicates I'm six miles from Petaluma. What greets me on the far side of the bridge is a detour sign. Google's six-mile calculation is via a road that, by all appearances, is presently closed. I am not alone in my displeasure over this eventuality. By the grimaces I see through windshields, the parade of drivers attempting to bypass the congested freeway are all experiencing regret over choosing this particular route for that purpose. And, having to circumvent a cart-pushing pilgrim trekking down the edge of a now totally shoulder-less country road is not making the overriding mood any cheerier.

When a foot traveler is negotiating an already restricted stretch of blacktop, there is nothing less welcome than a yellow, diamond-shaped sign posted by the roadside that reads, *Pavement Narrows*. At this point, no shoulder at all would be a luxury. This road has no edge. The blacktop is eroded, ragged, uneven, and butts up against an abrupt, precipitous drop straight down into a snarled forest of scrub oaks and underbrush. In order to prevent the Pilgrimmobile from teetering off the road and tumbling into the wild tangle below, I have no choice but to walk in the lane of oncoming traffic. This requires approaching motorists to stop and wait for vehicles traveling in the opposite direction to pass by before steering around me. And, since the opposite lane is presently facilitating a caravan of frazzled, hurried freeway by-passers, the wait for drivers in my lane is often a tedious one. I paste a strained smile on my face, wave, and flash the peace sign, in a hopeful attempt to alleviate some of the mounting acrimony.

My peace-making efforts are futile, however, as few drivers respond with much else but resentful, fiery-eyed glowers. For several of them, an angry glare is not sufficient. They throw up their hands as they pass, in that universal gesture that asks, *What the (bleep) are you doing, asshole?* I find this gesture to be particularly ironic, especially under these precarious circumstances — because if there's any time when it's of ultra-importance to keep both hands on the wheel, it's when you're circumventing a defenseless pedestrian on a narrow, decaying road that plunges off at its jagged edge into a jungle.

This frightening unpleasantness hits its apex when an older-model BMW sedan is forced to stop in the lane ahead to wait out a particularly lengthy train of north-bounders. Finally, there's a break in the northbound traffic. However, the beamer driver, a man of approximately my own age, with a face as round, pale, and doughy as an uncooked piecrust, doesn't snatch the opportunity to swing around me. Instead, he pulls up right next to the Pilgrimmobile and rolls down his front-pedestrian-side window. Although this is perhaps the worst possible spot in the Western United States at this particular moment to engage in a pedestrian-driver chat, I certainly don't want to blow the guy off. After all, I am out here risking life and limb for the stated purpose of inspiring civil, constructive dialogue. Wearing a smile that naively presumes I'm about to meet yet another kind, concerned soul who wants to know if

I need help, or perhaps feels a magnanimous impulse to make a Sabbath-day donation, I poke my head into the open window.

While the pie-faced motorist is most definitely concerned, one might even say passionately so, the object of that concern is not at all what I was expecting. Through clenched jaw, with crimson-faced wrath, he bellows at ear-shattering volume, *"You could cause an accident, GODDAMMIT!"* Now, *I'm* concerned — that the poor, incensed fellow's skull is about to explode. He, however, provides a cranial safety valve by spitting in my face, before stomping down on his accelerator and pealing out. Thankfully, my quick instincts avoid decapitation via the open window and I observe the BMW fishtailing down the slender lane, miraculously avoiding colliding with oncoming traffic or careening off into the ditch.

Yes, I'm thinking, the fellow is absolutely correct. I *could* cause an accident. However, if he's genuinely committed to promoting highway safety, he might begin by taking control of what appears to be a very dangerous case of road rage.

Having been out of cellular range for some time, I have no clue how much further it is to Petaluma. I do, however, remember that I'm supposed to take a right turn on D Street, which, much to my relief, turns out to be a well-maintained road with decent bike lanes. While delighted to finally get a cell signal, I'm disturbed to discover that I have three miles yet to go. This seems impossible. It's odd how, when I'm feeling fresh and exhilarated, the morning miles seem to breeze by so quickly. Then, into the mid-to-late afternoon, as my foot pain intensifies and fatigue drags down every stride, the clock slips into slow motion and the remaining distance stretches out in front of me, like an ever-elongating rubber band.

My iPhone dings. It's a text message — from Alice Bailey. My response: *Absolutely! Yes!*

Just a few hours ago, I was standing on the edge of a precarious, decaying, country two-lane, getting screamed at and spat upon by an enraged motorist. A mere 30 minutes ago, I was stewing in my late-afternoon malaise, wondering if any of this self-inflicted misery is worth it. Now, I'm sitting in the passenger seat of a mini-van on my way to a party.

The man at the helm of the vehicle is Tom Bailey, husband of the lady with the translucent complexion and shoulder length, white hair, smiling warmly from the rear bench seat. Alice Bailey always seems to be wearing a smile. But, not just a smile-smile, mind you. There's something else behind the sparkle of her eyes, as if she is imbued with a knowing that the burdens of this physical life are only temporary. Whenever the Creator decides to put an end to her Earthly tribulations, Alice seems content that her holy spirit will be swept up to Heaven for all eternity. Yes, Alice is a Christian woman. And, even if I hadn't been informed in advance, I think I would have known right away. Alice's faith is evident in everything about her — her gentle voice, her modest, doe-eyed gaze, her very aura.

Although Sebra and I have been in a relationship for several years now, I had never actually met her younger sister until 10 minutes ago, when this borrowed van pulled onto the shoulder of D Street to rescue me. No, I was not in peril. I was, however, worn out, disheartened from the experiences of the day, and stressing about finding shelter for the night. And, while I still don't know where I'll be laying my head, things are looking up in that regard. We're on our way to a backyard anniversary celebration where, Alice tells me, folks are passing guitars and sharing songs. A gathering of musicians unpacks a logo rhythm of possibilities. Peace Pilgrim said, "A pilgrim not only walks prayerfully, but as an opportunity to contact people." After nearly seven hours of schlepping in solitude, with no human interaction — aside from one brief, furious harangue from a pie-faced Beamer driver — an opportunity to contact people sounds like a very enticing proposition.

It's Frank and Shannon Van Meter's 23rd wedding anniversary. If I were casting one of those ads for the erectile-dysfunction medication Cialis, this couple would get the gig. They'd look perfect reclining in those parallel, claw-footed bathtubs, holding hands, trading knowing, post-coital grins.

Shannon, blond, fit, and considerably younger than her tall, handsome, salt-and-pepper-haired husband, shows me to the pot-luck buffet. The Van Meter backyard is like a vast faerie wonderland. Gravel pathways snake between beautifully landscaped natural gardens and shade trees, curving past a patio, to a fire pit, on to an outdoor bar and barbecue grill. When I marvel at the storybook beauty, Shannon informs me this has been her project since they leased this house more than a year ago. The property's owner had let nature take its course, allowing the paths to disappear beneath brambles and underbrush, leaving the gardens to be invaded and strangled by vines. And, after months of toil, Shannon shares, today marks the unveiling of her labor of love.

I fill a small, paper plate with fresh fruit and vegetables, pour a cup of homemade lemonade, and pull a patio chair into the circle. Frank finishes telling everyone about a new perspective he has recently gained from re-reading a certain biblical passage. Alice introduces me to the guests, informing them that I'm on a pilgrimage. This naturally steers the subject at hand away from Frank's scriptural revelation to a group curiosity about my mission.

As always, I pick my language carefully so as to not express any particular political bias. From Sebra, I know that her sister and brother-in-law supported Trump. As these are Alice and Tom's friends, it stands to reason that most of them are also politically conservative. Still, no one disagrees when I suggest that the tone in America has grown considerably more hostile of late. And not one person takes issue when I suggest that we all need to start communicating respectfully and cooperating if we're ever going to solve the many problems we face as a nation.

Then, while my pilgrimage remains the focus of the conversation, the sub-theme shifts to one with less potential for friction: what a long-distance hiker, like myself, should and shouldn't be eating. Several of the guests are eager to share their tips on sustaining energy, keeping up the calorie intake, maintaining the correct balance between carbs and proteins, hydration, etc.

No one, however, has yet picked up an instrument. In fact, I don't see a guitar or a mandolin anywhere — until Frank emerges from the house carrying a lovely, blond, jumbo, acoustic six-string.

He announces that he'd like to dedicate a song to his beautiful bride of more than two decades. Frank proves to be an adequate guitarist and singer who makes up for his lack of virtuosity with absolute sincerity. His performance is enhanced considerably when Shannon pitches in sweetly on harmonies. By the time the host/hostess duo finishes their set, several guests are bidding their gracious, fond farewells.

"Would you mind if I played a song?" I ask. My guitar is still packed away in the box, which is locked inside the van. With some hesitation, Frank hands me the jumbo.

I'm vamping in six-eight waltz time on a G chord. "This is something I wrote for someone special," I share, with a wink in Alice's direction. By her smile, it's clear that Alice knows that the special someone to whom I'm referring is her sister, who I haven't seen in six weeks and miss horribly. The chorus to "It All Goes Away" goes thusly...

With you, it all goes away
The stress and the worry, the fear, and the pain
Because you are my safe place
Your love gives me shelter, a roof from the rain
Trouble comes 'round, it's true
But, with you, it all goes away

— RAND BISHOP, © 2016
WEIGHTLESS CARGO MUSIC, BMI

As I conclude the tune, the group offers up a nice round of applause. When I stand to return Frank's instrument, Shannon insists on an encore. It occurs to me that I have the perfect number for the occasion.

I have come to realize that most everything I've done in my life, up to and including this pilgrimage, has been at least partially motivated by the desire to re-create and re-experience that original family circle, the one I was born into: my parents and paternal grandparents, in whose adoring eyes I, their cherubic, firstborn son/grandson, was peerless...

In certain circles, I can do no wrong
There's something special 'bout the ground I walk on
Those uncertainties, they're all gone in certain circles

— RAND BISHOP/KIM PATTON, ©1997
MIKE CURB/POSTER CHILD MUSIC, BMI
KIM MCCLEAN MUSIC, ASCAP

My first bitter disillusionment in life came with the shocking and unexpected whack-in-the-gut realization that I was not, as I had been brainwashed to believe by the persistent adulation of those first four adoring fans, perfect. A child gets his little ego pumped up day after day, it's bound to get over-inflated — especially when the source of that hot air is the puckered lips of doting, grown-up, authority figures. However, while it's a fine thing to bolster a kid's confidence, blowing an innocent little one up with the certainty that he is innately superior and therefore incapable of failure does him a disservice. It's a set-up for an explosive bubble bursting. I was that deluded, puffed-up boy, cruising along, convinced of my flawlessness, expecting continuous adoration, and assuming that success, even fame and fortune, was my birthright.

Then, the real world bludgeoned me with the awful, devastating reality that I am just as human, therefore just as flawed, as everyone else. I discovered that I was not, after all, destined to trace an easy glide path to the top of the mountain, to sit upon a golden throne while commoners scrambled up the steep, rocky path for the privilege of prostrating themselves at my feet and kissing my ring. I, too, it turned out, was destined to do some mountain climbing, prostrating, and ring-kissing of my own. To achieve my life's goals, I would have to suffer shortfalls, survive setbacks, pick up the pieces, recover, regroup and start all over — time and time again.

But what real satisfaction can be found in an accomplishment that requires little or no effort? What fulfillment can be gained from winning when the race is fixed? To feel deserving is a good thing. Everyone deserves the chance to make his or her dreams come true. Feeling entitled is something else altogether.

But, I've meandered from the story. So, I'm vamping, finger-picking the introductory chord progression. However, even though I'm about to launch into a command performance at the bequest of the queen of the house, folks are not paying attention. *Don't these people know who I am?* cries the entitled little boy from my disillusioned past.

"I'd like to dedicate this song to Frank and Shannon," I interject. After expressing how much I appreciate being welcomed into this circle of friends, I begin to sing, "Wheels are turning on the interstate. Clock is ticking on the wall. Another day slips away on this blue ball." By now, I've re-captured the group's full attention.

JUNE 5 · DAY THIRTY-SIX

Frank Van Meter is something of a genius. As he takes the first sips of morning coffee in his Penngrove, California, living room, Frank's long, spidery frame is draped casually across the couch cushions like a marionette between puppet shows. At 65, Frank's cheeks and mouth still retain the smooth blush of a much younger man, even when encircled by a grey Abe-Lincoln beard and salt-and-pepper hair. Poised on the adjacent divan, nursing a mug of English breakfast tea, I sit transfixed. Dominating the space, and my attention, from the opposite corner, illuminated by amber sunlight splashing in from a pair of floor-to-ceiling windows, stands an astounding sculpture. Or, perhaps it would be more accurate to describe the object of my fascination as an amazing work of functional art in the guise of a 3D puzzle.

Frank conceived this working Ferris wheel, a full six-feet in diameter, fashioning it out of hundreds of small, painstakingly shaped hunks of pine, all somehow fitting and connecting together without the benefit of a single dab of glue, nail, pin, or staple. This, Frank explains, is the prototype, the display model, intended only for trade shows and craft fairs. The product itself, intended for public consumption, is the identical, but considerably smaller, tabletop version.

Woodworking is only one of Frank's many creative passions. He loves taking pieces of wood and shaping into something not only aesthetically pleasing, but useful as well. He shows me another artful invention, one, as a musician, I find particularly interesting. Seeing these oddly shaped, inlaid, finely finished wooden components separately, one would be hard-pressed to guess what they become when assembled. After a few stabs at decoding this brainteaser of his own devising, Frank manages to configure his portable guitar stand — and a very beautiful one indeed. He had hoped to make a profitable business selling products like the 3D Ferris-wheel puzzle and the guitar stand. So far, he's achieved the working prototypes, while realizing none of the profits.

The many paintings adorning these walls, wondrous in their color, texture, and detail, are all Van Meter originals as well. It's obvious how unfettered and limitless Frank's creative talents are. However, he confesses, like so many artists, he lacks the natural inclination or proclivity for marketing his own work. A big idea will rise in his head as brightly and vividly as the sun at dawn. Not only can he see it, he knows what it's made of and precisely how he can give it three dimensions. It stirs his gut, quickens his heart, and sucks him into its magical, swirling vortex. It would be futile to struggle against it. This is the very reason he lives and breathes.

Then, after having made the picture in his head manifest, he finds himself saying, "Well, that was fun! What's next?" So, rather than summoning up and sustaining the energy and effort it takes to turn inspiration into commerce, his default is to move on — excited and energized by the next, bigger, even-better idea.

I tell Frank how familiar this syndrome is to me; how similar, it seems, my fickle, creative temperament is to his. Like him, I'm in constant need of a major project to inspire me, to motivate me. It's amazing to look back and see how many credits dot my résumé with such an embarrassing minority of the endeavors I've initiated having reached completion. Invariably, somewhere along the way, fear sets in — whether it's fear of success or failure matters not. Or, another apparently shinier object catches my eye, one that, from here, looks even more promising. This causes me to lose focus on the task at hand before I've given it any real shot at success. Regardless, even when I actually do bring a creative work to its completion, like Frank, I tend to peter out before devoting requisite energy to the equally important marketing/money-making stage.

I'm surprised to find out that, at an age when many men are ready to couch potato, travel, play golf, or putter in the garden, Frank Van Meter's primary bread-and-butter vocation is in construction. And, not as a contractor. He's a hammer-and-nail guy. This is a quality that sets him apart from me. Although I've put shoulder to grindstone now and then, I'm not built for heavy labor. I ask him how, in his mid-sixties, his body can withstand all that daily toil. "I just take my time," he responds, with calm, Zen self-awareness. "I get my work done. But I don't push it."

By now, the dining room is resounding with the rapid-fire cadence of youthful, female repartee. The three Van Meter daughters, all in their late teens, and a fourth young lady, who just moved here from Texas, sit around the table, chipmunk chattering in some indiscernible, generational Pig Latin. Last evening, this same bunch showed up in the garden armed with ukuleles to treat their parents to some loose, ensemble renditions of their current pop favs. That was a language I understood. Their vocal harmonies were sweet and I told them as much. This morning, however, I'm the ancient alien who just dropped in from a galaxy light years away. Sitting quietly, noshing oatmeal, I nod my head and grin, as if I have a single centile of comprehension.

There is one clear observation, however, that I can and will make: these young women are steeped in Christian doctrine, hardwired to give the Good Lord top billing, even while bantering about the most secular of subjects. Never have I heard teenagers inclined to give such consistent credit to the Heavenly Father's divine Grace. By the beatific grin on Frank's face, it's evident that their Earthly father also takes enormous gratification in his children's spontaneous, voluntary testimonials of devotion.

☮   ☮   ☮   ☮   ☮

A pilgrim's emotional journey is as dynamic and ever-changing as the path he travels. Over the previous, eventful 24 hours,

I trekked in solitude, through isolation and alienation, to arrive at the end of the day at acceptance and connection. I have been strengthened and emboldened by the solo hours, only to be softened and humbled in the nourishing folds of human kindness and attention.

Frank swings open the gate. As we bro hug, he prays out loud: "May the Good Lord guide you and protect you."

"Well," I remark, "the angels have definitely been watching over me." This is my diplomatic way of accepting his blessing, while holding to my own pagan beliefs.

"That may be true," Frank affirms. "But the Heavenly Father is in charge. He tells those angels what to do." Although I bridle at this statement, I choose to keep it to myself.

I've spent a good deal of time on this trip with Evangelical Christians. Almost without exception, they've been kind, giving, and genuinely concerned — all admirable, Christ-like traits. However, so many of them never pass up an opportunity to flaunt their faith. Like every subculture, Christians use coded language to identify themselves to one another. But, unlike other subcultures, everyday phrases like, "Since I found Jesus…" or "I was reading my *Bible* when it occurred to me…" or "Praise our Heavenly Father…" can also be interpreted — by pagans, agnostics, and atheists — as not-so-subtle warnings: *Better start cleaning up your act, Sinner, because Judgment Day is nigh.*

As I begin another day's journey into the yet to be known, Frank's parting statement, so absolute and unequivocal, ping-pongs around in my head… *If God's will is the only way,* I'm thinking, *why then did He create each human with his or her own individual will?*

Certainly, God (whatever those three letters represent) *must be omniscient and omnipotent. But, is He — or She, or It — literally barking marching orders on a split-second by split-second basis? Is it really Frank's contention* that every angel surrenders its will and, for eternity, supplicates every thought and action to a benevolent boss-dictator called God? Is it really comprehensible that, by handing over all of our native human frailties to the one and only Savior, we are rewarded in the end with a backstage pass to spend eternity under God's absolute, authoritarian control? *I don't know, Frank. Doesn't sound much like Heaven to me.*

In my belief system, every person's every thought and action contributes to the unfathomably infinite energy of one universal God Force. The God I believe in doesn't tell me what to think. The God I believe in *is* what I think, added to the sum total of every thought that has ever been conceived or ever will be conceived. In my universe, a brilliant mind like Frank Van Meter's has contributed at least as much to the essence of God as the Heavenly Father has given to Frank Van Meter.

Anyway, that's where this pilgrim stands — at least, until further notice.

CHAPTER 20

Sweet Honeysuckle and Sour Grapes

JUNE 5 · DAY THIRTY-SIX, *CONTINUED*

Although today's Penngrove-to-Sonoma trek didn't necessitate pushing the weighty, meandering Pilgrimmobile up or down steep grades, it has been grueling nonetheless, simply due to its length and monotony, and my constant exposure to the sun. At the risk of sounding whiney, I might coin a word to define this, the 36th day of my journey — it's been "trudgery."

With the skyline of Petaluma on the southern horizon, Old Adobe Road rolled out ahead like an infinite tape measure. Even the smallest patch of shade was a rarity. In fact, the route offered not a single wayside to take the briefest break from those blistering rays. At one juncture, with the sun at its zenith, I came upon a tiny patch of scrub oaks by the shoulder of the road. In the shadow of this prickly leafed umbrella, I assembled my Monarch Chair in the gravel and kicked back to bolster my saline intake with a bag of Trader Joe's organic potato chips. My resting place offered only a few feet of separation between my feet and a raging river of vehicles gushing along the eastbound lane. Every few minutes, a convoy of trucks and trailers hauling heavy construction equipment would blast by, whipping up walls of hot air that quaked the parked Pilgrimmobile and buffeted my supply bags like windsocks at a prairie airport.

I found this periodic assault so jarring that I captured one such blast-by on video and uploaded it to Facebook. "This, my friends," I posted, "is a typical day on a typical rural road in California." My point: Even on a remote, two-lane road, on a Monday afternoon in June, the noisy, violent, polluting, gas-guzzling race rolls on, unabated.

With miles still to go, I hoisted myself from my dusty, roadside respite and proceeded to roll the Pilgrimmobile down the shoulder of the road — until I realized there was something I'd forgotten. Although my hands are strong from decades of playing the guitar and piano, they are also tender. Gripping the dimpled-rubber handle of the jogging stroller hour after hour tends to irritate my palms. So, while pushing the Pilgrimmobile, I always wear a pair of leather, fingerless weight-lifting gloves to prevent blisters.

I was crouching on the side of the highway, rifling through the outside pockets of my backpack, mumbling self-castigations for mislaying the protective gloves, when a semi-truck, pulling a long, extra-wide aluminum trailer — the kind designed to haul a massive bulldozer — roared past me. No more than 100 feet ahead, the trailer tires hit a bump in the pavement. With no bulldozer to weigh it down, the entire trailer lifted off the ground and swung several feet to the right, skidding at least four feet off the pavement onto the shoulder, and bouncing several times in the dirt and gravel, before the speeding truck cab yanked it back between the lines of the eastbound lane.

Even with the sun blaring on my back, a shiver ran across my shoulders and down my spine. Had I not stopped to look for my fingerless gloves, I might have been walking at the exact spot where that huge, heavy-metal trailer just bounced wildly off the pavement. Is it possible that angels conspire to make a pilgrim absent minded? Perhaps they do — when that pilgrim's survival calls for it.

Now, as I bump the Pilgrimmobile alongside Sonoma Creek, I'm happy to be out of the unrelenting sun, distanced from the racket, the strangling exhaust, and those stiff, truck-stirred blasts of hot wind. However, these narrow, irregular, residential lanes present a cart-pushing pilgrim with another kind of challenge. Marin, Sonoma, and Napa counties are reputed to be some of the most desirable areas in a very abundant state. And yet, consistently, sidewalks and city streets here have been allowed to erode and decay to a shameful degree. The U.S. borrows hundreds of billions from China to purchase jets and bombs. With little or no debate, our nation foots the bill for exorbitant, no-bid contracts to build roads, schools, and hospitals half a world away. The government has sent truckloads of our tax dollars to win the fealty of middle-eastern war lords. Is it even possible that we can't afford to pave and maintain our own streets?

Come on, Americans, we can do it! We put men on the moon with less computer power than exists in a pocket calculator. We can set aside our party loyalties long enough to rally together and get down to fixing this mess. What d'ya say?

JUNE 7 · DAY THIRTY-EIGHT

The unforgiving living room floor of Tom and Alice Bailey's cozy Santa Rosa home wasn't the only factor preventing me from slumbering soundly. It seems silly, even juvenile for two mulish, 60-something pals to get caught up in an irreconcilable squabble. A senior-citizen spat, however, was the primary source of last night's insomnia.

Charlie Pullman and I have been friends for nearly 30 years. The jovial, brash South Philly native fancies himself as an "idea guy." It was 1989, when one of those ideas lured me into Mr. Pullman's universe.

Released by Sony Kids Records in 1991, the compilation album "Put on Your Green Shoes," features Cyndi Lauper, Kenny Loggins, Willie Nelson, Dr. John, Indigo Girls, and Olivia Newton-John, among others. I acted in the role of A&R Director (in layman's terms, creative coordinator), contributed several original compositions, and produced many of the new tracks. While most of the production took place in Los Angeles, Charlie and I helmed memorable sessions in New York and Seattle as well. And, while the two-year process of birthing "Green Shoes" left me bankrupt, Charlie remained a steadfast, compassionate friend, doing everything he could within his means to keep my family afloat. So, when our daughter Glendyn was born in 1993, Stacey and I chose Charlie and his then-wife/business partner Kate Cunningham as her godparents.

Flash forward to last December… From the beginning, Charlie couldn't get his head around this crazy pilgrimage idea. Still, true to his idea-guy nature, as my departure date approached, he was a veritable fountain of suggestions, and a well of unfulfilled promises. Charlie was 100% idea — all-talk, no-action. I'd long ago lost patience with my old pal. Last night's text message was the final straw…

"I think you need to re-think your mission," he wrote. "You've already gone beyond expectations." The remainder of Charlie's message lectured me to pull the plug and cut my losses, or at least postpone the remainder of my trek until I actually had all the funds in hand to support it. These words of discouragement from a close friend of three decades were difficult to accept, especially landing, as they did, with a leaden thud, smack-dab in the middle of my journey.

Even so, I might have been able to sleep last night, had Charlie not capped off his missive thusly: "Why would you even want to talk to those people? They're the American Taliban!"

My dear friend lives in a bubble, paying attention only to information that reinforces his rigidly held beliefs. Therefore, Charlie views anyone who sees the world through an alternative lens as not merely dimwitted and uninformed, but as an actual threat. That his buddy seems so willing, eager in fact, to engage with "the other side" has him flummoxed. And now, he fears, I'm teetering on the verge of becoming one of *"THEM!"* — as if, through exposure, I might contract the virus that causes wingnut brain rot.

Admittedly, I, too, have tossed more than my share of inflammatory word grenades toward those with whom I disagree. As recently as six months ago, I suggested that anyone who voted for the Trump ticket must be as guilty of bigotry, misogyny, homophobia, and xenophobia as the candidate himself. Without question, there are some who feel the new president's election has given them permission to hate from the rooftops. And I still strongly believe it is incumbent upon people of conscience to decry bigotry, misogyny, homophobia, and xenophobia whenever and wherever those antediluvian monsters rear their ugly heads. However, now I recognize that my verbal assaults against all Trump supporters were based upon rash, intellectually lazy generalizations made about people I had yet to meet.

> *"Biases are the stories we make up about*
> *people before we know who they are."*
> — Vernā Myers

By making those kinds of gross, general assumptions, I was only revealing my own prejudice, my own bigotry. And, even if I was taking the righteous side of the issue — as I still wholeheartedly believe I was — what good could it possibly do to be in the right if, by choosing to express my position in such presumptuous, judgmental language, I was cutting off any chance of being heard by anyone who didn't already share my point of view? And, finally, by calling *"THEM"* names, I was also giving *them* additional fodder to support their blanket belief that all of us out here on the left fringe are just a bunch of elitist, pretentious, intellectual snobs.

On countless occasions, I've been categorized as one of those "… commie pinkos just looking for a government handout," or part of a "… socialist plot promoting a homosexual agenda," or just another "… vegan tree-hugger who hates free enterprise." It's not the least bit pleasant to be painted as some simplistic cliché of what some misinformed boob thinks liberalism stands for. Ironically, since I began making a concerted effort to discipline my language, refrain from name-calling, and actually empathize and reason with those on the opposite end of the spectrum, I've received some vicious harangues from folks in my own camp as well. And one of the most painful and befuddling of these barbs came from my friend Charlie just last night.

Over the course of the last 38 days, I've been able to engage respectfully with people from many different points of view and walks of life. It's not only ironic, but totally exasperating that the person with whom I've had the most difficulty seeing eye-to-eye thus far is one of my closest friends, someone with whom I actually agree regarding almost every issue.

But, as I'm always on the lookout for common ground, I'll toss this little conciliatory hunk out there. Maybe this will re-prime the pump for further, more constructive discussion: Yes, Charlie, there are those in positions of power in this administration, as well as others emboldened by the 2016 election, who espouse the philosophy that America would be "greater" if we were a more Christian, more European — read "Caucasian" — nation. And, the most radical voices among this regressive cabal would probably be a whole lot happier if these United States magically transformed into a Christian theocracy.

Now it's my turn to lecture you, Charlie. Making this accusation discredits your entire position, which automatically makes you the loser in this debate. Perhaps you're attempting to use the "American Taliban" thing as a metaphor. But it's also an absurd exaggeration, as well as a shameful example of liberal, west-coast Christian bashing.

After we finish our scrambled eggs, bacon, and toast, so lovingly prepared by Alice, her son Levi will take a look at the Pilgrimmobile to see if there is anything he can do to cure the stroller's pervasive insistence on veering to the left. By the look in the young man's eyes and the tone of his voice, he is eager to get his hands dirty.

Working with Levi to diagnose the stroller-wheel issue turns out to be an unexpected pleasure. We attack the problem seriously, but in a spirit of levity, brainstorming theories as to why the stroller has been behaving so uncooperatively. Our generational divide — of nearly half a century — evaporates. We're just two guys intent on solving a riddle. Ultimately, we arrive at a simple fix, a solution that requires no welding, looks all wrong, and makes no logical sense but, in the end, works like a charm. Levi and I scratch our heads and laugh, neither of us having the first clue why what looks so counter-intuitive works so well. Still, together, we've tamed the beast. And, if the solution holds, my trek from this point forward will be considerably less strenuous.

Six months ago, I had the self-righteous audacity to accuse folks like the Baileys of endorsing bigotry, misogyny, homophobia, and xenophobia, simply because they voted for a certain candidate. My friend Charlie continues to lump white, Christian conservatives like the Baileys together, calling them "the American Taliban."

Purely out of love and concern, this white, conservative, Christian family rescued a weary pagan from the side of the highway, welcomed him into their home, offered him food and drink, provided him shelter, and assisted him in every way they could. The Baileys, good neighbors and good people, have done a hell of a lot more to facilitate my pilgrimage than has Charlie Pullman.

So, until such time as Levi Bailey enlists in a Jihad, straps dynamite to his belly, and aspires to become a human bomb, I suggest we cool it with the "American Taliban" talk. It's not only offensive to the Baileys and every other good Christian family, it cuts off all opportunity for civil, constructive communication. And, it gives bigots, misogynists, homophobes, and xenophobes the perfect excuse to call liberal non-Christians like me some very ugly, inaccurate names. And... Charlie... that's something I'd just as soon avoid, thank you very much.

CHAPTER 21

Maybe It's a Chance

JUNE 9 · DAY FORTY

Two afternoons ago…

"Need a lift?" called a voice from within the truck cab. The dark-haired young man behind the wheel wore a baseball cap and a toothy smile. A large, brown dog in the passenger seat matched his master's sociable expression with a slobbery grin of its own.

"No, thanks," I answered. "That's very kind of you. But, I'm on a pilgrimage. I'm walking."

"Well, I just had to stop and ask," he responded.

I locked the wheels of my cart, approached his truck, and extended my hand, asking, "What's your name?"

"Jovan," he answered, as we shook.

After identifying myself, I said, "You're a good man, Jovan."

"Sometimes," he replied, pushing the bill of his cap back on his forehead. That's all he needed to say. Humility wasn't the only quality expressed in this kind young man's one-word admission. Wisdom and self-awareness echoed as well. Every human being struggles with contradictory impulses — the angel whispering into one ear, the devil hissing into the other.

"I know exactly what you mean," I related. "I'm a good man sometimes, too." Our conversation was succinct but packed with unspoken nuance. I handed him my postcard. "This kind of explains what my pilgrimage is all about," I said, before turning to shuffle back to my cart.

"You got water?" he asked. He wasn't going to let me go without making sure there wasn't something, anything at all, he could do for me.

"Yeah." I tossed my answer over my shoulder with a smile. "I'm set."

One of the greatest rewards of this journey is that nearly every day it introduces me to decent, generous human beings I would never otherwise have met. One ever-so-brief, highway-shoulder encounter with a humble, big-hearted, young man named Jovan fuels me through daily tests of physical stamina and trials of self-belief. Also profoundly meaningful have been the reconnections with personalities from the dustier chapters in my life's story: Marty Harris, Paula Williams, Nicholas Binion, Fritz Torp, and now, Ardythe Brandon.

Forty-five years ago, Ardythe was all of 15. Doing the math, I was 22, only recently married to Melanie, and living communally with my bandmates in an expansive, redwood-paneled lodge teetering on a hillside, above a sheep pasture in Eureka, California. For a period of time, those many years ago, this lovely, innocent nymph, who answered to the sonorous tag of Ardythe, was adopted by our band as a sort of mascot. On gig nights, our ladies, Melanie, Cheryl, and Cherie would doll "Ardy" up in flowing, vintage dresses and paint her freckled face with dramatic, glittery makeup. During our sets, these four beauties would execute their Isadora Duncan hippie twirls in front of the stage. Sometimes it seemed as if we were merely providing accompaniment to this all-girl dance company's graceful choreographic improvisations.

Decades later, Ardythe and I are both grandparents and I am sitting in the beautiful, stately Santa Rosa home she shares with Tom Brandon, her husband of 35 years. The Brandon children are grown, the house has become too big, and a *For Sale* sign is posted at the edge of the driveway.

Ardythe feels compelled to divulge something. It means a great deal to her that I interrupted my trek to stop here. For some yet-to-be-explained reason, it is important that I, someone she hadn't seen since the early 1970s, witness first-hand how her life turned out. Those teen years, she confides, had been extremely troubled. As, at the time, I was totally absorbed in making music and cultivating my own celebrity, our little mascot's distress naturally slipped beneath my radar. I'm suddenly concerned that Ardythe's troubles might have been due to questionable activities she'd been prematurely exposed to while hanging out with a band of debauched rockers — even though, as I recall, our rock 'n' roll family took extra care to shield our tiny, dancing sprite from such unseemly influences.

"Whatever happened with the band," she reveals, "was nothing compared to what else was going on in my life." Ardythe's lip quivers. Tears fill the corners of her sorrowful eyes, as she declares an unexpected and bitter truth: "Uncle Monty was not a good person." Monty (not her uncle's real name) had been a friend of the band, a sponsor, a patron. But this charming, dashing gentleman, who had treated our entourage so generously, was, apparently, also guilty of unspeakable things. Having accepted the responsibility of looking after and caring for his vulnerable, teenage niece, Monty had, instead, abused her sexually — routinely and repeatedly.

Thus, tagging along with the band and our ladies had not been a negative influence on Ardythe. In fact, we had provided a deeply scarred adolescent girl with a temporary escape from sexual slavery. And now, at 60, Ardythe is eager to show me how well she survived, how today, after a long, difficult recovery, she thrives as a strong, contented woman with a beautiful home, a highly responsible career, a husband she adores, kids launched out into the world, and grandkids to dote upon.

Of late, Ardythe has been confronted with yet another nemesis, brought on, I can only assume, by a conspiracy between genetics and that ornery scalawag known as Time. Lean and fit from her daily regime of jogging and yoga, her dark hair sweeping stylishly to her shoulders, the only visible evidence of this still strikingly beautiful woman's age lies in the twisted knuckles of her long fingers. Not as visible are the dozens of prescription drug vials hiding in the kitchen cupboard. "Does it hurt?" I ask.

"Not so much," she replies. I'm assuming rheumatoid arthritis. She tells me the diagnosis holds far more-serious implications. "But,

I won't accept that," she declares defiantly.

This evening, a small group gathers here in the Brandon living room to share some songs — three singing guitarists and an audience of two. It only seems right that the timeless, universal language of music once again re-unites an ex glam-rocker with the freckle-faced beauty who, 45 years ago, as an emotionally wounded teenager, whirled with such hypnotic abandon to escape her troubles. Also contributing to the song cycle: married songwriting duo, Marty Rainone and Carol Hache-Rainone. Friends from the Nashville Center for Spiritual Living, Marty and Carol relocated to Santa Rosa five years ago. The circle remains unbroken.

Ardythe has seized this event as an opportunity to demonstrate her top-flight hostessing chops. With effortless grace, she has manifested a delectable burrito buffet and a veritable mountain of homemade chocolate-chip cookies.

Some words about the lord of the manor… Tom Brandon began his career as an auto mechanic, got involved in organized labor, and ultimately ascended to become the west-coast top dog for the Machinists Union. Over decades of working on behalf of the labor alliance, Tom rubbed shoulders with top politicos, endured a thousand disingenuous promises, and confronted double-dealings on a monumental scale. He's seen first-hand how the gears of government turn, greased by cronyism, self-interest, and graft.

I picked out a special song for Tom tonight. Florence Reece's enduring 1931 folk ballad speaks through the voice of a labor organizer recruiting exploited coal miners in Harlan County, Kentucky. The refrain "Which side are you on, boys?" still resonates as authentically today as it did during the Great Depression. I'm pleased and proud when Tom posts a video online, sharing my living-room rendition with his union cohorts.

Before we call it a night, Carol makes a request…

You say your greatest dream
Came up against some hard and harsh realities
And there's a hole as big as Heaven inside your heart
But, you'll survive, and you might find, here in the dark…

Maybe it's a chance, maybe it's an opportunity
Maybe it's a path that winds its way to
where you're truly meant to be
The song isn't over, it's just the middle of the dance
You think that it's the end, oh, but think again
Maybe it's a chance

— RAND BISHOP AND IRENE KELLEY, © 2003
ASH STREET/BASH MUSIC, ASCAP,
WEIGHTLESS CARGO MUSIC BMI

"Maybe it's a Chance" turns out to be the perfect song to end the evening, comprising an extremely relatable message for a strong woman who has managed to recover from sexual abuse and now battles a degenerative disease, and a union organizer who spent his life doggedly confronting the powers that be, while never backing down.

JUNE 10 · DAY FORTY-ONE

Ardythe's adoration for her husband is evident, as well as her enormous pride in his selfless commitment to the cause of working men and women. However, she makes it clear that she doesn't mirror his left-leaning sensibilities. "If you really want to know what I'm concerned about," Ardythe remarks, "it's not global warming." I nod my head, encouraging her to elaborate. "And," she continues, "I don't think Social Security will run out of money." Ardythe expresses confidence that those issues will be sorted out in due course without excessive governmental intervention. The free market, she believes, will save the day. "What I am really very worried about," she clarifies with absolute seriousness, "is the National Park system. I'd hate to think those beautiful places won't be there for my grandchildren to visit. Now *that* would be a tragedy!"

While Ardythe's specific expression of concern is unique among folks I've met so far on my pilgrimage, it is consistent with a certain theme. When our great-grandchildren will most certainly rely on cleaner, more renewable sources of energy, why should we stand by and allow the decimation of our most precious and pristine landscapes for short-term corporate profit? We should not succumb to the myth that further exploration and extraction of oil and gas will create jobs and stimulate the economy. Wind, solar, and hydrogen will provide many more jobs and result in far greater economic growth for centuries to come — while allowing us to preserve the natural beauty of our federal land and national parks. And that, in this pilgrim's opinion, is how the free market can, and hopefully *will*, save the day.

CHAPTER 22

Grace, Sheila, and Liz

JUNE 12 · DAY FORTY-THREE

Am I thrilled about what I'm having for dinner? Frankly, no. But I will not complain. What I *am* over the moon about is the view from my campsite! Breeze-blown ripples on the jagged Warm Springs arm of Lake Sonoma glisten 500 feet below like Christmas tinsel in the early evening sun. My red bivy is set up for slumber. It's just past 6 Pm and I am sitting at a picnic table at site number 83 of the Liberty Glen campground, cobbling together the facsimile of a meal.

My hastily consumed appetizer comprised the dry, sinewy remains of a bag of turkey jerky leftover from my first night of wild camping — more than a month ago! Now, I'm cooking up my main course, squeezing Justin's peanut butter from a serving-sized packet onto a peanut-butter-and-dark-chocolate Kind bar — ingredients charity of Wendy Hunter, who so munificently gifted me a plethora of just-in-case supplies back at Jim Liao's Motel 6 in Santa Maria. As it inevitably does, just-in-case has arrived. And, to be honest, this recipe, washed down with a tepid Trader Joe's Simpler Times Lager, is genuinely delicious, especially at the end of long day's trek. As a capper to this improvised repast, I'm looking forward to a perfect dessert, plucked from a zip-lock baggie of homemade chocolate chip cookies lovingly baked in the Santa Rosa oven of Ardythe Brandon.

Having surpassed 400 miles, I'm reflecting with gratitude on the angels I've encountered thus far on this journey. And, since

I have no cellular or internet service in this remote spot, there's plenty of time for such reflection. It doesn't tax my memory in the least, however, to recall having been graced by Grace.

If Tracey Ullman were to concoct an impersonation of a Park Ranger, I've just met the perfect prototype. Topping out at no more than four-foot-ten, with one wandering eye behind black-rimmed, rectangular-shaped glasses, Grace exudes an energy one might describe as chipmunk-ish. She's the kind of person who nods and blinks as you speak, as if she intends to agree with you, even before you've completed your entire statement.

After eight hours of pavement-trekking under the June sun, my feet were screaming in protest and my legs were leadened with fatigue. Grace, in her official, bright-red Army Corps of Engineers volunteer vest, was scurrying to lock the public bathrooms at the Lake Sonoma Visitor Center. I took note of the posted hours: *Closing time, 4PM*. It was six minutes after. *Drat a pilgrim's unfortunate timing*! As Grace bustled back toward the main entrance to the building, she took notice of the tuckered-out cart pusher. "Can I help you?" she inquired.

"I hope so..." I responded. "Is there a tent site available?"

"Yes," she said, cheerfully. "At our Liberty Glen campground." Then, like a stoic Sacajawea might have for Lewis and Clarke, she gazed toward the horizon and pointed at an upward angle. "Five miles up the road." Although her answer made my heart sink, I managed to hide my disappointment behind a forced smile of cordiality. I explained that I'd been without cell phone or Internet service all afternoon, which prohibited me from finding out how far the campground was, that I was on foot and had walked a dozen miles already. "Yeah," she said, with evident sympathy, "and it's all up hill, too." To be helpful, she gave me the Visitor Center Wi-Fi code before scampering back inside.

With some rest, I might have been able to push on a little further. However, five more miles up a steep incline at this late hour was an endurance test I wasn't eager to accept. I sat surveying the surrounding area for potential wild-camping locations. A second woman, also red-vested, but literally double the size of petite Grace, emerged from the Visitor Center. Her nametag read *Emily*. Handing me a cold bottle of water, Emily smiled. "Wow, you've walked a long ways! So, are you interested in booking a campsite?"

I told her that, yes, I certainly was — but, only if there might be a park ranger willing to drive me up to the campground. Emily strode off to find out, while I laid down on the bench — for 10 minutes or so, until its wood planks became unbearably hard.

Then, busy-bee Grace buzzed out from the Visitor's Center. "The ranger with a truck has been called away," she said.

Once again, my heart sunk. This time, however, I was unable to hide my disappointment.

"But, I have an Isuzu, if that would work."

As it turns out, Grace actually lives at Liberty Glen. She volunteers at the Visitor Center in exchange for her RV site. "I can show you around the campground," she elaborated. "You can pick out whatever empty site appeals to you." That gush of very welcome information immediately sweetened my mood. Then she iced the cake: "And, we'll comp it for you."

I chose site #83, primarily because it featured the spectacular view I'm gazing at right now. A brisk wind is kicking up, the sun has all but disappeared over the western horizon, and the temperature is plummeting. I'd best crawl into my bivy and catch some shut-eye.

☮   ☮   ☮   ☮   ☮

There are degrees of quiet, not unlike the shades of a color. You say you want to paint the room white. Then, you discover there are 39 whites from which to choose — the eggshells, the ivories, and the creams being the most appealing. A true white is garish, bright, blinding. Such is the quality of quiet I listen to as I attempt to fall sleep.

Until one actually has the experience, it's impossible to imagine how intensely loud absolute quiet can be. What we perceive as quiet is invariably impure, off-white, muddled with churning tires on a distant highway, birds chirping, a jet plane at high altitude, and/or wind rustling leaves. On this night, high over the reservoir called Lake Sonoma, at campsite #83, for minutes at a time, seemingly endless minutes, the white-white quiet is deafening.

Silence is broken. I'm awake. It's the unmistakable sound of somebody — or some *thing!* — outside my tent rooting through my stuff. My heart races as my auditory senses become intensely acute. *Damn!* I suddenly remember. Foolishly, I left my supply bags out there, on the ground.

I grab a flashlight, hastily unzip my tent door, and poke my head out into the brisk night air. The flashlight beam reveals a furry creature with a long tail, its head burrowed deeply into one of my supply bags. "Get out of here!" I demand. My deep, gruff, boisterous command almost frightens *me*. "Go AWAY!"

I've polluted the quiet. Surely, my voice can be heard for miles. I wave my flashlight beam at the thieves. Now, I can make out two of them, the largest raccoons I'd ever seen, as big as small bears. They slip some distance into the darkness. I locate my flip-flops and slither nervously out of my bivy to take stock. By now, one of the marauders has returned. He's standing up on his hind legs, staring back, taunting me like a brazen cat burglar. Although my knees quaver, I stand my ground, aiming the flashlight beam directly into his glowing eyes. After a minute-long standoff, he turns and waddles off.

A brilliant full moon hangs over the lake like a paper lantern, illuminating the crime scene. Wrappers and trash are strewn everywhere. I gather up what I can see, fetch the two now-considerably-lighter supply bags, toss them into the furthest back corner of my tent and crawl back inside. An hour passes before I can calm the pace of my heart and get back to sleep.

JUNE 13 · DAY FORTY-FOUR

In the first light of dawn, I'm gathering up the remainder of the detritus left behind by my litterbug night visitors. Granola bar wrappers, plastic zip-lock bags, fragments of cardboard are strewn in a 50-foot semi-circle around my tent. Raccoon hands have such dexterity that the clever scavengers tore wrappers open and gobbled the contents just like humans. My biggest disappointment is that every one of the delectable chocolate-chip cookies Ardythe so lovingly made and packed for me is gone. Seeing that the thieves also devoured an entire bag of dark-chocolate-covered espresso beans, I can't help but chuckle, picturing those nocturnal creatures by daylight, wide-eyed, wired, and confused. It's proper justice after last night's mischief that they should be having an equally tough time as I did getting satisfactory shuteye.

It's a five-mile, mostly downhill trek on Rockpile Road to the Visitor Center. As always, guiding the Pilgrimmobile down a steep downgrade is slow going.

A bicyclist comes huffing/puffing around a corner. He looks up, obviously surprised to see a pilgrim and his cart out here so far from anything. "What are *you* up to?" he inquires, stopping to straddle his bike. As he catches his breath, I give my little spiel about inspiring civil, constructive dialogue.

Bryan's reason for riding Rockpile Road is simple. He had to climb this grade to find out for himself what was up here. Bryan lives in a small, artsy community on the Russian River. There, he feels alienated, out of step with the dominant, preponderantly left-leaning, politically correct culture. Any point of view other than hardcore liberalism, he says, is maligned, mocked, and ridiculed. Bryan believes Mr. Trump might be a better president than Mrs. Clinton would have been. He thinks the new president's business acumen could be positive for the economy. "Except," he qualifies, "that the way he acts is so embarrassing. He's gotta cut that crap out!" Then, Bryan makes certain I'm aware that, "I didn't vote for him. I voted for the third-party candidate." He muses, "Everybody said I was throwing my vote away."

I tell him, as far as I'm concerned, it's time for this country to evolve beyond hyper-partisanship. No more handing over campaign contributions, giving support to our party's candidates every election cycle, just so they can head off to DC to represent corporate interests and neglect the folks who voted them into office. Bryan totally concurs before resuming his upward trajectory, while I continue my cautious, one-painful-step-at-a-time descent.

Another half mile down the road, a familiar white Isuzu SUV pulls up. From behind her rectangular, black spectacles, Grace queries, "Want a ride to the Visitor Center?" When I ask how far it is, she guesses about a mile. I see no sense in completely disassembling the Pilgrimmobile, only to put the whole thing back together again at the bottom of the hill — not for a mere mile's lift.

"I had an invasion last night," I inform her. "Raccoons."

"You're lucky it wasn't coyotes. Or, worse yet, wild pigs!"

Grace spoke a mouthful there. What if I'd unzipped my tent flap and shined my flashlight beam on a couple of voracious, fiery-eyed, feral swine? However, as my masked marauders did devour all of my edibles, what I really need, I tell Grace, is a meal of some substance — and *soon*!

"We sell snacks at the Visitor Center," she informs me, "but that's about all. After that, the nearest market would be in Cloverdale." As Cloverdale is 10 miles from here, this is not welcome news.

Much to the consternation of my feet and knees, Grace's off-the-cuff guesstimation of one mile to the Visitor's Center was off by 100%. Thus, the plodding, painful, downhill trek takes an extra hour. I hobble into the Visitor Center at half past 12, weak, dispirited, and famished. The toenail on my badly blistered right pinky is hanging by a final fiber. Although it's the tiniest digit in my body, the pain is huge, with inflammation spreading all the way down the side of the foot to the heel. I toss a wave to Grace — she's giving a tourist a look-see around the facility — and park myself in the exhibit hall to put my feet up and take advantage of the Wi-Fi. When I emerge, Grace hands me two cold bottles of water. "There's a paper bag next to your cart," she informs me, with a wink. I examine the sack's contents: a can of tuna, a package of crackers, and an apple.

Last night, a miniature, blinky-eyed woman I'd never met

before taxied me and my load to the Liberty Glen campground and took me on a tour, so I could pick out an ideal spot, at no charge. Earlier today, she offered to give me another ride. Then, hearing I was in need, she returned to her own camp to fetch what sustenance she could offer me. All this, purely out of the goodness of her heart. When a pilgrim meets someone like Grace, the suffering is made bearable. And, now, thanks to her kindness, I have strength enough to trek the remaining nine miles to Cloverdale.

JUNE 15 · DAY FORTY-SIX

As I push through the compact, tidy downtown area of Cloverdale, I am particularly impressed by the many beautifully restored Victorian structures dating back to the 1870s, when the San Francisco and North Pacific railroads first arrived. Some are family homes. The larger vintage structures house law practices, medical offices, even a few churches. Art galleries, yoga studios, and wine shops selling Zinfandels from local wineries line the main street. Even with its anachronistic charm, Cloverdale seems cool.

In the interest of sparing my inflamed right foot from yet another consecutive, punishing, 12- to 15-mile jaunt, I've decided to reduce today's goal — a nearby KOA campground — to a more do-able six miles. Trekking the last residential block on the edge of town, I observe an intriguing figure — tall, with the slender, but broad-shouldered body of a man, with feminine facial features and short-cropped hair, topped with a beige, canvas, Norman Lear boating hat.

The androgynous one comes running across the road, waving slender, awkward arms toward the sky, like a tube man at a used-car lot. "Are you really a peace pilgrim?" she inquires — high-pitched vocal timbre revealing her gender. Energy frenetic, giddy with excitement, the woman exudes, "Nobody ever talks about peace anymore!"

Liz asks if I'd like to come up to her place "to rest and talk about peace." I've barely begun today's jaunt. Tomorrow, I might have some time to visit on my way back through. I fish a postcard out of my pocket. Not wearing her glasses, Liz re-pockets it.

"Well," she says, "Feel free to knock on my door then. But knock loud!" This begins a series of advance apologies. Liz informs me she's a night person and sleeps by day. As she medicates with marijuana to ease symptoms of a chronic digestive ailment, she hopes I won't judge her for that. I assure her that I would not. She demands a hug before I trek on.

Having found a fairly level patch of shade on the edge of North River Road, I'm mid-sandwich when a VW Golf pulls up across the lane and stops. The driver saunters over. "Hello," she hails me. The woman is blond, 60-ish, with extremely large, very white teeth. Her T-shirt, silk-screened with an artist's rendering of a large honeybee, tents a voluptuous pair of breasts, while her hips are so slender, you'd think she'd topple right over. "I saw you a few days ago," she says. "In Sonoma. And, here you are again. So, I had to stop and meet you."

Sheila has the aristocratic carriage and the throaty vocal texture of the splendid character-actress Holland Taylor. Her passion is a vineyard called Eco Terrena and its natural bee garden. She rants about the oil-based fertilizers vineyards use, how it kills the bees, gets into the watershed, and even pollutes the wine. Eco Terrena's fields are fertilized with organic compost. This coming Saturday, she informs me, is the big launch party for her enterprise, an event to show her neighboring grape growers how, in her strong, unbridled opinion, it really *should* be done.

Sheila is quite the entrepreneur. After getting her start in banking, she opened a financial planning firm. Apparently, her personal financial plans have reaped enough abundance to branch out into organic viticulture and beekeeping.

"So, what about the signs I see along the road," I ask, "labeling all those Sonoma County farms as sustainable and organic?"

"That's all bullshit!" Sheila declares with self-righteous certitude. "We're the only ones who do it right."

Organic grape growing is not the only subject Sheila is certain about. She proceeds to make two startling, apocalyptic predictions — both, she purports, due to take place within the next three years. First, the dollar will lose its world-currency status, plunging the U.S. economy into crisis. That prophecy, however, as dire as it may sound, is not even the worst of it. World war, she declares, is imminent, which will reduce global population by half, perhaps even by two-thirds. However, she envisions a happy ending to these mega tragedies. According to a guru with whom she's been studying for decades, these cataclysms will finally force humankind to co-exist harmoniously.

Meanwhile, in the shorter term, Sheila is on her way back to Eco Terrena with a Thai food lunch for herself and her business partner son. "You should drop by," she suggests. "Are you hungry?" I only wish I'd received this invitation before filling my belly with Quick-Stop tuna.

☮   ☮   ☮   ☮   ☮

"Go ahead and say hi." The woman's voice emits mother-child kid-speak in an unmistakable Irish lilt. The adorable little girl, raven-haired and impish faced, does just that. I return her greeting cheerfully. Then, she and her even tinier brother scurry toward my little, red bivouac with wonder in their eyes. "They were really curious earlier," the mother tells me, as the two children marvel at the miniature tent like it's something out of a faery story.

The mother, slender, dark-haired, naturally beautiful, introduces herself as Tracey. The large, broad-chested, shaved-headed fellow is her husband Ed. Hailing from Ireland, they live in San Francisco. Poppi is their daughter, Alfie, their son. They've taken a cabin here at the KOA for two nights, on their way to a Reggae festival in nearby Booneville.

"Can I make a contribution to your cause?" Tracey asks. "I'm not a rich woman," she confesses, "but I'm all about peace." Then comes an even more-immediately appealing offer: "Would you like a beer?" The ice-cold Corona is the best thing I've tasted all day.

Sated, with some evening to spare, I carry my guitar down to a patio above the pool and hot tub. There, I embark upon some instrumental improvisation and segue into a short set of songs. While the last straggling bathers of the day glance up at me with cursory attention, one boy, 11 or 12, circles below on his bicycle for a full 20 minutes. He's pretending to be too cool to be listening. However, it's clear that he is enthralled by the music as he keeps his tight two-wheel oval within earshot. Perhaps he's a budding guitarist himself. Or, maybe he is suddenly feeling inspired to ask for an instrument for his next birthday.

JUNE 16 · DAY FORTY-SEVEN

Poppi is attempting to give her little brother a ride in a red-plastic wagon. Gravity, however, keeps thwarting her efforts, leaving the wagon's front wheels crimped against the logs that divide the campsites from the road. When little Alfie jumps out to allow his sister to straighten the wheels, he steps barefoot into the tiny stickers that hide under the crabgrass. He thinks if he continues to walk, he'll escape this prickly peril. Instead, every step results in more needle pokes into his pudgy feet. One would think the now-crying boy would figure out this simple reality and stop walking. Then again, in the last 12 hours, I've banged my head at least six times on the shelter roof over my picnic table. Some lessons, it seems, take longer to learn than others.

Before I lock up my box, I carry my guitar across the lane. "I was wondering," I ask, "if it would be okay if I sang a song for the kids."

"Sure," Tracey says. "Kids! Wanna hear a song?" The family gathers around their sheltered picnic table.

"Okay," I begin, "this is a song about a tree. But not just any tree..." I tell the kids about the tree in my friend Stephen's backyard and how, every summer, it sprouted little yellow loquats. While the fruit was far too bitter for most people's taste, when it ripened, the tree would swarm with hungry creatures...

The squirrel and the sparrow and the mouse and the bee
All havin' a party in the loquat tree
Eatin' all the yellow fruit they can see
It's a wild, wild party in the loquat tree

— RAND BISHOP, © 1989
WEIGHTLESS CARGO MUSIC, BMI

The Indigo Girls' wonderfully imaginative rendition of "Wild, Wild Party in the Loquat Tree" was featured on the *Put on Your Green Shoes* album. Alfie is way into it, as are Ed and Tracey. Poppi seems confused, shy, wondering why some old, grey-bearded man is singing and playing guitar at their shelter table. Ed and Tracey reward my performance with hoots and hollers and enthusiastic applause.

"This next one is for all of you," I say, "since you're enroute to a reggae festival." I launch into Bob Marley's "One Love" medley-ed with Curtis Mayfield's "People Get Ready." Brawny, bald-headed Ed sings along, playing spoon-on-bowl percussion. Alfie bobs his head and emulates his daddy by pounding his hands in time to the music. One errant beat sends a plastic bowl spinning off the table to the ground, scattering Pepperidge Farm goldfish crackers this way and that.

☮   ☮   ☮   ☮   ☮

I get the impression that Liz is not accustomed to guests. The miniscule, above-the-garage apartment she calls Studio B is not, she informs me, a legal rental. After taking quick inventory of the clutter, she removes an accumulation of books, newspapers, and cast-aside clothing from a chair to provide a place for me to sit, a gesture for which my feet are most appreciative. My hostess is in a spacey, post-afternoon-nap state. Still, it soon becomes clear that she's actually put considerable thought into preparing for my visit. Not only has she perused my postcard thoroughly, she has watched my YouTube videos.

Only two minutes since plopping down on the newly unburied chair and I have reams of reading matter stacked on my lap. Meanwhile, Liz is motor-mouthing six subjects at once, her tongue whipping around so fast, I worry it might tie itself in a knot and impede her windpipe. Calmly, I lay aside one volume at a time, finally unearthing the thick, musty, academic-looking tome at the bottom of the pile. "Oh, good!" she exclaims, pointing to the weighty volume I've just opened, "I have to tell you about my grandfather!"

Liz hails from generations of Bay Area aristocracy. The grandfather in question, Franklin A. Griffin, whose hefty biography I am now leafing through, was a San Francisco superior court judge. Granddad's primary fame — and shame, as it turns out — stems from having sentenced notorious socialist-labor revolutionary Tom Mooney to be hanged. Liz describes her grandparent's mansion, one of the poshest addresses in old San Francisco, and her rigid, Episcopalian upbringing, growing up under the constant pressure to rise to and uphold a patrician family's social status. For a gangly tomboy with no debutante aspirations, it must have been difficult — not to mention lonely.

"I need to medicate," Liz says, clutching her abdomen. With her first exhalation of marijuana smoke, Liz rambles on to another family member: her uncle, surrealist painter Ed Cunningham. Liz and her siblings were bestowed their artist uncle's estate by his widow. Liz's share of that largess is long gone.

"Okay, constructive dialogue," the lanky lady blurts, snatching up a list of topics, evidently scribbled down while contemplating a potential face-to-face encounter with Peace Pilgrim 2017. "What about immigration?" she asks, tossing an open-ended question into the cannabis-tainted air. Not waiting for my response, she declares, "There's just too many of them. What are we going to do about it?" She hopscotches on… "What about feminism?"

Once again, before I can even open my mouth, she segues to, "Same-sex-marriage. I married my partner before it was legal. We were together for ten years." Since this revelation confirms something I suspected from the get-go — that Liz is a lesbian — it comes without surprise. Her next unequivocal pronouncement, however, comes out of deep left field. "Marriage is a financial arrangement, you know. Pure and simple."

I still can't find a breath between blathers to squeeze in a word. This dialogue, if one can call it that, is hardly constructive. Perhaps a more accurate term for this solo rant might be "frenetic monologue" or, using a more charitable definition, "constructive catharsis."

This, I'm realizing, *is a lonely, frightened, self-possessed person.* I'm Jane Goodall, studying my subject in her own habitat, not forcing myself into the conversation, but interacting only when she invites me to participate.

☮ ☮ ☮ ☮ ☮

Liz and I are walking to the market. "See," she says, nodding her head toward the house on the corner, "that's the problem." Up until recently, she explains, this modest, one-story, masonry structure had been owner-occupied. When the owner passed on, a speculator snapped up the property, did the requisite HGTV renovations, and posted a *For Lease* sign behind its white picket fence. "You know how much it rents for now?"

I don't have a clue.

"Thirty-five hundred! Now *my* rent's gonna go up," Liz pines. "I won't be able to afford it. Then, where will I go?"

Flight from San Francisco's severely inflated real estate market in search of anything affordable now extends this far: 90 miles from the city. Meanwhile, investors are making above-list-price offers on every fixer-upper in the North Bay area, with plans to convert them into rentals or Airbnbs. This rampant speculation takes property off the market, while supply and demand drives rents and purchase prices out of range for the middle class. A local publication, Liz informs me, recently published a list of 40 professions — good jobs, respectable jobs — all paying at least $40,000 per year, none of which provide enough income to pay rent and make ends meet in Sonoma County.

☮   ☮   ☮   ☮   ☮

Liz insists that I watch a documentary with her, entitled *Hyper-Normalisation*. She's the host. She's a night person. We're in tight quarters. So, I acquiesce, expressing the proviso that I doubt I'll be able to stay awake for the duration. At an interminable two and a half hours in length, this bizarre, paranoiac film is an epic, meandering attempt to free-associate a thread of seemingly random historical events. Liz, apparently, has swallowed the film's premise, hook, line, and sinker, believing that, for a half century, a cabal of government leaders, bankers, and think-tank utopians have been engaging in an insidious, coordinated plot to hand control of the entire world to multi-national corporations and banks.

Henry Kissinger, Iran's Ayatollah Khomeini, Syria's Hafez al-Assad, Libya's Muammar Gaddafi and, yes, even Donald Trump play key roles in this docu-melodrama. Kissinger's Vietnam-era shuttle-diplomacy, suicide bombing, LSD research, and Trump borrowing billions to give Manhattan a luxury-condo makeover are all somehow connected. Finally, the Internet hijacking our personal privacy completes this devious design. In a hyper-stroke of hyper-irony, if not for the Internet, *HyperNormalisation* would not be available for us to watch.

"I can't believe how great I'm feeling!" Liz exudes. She has been self-medicating all afternoon and evening — but not, she notes, nearly as much as normal. Earlier, over a makeshift dinner, she confided that, at 58, she feels as if she has nothing left to contribute to the world. There are no jobs available for a woman of her experience and maturity. Hers is primarily an isolated existence. Living on a meager fixed income, on the verge of bankruptcy, she suffers from a chronic intestinal disorder and often slips into clinical depression. Admittedly, she confesses, at times, she contemplates suicide.

It saddens me to ponder how many solitary folks experience similar quandaries, similar despair. Tonight, however, the rare, simple experience of having someone to talk to has eased this woman's pain and anxiety. Listening is an act of kindness. Listening costs nothing but time. Listening is a skill every person has the capability to practice and develop. Just being there, present, alert, responsive, and willing to pay attention is a priceless gift.

From the very outset of this pilgrimage, I was fully aware that this journey would push my physical fortitude to its limit, perhaps beyond. Putting myself out here to interact with someone like Liz demands an altogether different kind of stamina.

CHAPTER 23

Green River, the KKK, and a Cannonball

JUNE 17 · DAY FORTY-EIGHT

The rising temperature is made significantly more intense by the heat-absorbing blacktop and the constant rush of traffic. With the highway paralleling the Russian River, a plunge into the translucent, pale-emerald water proves irresistible. Taking even a dozen steps across the pebbled riverbank was torture for these very tender, bare feet. But that minute of agony was worth it.

I'm luxuriating in the cool currents, when a pair of young men appear, trudging loudly across the rocky beach. The taller one, with sandy-colored, wavy hair, catches his first close-up glimpse of the aqua eddy, sheds his T-shirt and shoes, walks out of his jeans, takes six long, swift strides, and chest-flops in. He floats on his belly for a few seconds, then bounces off of the river bottom on tiptoe, whipping sopping hair from his flushed face with a swift twist of his lithe, muscular neck. "Come on in," he beckons to his friend. "It's great!"

My tranquility having been disturbed, I tread water and observe, as the young man dives back under, surfaces, rolls, and splashes like a playful sea otter.

With my body temperature now satisfactorily lowered, I wade to the shore, plop down in the Monarch Chair to dry off and sip the caffeinated beverage I hope will energize the remainder of today's hike. Sitting here in the shade, listening to the water lapping on the rocks, a Credence Clearwater song begins playing in my head. Surely, John Fogarty was inspired by a sight exactly like this when he penned his classic "Green River."

✳   ✳   ✳   ✳   ✳

Males flatter themselves as the more rational gender. Yet, the way some men behave — especially young men — often defies logic. Sociopathic conduct — devilish mischief, vandalism, or overt cruelty — comes all too naturally for males in pre-adulthood. This syndrome is particularly prevalent when boys gather together in groups. What follows is my half-serious theory explaining the syndrome I call Male Pack Stupidity...

In every meeting of the Penis and Testicles Club, there is a finite level of intelligence, a maximum, gross-total IQ, as it were. Think of it as one common brain, shared by all the individuals in the group. The more males gathering in one place, the less brain power is available for each individual. There comes a point when everyone present becomes as dumb as the dumbest guy in the room. That's when idiotic ideas begin to sound brilliant and, therefore, become impossible to resist. Primitive, base, mob impulse obliterates good sense. Any rational voice is swiftly smothered under the weight of peer pressure. *Voila!* The result? Ladies and gents, I give you *Male Pack Stupidity.*

In the early seventies, a fellow musician recalled a pastime in which he and his pals indulged as Mississippi teenagers. This posse of good ol' boys spent their idle summer evenings cruising a rural highway on the lookout for a "colored" hitchhiker. Having located their victim, they'd pull to the side of the road and slow down, as if they were about to pick him up. Naturally, the hitchhiker would approach their vehicle with the reasonable expectation of being welcomed aboard. Instead, the young delinquents would peel out, extend a broom handle out from the passenger window, and try to whack the unwary fellow in the head. The storyteller belly laughed as told me this cruel game was called "nigger knocking." In a premier stroke of irony — or, perhaps, karma — this same musician's very next gig was in the back-up band for a black, transvestite singer.

In my youth, I too did some extremely foolish things, stuff I'm not at all proud of. Once, to impress some high-school peers, I shoplifted a water ski. In my college years, during a protest march,

I dented a U.S. Post Office box with a baseball bat. But I never initiated or participated in an intentional act aimed at frightening, humiliating, or hurting another person.

The sustained horn honk and verbal taunting deliberately directed at me by a car full of callous juveniles was nowhere near as malicious as a racially motivated head bashing. It was, however, mean-spirited, and hurtful. Now, I hear another raised voice. Across the highway, on the shoulder of the northbound lanes, a man stands behind a basic, beat-up white pickup, waving his hands in the air, and calling out to me. With a momentary gap in traffic, I strain my ears to make out, *"Do you need a ride to the next town?"*

Over the course of this journey, a number of kind-hearted Samaritans have offered to give me a lift. And, while I've been moved by these gestures, so far, my response has been a sincerely grateful thanks-but-no-thanks. I promised to accept rides only over stretches where the roadway is too dangerous, through remote, desolate areas, or when the weather gets too severe. The present situation doesn't exactly meet those criteria. However, pushing myself beyond my physical endurance and emotional fortitude would also be unwise. Presently, I'm overheated, exhausted, disheartened, and lonesome. Not only could I use a lift physically, my heart could use some lifting as well. The man waving and calling out to me from across four busy lanes of highway traffic was observant and sensitive enough to detect the plight of a fellow human. Who am I to wave him away and deny him the fulfillment of helping a person in need?

I've trekked a dozen grueling miles today on blistering blacktop without serious mishap, arriving at this place in one piece. The next 100 feet, across Highway 101, with a blazing, orange sun sinking over my shoulder and streams of hurried vehicles streaking in both directions, looks to be the longest yard of the day. As I dart out onto the pavement, it suddenly occurs to me that, at this moment, I am actually breaking my promise by putting myself in unnecessary jeopardy. This foray, in fact, could be my most foolhardy yet. With my heartbeat suddenly accelerated to puppy-chasing-squirrel pace, I make it to the island between the south- and northbound lanes.

Now fully committed to this ill-advised stunt, turning back makes no sense at all. Fording the final 40 feet will require precise timing and nifty maneuvering and, no doubt, some aid and assistance from my guardian angels.

After a couple of false starts and retreats, I make my bid and charge into the home stretch. The driver of a delivery truck lays on his horn — as if I could possibly be unaware that his vehicle is barreling toward me at 70 miles-per-hour! That the truck fails to slow down at all indicates that the driver is totally cognizant of the algebra in this equation. His honking isn't a warning that he might run me down. He's staking claim to the highway, cautioning the wayward pedestrian in no unsubtle terms to refrain from trespassing on his exclusive property.

Tim is rotund and dripping with perspiration. He's clad in a sweat-and-grease-stained XXXL-sized, formerly white, cheap-cotton T-shirt and a pair of equally soiled, shapeless, baggy Bermuda shorts.

"Thank you…" I utter, gasping for breath, "for stopping."

"Well," Tim responds, "you looked like you might need help."

Yes, I confess, I was, in fact, in distress. Tim is helping me lift the storage box into the truck bed, when he inquires, "Do you know anything about these communities?"

I ask for clarification: "These communities?"

"Yeah," he says, "these towns around here, they're all run by the Klan."

I'm bewildered by this out-of-the-blue declaration. The ride to Hopland is brief, but informative. I'm hoping what Tim is telling me isn't true. Yet, if this is all in his imagination, what does that say about the mental state of the man I am now entrusting with my life?

The police and fire departments, city councils, and every mayor of every town in this area, Tim swears, are card-carrying white supremacists. Even the U.S. Department of Homeland Security is staffed by KKK members, in cahoots with the locals. Tim worked as a landscaper for an outfit that regularly contracted for Homeland Security. Federal agents, he says, arrived at his trailer unannounced to grill him aggressively about what he might have observed or overheard. Their questions made one thing obvious: it would be highly advisable for Tim to keep his mouth shut about any racial intolerance he'd been privy to. Now, here he is, yacking about it to a stranger he just picked up on the highway. "I just thought," Tim says, "since you're walking for peace and all that, you should know." He assures me that he's on my side 100% and doesn't condone bigotry of any kind.

My chauffer is on his way to his girlfriend's place for dinner. I'm noticing that he didn't bother to tidy up for his date. Catching my sidelong glance, he explains that he pretty much lives off the grid. His trailer has no running water, and one single extension cord provides all his electricity. With a shower, a hot meal, and his lady awaiting, he seems eager to jettison me at his first opportunity.

As the sweaty, corpulent man helps me unload my gear from the truck bed, I detect a grin of self-satisfaction on his face — for having done a good deed. That's when he decides to share another random morsel of information...

"I didn't learn to read and write till I was fifty-eight."

I congratulate him for making a better-late-than-never effort to improve himself.

Then, he delivers his punch line: "I'm sixty now."

JUNE 18 · DAY FORTY-NINE

Morning's first light couldn't come soon enough. I didn't want to believe Tim's claim that these communities are all run by the Klan. However, I've seen plenty of movies about unsuspecting travelers discovering ugly, small-town secrets and becoming victimized by local cultists. So, it didn't calm my paranoia when the only place I could find to bed down was midway between the trees lining the highway and some railroad tracks. On the more-positive flip side, lying out under the stars allowed me a front-row, recliner seat to a spectacular, pastel, watercolor sunset. Last evening's entertainment was the twilight sky, in streaks of pink, yellow, and purple against a Maya blue background, gradually giving way to a twinkling tapestry of celestial bodies. Unfortunately, however, with tires speeding over warning bumps on the centerline of the highway, it was like trying to sleep through nearby machine-gun fire.

With my newly purchased lunch packed away in my supply bags, I'm about to push the Pilgrimmobile northward, when a large, bald-pated man emerges from the market balancing two corn dogs on a white paper tray. In a raspy, overly exuberant voice, he wants to know, "How far ya pushing that thing?"

"Well," I inform him, "Four hundred and thirty miles so far."

"What are ya, nuts?" he asks, with more wonder than humor.

"Yes," I chuckle, "I must be. Pretty much every day at some point, that very thought passes through my head."

"Want a corn dog?" he offers, extending the paper tray. I decline. "I've got two," he points out. I decline again with a *thanks anyway*. He shrugs and opens the door of his truck, saying, "Well, you have a good day."

As he swivels into the driver's seat, I feel compelled to explain, "I'm on a pilgrimage hoping to meet some nice people."

"I bet you're gonna meet a lot of 'em," he surmises, with a smile, then immediately indulges in a bite that vanishes half of corn dog number one.

"I already have," I respond. And, I mean it.

Case in point... The minivan's license plate reads, *Utah, Life Elevated.* A young man bounds out from the driver-side door. He looks like a monk: head shaved, baggy sweats, flip-flops, and a serene, Dalai Lama smile. "We don't have anything in the car," he says, "but is there anything you need?" Odd statement. He has nothing to offer, yet he's offering whatever I might need.

Brad tells me he walked the Appalachian Trail last year. This prompts me to confess that I hadn't even known how to pack a backpack when I started out. I tell him how much weight I've lost, how I learned about the necessity of taking zero days for physical recuperation and caloric replenishment. After a brisk interchange, he wishes me well, climbs back in his vehicle, pulls across the highway, and heads south. The young man had U-turned and stopped to make sure the stranger trekking in the opposite direction was all right before turning back again to resume his own journey. *Who does that?* Yes, Corn Dog Man, I'm meeting some very nice people. Some of them, believe it or not, are even from Utah.

The temperature is skyrocketing. Long segments of highway provide little or no shade. With the blacktop re-radiating the sun's rays, it feels as if I'm slogging through a blast furnace. Spying a fruit stand ahead, I cross the highway and trundle down a dry-dirt driveway.

"What are Ollalie berries?" I ask the oval-faced, brown-skinned young woman.

"Well," she explains, "they're kind of like a blackberry crossed with a boysenberry."

I taste one — tart, juicy, delicious. I'm sold. I lean the Monarch Chair against the side of the little shack in a sliver of shade to indulge. Today is my father's ninety-first birthday. I call. My parents are always comforted to hear from me, which always buoys my flagging spirits.

A man parks his black Escalade, and strolls past. To be friendly, he feels obliged to make the most blatantly obvious observation of all: "Hot day for walking."

I'm slipping my weight-lifting gloves over berry-stained fingers. A white Toyota pulls in, wafting a small cloud of fine dust over me. The petite, white-haired woman stops to talk — Caroline from Eureka, nice smile. The Ollalie berries are particularly good, I inform her. Now I'm the one stating the obvious. This, she says, is her favorite fruit stand. She always stops here. "Thank you for what you're doing," she says, sincerely. Fueled by natural sucrose, hydrated by berry juice, encouraged by Caroline's kind words, I push my cart across dry dirt to the highway.

I'm rolling the Pilgrimmobile up the ramp onto 101. Out of courtesy, a driver exiting the freeway slows to a crawl. The driver of the car directly behind him, evidently not paying attention, is closing in all-too-rapidly. At the very last second, he jams on his brakes, and swerves to avoid rear-ending the first car. From my vantage point, only a few feet away, the screech of tires skidding on pavement is terrifying. My heart accelerates into double time, as what appeared to be a certain collision has miraculously been averted. And this was not merely an extremely close call for these two vehicles. Had they collided, there is little question that I, too, would have suffered some, possibly serious, collateral injury.

Putrid, ebony smoke rises from black skid marks on the fiery pavement. The equally heated glare I'm receiving from the neglectful driver of the now-stationary second car indicates that he places the blame for this near calamity on me. It's tempting to return the angry fellow's glare with one of my own. Instead, I summon a smile and flash him the peace sign.

The morbidly obese woman at the lobby's front desk demonstrates a friendly, respectful, professional demeanor as she informs me that my room is not yet ready. As I wait, I'm a fly on the wall for some rather unpleasant goings on. A young man, who has been permanently banned from this Motel 6 in Ukiah, California, for previous suspicious behavior, is on the property. There is a heated phone conversation between the manager and the trespasser. Then, the motel security guard — whose boyishness would probably make him more suited to life guarding at a YMCA pool — is dispatched to expel the offender from campus.

Soon, the villain of this drama, a wiry, tightly wound young man with tattoos on his neck, charges into the lobby to confront the manager face-to-face. It's a 10-minute-long verbal skirmish, during which the guy repeatedly insists on his absolute innocence, while demanding his legitimate right to remain on the property. The manager, however, stands her ground, not yielding an inch. As Neck Tattoo refuses to vacate the premises, she makes good on her threat to call the police. By the time the black-and-white pulls into the parking lot, the unwelcome party crasher has wisely vamoosed.

It's 5:30PM by the time I get the key to my room. While my laundry is spinning in the motel laundromat, I decide to take a dip in the pool. The water is refreshing. However, relaxation seems out of the question. Two pre-adolescent children — brother and sister

I surmise — are engaged in an exuberant game of dunking and splashing. A man sits on a chair in the shade of a beach umbrella, "supervising" the young swimmers. Unfortunately for me, he is less interested in that obligation than he is in the smart phone in his hand. I look to him in a silent plea to exercise some control over the children's shenanigans. He mumbles something to them about calming down. They don't listen. He goes back to his phone. I decide to cut my swim short.

I'm drip-drying on a chaise lounge on the pool deck, trying to dial out the din of children's water play. I'm still thinking about the real-life theatrics I just observed in the motel lobby. Admittedly, the scene provided some distraction from the tedium of an hour-and-a-half wait. However, in retrospect, I find it curious that the hotel staff lacked any inhibition about exposing me, a paying guest, obviously fatigued, already inconvenienced, to a genuinely disturbing situation that might easily have become dangerous.

An ugly thought enters my head: *What if the disgruntled, neck-tatted dude had charged into the lobby with a gun? What if he'd taken hostages?* I hear the sound of bare feet slapping rapidly on wet cement, followed by a huge splash. Startled, I open my eyes to see the brother of the siblings coming to the water's choppy surface. He's wiping chlorinated water out of his eyes, eager to see if the spray from his cannonball has done its job of drenching the unwary, grey-bearded man on the chaise lounge.

"Did I get you wet?" the boy asks, breathlessly.

A little bit, I tell him.

"I'm sorry," he says, with an impish grin, as if he hadn't meant to splash me at all. Then, the punky little mischief-maker fish flops and swims away to resume dunking his sister.

By the time I've folded my laundry and washed down a sandpaper-dry sandwich with cold beer, I'm shot. But when I turn off the tube, I realize how noisy it is. TVs from other rooms; the coughing and wheezing of the woman in the handicapped room next door;

a man baby-talking to a dog; the dog barking, then whimpering. As bone-tired as I am, I wonder if I'll be able to sleep.

The answer comes quickly. The answer is yes.

CHAPTER 24

Mendocino County Layer Cake

JUNE 21 · DAY FIFTY-TWO

"This looks good. Let's pull over here."

I resist even a brief, leftward glance at the beautiful woman at the wheel. If our eyes should meet, tears will flow. As the turn signal pings, Sebra glides her periwinkle-blue hybrid Toyota Highlander off the road and slows to a stop on the shoulder of California Highway 1.

We've shoved this moment into the near future for as long as possible. Now, after three long-awaited days and nights together, that near future has arrived. Saying goodbye has always been hard for my lady and me, living 100 miles apart as we do. Back in Oregon, whenever we can, we'll spend a weekend sharing space, being a couple, only to be yanked apart by the demands of our separate lives. The emotional dynamics in a long-distance relationship are tough.

Up until 72 hours ago, we hadn't looked into one another's eyes, touched one another, laughed together, or shared meals and a bed for what felt like a lifetime — nearly eight interminable weeks. While I was out here trekking a daunting 450 California miles, pushing my body to the limit, alternatively enduring intense solitude, then connecting just as intensely with old friends and new, Sebra was holding down her own fort, dealing with her business, her family, doing a lone physical/emotional balancing act, while continuing to recover from injuries suffered in the serious auto accident she'd had just before the New Year. Our two nights hiding away in a converted backyard-garage Airbnb in Ukiah was emotional comfort food.

*"I'm experiencing this very odd feel-
ing. I think it might be happiness."*

— ALAN ARKIN, AS "AL" IN *GOING IN STYLE*

I'm wearing a new accoutrement. My lady and I spent an entire
afternoon scouring the shops of Ukiah for the perfect chapeau for
a summertime trek: a hat to shield my face, ears, and neck from
UV exposure, while also allowing my overheated pate to breathe.
We ended up driving 17 miles south to the Real Goods Store in
Hopland to find this ever-so-cool straw cowboy hat. To make the
score even sweeter, my lady insisted on making it her gift. "It makes
you look more friendly," she observes, "but, at the same time, like
a guy you don't want to mess with, somebody who can take care
of himself." I've always wanted a hat just like this. I *love* it.

This farewell embrace, standing on the shoulder of the Pacific
Coast Highway, is neither bitter nor sweet. It just hurts like hell. I
muster the fortitude to extricate myself from her, turn away, push
my cart across the two-lane road, and begin trekking northward.
I hear her car door shut behind me. I'm pretty sure that, like me,
she is crying.

For the next five days, the temperature east of the Coast Range
is expected to climb as high as 107. Here, the forecast is breezy, in
the high sixties. That's why, at least for this stretch, I'll be traipsing
along the coastline of Mendocino County.

This part of California is one of my favorite places on Earth.
Here, the highway weaves along cliff sides that plunge directly
down to the vast, roiling Pacific Ocean. The views are spectacular and the experience is humbling. A pilgrim can't help but feel
miniscule, insignificant, in awe of the massiveness of everything.
After an hour, the dramatic cliffs of Mendocino come into view,
topped with the toy-like village perched high above the sea. The
Pacific glimmers like pirate's booty in the sunlight, its foam-topped
waves crashing onto jagged stone and rolling onto khaki-colored
sand. It's a holographic vision out of a fantasy book, almost unreal.

Soon, I'm rolling the Pilgrimmobile into this picturesque
colony, flashing back to my high-school graduation year — 1967,

the "Summer of Love." A dozen hippies congregate in a park area
by the bluff, clad in loose-fitting hemp-cloth, draw-string trousers,
tie-dyed T-shirts, flowing skirts, and sandals. Acoustic guitars, hand
drums, tambourines, and lifted voices resound. The unmistakable
aromatic blend of cannabis smoke and sandalwood incense wafts
in the cool, salty breeze. The hippie jammers send me bloodshot,
squint-eyed smiles, waves, and peace signs. Artisans line the sidewalk, displaying photo prints, paintings, baskets, macramé, and
handcrafted jewelry. They banter among themselves with collegial
familiarity, while keeping eyes peeled for the next tourist with a
spare dollar to spend.

As romantic a notion as busking is, in my half-century as a
performing musician, I've never actually done it. As a longtime
professional, I prefer a stage, a proper introduction and, ideally,
a focused, captive audience. I give Sebra credit for opening my
mind to the possibility of such an experience. She simply doesn't
understand why I'd want to keep my musical gifts to myself. "Just
take out your guitar and start playing," she says, "and everyone
will love you." Presently, I'm somewhat at loose ends, with no set
distance goal for the day, or even a specific destination. On this
trip, with my lady's loving encouragement ringing in my head, I've
been eager for any chance to share my music and my message. It's
a beautiful day. This looks like an ideal opportunity to give street
performing a shot.

I park my cart next to an affable, chatty purveyor of polished
stones and petrified rock. I set up my music stand and lay my
guitar case on the sidewalk to collect tips, alongside some CDs
to sell. Timidly, I begin some instrumental improvisation. There's
the occasional, random smile from a passing tourist. But no one
stops to listen. I get bolder and break into my "One Love/People
Get Ready" medley.

One longhaired fellow plops down on the bus bench across the
road, listening intently, nodding his head, tapping his foot. After

20 minutes or so, the longhaired fellow traipses across the street and drops a dollar bill into my guitar case. "Cool stuff, man," he says. I thank him. He shuffles on. Now, I've lost my audience of one. A few more tunes later, a clean-cut, elderly gentleman drops a second dollar in my case. I'm beginning to feel hungry. I pack up my gear with two more greenbacks in my pocket than I had when I started picking my axe some 90 minutes ago. I conquered my fear of street performing, had myself a cathartic little solo jam, and the street merchants seemed to appreciate it.

As I bump the Pilgrimmobile down the sidewalk, I hear the sound of a slide acoustic guitar and a bluesy harmonica. A musician, sitting on the curb, is improvising, making it up as he goes along. As I get closer, I recognize the fellow. It's the toe-tapping longhair, my audience of one, who dropped the first dollar bill in my guitar case. As I pass, I pull my two busking bucks from my pocket and deposit both in his tip jar, which is already filling up. We make eye contact and exchange nods. My expression is one of camaraderie and respect, a wordless admission that, when it comes to pickin' 'n' grinnin' on the street, I'm the dilettante. He is the pro.

JUNE 22 · DAY FIFTY-THREE

Sock never walks. He runs. And he clomps when he runs. And he smiles as he clomps as he runs. Grizzly barks at everything — any discernible sound, a slightly shifting shadow, even a flashlight beam. Sock, a strapping young dude from Moab, Utah, is broad-shouldered, fair-haired, and rustically handsome. He sheaths his long, slender legs in synthetic-fabric pants that fit so snuggly, it is evident that he is indeed circumcised. He prefers to keep the size of his ears and the length of his hair a mystery, however, by pulling a tight, knitted cap down over his skull. Sock, Michaela, and their large, shaggy, clumsy, constantly drooling golden retriever have been my overnight next-door neighbors here at Caspar Beach.

As he did while setting up their campsite last evening, Sock traverses the pathway to and from the parking lot as if he's vying to win TV's *The Amazing Race*, his arms loaded with gear and/or supplies on each pass. Meanwhile, Grizzly remains tethered to the leg of a picnic table sending out deep-throated roars to the unseen world.

Michaela, considerably less kinetic than her boyfriend and a great deal quieter than her dog, radiates a peaceful countenance, while bearing an earthy beauty. During their move-in last evening, Michaela stopped to chat, expressing sincere interest in my pilgrimage. Walking the Appalachian Trail, more than 500 miles, has gained her intimate familiarity with long-distance hiking. Presently, the quirky little family unit is mid-adventure, rolling along the coast without a plan, going wherever their hearts lead them. Next stop? Maybe San Francisco. They'll see.

Even in a little town like Mojab, Sock informed me, in the ultra-conservative state of Utah, a lot of people are troubled about the direction our nation has been taking. The environment and climate change are of special concern. Again, it was reassuring to be reminded that not all Utahns are stridently right-wing — or Mormon, for that matter.

Although I would have much preferred more privacy to get some real writing done, the only place on the camp-store porch, out of the late-afternoon sun's glare was not remotely isolated. At a nearby table, a woman had spread out an array of clothing and shoes — for sale. Forty-ish, I estimated, and still undeniably attractive, even after what must have been some hard living, she snuck a swig from a liter bottle of Miller High Life. Then, without provocation, she proceeded to share the details of her circumstance. In a rasp confessing of a million cigarettes, Cata explained that she's "getting rid of stuff," preparing "to travel light." After losing her house, she's returned to her hometown of Caspar Beach and finds herself living hand-to-mouth, temporarily ensconced in a poached spot on the above hillside. After spending a couple of nights in a legitimate site, she could no longer afford the daily fee. "Really nice place," she told me. "You're gonna enjoy it."

Anita, the friendly, zaftig, dark-haired lady who had earlier checked me into Tent Site G, emerged from the store. She and Cata engaged in casual, familiar banter, while Anita browsed the merchandise. A pair of shoes caught Anita's fancy and the two women quickly bartered a mutually acceptable exchange — which included Cata receiving another liter bottle of Miller High Life.

Amazingly, Cata never stopped smiling. It was a smile of defiance, an unspoken declaration that... *Life's a bitch! But it ain't gonna beat me!* Still, in everything she said, her facial expressions, and how she moved, there was a suggestive, somewhat desperate hint of seduction. This impulse was even more evident when a younger man arrived on the scene. Cata sprang to her bare feet and intercepted the unwary fellow before he could enter the store, to ask coyly if she could bum a smoke. The cigarette seemed less important than her flagrant attempt to attract a potentially available man's attention.

Here, I couldn't help but suspect, was a woman accustomed to using her feminine wiles for self-preservation. Most likely she's always been able to find a guy willing to foot the bill, to put a roof over her head, and provide her with the quick fixes that eventually mount up to a life squandered in a series of pleasurable short-term distractions. Now, with her once milky-smooth skin beginning to wrinkle and her previously nubile body giving way to gravity, the only native resource she can call upon is that killer smile — and the last remnants of a table-top flea market.

After hastily packing up her remaining inventory in a cardboard box, Cata placed what sounded like an obligatory reporting-in call to her father. Pacing the porch deck like a convicted felon awaiting sentencing, she puffed manically on her bummed cig. It was evident that the wayward daughter was having to swallow some tough love from Daddy. Although I got the impression that Cata could easily have erupted into rage, she kept a lid on it, while putting on a show of cheerful optimism for the old man's benefit.

After terminating this stressful exchange, she tromped down the stairs and around the building. Then, she abruptly reappeared, marched back up the stairs, and snuffed out her cigarette in a proper ashtray. There was a second false departure, then a third. All the while, her expression remained fixed in that never-say-die smile. Finally, Cata was gone, and the absence of her smoldering energy left me in the fading glare of a summer-solstice sun, feeling chilled.

Imagine a 20-mile-long, five-tiered, earthen wedding cake on the edge of the Pacific, a section of the Northern California Coast, baked, frosted, and decorated over the millennia by wave action, fluctuating sea level, and tectonic shift. The base tier, the beach, is being stirred, shaped, and re-shaped in the present tense. The second tier, the soil, a mere 100,000 years old, remains rich in nutrients, ideal for tall, prairie grasses to thrive. The soil on the third plateau is yet another 100,000 years depleted, which makes a perfect environment for tall, coastal redwoods. Finally, we have the top three tiers, where millions of seasons have sapped the soil so completely that the cypresses and pines growing here have literally been starved and stunted. This is Jug Handle Creek State Reserve, the location of the world's largest pygmy forest ecological staircase.

I'm sitting at a picnic table in the shade, laying out my midday meal: a day-old, pre-prepared, cellophane-wrapped sandwich from the Caspar Beach camp store, what's left of a bag of barbecue-flavored Fritos, and a bottle of lukewarm tea. Meanwhile, two women and three kids have commandeered the adjacent table — all dressed as if they've just been beamed in from previous eras. One woman, thin, diminutive, with a wild bush of greying, wavy hair, is 100% hippie, clad in loose-fitting, cotton pantaloons, a tie-dyed T-shirt, and a floppy, broad-brimmed hat. The other, tall, shapely, dark-haired, perhaps a decade younger, is draped in a skin-hugging, brown, sarong-like dress. The children, three girls, eight, nine, 10-ish, wear identical, ankle-length, cotton dresses. They could be on lunch break from shooting a redux of *Little House on the Prairie*.

The women have immersed themselves in an intense confab about their dietary habits. The petite, floppy-hatted one speaks with a slight English accent. One of the children slips away from the table to do some tightrope walking on the top rail of a wooden fence. As she is a full four feet above the ground, a misstep could easily lead to a cracked skull, and/or a broken arm. I'm wondering if I should say something, when, while barely looking up, the English-accented woman calls out, "Don't you want to finish your kefir?" Although she asks again — twice, in fact — the little acrobat continues her gravity-defying routine, totally disregarding the repeated question.

At this point, no doubt encouraged by the first girl's expression of independence, the two others bolt from the table and skitter toward a pile of large boulders at the edge of the parking lot. After quickly clamoring to the top, they proceed to leap to and fro like Olympic gymnasts, performing a spontaneous floor-exercise routine eight feet above the gravel. Without demonstrating any discernible level of concern, Floppy-Hat Woman asks, "Do you want to go with Marcella to the beach while I finish my lunch?" *Bingo!* To my relief, this query receives a response, and a cooperative one at that. A few, expertly chosen words from a cool, calm, unflappable mom, and potential disaster has been averted. The prairie-girl trio traipses gaily down the trail into the pygmy forest, accompanied by the tall woman in the snug, brown sarong.

The floppy-hatted mother's name is Samantha. She lives south of here in Albion. In telling her about my pilgrimage, I reveal my age. "Sixty-seven is nothing," she remarks. "My trapeze instructor is seventy-one!"

Hearing "trapeze," I muse about the circus act the girls had been performing earlier.

"Oh, yeah," Samantha notes. "I think Mendocino County has more circus performers than anywhere. Everybody's into it, the parents *and* the kids. It's just something people around here do."

I've just handed Samantha my postcard, when a panting, perspiring bicyclist pushes his two-wheeler between our tables. Without waiting for a cue, the fellow delves into stream-of-consciousness blathering. He resides in Oakland, he overshares, but he's seriously considering giving up his place for a year to travel via bicycle. These, I figure, are the private visions he's been seeing in an endorphin-ized brain while pedaling alone, hour after solitary hour. He's giving his heretofore silent ruminations a test run, making an imagined future a little more real, by telling someone about it. Unwittingly, simply by virtue of being at this place at this moment, the hippie mom on the flying trapeze and the peace pilgrim have become the sounding board for an absolute stranger's fantasy plans.

"Well," Samantha informs the cyclist, "this man is walking." It's as if she's boasting about having met me first.

"You're walking?" he wants to know.

"The coast," Samantha clarifies on my behalf. As she begs off and slips down the trail to join her party, I realize that she wasn't boasting at all. She was slyly directing the obviously self-possessed fellow's attention to me so she could make a quick escape. Modern moms are very clever, indeed.

"About four-hundred-sixty miles so far," I hear myself tell the bicyclist. Now, it seems I'm the one who needs to hear my own words spoken out loud to make the thoughts in my head more real. Sometimes it's not all that easy to convince myself that I've trekked such a distance. The cyclist begins peppering me with questions, like a kindergartener who wants to know why rain is wet. Unfortunately, he has the attention span of a two-year-old and keeps interrupting me midsentence to tell me why he thinks we have so very much in common.

Our presumed fraternal bond hits maximum intensity when I inform him that I'm a songwriter.

"Are you kidding me?" he exudes. "*I'm* a songwriter!" To be clear, he *was* a school teacher but, since retiring from the classroom, he's been pursuing the singer/songwriter thing. When he talks about "selling his songs," it becomes clear that this fellow actually knows little or nothing about the music business. I can't help but wax pedantically with some *how-to's* and *what-to-avoids*. He responds to every piece of advice I hand out with one version or another of "Oh, yeah, I know. I'm already doing that." He is, after all, being produced by a guy who used to be in the Electric Prunes. Through Facebook, he's made some connections in Germany and is waiting to hear back about booking an opening slot on Bob Dylan's next European tour. Hopefully, he has the thick skin required for show business survival. I give him one of my CDs. We take a selfie. I wish him every success and fulfillment in his creative pursuits, and push on.

You'd assume the streets of a town called Fort Bragg would be lined with big pickup trucks. And, you'd be right. However, for the first time on my journey, there are also beaters on the road — dented, rusty cars with cracked windshields, duct-taped bumpers, and sagging tailpipes. It appears that the down and out 'round these parts are predominately white and relatively young. One such young man, wobbling up the street on a big-tired bicycle, holds a loaf of bread like a tailback carrying a football. A small, unwashed fellow with dreadlocks picks up something off the side-walk, examines it, then tosses it aside. Through the loudspeaker of a passing police car, an officer orders him to, "Pick it up!" The unwashed man keeps his natty head down, ignoring the cop for a few strides. Then, he abruptly stops, turns around, waves mockingly at the police cruiser, and trudges on.

Earlier, I was pleased when a local minister and his wife, friends of a friend — not naming names here — extended an offer for me to pitch my tent in their backyard and join them for dinner. However, the invite came too late for me to cancel my motel res-ervation. I might as well sleep in the bed I'm paying $75 for, and take a shower. Meanwhile, perhaps the dinner offer remains on the table. It would be great to visit with a local family. And, a pilgrim seldom passes up a free meal.

The owner of the Ebb Tide Motel, a septuagenarian of East Indian descent, informs me that he moved to the states from Fiji four years ago, ultimately landing here in Fort Bragg, after stop-overs in Florida and Kansas. "Kansas?" I tease. "Why would you ever want to live in Kansas?"

"When you need work, you'll go anywhere," he answers. Unfor-tunately, the motel has no more ground-floor rooms available. This means dissembling the Pilgrimmobile and hoisting the heavy box up a flight of stairs. To help me in this task, the man at the desk enlists his nephew, who seems pleased to take a break from making beds to lend a hand.

I call the local family, not at all surprised to hear the high-pitched, syrupy-sweet tone of a preacher's wife. I explain that I was unable to cancel my room without being charged. "I'm at the ever-so lovely Ebb Tide Motel," I inform her. There is a brief, uncomfortable pause. I feel the need to fill the silence with a not-so-subtle hint that I'm still open for dinner: "I'd really like to meet you guys." Either she's not following my verbal breadcrumbs, or she's avoiding the subject altogether.

"You know what," she suggests, "while you're in the area, you should check out the new walking trails by the coast. I hear they're really lovely" — as if, after trekking 15 miles on pavement, the first thing I want to do is run right out and take a hike. There is yet another uncomfortable lull.

It's becoming clear that she has no plans to follow through with the dinner offer. So, I reach out with another request: "If you know anyone between here and Leggett who might want to give a pilgrim a place to rest, I'd appreciate you making the connection."

"Hmmm," she muses, "Pretty much everybody we know lives south of here." Maybe, I suggest, if she thinks about it, someone might occur to her. Then, she whips out the perfect, convenient Christian cop out to rid herself of any further potential commitment or involvement: "Well, I can't help you there," she bubbles. "But, I'll tell you what. I'm just going to pray that God takes good care of you and He provides you with exactly what you need."

And, with that, she's washed her hands of me altogether with a clean conscience. As I disconnect the call, I'm absolutely certain that, as soon as the Man Upstairs hears this good, sweet, Christian woman's promised supplication, a certain pilgrim's well-being will leap right to the top of His list of concerns. (Sarcasm fully intentional.)

CHAPTER 25

Blue Whale on Wheel

JUNE 23 · DAY FIFTY-FOUR

I knew today's trek — 17-plus miles from Fort Bragg to the campground at Westport — would be a trial. The jaunt began on smooth blacktop with wide bike lanes. Now, it's rough and uneven, with no shoulder at all. For some stretches, even the painted white line at the pavement's edge has eroded away.

I'm trucking up a steep grade on a serpentine, cliff-side segment of road, when a light-blue Prius pulls past, abruptly slows to a crawl, before vanishing around the next bend. A minute later, the same vehicle reappears, now traveling in the opposite direction, and stops in the middle of the southbound lane. The woman at the wheel, blond, probably in her fifties, rolls down her window. "Wow!" she exclaims, wide eyes focused on the *Peace Pilgrim 2017* banner wrapped around my cart, "I read the original book."

Yes, I tell her, I was inspired by the author of that book, the woman called Peace Pilgrim. Seemingly at a loss for words, the blond woman presses her hands together in a praying gesture, directs a reverent, Buddhist-monk head-nod in my direction, then drives on. A few minutes later, the same vehicle shows up for a third time having resumed its original northern trajectory. "Trader Joe's should sponsor you!" the blond woman jokes. She's referring to the colorful, vinyl Trader Joe's shopping bags, dangling from each side of the Pilgrimmobile. As she snaps a quick photo, I notice kids in the backseat — grandchildren, I'm guessing. Then she disappears around the bend again, for the last time.

Periodically, earth slides have reduced the road to a single lane. As northbound cars, SUVs, trucks, buses, and RVs slither cautiously through a concrete-barricaded, one-lane corridor, a cue of vehicles waiting to squeeze through in the southward direction grows longer. Meanwhile, hard-hatted construction workers and heavy equipment operators toil cacophonously in the dust, attempting to sculpt some kind of functional roadway out of this fickle, untrustworthy hunk of dirt and rock. A cart-pushing pilgrim is both a source of curiosity and an annoyance to the impatient drivers navigating through these inconvenient, mandatory slowdowns. Their vehicles, in turn, provide an entirely unwanted source of noise, dust, and noxious fumes for me. No friendly waves or peace signs here. We're all concentrating on one task: making it through the maze without suffering dents and scratches.

It's two-lane road again. I'm laboring up a steep, vertical slope against traffic on the ocean side. As the summer travel season is now earnestly underway, I've identified a new nemesis. They used to call them motor homes, or — consistent with how the brand name Kleenex became common parlance for facial tissue — Winnebagos. At some point, for some inexplicable reason (perhaps to make these road-hogging monstrosities sound more fun) motor homes were re-tagged as "recreational vehicles."

From my vantage point, I fail to see anything whatsoever "recreational" about the vehicle looming in the lane ahead. It looks like someone put four tires on Moby Dick. The white-haired gentleman staring down at me from the captain's chair of this aircraft carrier on wheels — the fellow is 80 if he's a day — appears to be even more frightened than I am at this moment, and clueless, as if he's just been jarred awake from a peaceful, two-hour afternoon nap, only to realize that his house is on fire.

It's a David-and-Goliath standoff. This road ain't big enough for him alone. I'm already squeezing myself and my cart as close as possible to the waist-high guardrail. Slipping that monstrosity past me without making some contact would be a feat worthy of Hans Solo in his prime — which, incidentally, perhaps even coincidentally, was 40 years ago. And, any contact whatsoever with a moving force of this size and weight, could easily send me, at a mere 160 pounds, over the rail, plummeting down 150 feet of vertical, rocky cliff to certain death.

As the blue whale on wheels begins rolling ever-so-slowly down the narrow incline, my alarm increases. Someone — guess *who* — has forgotten to retract the motor home's side stairs! Having not been gifted with the ability to levitate, I am left with no other choice but to hang on for dear life, hoping against hope for the best possible outcome. With my heart throbbing in my throat, I murmur an affirmation: "I am strong; I am loving; I have nothing to fear." *Hallelujah!* The front section of the motor home slips past, clearing my cart by six inches. "God is within me," I affirm. "I am within God." Miraculously, the un-retracted stairs miss the stroller's right rear tricycle wheel by an inch. *Maybe I'm home free!* But, no. The side panel of the RV starts scraping and dragging against my Trader Joe's supply bag, lifting the Pilgrimmobile up off of its right wheel, tilting the cart toward the guard rail. I'm tugging at the bag in a belated attempt to make space. But the stuffed sack is now so firmly wedged between the RV and the side of the storage box that my effort goes for naught.

I clench my eyes closed, anticipating the worst. For several more everlasting seconds, all my senses perceive is the grating sound of fiberglass dragging against vinyl. I'm summoning every desperate morsel of strength, gripping the stroller handle. Still, the Pilgrimmobile lurches, teetering another inch closer to the guard-rail. Then, all of a sudden, the scraping stops and the stroller frame springs back onto all three wheels. With my ears now drinking in the familiar, soothing white noise of surf pounding the rocks below, I open my eyes. *I'm in the clear!*

"Thank you, thank you, thank you, God," I expound, "for all the wonderful blessings of this life." If I weren't still leaning my body weight against the handle of this heavy cart to prevent it from running and tumbling away, I would kick up my heels and dance a jig to the audible beat of my own elated, still-pounding heart.

JUNE 24 · DAY FIFTY-FIVE

Greg calls his wife Grandma. They, along with two very active, pre-adolescent grandsons, are my next-door neighbors at the West-port Beach RV Park and Campground. Greg is a large, burly fellow, unguarded, and gregarious. Grandma seems demure, less forth-coming. I wonder if he calls her Grandma when the grandkids aren't around. Regardless, as far as grandmas go, she's a good one. I can tell by the way she relates to the boys — gently, but firmly, respectfully, but always maintaining authority. Those kids mind their grandma, without whining or complaint. And, they adore Grampa. At least five times last night, I heard a boy's lugubrious, soprano voice call out from within the camper next door, "I love you, Grampa."

"I love you, too," Greg responded every time. "G'night. Now, go to sleep."

Greg and Grandma reside in Brandscome, California, near Laytonville. Brandscome used to be a saw-milling town. Now, it's not much of a town at all. Greg tells me they moved from Santa Rosa some years back. "Too big," he says. Now, they live off the grid, procuring their water from the creek that flows past their cabin. That same, swift current also provides a primary source of electric-ity — via a portable hydropower generator the size of an orange crate. Supplemented by three solar panels, Greg says the mini-gen-erator cranks out more juice than they'll ever need — which isn't much — to light the place and listen to local news and San Fran-cisco Giants games on the radio. They don't have a TV. "Every time I go to my Mom's in Santa Rosa and watch the news," Greg remarks, "it's all bad. Gets me down."

"The media feeds on conflict," I observe. "Anything that divides us." I tell him my pilgrimage was originally inspired by my own dismay after the election.

Last November, Greg left his presidential pick blank. "I voted on every other thing on the ballot," he confides, shaking his head in bewilderment. "But I couldn't vote for either o' those people. First time since I was eighteen that I didn't vote for president."

"Too bad those were the choices we got," I commiserate.

"Yep," Greg agrees. "The good one faded away." Then, he finally lays his cards on the table: "If Bernie would-a got the nomination, I think he might-a won."

I'm locking up my storage box when a woman strolls by, leading her Bijon Frise. With her shoulder-length, dyed-purple hair and chic, black-knit dress, she seems more appropriately dressed for window shopping at an upscale mall, than a campground dog walk. The woman stops and gazes at the Pilgrimmobile through squinted eyes. "So, you're walking?" she asks. Heidi, 50-ish I'm guessing, is a rep for an essential oils company. Hearing that I'm a musician, she informs me that her 10-year-old son, Jake, is a drummer.

"Every mother's worst nightmare," I josh, painfully aware of how much racket a kid can make with a kit of drums.

Heidi explains that young Jake's passion for percussion, as noisy is it gets sometimes, is actually a blessing. "He's on the spectrum," she informs me.

I immediately understand what she's saying. Drumming helps the boy make sense of things and connects him with the world around him. It's a means of non-verbal, yet-direct communication with his peers. Recently, she recounts, he performed at a school talent show. After pounding out time to ACDC's "Back in Black," there wasn't a dry eye in the auditorium. "You know what he told me afterwards?" she asks, wistfully. "He said, 'I've got some fans, Mom.'"

I'm sitting in my Monarch Chair, glomming what's left of the chicken wrap I purchased yesterday morning in Fort Bragg. Even though my lunch is a day old, it tastes especially delicious. The view from this vista point, however, could never get stale. Nature's display is as spectacular today as I'm sure it's been every day for a million years. Up to and over the curvature of the globe, the vast, unfathomable, azure, white-capped Pacific Ocean glimmers in the unhindered radiance of an early-summer sun. The ever-persistent surf exploding on the rocks a dozen stories below sends spritzes of salty mist floating up on gentle breezes to cool my face. This, I decide, is an excellent time to shoot a commemorative video. While necessity makes me both cinematographer and director, the real star is the Mendocino County coastline. The grinning, grey-bearded fellow in the straw cowboy hat is only making a cameo appearance.

"So, here I am," I begin in close-up, "having a celebratory lunch. The occasion? I've just achieved my five-hundredth mile." The pilgrim in the minute-long clip comes off as jolly and relaxed, even a bit cocky. He finishes off his brief report by bursting into the raspy "Ba-da-da-tah" refrain from the Proclaimers' song, "I'm Gonna Be," then signs off with a convivial, "Peace out."

As I push the Pilgrimmobile toward the highway to resume today's travels, my mind flashes back to Trek week one when, on a coastal bike path in Ventura County, Millie and I encountered the woman named Pat, walking in remembrance of her mother's fatal breast cancer. That Pat and her companion had covered more than 500 miles seemed unreal, almost incomprehensible. And now, by taking one step at a time, day-by-day-by-day, I've managed to pull off an equivalent feat.

A van bumps up in a cloud of dust and skids to a halt. The smiling, ponytailed young driver leans out the window. "How far are you walking?" he inquires. Oregon, I tell him. He informs me that he's driven all the way from Manitoba, well over 2,000 miles. Adventurers always seem to want to share their adventures with other adventurers. "You'll make it," he declares, giving me a salute of encouragement, before pulling back out onto the highway.

As well-meaning as Ponytail's words are, I find his statement odd. It's something a coach would say, while sending his back-up quarterback out onto the gridiron with a brisk pat on the butt to toss a desperate, last-second Hail Mary. While I welcome the positive reassurance, the fact that this sojourner from Canada feels the spontaneous inclination to say those particular words to a traveling stranger suddenly plants a seed of doubt in my mind. *What does he know that I don't know? How can he make such a definitive promise?* Only a minute ago, I was feeling buoyed by a sense of certitude. Now, I'm worried, wondering if I actually *can* make it.

⊕   ⊕   ⊕   ⊕   ⊕

In a matter of a couple of hours, it's as if that little seed of doubt has germinated, taken root, and sprung forth in the form of a tangled sticker bush of uncertainty. My worries are literally manifesting in reality. The highway has turned east, away from the ocean. Two extremely tight lanes curl their way up, up, and up some more, under a thick forest of towering evergreens. The grade is so severe, so uninterrupted, I have to stop frequently to catch my breath.

Over the course of my journey, I've developed a critical survival skill: the ability to hear tires on pavement from a distance away. This enhanced auditory sense is particularly important in a circumstance like this because, with the constant curvature of the road, it's beneficial to cross the highway frequently to provide optimum sight lines to approaching motorists. Presumably, the sun still blazes above the trees. But shade from the dense forest cover puts the road in permanent twilight, severely limiting visibility. I may not be able to see vehicles coming from either direction. However, I can always hear them, which helps me get to where *they* can best see *me*.

This climb is one of the most arduous tests of my trek thus far. Here I am, alone in the wilderness. Cell service is sporadic and weak. Impatient drivers often glare at me and make gestures that ask, *What the hell are you doing?* Even though the breeze is cool and damp, I'm drenched in sweat. Still, I have no other option but to keep my head down and push on against gravity.

Periodically, large signs are posted in the trees, clearly visible from the road. *Private Property. No Trespassing.* Can all of this land, so abundant with primordial forest and natural habitat, actually be owned by private interests? I come upon another sign displayed on a tree, this one not posted by a corporate property owner. Wrapped in protective plastic is the sad, faded picture of a missing man, last seen some months ago in a nearby town. Accompanying information indicates that he has mental problems and is dependent on medication. *What if I were to wander from the beaten path into the uncharted jungle? Supposing I got myself hopelessly lost? How many days would it take for someone to notice that, like the unfortunate, mentally challenged man in the photo, I was unaccounted for? Then, how long would it take for me to be found? Or, would I ever be found at all?* A shiver races up my spine at this macabre speculation.

Finally, after plodding three unforgiving, uphill miles, I reach the summit. Now, the really painful part begins. The downgrade is as severe as the trip up and the going equally as slow. With my tender toes jamming into the ends of my shoes and my knees throbbing with each stride, I make sure to keep my feet flat, firmly on the ground. Should the Pilgrimmobile get moving just a little too fast and the stroller wheels gain enough momentum, control could easily be lost.

I'm approaching yet another blind curve. For sight lines, it would be wise to cross to the opposite side of the road. Although I detect the sound of an internal combustion engine, my finely tuned aural radar gauges the approaching vehicle to be a safe distance away. There should be plenty of time to cross. I begin steering the Pilgrimmobile out across the blacktop. As I reach the center line of the road, the revving of eight muscular cylinders roars like the MGM lion in Dolby Surround Sound. I look over my shoulder, startled to see a shiny, metallic-blue Chevy Camaro screeching around the bend, fishtailing in my direction at Grand-Prix speed.

Certainly, the pilot of this rocket must be as surprised to see a cart-pushing pilgrim in the middle of the highway as I am to suddenly find myself in the direct path of a speeding street racer. My natural survival response is to shift my pace into overdrive and apply every muscle in my body to scrambling forward. In this rare instance, gravity is my ally, providing me just enough extra speed and momentum to reach the shoulder a split second before the Camaro rips past. Through tinted windows, I think I see a Jeff

Gordon wannabe, with bugged saucer eyes and jaw agape. But maybe that's just my imagination.

Although there are dots on the map with names, no town ever seems to materialize. At the bottom of the grade, I arrive at one such dot: Rockport. There's a road intersecting the highway next to a bridge over a large creek. No structures, however, are visible. Although I've walked only 10 miles today, every single one proved especially grueling. This, I decide, is as far as my pained feet will take me. It's closing in on five. Hopefully, my ride will be here within a half hour. I assemble my Monarch Chair and sit by the bridge to wait.

A man in a four-wheeler loaded with supplies comes tooling out of the side road. He stops momentarily, then pulls out, crossing the highway. Other than a brief side glance, he pays me no mind. An SUV turns off the highway, and stops directly in front of me. The passenger window rolls down. I'm prepared to tell the nice, concerned folks within that I'm okay, that somebody is on their way to pick me up.

"Hi, Babe."

It's Sebra's voice. That's how fatigued I am. The light is so strange, I failed to recognize my lady's vehicle.

As we enter the lobby, I wonder if the motelier is operating a consignment store to supplement his income. On closer examination, it's more likely that he's taking inventory for an everything-must-go, going-out-of-business sale. The floor, every bench, chair, and countertop is strewn with random items — industrial grade coffee makers, toasters, juice dispensers, cereal bins, and empty display cases. Treadmills and stair climbers recline on couches. Then, inexplicably, right in the center of Ye Olde Junque Mart, there is a Christmas tree, dead, dry, and drooping, almost six months to the day since it would have served as appropriate holiday decor.

It's approaching 8PM, presumably prime hour for walk-in business. Yet, no one mans the front desk of the Travel Inn in Fortuna, California. I ring the bell. No response. I ring again. "Hello," I call out, "anybody here?" Finally, a figure shuffles drowsily out from a back room, scratching himself. Brown-skinned, bald-headed, and barefoot, his soiled T-shirt drapes almost to his knees, tarping a slight torso and pencil-thin arms. To call this man gaunt would put extra pounds on his frame. He looks like Mahatma Gandhi broke a 60-day fast with a three-day bender.

A grunted greeting invites me to identify myself, which sends the disheveled, half-awake fellow to locate a stack of printed sheets of paper. He shuffles through the pile several times, finally located my reservation. He asks me something in an accent — Indian? Pakistani? — that seems unusually thick and heavy. Or, maybe his dentures are slipping. Every step of the check-in process is executed old-school, hand-written on paper. My mounting impatience makes me aware of how accustomed we've become to the expedition provided us by computers. Only 25 years ago, this paperwork routine would have been just that: routine. Now, it feels like an absolute waste of time, not to mention paper.

At last, my lady and I exit the motel office, receipt and room key in hand. And, as we have in so many other less-than-perfect situations, we share chuckles over this bizarre happenstance. Relieved to find our room satisfactory and clean, we make a Safeway run for fresh fruit and yogurt for breakfast. Upon returning, I open the mini-fridge to discover that it's stuffed with plastic jugs of milk, cream, and drinkable yogurt. Not a cubic inch is available for our use.

Back in the lobby, re-arousing our slovenly, sleepy-eyed hotelier takes another bell ring and call-out. I inform him that someone, perhaps the previous occupant, has left an entire stock of dairy products in our fridge. *But, oh no!* The vessels belong to the proprietor himself. His fridge, he explains, is on the fritz. So, of course, he's using ours. He appears puzzled that I'm not the least bit cool with this arrangement, and seems equally perplexed that people who are forking out top dollar for a room have need for refrigeration at all. Somewhat petulantly, he follows me to the room where

I help him remove his moo-juice from our fridge.

Meanwhile, Sebra is drawing a bath. And, although she has kept the spigot running wide open for a full five minutes, the tap is not yielding a drop of hot water. This sends me on yet another trip to the lobby to alert the hapless manager. Keep running the water, he tells me, and it will eventually heat up.

When I explain that we've done that already, he locates a huge crescent wrench. I follow him to the furnace room, where he bangs around, making a huge clamor, then grumbles something about calling a plumber. By the time I get back to the room, Sebra is slipping into the tub. While it took 15 minutes for heated liquid to make its Amazon-long journey through the pipes, it did finally reach our tub after all. I have to admit that the proprietor was right about something.

As I undress to join her in the bath, a new irritant commences: the sound of a revving engine and tires screeching on pavement. I look out through the bathroom window to see the source of the noise: a car spinning donuts in the empty parking lot next door. As the delinquent driver continues to get his jollies, the aroma of burnt rubber wafts through the open window, and I slide into the steamy water with Sebra to share some healthy, cleansing guffaws.

CHAPTER 26

Moral Relativity

JUNE 25 · DAY FIFTY-SIX

The weather during today's 14-mile trek from Loleta to Eureka was typical of Humboldt County — overcast, damp, and chilly. This made walking the first few miles of scenic, pastoral, rural lanes invigorating. At one juncture, I was relieving my bladder behind a bulldozed pile of tree stumps, roots, and dirt when I heard a sudden and surprising crash. I peeked around the mound, alarmed to see the Pilgrimmobile tipped over, the fiberglass storage box dislodged from the stroller base and rolling out onto the road. Zipping up on the run, I jogged to the wreckage, spouting some choice expletives to no one in particular. Fortunately, the only fatality was one of my Trader Joe's supply bags, its contents crushed by the weight of the box.

Soon, the route took me onto the freeway. The shoulder was smooth and wide. A constant whoosh of passing vehicles lulled me into a somnambulant trance until I came to a stretch where cattails and pussywillows bordered the road. There, mosquitoes began to swarm. One ferocious little bugger managed to poke its beak through my weight-lifting gloves into the flesh between my thumb and pointer finger. The sleep walk was over. I was far too busy swatting away those bloodsuckers. My feet began to hurt. Then, for a while, the discomfort went away. But the pain returned, only worse — accumulative wear and tear, this being the sixth consecutive day of trekking pavement, much of it up and down steep hills.

At the bottom of an off ramp, I was Googling for a nearby eatery, when an extended-cab pickup roared up and skidded to a stop right next to me. Both cab doors swung open. The driver popped out first, 20-something, male. As he careened around the front of the idling vehicle, his vague grin and slight stagger suggested that he'd been indulging in some day drinking. His passenger, female, of similar age, apparently less impaired, reversed her partner's path and replaced him behind the wheel.

Before this Chinese fire drill could be completed, a man's face emerged from the second-row bench behind the truck's passenger seat. Older and grizzlier than his traveling companions, this fellow recalled Huck Finn's mean-drunk Pappy sprung off Mark Twain's page. He glared at me with daggers in his eyes and demanded to know, "Wha-da you think *yer* doin'?" The drool on his chin and the slur of his words left no doubt that he was well into the sauce.

This is it! I dared to imagine. *After more than 500 miles of walking the roads of California, here, on an exit ramp in Humboldt County, I'm about to suffer my first physical assault.* If there was ever an occasion for a peace pilgrim to inspire civil, constructive dialogue, this was it.

"I'm just walking," I explained. "Just walking from one place to another."

Fortunately, happy-drunk Huck saw the logic in stepping between mean-drunk Pappy and sitting-duck me. "Come on, Dad," the younger man said, with an inebriated chuckle. "Take it easy. He's cool."

Minutes later, I was back pushing the Pilgrimmobile along the shoulder of the freeway. Oddly, I pondered, walking next to a steady flow of speeding traffic made me feel a great deal safer.

☮   ☮   ☮   ☮   ☮

It seemed logical that the town I called home for two years would look familiar. Eureka is where The Wackers wrote our first songs, where we played our first gigs at a dive bar called the Purple Haze. I got married here for the first time. Yet, as I roll my load along Broadway, nothing is recognizable. Not a single touchstone connects today to 45 years ago. I stop at a gas station convenience store. Posted: *Rest Rooms for Customers Only.* To earn the legitimate right to ask for the men's room key, I pick out a can of Yerba Mate tea and lay it on the counter. "Will that be all?" the cashier asks. There is no doubt that this smiling woman is in the process of gender transition, male-to-female. I'm impressed that the petroleum company has put a trans person out here behind the counter to interact with the public.

Maybe she is my touchstone. After all, Eureka was where, as a 21-year-old glam rocker, I first started experimenting with make-up and androgynous stage garb. For whatever reason, here in this rough-and-tumble seaport town, I felt inspired to initiate a personal campaign to blur traditional gender roles — a mission that would eventually lead me to suffer several violent attacks from insecure, intolerant men. Maybe my pioneer gender-bending back in 1971 put some preliminary cracks in the ice, so that this person can live openly as herself and serve customers in a convenience store.

Due to the unpredictability of my daily progress, almost all my accommodations thus far have been arranged on the day-of or last-minute, on-the-fly. It's a comfort knowing more than a day or two in advance where I'll be staying. In contrast, thanks to my friend CM Hall, my Eureka lodgings were set up months before I even put foot to pavement.

My host Loren is 40-something, small and slight, with a sparse, curly beard. Wearing a cabby hat, he is extremely friendly, energetic, and welcoming. I'm surprised to learn that Loren has only just returned from a three-week backpacking trip — in Nepal, of all places, where he served in the Peace Corps in his early twenties. This makes him totally familiar, freshly so, with the rigors of long-distance hiking. Loren reports that his wife Jessica, a motivational speaker, is on the road. Two, large, drooling dogs, however, are delighted to have a pair of canine-loving hands on campus. One immediately petitions me for scratches behind the ears, while the other drops a slobbery ball at my feet in hopes of a game of fetch.

"We'll take the Cadillac," Loren jokes. We proceed to hop into one of the most dilapidated vehicles I've ever ridden in. The front seat of this rusted-out Toyota pickup has been replaced by a sheet of plywood. The driver sits on a cushion from a chaise lounge. The passenger's posterior gets no padding whatsoever — other than an Indian blanket. After trekking through Southern California, where the automobile represents a person's most important status symbol, my host's complete lack of pretense is refreshing. Bicycle, he informs me, is his go-to means of local transport.

Loren is smart and extremely opinionated. What else would one expect from a professor of Ethical Philosophy? We immediately leap headlong into a series of deep topics, volleying theories and observations back and forth across the table at the Lone Coast Brewery. I'm as starved for conversation with a highly-educated adult as I am for the Santa Fe Chicken Salad.

To illustrate one of his greatest concerns, Loren begins an anecdote about one of his students by explaining that most of the work in his classes is done in essay form. "His writing was good," the professor recalls. "Good sentence structure, complete paragraphs. But I had to give him a D." Naturally, the student was upset by the low mark. So, Loren called him into his office. After clarifying that the young man's paper offered no thought process or point of view, the student burst into tears. He had never, over the entire course of his education, been asked to actually think something through to a logical solution, to actually solve a problem. This, one of the most fundamental skills with which every successful adult should be equipped, was enigmatic to the young man.

What gets the professor even hotter under the collar is the concept of moral relativism. A moral relativist, he says, will justify such deplorable customs as mercy killing and female castration on the basis of cultural tradition. "A logical analysis based on simple ethics," Loren declares, "concludes that brutal practices like these cannot be excused on *any* basis." By now, under the influence of his second pint of micro-brew draft, my dinner companion is opining with increasing volume and vigor.

I agree with Loren on both points. Absolutely, students should be taught analytical thinking. We shouldn't expect them to simply regurgitate "correct" answers. Too, some cultural traditions are ethically unacceptable in a modern world. It occurs to me that, here in the U.S.A., these two themes actually coincide in a long-established tradition I call "willful ignorance." This nation takes perverse pride in anti-intellectualism. For far too many Americans, an eager, curious mind is less an asset than a character flaw. Smart kids are tormented and ostracized for being weak, nerdy, or gay. Our heroes are not thinkers. We idolize cowboys, renegades, and silent, brooding loners.

Brawn-over-brain-ism is as American as red, white, and blue. Working for years on Nashville's Music Row exposed me to song after song on the theme of... *If it was good enough for Granddaddy, it's good enough for me.* Don't get me wrong. I think carrying on family tradition is great. But, when that tradition is all about remaining ignorant, maybe it's time to shed custom, break free from the devolutionary cycle, lift those knuckles up outta the dirt, and crack a book.

> *"We were all born ignorant. But one must*
> *work hard to remain stupid."*
>
> — BENJAMIN FRANKLIN

Ten days ago, on a 100-degree-plus afternoon, I was pushing the Pilgrimmobile through Ukiah, California, when I came upon the Yokaho Elementary School. There, I felt compelled to stop and snap a photo. The subject of my interest was a large banner, hanging across the front, exterior wall of the building. Displayed was an axiom most parents presumably want their children to believe and live by: *Character Always Counts.* I should have felt inspired and encouraged, knowing Ukiah's kids were being instilled with such substantive and timeless values. Sadly, instead, I began wondering whether this fundamental platitude, one we *should* be able to take for granted, actually remains valid. Perhaps, I worried, this idealistic concept has been reduced to a quaint anachronism.

When vanity and greed are flaunted as virtues, when self-serving lies and rigging the system elevate people into positions of ultimate power and wealth, how can we possibly demonstrate there is any tangible return for acting with integrity and civic responsibility? If our kids observe people being so richly rewarded for short-sighted, selfish, even outright mean-spirited behavior, who are they likely to emulate when they grow up?

Supposing we take a hard look at the good ol' USA, the self-christened *Greatest Nation on Earth*, through the lens of moral relativism. Can we possibly defend the dumbing down of this nation or the spineless self-servitude of our elected representatives as American cultural traditions? Can we forgive bigotry because our nation was founded on racism? Can we excuse misogyny and homophobia because that's how our forefathers behaved? Loren is absolutely right. Some attitudes and practices cannot be excused. And, those customs must be opposed and stopped.

As we bump along the dark, rutted streets of Eureka in a rusted-out, tin-can Toyota pickup, I sit on a hunk of plywood covered in an Indian blanket, buzzing over inspiring conversation shared over a fine meal. I feel nourished in body, mind, and soul. And, for that, I am deeply grateful.

JUNE 26 · DAY FIFTY-SEVEN

Perusing the spines of the books in a Dollar Store is not unlike dropping by the dog pound. If you dare to make eye contact, mongrel after mongrel seems to be looking at you with big, heartrendingly sad, tear-filled orbs, silently begging you to take pity and spring it from this cold, brightly lit prison. This title — the only copy of this slender paperback on the shelf — tugged at my heartstrings for obvious reasons. And, I knew, without a doubt, *The End of War: How Waging Peace Can Save Humanity, Our Planet, and Our Future* by Captain Paul K. Chappell, U.S. Army, had been waiting here just for me.

I'm taking advantage of what has turned out to be an unusually pleasant, warm Humboldt County day to kick back, barefoot and shirtless in the afternoon sun. As I open my newly purchased one-buck paperback, I get immediate confirmation that the words on these pages were meant for my eyes. In the final paragraph of the book's foreword, renowned authority on human violence Gavin de Becker writes, "Paul K. Chappell offers us a view through the heart's eye." Last evening, Loren and I traded considerable verbiage about how America needs to open up its "mind's eye." However, as evidenced by the epidemic of meanness in this country, the brain is not our only underused organ. Our nation has developed some serious heart deficiencies as well.

Meanwhile, I'll set metaphor aside because the actual view from Loren and Jessica's backyard — right now, through my real eyes, in real time — is genuinely spectacular. Loren strolls out from his converted-backyard-shed office. I set down my book and amble with him to the edge of the bluff-side lot. There, across the horizon, under a sinking sun, expands the largest protected body of water on the west coast north of San Francisco. Humboldt Bay stretches 10 miles from Eureka to Arcata, providing habitat for hundreds of species of plants, invertebrates, fish, and birds. More than half of the oysters farmed in California are harvested from this estuary.

Recently, Loren informs me, one invasive species was eradicated from the bay ecology. For some time, the expansive marshes on the bay's edge provided safe haven for the area's homeless population. As recently as 12 months ago, he says, the view from here looked out over a tent city. To remove this embarrassing eyesore, police officers were dispatched to remove the itinerates, followed by bulldozers to bury any trace the undesirables might have left behind. Supposedly, the tent city residents were to be moved to another location. A year later, Loren says he's yet to hear where that location is.

CHAPTER 27

Gravy From a Jar

JUNE 28 · DAY FIFTY-NINE

Today began with a series of miscalculations. Instead of steering onto the quieter, less frantic frontage road, I got stuck on the freeway — on a stretch where pedestrians and cyclists are forbidden. Fortunately, I avoided getting busted. Jumping off at the first possible exit sent me on a circuitous course through the business loop of McKinleyville, past gas stations, fast food restaurants, convenience stores, mattress outlets, body shops, and used car dealers. After two hours of inhaling exhaust, I took a wrong turn into a residential neighborhood, only to meander for yet another half hour, lost in a maze of cul-de-sacs. Now, I'm finally back on course, pushing the Pilgrimmobile northward along a placid ribbon of smooth blacktop, sheltered by a canopy of coastal forest. This is Hammond Trail, a five-and-a-half-mile pathway provided for cyclists, hikers, and peace pilgrims traversing the Humboldt County coastline.

Ahead, someone is poking along in a motorized wheelchair. As I draw nearer, I notice that the person, a woman, is gripping a pair of leashes, like Spartacus holding the reins in a slow motion, miniature chariot race. Her team of stallions: two small dogs. The woman identifies herself as Sharon. I immediately notice that Sharon has a bit of a beard on her chin and that one half of her canine team, Scooter, a black, short-legged rag mop of a terrier, seems to be laboring, struggling for breath. Turns out the old boy is suffering from chronic heart failure. The vet said, yes, she could walk him, but only at Scooter's pace — which is not much of a pace at all.

I remark at how lovely this trail is. Sharon's response: "I thank my lucky stars every day that they did something right for a change." She asks me if I know if the new path will be as good. I tell her I didn't know about this one until this morning, that I'm from Oregon. "Oh, I *love* Oregon!" the goateed woman exudes. "My husband's relatives lived there." Back in the good old days, she recalls, they always enjoyed their visits to the Pacific Northwest.

Leaving the Sharon's slo-mo chariot behind, I follow Hammond Trail as it breaks out of the trees to paint a stripe along the sand. Nearing Clam Beach, the pathway's surface segues from pavement to gravel, winding uphill and down on the edge of the dunes, ending at Little River State Park. At this point, the route kicks me back onto the freeway. Although every step puts my feet in further distress, a drizzly morning has given way to a clear blue sky, with the temperature in the mid-seventies. The weather is beautiful — ideal, in fact.

Just south of Trinidad, I park the cart by the highway and scramble up a steep embankment to a massive redwood stump. There, overlooking the river of traffic, I rest just long enough to imbibe an energy drink. As I rise up from my perch, my first few steps send my sore feet into spasms. While making my way gingerly back down the slope, I slip in the damp pine needles and stumble. Fortunately, I land feet first on the shoulder of the road, stabilize myself, and regain my balance. Fall averted.

As I push on, I hear an odd, irritating, distorted, buzzing noise. A glance over my shoulder reveals the sound is coming from one of two CHP cars pulling up behind me.

So far, my interactions with the California Highway Patrol have been respectful and convivial. I have no reason to believe this will be any different. An officer swaggers toward me, youngish, perhaps even shy of 30, very good-looking, sporting a CPH regulation buzz-cut, and cocky as hell. "We've been getting calls," he informs me. "Reports of a man matching your description staggering on the shoulder of the highway." More than likely, I'm surmising, some concerned driver witnessed my tender-footed near slip-and-fall a mile back. "We can't allow you to walk on this section of the freeway," Officer Cocky states. "When there are two lanes on both sides of the divider, pedestrians are not allowed." Tactfully, I inform him that this contradicts what every other CHP officer has previously told me. "There were *No Pedestrian* signs posted on the on ramp," he contends. *Not where I entered the freeway, there weren't.*

This guy is young, probably relatively new on the job. I honestly don't think he knows what he's talking about. "I saw you earlier, just outside Arcata," he says. *Aha! That was when I made the mistake of entering that forbidden section of divided highway instead of taking the frontage road.* "I'd offer to give you a ride. But…" — he's pointing to the Pilgrimmobile — "*that* would be a bit of a problem." Officer Cocky offers a reasonable compromise… "Do me a favor," he suggests. "Get off at the next exit in a half mile."

That was my intent anyway. I smile, agree to, and comply with his request.

Nestled in a canyon glen, surrounded by redwoods, Sylvan Harbor RV Park deserves the "sylvan" part of its moniker. However, there is no harbor or body of water anywhere in sight, just dozens of motor homes and camper trailers parked side-by-side-by-side. In a vintage, white, wood-framed house fronting Patricks Point Road, I find the office unattended. Christian literature abounds everywhere, on shelves and tables. Biblical platitudes adorn the walls.

I follow the high-pitched zing of an electric saw to a courtyard next to the house. There, a thin man in a baseball cap, protective goggles, and earphones is fully absorbed in the craft of woodworking. It's Sean, the fellow I spoke to on the phone yesterday. He's a boyish 40, unassuming, and compulsively apologetic. As he checks me in, he kindly offers me a can of soda. I'm getting the impression that this man has no spouse or family, that he manages and maintains this enterprise on his own — with the implicit aid and comfort of his Lord and Savior, Jesus Christ, of course.

I pick out a tent site on the one-lane, gravel loop at the very rear of the property. There is no discernible activity at the pair of tents situated around the fire pit next door. Sean has informed firewood is free for campers. That the host has chopped and stacked wood is not unusual. That firewood is gratis is unprecedented — yet more evidence of Sean's truly charitable, Christian nature.

I'm cradling an armful of wood when a pair of cars pull up and park at the campsite next door. As the five-person entourage emerges into the damp, chilly air, I wave and call out a cheerful *Hi!* A round woman with shoulder-length, dark hair ambles over. Looking at me suspiciously through owlish eyes, she grumbles, "I guess we're neighbors."

"Yep. Looks like it," I respond, restraining myself from pointing out the obviousness of her statement. She identifies herself as Kathy, mentions that her family is here from Chico, then proceeds to introduce Raul, her husband. Raul, she explains, is suffering from temporary hearing loss, due to water in his ears from snorkeling in the ocean. In a thick Hispanic accent, Raul asks me if I need something to help start my fire. The free firewood, it turns out, is quite damp. Raul tells me he has what he calls, "these leettle steeks." I inform him that I already have a fire-starter. Deaf to my response, Raul strides over and fetches one of his "leettle steeks" anyway.

Accepting my neighbor's gift, I tell him, "You're very kind." Raul just stands there grinning vaguely and nodding his head. In a raised voice, Kathy repeats what I just said, then feels the need to articulate it one more time for good measure — at least, I'm assuming that's what she's saying, as she's speaking in Spanish. Raul's smile broadens, and he continues nodding his head.

A few minutes later, Kathy ushers her young son over. "Go ahead," she prompts the boy, "tell him."

Nearly bursting with pride, the chunky, dark-haired 10-year-old informs me that he, too, has been on a pilgrimage. "It was for the Mormon Church," he elaborates. "We walked twenty miles… to show how the Mormons came across the country." The youngster seems surprised to find out how well-versed I am on the plight of the prophet John Smith and his disciples, that I know all about the persecution suffered by the early Mormons while migrating westward from New York to their ultimate settlement in Utah.

☮   ☮   ☮   ☮   ☮

Time tends to evaporate when one is "in the flow." I've been journaling for hours, twilight is fading, and my stomach is rumbling. Kathy, Raul, and their brood come shuffling up the road, chattering busily amongst themselves. "You like pork chops and mashed potatoes?" Kathy asks me, balancing a paper plate in her hands.

"Damn straight, I do!" I answer, already salivating at the thought. The chops are breaded, the taters are instant, and the gravy obviously came out of a jar. But, at this moment, even a barely hot supper beats the soggy sandwich I saved for my evening repast.

I'm sitting at my picnic table, hunkered over this paper plate, gobbling up my charity meal like a stray dog. I take a moment between bites to call out gratefully to the campfire next door: "This hits the spot!" Kathy acknowledges my expression of gratitude with a brief glance out of the corners of her dark eyes.

JUNE 29 · DAY SIXTY

My next-door neighbors are entertaining guests. Parents jabber in between periodic hollers at kids just being kids, chasing one another, shrieking and laughing. I've begun breaking down my site, when Kathy cuts loose from the boisterous festivities and sidles over to pepper me with a dozen questions about my pilgrimage. The simplest of her many queries to answer is how far I plan to walk today. It's now past three o'clock. Fortunately, there is less than five miles to tonight's destination: Patricks Point State Park. Barring any unforeseen delays, a solid two-to-three hours of walking should get me there. "Hey, would it be all right before I leave," I ask her, "if I came over and played a song for the kids?"

"We'd love it!" Kathy replies. I'm pretty sure this is the first time I've seen the stout, stern woman smile. She promptly bustles back over to inform her party that they are about to be treated to a mini-concert by the Peace Pilgrim.

The children sit in a row like birds on a log, a quiet, focused, attentive audience. I strum the song's final guitar chord. The entire group bursts into enthusiastic applause. I compliment the kids for sitting so still and listening. And, after handing Kathy one of my CDs, I pack my guitar into the storage box for this afternoon's trek. I'm pushing the Pilgrimmobile down the gravel lane toward Patricks Point Road, when my voice suddenly comes booming out of Kathy and Raul's pickup. "The kids wanted to hear your CD," Kathy calls out after me.

"Hope you guys enjoy it," I respond with a parting wave and an ear-to-ear grin. Amazing how strangers on a campground can so easily and naturally burgeon a neighborly connection. It was a stroke of good fortune pitching my tent next to these very kind, generous folks here at the Sylvan Harbor RV Park.

Patricks Point State Park, a forested promontory extending out into and over the Pacific Ocean, covers 640 acres. I've pushed the Pilgrimmobile across the entire peninsula by the time I reach the hike-and-bike area. Chad, my only neighbor, is here on a detour from the Pacific Crest Trail, where the winter's extraordinary snowfall has left areas of the Sierra Nevadas, Siskiyous, and Cascades impassable. To make the route even less hospitable, excess runoff has swollen rivers and streams to flood levels. Before detouring to the coast, Chad covered more than 600 miles of the PCT.

The area is extremely rocky, making it nearly impossible to pound and secure tent stakes into the ground. Through dogged perseverance, I finally manage to find angles to get the spikes to hold. After getting my bivy set up and rolling out my bedding, I sit down for dinner — a sandwich purchased yesterday morning in Arcata, and a bag of chips. Clyde, the affable, soft-spoken camp host, arrives with my firewood delivery. Walking with a decided limp, he fetches a bundle from the back of his four-wheeler. Thoughtfully, he's brought along some twigs and newspaper, too, to get the blaze started.

I invite Chad to share my fire. He, however, has strapped on a backpack and is headed out for a night hike. I'm left in solitude, dwarfed by natural wildness, engulfed by encroaching darkness, reading words of wisdom by firelight…

"There are so many gifts in life we can
appreciate but never own,
such as the sunrise, the sunset, a beautiful day, other people,
and the magnificent planet we inhabit.
Appreciation, not ownership, is the doorway to happiness."

— Captain Paul K. Chappell
The End of War (2010, Easton Studio Press)

JUNE 30 · DAY SIXTY-ONE

"Appreciation," Captain Chappell writes, "is the doorway to happiness." I will agree with the author of *The End of War* that appreciation is important. I will also, however, purport that a step above and beyond the mindset of appreciation is the feeling of gratitude. And, certainly, happiness is a desirable and pleasant experience. But happiness is impermanent, as fleeting and transitory as sadness or despair. And, if not for the contrast of other, less-desirable, less-pleasant, but equally valid and sincere emotions, happiness could easily become a normal, even mundane state of existence. Happiness is like a warm, sunny, spring day after a cold, stormy winter. Thus, it should not be our end goal. Rather, we should think of happiness as a sunshiny rest stop, a lovely oasis, a place to linger, but only as long as it lasts. And, although the warm glow of happiness can't be trusted or expected to last forever, and we know the chill will inevitably return, we can also be sure we'll find our way back there again.

Appreciating the awesome, miraculous display of a sunrise or a sunset is easy. Appreciating other people can, at times, be more of a challenge. However, these days, for this pilgrim, the recognition, acknowledgment, and appreciation of just how good, kind, and generous people can be, and so often are, has become, for me, to borrow a phrase from Captain Chappell, a "doorway to happiness."

So, on that theme, what can I say about the man at the wheel of this Toyota pickup? Gary Lahman is a jolly, pink-cheeked, round-bellied fellow, with a full, snowy beard, and long-ish, white hair. He might be mistaken for Saint Nicholas's sprier younger brother. Gary is the kind of guy who almost always responds "No!" first, then ends up getting involved anyway. And by involved, I mean *very* involved! He gets elected to the board of directors or accepts extra responsibility as a committee chair.

Gary and his beautiful, multi-talented wife, Cynthia Jacobi were gracious enough to host my pre-pilgrimage house-concert fundraiser at their spectacular, bluff-side home above Agate Beach. When I first suggested that the Lahman-Jacobi abode would make a perfect venue for a house concert, Gary's kneejerk was negative: "We really don't do fundraisers at our house," he stated.

A week later, I was surprised when Cynthia approached me to schedule a concert date. I asked her if Gary was okay with the idea. "Oh, he always comes around," she said, with a loving wife's knowing smile. Nonetheless, even when my walk was in its earliest preparation phase, Gary was eager to sit down with the map, offer advice on my route, all the while suggesting that he would be willing to join me at some point along the way — if and when I might need his help. That point has arrived. And, now I'm sitting in the passenger seat of this truck, in full appreciation — hear that, Captain Chappell? — of my friend's willingness to follow through on his word.

Highway 101 south of Crescent City is plagued with multiple slides and washouts. And, between spots where the road is severely damaged and/or under reparation, there is a five-mile segment of extremely steep incline, which, it stands to reason, is followed on the other side by an equivalent length of steep downhill grade. With my feet already under extreme duress, avoiding such an arduous climb and potentially painful descent would be extremely advantageous. So, to save the day, my hero Gary drove from Newport to Gold Beach, Oregon, yesterday, spent last night at a motel, then motored the rest of the way this morning to pick up a pal at Patricks Point State Park.

Falling asleep last night was difficult. Although my body was tired, I found myself fretting about the safety of my neighbor Chad, who had set out on a hike at nightfall and was, several hours later, still traipsing God knows where, through the woods in pitch darkness. I was lying on the rocky ground, imagining being interviewed by the head of a search-and-rescue squad — *Well, he took off at twilight and I haven't seen him since.* Then, around 2 AM, I heard my intrepid neighbor literally bounding into the hike-and-bike area like an antelope, loudly unzipping his tent flap, and diving into his bed roll. At that late hour, I was finally able to put my mind to rest, along with my body.

By the time I emerged into the damp morning air, Chad had already pulled off a magic trick I wouldn't have thought possible, by stowing his tent and all his camping gear into his backpack. He informed me that he'd already used up his maximum stay at the five-buck hike-and-bike and was headed off to catch a bus at the park entrance. I noticed that, in spite of the enormous pack on his back, he wasn't using trekking poles, the retractable, aluminum ski-pole-like devices commonly used by long-distance hikers for support, balance, and propulsion. I asked him why. His poles, he explained, had been stolen. "I have a brand-new pair," I declared, "really nice ones. You can have them. For free." As my hands are always employed with pushing the Pilgrimmobile, the poles I purchased months earlier have been riding at the bottom of my storage box for two full months, unused.

As Chad checked out the poles, my heart was swelling with a feeling of beneficence. I've been the recipient of so much generosity over the last 60 days, this, it seemed, was a perfect opportunity for me to pass a little bit of that good will forward. "They're really nice," Chad observed, showing a distinct lack of enthusiasm. "But, right now, I'm kinda into traveling light."

"Are you sure?" I was almost pleading with him to accept the gift. He reconsidered for a few seconds, then handed the poles back. If and when he needed a pair, he said, he'd buy some. As I stuffed the poles into their fabric carry bag, and re-buried them in the bottom of the storage box, the sunny elation I'd just experienced disappeared behind a cloud of melancholy. Happiness is indeed fleeting.

I was 20 minutes late as I pushed the Pilgrimmobile into the parking lot of the Patricks Point Visitor Center. There, I found my always-affable friend Gary Lahman engaged in conversation with none other than my camp neighbor Chad. Today's bus schedule, it seems, had been changed. Chad would have to wait until mid-afternoon for transport. Gary, generous soul that he is, had already volunteered to give Chad a ride with us to Crescent City. Ever the stoic loner, Chad turned down Gary's offer, just as he had every one of mine.

I'm in dire need of new sneakers. A Google search informs me that Crescent City's only half-decent selection of athletic shoes is Big 5. Although I try to shy away from using such absolute and negative language, I hate Big 5. After an extremely unpleasant encounter at their Thousand Oaks location, on Day One of my pilgrimage, I stomped out of the store, swearing I'd never set foot in a Big 5 again. Now, here I am 61 days later, not only setting foot in a Big 5 store, but hobbling in on two very unhappy feet, with a sour disposition, and harboring a pessimistic expectation of the experience to come. One can't help but wonder if this shopping venture might be doomed from the get-go.

But, soft. The sales associate approacheth. This fellow looks as though he's never exercised in his life, let alone played any sport requiring more exertion than tiddlywinks or marbles. "Can I help you with something?" the flabby, corpulent fellow asks. I'm standing at the back wall of the store, staring at shelves of sneakers on display, next to a sign that reads, *Walking*.

My answer is clear and succinct: "I'm looking for some walking shoes."

"Well, the walking shoes are over here," he says, ushering me 10 feet down the wall to the display labeled, *Running*. When I point out the signs, he explains, "They're all mixed in." *Great! We're off to a flying start!*

"If you were going on a very long walk," I inquire, "which shoe would you wear?"

"Well," he expounds, "I'd go with the Asics, or the Adidas."

I proceed to articulate all the very specific qualities I'm looking for in a shoe: enough room for the toes to spread out, so to avoid more blisters and toenail loss, a design that would accommodate my Good Feet inserts and keep them in place, etc. "Which shoe would you recommend?" Asics, he reiterates, would be a good choice.

"Which one?" I ask.

He begins pointing out various shoes on the wall. "This is Asics. This is Asics, This is Asics," etc. "Just pick the color and style you like," he advises, "and try it on." Either he simply didn't listen to the very specific qualities I'm looking for, or he has no idea which shoe might fill those specific needs. Either way, he is demonstrating the kind of unprofessionalism that drives me batty. My patience level, which had been hovering at E-for-empty when I walked in, is now dipping into the reserve tank. I've yet to try on a single shoe, and I'm already on the verge of losing it. I select a New Balance model and ask him if he could bring me a pair, in size 12. These are not quite perfect, which leaves me waiting interminably for the sales associate to return, so I can try on something else. This try-on, reject, and wait routine repeats itself with two more shoe styles.

I'm muzzling a scream of anguish, when Gary hands me a New Balance sample I hadn't noticed. "This one looks like it has plenty of room in the toe," he suggests. I finally flag down the associate. He fetches this model. I try them on and decide to buy them, not the least bit confident that I'm not making a huge mistake.

As Gary drops me at the Front Street Inn, he leaves me with contact information for three friends along my route and promises to phone them in advance, so my call won't take them by surprise.

The remainder of the evening is all about trying to get the free Wi-Fi to work. Three hours attempting to put up one single Facebook post ends in failure and frustration, with the Apple "spinning wheel of death" turning and turning interminably. I shut the whole thing down and call Sebra. After listening to my snit fit, she's able to talk me down from the ledge. A half hour later, I'm laughing again, lifted out of my melancholic, unappreciative frame of mind — at least, for the moment.

CHAPTER 28

Born Again

JUNE 30 · DAY SIXTY-ONE

Trekking the highways of America for 61 days invariably leads to encounters with all kinds of drivers. Most are considerate. Some are rude. Rarely will a motorist cross over the line into meanness. Today, I was subjected to an overt act of intentional cruelty.

The two-lane bridge spanning the mouth of the Smith River is narrow enough that a motion sensor at its entrance triggers a bright, flashing strobe light alerting drivers to the presence of cyclists or pedestrians. I was approximately three-quarters of the way across its quarter-mile span, when a black Dodge Ram 2500 king-cab pickup pulled its over-sized tires up next to me and slowed to my pace — unusual, and more than a little bit intimidating. After a minute or so, the driver pulled up so that I was behind his right, rear bumper, then suddenly gunned his engine and peeled out. Tire tread spun on pavement, burning rubber and spattering gravel onto my bare legs and arms, while a thick cloud of black, diesel exhaust bilged from the vehicle's tailpipe. I was left, engulfed in a dark, putrid bank of heavy-metal soot, gagging and coughing, as the truck sped off the north end of the bridge,

What, I couldn't help but wonder, *could possibly have compelled the pilot of that long-gone pickup to do such a heinous thing? Did he* — I'm assuming the driver was male — *actually get a kick out of it? And, if so, why?* As the vehicle had approached me from behind, and its cab looked down from such a lofty angle, the driver couldn't possibly have seen the *Peace Pilgrim 2017* banner wrapped around my cart. So, that eliminates the possibility of this act having been an expression of displeasure with the purpose of my mission. He certainly couldn't have divined that I had made a conscious, willing choice to leave my vehicle at home and travel by foot. So, the only logical conclusion is that this person assumed he had come upon a less fortunate, possibly homeless man pushing a cart containing all of his meager possessions. And, from that driver's superior vantage point, sitting behind the wheel of a tricked-out $50,000-plus road machine, he must have thought it would be a laugh riot to make a downtrodden, forlorn fellow human's day that much more unpleasant.

> *I WOULD SOON learn that the black cloud emitted from this particular tailpipe came from an adaptation marketed to truck owners, called a smoke switch. This device fools the diesel engine into thinking it needs more fuel, thus causing it to expel an excessive, ultra-concentrated cloud of black exhaust. They call it "coal rolling" and those who indulge in this smoky practice proudly identify themselves as "coal rollers." Typically, they single out hybrid and/or electric vehicles as their targets, as their way of protesting compulsory emission standards. However, this particular fellow was not simply demonstrating his opposition to pollution regulations, he was using his exhaust-bilging mechanism as a weapon, to exert his dominance over another, more-vulnerable human being, someone with no means of defense or retaliation. This was not merely a statement of protest, nor was it just a demonstration of unabashed cruelty. This was an act of pure cowardice.*

As I trudged off of the Smith River span, a toxic mishmash of anger, sorrow, disappointment, alienation, and confusion bubbled in my gut. Now, however, only a few hours after that regrettable experience, my demeanor has transformed. I couldn't wipe this smile off my face if I tried. Nor would I want to.

What could possibly have, in a matter of hours, soothed

my fractured soul and enabled me to rediscover the simple joy of being alive? Well, it wasn't one of those everyday miracles of nature described in Captain Chappell's book — a sunrise or a sunset, or catching sight of an eagle soaring over the white-capped surf — nor was it yet another helping hand extended by an angelic Good Samaritan. Ironically, I'm filled with renewed elation because of an occurrence even more terrifying, more random, and potentially even more traumatic than getting smoke bombed by a bully in a pickup.

I was in the home stretch, seven hours into today's trek, when I noticed an open gate leading to a dirt farm road running perpendicular to the highway. A pilgrim is well advised to take advantage of every opportunity to relieve his bladder. So, I left the Pilgrimmobile parked on the shoulder of the two-lane highway and shuffled through the open gate.

After taking care of business, I was ambling back toward the highway, busying myself double-checking Google Maps on my iPhone when, suddenly, the Earth gave way. In a split second, my right leg disappeared up to my knee — a freakish occurrence with the definite potential for sprain or fracture. Thankfully, my foot had landed on something solid. Unfortunately, before I could shift my weight and uproot my appendage from the hole, the unseen layer beneath my buried foot gave way. It's a helpless feeling, realizing you're beyond the tipping point, well past any chance of regaining equilibrium. Twisting and tumbling, I crashed noisily, backside-first, through a tangle of brambles, finally landing with a heavy thump on my shoulder blades, while dirt and rocks tumbled down after me onto my legs, arms, chest, and face.

When the dust settled, I found myself lying flat on my back, half buried, looking up from an instant grave, approximately four feet below the surface of the farm road. But, that wasn't even the worst of it. I was also strapped down by blackberry vines — big, fat ones. The strand across my chest and arms matched the circumference of my thumb, with stout, rapier-sharp thorns a half-inch long poking into my flesh. Any movement at all, and the barbs penetrating my arms, chest, bare legs, and back would surely rip my skin.

Fortunately, my iPhone was still clenched in my fist. First thought: *Call 911! But, wait! Why not try using the high-tech device for a lower-tech purpose?* Ever so gradually, using the side edge of the phone, I was able to bend and break up the vines. Then, carefully, surgically, I extracted each thorn, one by one, freeing my arms, torso, and legs.

My next challenge was to somehow, in this extremely confined space, get to my feet. Every slightest move had to be executed slowly and meticulously to avoid re-snagging my skin or clothing. A rope-sized segment of broken root dangled above, like the tail of a Jack Russell terrier. When I reached up and yanked, another mini-avalanche of rocks and dirt plummeted down onto my face and chest. Still, the dog's tail seemed relatively well-anchored. If I could somehow push down on the ground with my right hand, while pulling up on the root with my left, I might be able to get my feet underneath me. This would definitely be a gamble. If the root were to break or give way, I'd go careening backwards, sinking deeper and further into the vines, becoming even more buried and, once again, straightjacketed in blackberry thorns. If that happened, and if I somehow managed to cling to my iPhone, calling 911 would be my one last resort.

Grasping the root firmly in my left hand, I placed my right hand down under my buttocks. *Ouch!* I was pushing down on a carpet of prickly vines. Another dumbing down of my smart phone was called for. It became a shield underneath my palm. Thankfully, this coordinated pushing-down-while-pulling-up enabled me to get my feet securely underneath me. I placed one of my brand-new sneakers — now caked in mud and dirt — on a protruding stone, rocked forward and back, once, twice… then, throwing all my weight forward, I clamored up and out of the tomb into the sunshine.

Now, here I am, standing on the farm road, looking down into the yawning, dirty mouth that had attempted to eat me alive. The iPhone in my hand is smeared with blood. My arms are dotted in crimson puncture wounds and streaks of mud. My socks and shoes are filled with pebbles, dirt, and broken segments of barbed blackberry vine. My calves are a chaotic map of jagged, scarlet scratches. And I feel rivulets of warm blood rolling down my back.

A shiver races through my entire body, as I attempt to make sense of the strange ordeal I've just survived — all alone, yet only a few feet from a major highway. A physical sensation bubbles in my abdomen. Effervescent, effusive, and jubilant, the feeling ripples up through my belly, rises into my chest, and comes bursting into the air as laughter — goofy, uncontrollable, grateful peals of it. "Oh, my God! Oh, my *God!*" I am standing next the sepulcher from which, just a few seconds ago, I willed myself to rise again. Trembling hands on trembling knees, my shoulders heaving, convulsing, I am laughing out loud, yet weeping at the same time.

This peace pilgrim is as filthy as a coal miner at the end of a 10-hour shift. My back, arms, and legs sting from a hundred, bleeding lacerations. But I am ecstatic to be freed from that cave — the physical one, as well as the emotional pit in which I've been wallowing for days.

Yes. Life is good.

JULY 1 · DAY SIXTY-TWO

After two months of trekking from Southern to Central, and finally across Northern California, inland and coastal, through cities and villages, on highways, byways, and remote rural roads, I've crossed the border into my home state. Suddenly, inexplicably, everything seems noticeably different. The forest has more density, the ocean is a darker green, and the air itself smells richer and thicker. The corporate farms are gone. The barns and farmhouses take on a timeless, American-gothic character, almost as if they've been oil painted onto the landscape. And… I begin to see other pedestrians on the road.

I accelerate my pace to catch up with a pair of backpackers. I recognize this female duo, having overheard a conversation as they decamped and departed earlier from Clifford Kamph Memorial Park. Like Chad, my reclusive neighbor at the Patricks Point hike-and-bike, these two women detoured to the coast due to unpassable conditions on the Pacific Crest Trail.

The elder of the couple introduces herself as Yukon Barb. Sixty-ish, with spiked, bleached-blond hair, the stout woman sports a rather nice little goatee. Barb says she set out from the Mexican border in March and, thus far, has covered 1,000 miles on foot. Somewhere along the way, she teamed up with her companion, a muscular dishwater blond half Barb's age who has chosen the tag Trail Mix.

Interestingly, the deep Sierra snowpack wasn't the only impediment that chased Barb and her young cohort out of the mountains. The 100-degree-plus temperature factored in as well. Barb, who hails from Alaska — her hiker nickname is Yukon Barb, after all — is not accustomed to hot weather. And, as if freezing one's tootsies off while simultaneously sweating bullets wasn't enough of a dissuasion, the rapid snow melt has rendered streams and rivers far too precarious to cross.

When Barb hears about my mission, she remarks, "You know, we've got people on both sides in Alaska. Folks like me, outdoor types, who are all about environmental protections. Then, there's the 'drill, baby, drill' gang." The Pacific Crest Trail, she reminds me, passes through territory where most folks tend to be way out on the far-right political fringe. "I'm in a diner or a pub," she shares. "Fox News is on the tube and everybody's cheering the president, repeating all these whacky conspiracy theories. Then," she muses, "these same people offer me rides in their pickups."

The Alaskan woman's presence unabashedly announces, *Here I am, folks, your prototypical 21st century lesbian; so, deal with it!* Still, she hiked, alone, flying her flag of androgyny, through hundreds of miles populated by supposedly hostile tribes people. Her report? Yes, as a group, the natives adhere to some extremely dubious mythology. Individually, however, they actually report themselves as nice, kind, and oftentimes generous.

The tall-ish man standing in the front doorway is clad in a Green Bay Packers sweatshirt, tucked into baggy red athletic shorts, multi-colored running shoes, and a yellow San Francisco Giants World Series Championship cap. Hesitantly, I mutter, "Is there a Bob here?"

"That's me," answers the oddly dressed fellow, matter-of-factly, without a hint of a smile.

"I'm Rand."

"Yes, I know," he says, shaking my hand. "I passed by you on the highway."

Okay, I'm thinking, *evidently, my couch-surfing host motored right past me as I labored up a six-mile grade, without thinking to offer so much as a wave or a thumbs-up.*

"Anyway," Bob announces, "I have to go to the bathroom." He performs an abrupt about face and takes a few strides into the house. Then, as if it's an afterthought — once again, without a hint of a smile or any discernible welcome in his voice — he turns back and says, "You can come in if you want."

If I want? I've walked 15 miles today... to get to this house... at YOUR invitation! Yes, I would like to come in! I didn't say those words aloud. But that's definitely what I was thinking.

In my mind's eye, the couch-surfing host I expected to meet was friendly, fit, ambitious, entrepreneurial, fastidious, and gay. After all, his couchsurfing.com profile photo depicted two clean-cut, smiling, athletic-looking men, arms around each other's shoulders. His *ABOUT ME* described "... an ultra-friendly, outgoing type who loves traveling and meeting people."

The "fastidious" part of my mental image was immediately dashed as I bumped my cart past a dilapidated Trump/Pence *Make America Great* yard sign, down a rough, rutted, gravel driveway to behold a deck cluttered with haphazardly stacked cardboard boxes, rusted bicycles, exercise equipment, and disconnected appliances.

Squeezing past boxes of bulk food items stacked up against a two-by-four, interior wall frame, Bob ushers me into his living room, which, at present, has no dry wall or flooring. Three pieces of furniture are tucked into a corner alcove: a couch, a coffee table, and a single chair. A game of Risk and an open tray of Monopoly money lay catawampus on the floor. The sofa cushions are strewn with books, coin-collector magazines, and various knickknacks. Monopoly pieces clutter the coffee table. While Bob exits to the bathroom, I plop down heavily on the chair and check my phone. *No service. What,* I wonder, *have I gotten myself into?*

Someone bursts in noisily from outside. The swarthy, overly tanned young man's sweat-drenched tank top clings to his broad, muscular shoulders. He takes long, purposeful strides across the plywood subfloor, then pauses for a second to acknowledge my presence with a grin and a brief wave. *Who is this silent, perspiring fellow? What is his relationship to the owner of this house?*

After shoving the mess aside, Bob plops down on the couch and proceeds to obliterate most every preconception I'd made about him. He launches into a tirade about his erstwhile girlfriend who, he over shares, has gone back to her loser ex. *Evidently, he's not gay.* The tanned, muscle-bound, 20-something lad in the kitchen, I'm informed, is one of Bob's employees. Julio and his brother are renting rooms — if you can call them rooms, as this part of the Haas house lacks actual walls. Although Bob is "retired," he operates a moving company that serves much of the southern Oregon coast. This enterprise, however, is not my host's only going concern. He also deals in rare coins out of a Brookings storefront. At least I was correct about my host being "ambitious" and "entrepreneurial."

Bob *is* out and proud about one thing: his Christianity. He believes fervently that his beloved, recently passed parents, have been reunited in Heaven for eternity. Oddly enough, ultra-conservative, born-again Bob restricts his diet to organic food only. His fanaticism for good health also leads him to advocate outlawing any and every drug capable of altering human consciousness — including alcohol! "How can you be a conservative and support such strict governmental regulations?" I inquire.

"Simple," he retorts, "it's the right thing to do." To distance himself even further from a traditionally conservative, free-market posture, Bob declares that enemies to public health — like Monsanto and McDonalds — should be put out of business. This fellow is not the least bit shy about espousing some atypical, sometimes radical viewpoints. He does, however, fall in lockstep with hard-line right-wingers on other issues. For instance, he purports that every single illegal alien, as he calls them, should be sent packing.

"Who would harvest the crops?" I ask. "Bus the tables? Mow the lawns? Make hotel beds? Frame the houses?"

"Throw people off welfare and get rid of food stamps," Bob pontificates. "If you're hungry enough, you'll do anything to put food on the table for your family. Or," he suggests, "put 'em to work fixing the highway!"

Eureka! We may very well have stumbled upon an elusive sliver of common ground. Still, I feel obliged to play devil's advocate. "But," I point out, "our government doesn't spend money on infrastructure. We invest in weaponry and regime change."

At this juncture, our sliver of common ground expands to a healthy slice. "Like I say to my girlfriend," my opinionated host cracks through a wry grin, "if I think you're wrong, I'll argue with you." On this point, he doesn't.

Bob, who boasts of having been accepted by every top college — including M.I.T. — before attending Rutgers, is midway through a book entitled, *The Last Two Million Years*. "But it's basically fictional," he postulates. "Nobody was there to see evolution. So, how can they prove it? It's just another religion."

On one hand, I'm impressed that Bob is curious enough to read about the Big Bang, black holes, and the origin of the species. On the other hand, I marvel that someone who brags of a superior IQ so carelessly tosses sound scientific research into the same bag with Biblical mythology.

Bob is far, far to the right on the political spectrum and expresses his views with absolute certitude. However, he also listens to my opinions and answers my questions with respect. He restrains from taking intransigent, argumentative stances, and never comes off as judgmental. An hour earlier, meeting Bob filled me with apprehension. Now, in spite of our very different viewpoints, I'm actually beginning to like the guy. So much for preconceptions and first impressions.

JULY 2 · DAY SIXTY-THREE

Before I hit the road, there's a question burning in my craw, something I've been dying to ask a Trump supporter for two years…

"What," I inquire, "does Make America Great Again mean to you?"

"That's a very good question," Bob responds, squinting and nodding, obviously taking my query seriously. "Well," he begins. "I'd like to see us be a country that makes things, you know, manufacturing products. I'd like to see kids getting a better education, a real education. And, I think we need to get back to our core values."

"I can't disagree with any of that," I respond, with absolute sincerity — although I suspect he and I would butt heads when it comes to the exact definition of "core values." "But, what about the word 'again?'" Bob nods, as if he knows exactly where I'm going here. Still, I make sure we're on the same page. "The word 'again' implies there was a time when America actually *was* great. When do you think that was? And why?"

"Well…" Bob takes another moment to consider his response. "I guess it was probably around the end of World War Two, and just after… Late Forties, early Fifties. After that," Bob surmises, regretfully, "things started to change."

I totally understand what he's saying. In fact, I would have predicted this very answer. The America Bob recalls was an overwhelmingly white, Christian, patriarchal culture. It seemed like a much more innocent time. Parents didn't think twice about letting their kids play outside until dark. A high school graduate could get a job at the local plant, make enough to buy a decent house and a new car, while looking forward to an adequate and dignified retirement. His obedient little wife stayed home, cooking meals, raising kids, and keeping house. Marriages almost never ended in divorce, teens rarely used drugs or got pregnant, and homosexuals stayed in the closet.

"But," I remind Bob, "that was before Civil Rights. So, for people of color, America wasn't so great, was it?"

Bob admits this is a factor he hadn't considered. "But, I don't see race," he feels the need to add. "If I moved to Africa, after a couple of generations, my great-great grandchildren would be just as black as the natives."

"So, you *do* believe in evolution," I observe.

"Not evolution," he corrects me, "adaptation."

I resist pointing out that those adaptations he's just admitted to believing in eventually, over hundreds of generations, add up to evolution. Instead, I take this opportunity to remind Bob that back in those long-gone good ol' days, when he says America last experienced greatness, polio victims were lying in iron lungs, acid rain was beginning to fall, polluted rivers were bursting into flames, and women who had ambitions outside the home were limited to subservient, low-wage, secretarial, teaching, or nursing careers.

"Don't get me wrong," Bob comes to his own defense. "I think women should be paid as much as men."

Again, Bob is inadvertently admitting that things weren't all that perfect back then after all. Surely, in a number of sentimental ways, the America of the late Forties, early Fifties, was great — for white boys like Bob and myself, and our fathers. However, nostalgia is a rose-colored rear-view mirror. And, let's face it. We can't just hang a U-turn and jet back to live in an endless loop of *Happy Days* reruns. And, although many long to do just that, perhaps it's more realistic and pragmatic for us to keep working together, not to make America great again, but to make an already great nation a little bit greater every day.

CHAPTER 29

Friendly Pain, Foggy Fireworks, and Card Tricks

JULY 4 · DAY SIXTY-FIVE

I've reached the crest of Cape San Sebastian, breathless, fatigued, and drenched in sweat, but feeling the self-satisfaction of having conquered yet another mountain. Descending the northern slope brings me face-to-face with a bicyclist battling gravity in the opposite direction. Surely, he must be as long in the tooth as Yours Truly. He stops to catch his breath and express admiration for the Pilgrimmobile.

"Thanks," I respond. "Yeah, the jogging-stroller setup works pretty well."

Mopping his perspiring brow, he quips, "But, you can't coast!" *Oh, so true!* A cyclist's legs and lungs may burn on the way to the top. But he always has that easy glide to look forward to on the other side. The Pilgrimmobile offers no such respite.

Large, friendly, and gregarious, the seasoned cyclist's name is Richard. He calls Los Angeles home. Presently, he's en route from his vacation home in Gleneden Beach, Oregon, to San Francisco.

"I'm just trying to encourage people to stop shouting at each other."

"Well," chortles Richard, with a double dollop of big-city snark, "good luck with *that*!" Then, he queries, as if he's not quite certain it's true, "We do this because we love it, right?" Translation: *Are we insane to put our aging bodies through such ordeals?*

"I have to keep reminding myself," I confess, "that nobody made me do this. I've got nobody to blame but myself."

"Pain is our friend," Richard asserts, as if he assumes another old road dog will automatically concur with such a darkly existential declaration.

Instead, I'm taken aback. I've never looked at pain collegially, as an ally, a comrade. "Well, I guess," I respond, "if you don't sacrifice, if you don't suffer, at least little bit, you're just sitting on your ass, right?" Having no desire to delve any deeper into such Zen ruminations, I bid the sardonic gent a hail-fellow-well-met. But he insists on sharing a story…

It seems Richard was pedaling from Montana to Colorado — *this old dude gets around!* — when he encountered another fellow who, like me, was pushing a cart. Unlike me, this cart pusher was from Slovakia. "He was having the time of his life!" the cyclist recounts, affecting a generic, Eastern-European accent: "Back home, I work in factory. After work, I drink beer. Next day, same thing. Here? Not same thing."

The fundamental truth of this parable amuses me. "Yep," I chuckle, "it's all about perspective."

Now, I feel compelled to share something with Richard, an observation I've made numerous times back home. At the beach, for some magical reason, pretty much everything is fun — even back-breaking labor. Fathers will spend hour upon hour with their kids, blissfully digging trenches, creating mini-waterways, hauling buckets of heavy, wet sand, and erecting sandcastle kingdoms they know will be washed away with the next high tide. The exact same physical effort, under the eagle-eyed scrutiny of a boss, for the purpose of earning a meager paycheck, would be drudgery. Toil, voluntarily performed, with the playful wonderment of a child, while on a seaside vacation, can be pure pleasure. Herein lies the key to a positive, fulfilling life experience. "Yep," I repeat, "it's all about perspective."

As I push on, I ruminate on Richard's puzzling proclamation: *Pain is our friend…*

As the decades roll by, I find myself either unwilling or unable to fully accept the natural, inescapable process of aging. We can fight gravity. But we can't hold back time. However, regardless of how much resistance we put up, both of those immutable forces will end up victorious, having robbed us of our beauty, our strength, and our vitality, while steadily and stealthily diminishing the quality of our lives. As basketball great Mark Jackson so astutely points out, "Father Time is undefeated."

A few years back, I was having drinks with some new acquaintances. Rachel, 50-ish, and the mother of a grown daughter, asked me, "Does it hurt?" Confused, I requested clarification. She blushed a little, then made her cryptic query more specific: "Getting old. Does it hurt?"

The answer then was, and now is, most definitely *yes*. The aches and pains brought on by physical wear and tear are inevitable. You either accept that and live with it, or you don't. And, to be honest, I'm not a very good sport about it. There is profound sorrow in the realization that one's capacity is more limited with every passing day. And, for me, the pain of a body breaking down doesn't seem the least bit friendly — no matter what Richard or anybody else claims.

But maybe I'm out here putting my body through these daily tribulations to mask the agony of aging behind another, more-acceptable, albeit self-inflicted kind of pain — the pain I've willingly signed up for. If that's what Richard was saying, then, on further reflection, I must concur with his statement whole-heartedly. Pain *is* our friend, indeed!

From Day One of this trek, even with all the discomfort I've endured, I haven't, even for a moment, felt old. Perhaps that's what kept Peace Pilgrim walking for 28 years — because a pilgrim is absolutely ageless. The pain I'm inflicting on my body isn't a constant reminder that time and life are screaming by. A pilgrim's pain is what gets him to the top of the grade and back down again. It bridges adventure with adventure. It's the motor that moves me from one nourishing human encounter to the next.

The Azalea Lodge is no more a lodge than Sylvan Harbor was a harbor. But my room is clean, easily accessible and, for tonight at least, comes at no charge, having been generously gifted by a dear friend. From the moment I announced my plans to take on this mission, I got bombarded from every angle by well-meaning skeptics, naysayers, and worrywarts. However, no one made a more strident effort to talk me out of this pilgrimage than my martini-sipping, barstool confidante, Debbie Edwards.

Debbie and I both moved to Newport during the summer of 2012. Steve, Debbie's husband, best friend, and father of their twin daughters, had recently lost his prolonged battle with cancer. Fresh from my third divorce, I, too, had recently become single. However, the instant bond between Debbie and Rand had nothing to do with romance, or even flirtation. Our simpatico blossomed naturally, out of mutual interests — enjoying a cocktail being ice-breaker number one.

I think I was the first one to say it out loud. That detail, how-ever, matters not. It was probably around 2 AM. Debbie and I were goodbye hugging after another several-hour-long, heartrending tête-à-tête. "G'night," one of us said, "I love you." *I love you, too,* was the automatic response. It's easy to let those words slip out casually at closing time in a dive bar, when you're under the influence. But, for two friends who had grown so close and revealed so much to one another, these came from the heart. It was no big deal, mind you. Still, the sentiment wanted to be articulated. And, at least for me, it was a nice feeling to say it out loud.

It was clear from the start that Debbie's consternation about my planned pilgrimage was rooted in that love. And, I fully appre-ciated that. She shared much of my frustration about the troubled state of the nation, and therefore understood why I felt compelled to make a personal statement by taking some sort of meaningful action. The exact action I chose to take was what she questioned. As my planned departure date drew closer, this became a subject of dispute in nearly every post-midnight Sandbar chat. Ultimately though, after it became apparent that I wasn't about to adjust my game plan, Debbie's primary anxiety became less about my venture and more about her inability to make a financial contribution in support of it.

Still, all along, Debbie kept promising that, when she sold her Corvallis house, she would meet me on my trek, and treat me to a motel room and a nice dinner. That happy day, I'm pleased to report, has finally arrived. And, on the Fourth of July! So, tonight, I am not only blessed with accommodations and a delicious meal but, far more importantly, the easy company of a true-blue soulmate.

Unfortunately, no thanks to the fickle moods of Mother Nature on the Oregon Coast, the Gold Beach Independence Day fireworks display turns out to be a spectacular dud. The explosions and the crackle ring loud and clear. We can smell the smoke. The moisture in the air ignites, glowing red, then green, then gold. But the fog is so dense that the sparkle and the flash are barely visible. To me, this feels like a metaphor for the state of our nation. Come on, everybody, sing along! "Happy birthday, dear Americaaaaah… *We're lost in a fog.*"

JULY 5 · DAY SIXTY-SIX

As I take advantage of the "free continental breakfast," I'm chatting up the tiny, reed-thin, bushy-haired matriarch of the Indian family that owns and manages the Azalea Lodge.

"Why," I inquire, "is almost every motel owned by people of Indian or Asian heritage?"

"Because," she explains, "when you come to this country in your middle age, there are no jobs. And, this is hard work. People want to have weekends."

By "people," I immediately understand, she's referring to Americans. "So," I observe, "you don't get days off, do you?"

"No," she answers, with a wry smile that silently accuses every American of sloth. Her family, she elaborates, owns two motels in Gold Beach. They have no employees. Instead, every member of the clan does his or her part — cleaning, laundry, maintenance, security, bookkeeping, manning the desk, whatever it takes — 24/7/365. Here is yet another example of hard-working immigrants making very real and meaningful contributions to an American community.

JULY 6 · DAY SIXTY-SEVEN

Old Coast Road, just north of Gold Beach. In an expansive, vacant, barbed-wire-fenced field, directly across the lane from a tidy row of pristine, private, beachside homes, a weather-worn plank of wood, approximately eight-feet by three-feet, stands mounted on a pair of four-by-four posts. That the skirmish memorialized by the Curry County Historical Society happened within a stone's throw of the Pacific Ocean seems noteworthy, as it signifies that the theft of North America must have been nearing its completion right here, at a place called...

FORT MINOR

SHERIFF RILEY AND DR. HOLTON AND MINERS BUILT A FORT IN THE MIDDLE OF THIS FIELD. DRIFT LOGS WERE DRAGGED BY OXEN FROM THE BEACH. ON FEB 22, 1856, SETTLERS WERE ATTENDING THE WASHINGTON'S BIRTHDAY BALL IN ELLENSBURG. FIGHTING BROKE OUT BETWEEN INDIANS AND WHITES AND 23 WHITES WERE KILLED. PARTY GOERS RUSHED TO THE FORT AND WERE BESEIGED FOR 30 DAYS BEFORE BEING RESCUED.

As I stand here, I am flooded with a profound sense of sorrow and shame, reminded once again that this nation was built upon a foundation of genocide and racism. As happened throughout the Western Hemisphere, white, Christian Europeans invaded, slaughtered indigenous peoples, and took possession of their homeland. In what would become these United States of America, my European ancestors pushed their way across the continent, from east to west, systematically decimating native culture. And, to one degree or another, that brutal, merciless, incursion ended here in this field.

But the early settlers weren't satisfied with wiping out aboriginals and stealing this continent. They stole human beings from *another* continent. Africans were hunted down and captured, imported in the bellies of ships, to become the property of white landowners. They were sold like cattle, ripped apart from their families, and whipped into submission, to perform the backbreaking labor that would eventually make America, and white Americans, rich. I can't help but wonder what the karma must be for a nation founded on such inhumane treatment of other human beings. What amount of supplication and/or reparation could possibly make up for the injustice the Caucasian race has inflicted upon people of color?

And yet, the presumption of white privilege (Christian-white privilege, to be more precise) pervades. Last weekend, in Virginia, the Capital of the Confederacy, white nationalists rallied to "Unite the Right." Marchers waved swastika flags, brandished tiki torches, and shouted anti-Semitic chants. Event organizers brazenly declared their goal of inciting a race war. One participant was so emboldened by this fraternity of hate that he deliberately plowed his muscle car into a group of counter protestors, murdering an innocent young woman.

I can only hope that our more-enlightened children will break this regrettable cycle of hatred and lead America to a kinder, more enlightened way forward.

JULY 7 · DAY SIXTY-EIGHT

My bivy was the one and only tent pitched here last night at the Nasika Beach RV Park. I'm doing final-detail packing when I hear a voice...

"You look way too busy." The man is probably close to, if not beyond 80. Curiously, he carries a bucket in one hand and a chair in the other.

Keeping my nose to the task at hand, I inform him, "When I'm packing, I have to concentrate."

"Well then, I'll let you concentrate," the elderly man responds, his tone apologizing for bothering me.

"Oh, no, no, no," I protest, realizing how dismissive I must have sounded.

George's handshake is strong and firm. He places his chair in the middle of the gravel lane and sits, fully prepared to engage in conversation. "I got a new motor home," he announces, pointing to the Pinnacle model just across the road. "My brother gave it to me. My other one's not too far away. A travel trailer. I towed it with my Oldsmobile. But, I didn't need the car anymore, so I gave it away."

"You're paying it forward," I observe.

"Yep," George concurs, "and every time I do, I get something even better. I'm a very blessed man. I've got TV." I have no idea how to respond to this piece of info. But it doesn't matter, because George has more to share… "I had a thirty-five inch. But it was too big for the motor home, so my brother gave me one that was just the perfect size. So, I gave the thirty-five inch away. I was going to give the travel trailer away, too. But somebody offered me cash for it. I couldn't turn that down, could I?"

"So," I wonder, "are you ever gonna take your new motor home out on the road?"

"No," George responds, with a shake of his head, "it'll stay right there. I'll never move it." His smile is one of resignation. He knows his new digs just might be the last home he'll ever have. "They say I can't drive." He muses for few seconds, then remarks, "The Good Lord is kind, isn't He."

"Yes," I agree. And, even though I don't believe for a second that God has a gender, or any other Earthly qualities for that matter, I decide not to take issue with George. "He certainly is."

☮ ☮ ☮ ☮ ☮

I'm depositing the last of my trash when George emerges from his spiffy, new-to-him motor home. "Have a safe trip," he says. Accompanied by a large, blond woman, he shuffles toward a parked SUV.

"I'm Rand," I say, extending my hand to the woman. She, George informs me, is his sister.

"Flossy," George's sister elaborates, accepting my handshake with a smile.

As I push my cart down the gravel driveway out of the park, Flossy is driving brother George to a doctor's appointment. I stop to allow them to pass. Through the open passenger window, George points at me and winks. "May God be with you," he says.

Prehistoric Gardens is one of those tacky roadside attractions a parent acquiesces to stopping at out of sheer exasperation. When the kids in the backseat are going bonkers on the way to or from a family reunion where cousins are mean, uncles have bourbon on their breath, and great-grandparents are sadly senile, the life-sized, animatronic T-Rex in the parking lot must seem like the perfect distraction. For this pilgrim, the attraction's attraction is something else: the inviting rolling lawn, where I can get a load off and glom a sandwich.

But kids love dinosaurs. It's a fact. And, a ginger-haired toddler named Nico is no exception. Nico's grandmother, Kimberly, informs me that she owns a bookstore in the coastal town of Bandon. Then, she asks a most provocative question… "Has it been anything at all like you expected?"

I've actually put a great deal of thought into comparing the journey I originally envisioned to what I've experienced thus far. Still, I'm a wee bit flummoxed as I attempt to articulate an answer. "Well, I knew it was gonna hurt, that there'd be some pain," I manage. "So, in that way, I guess it's been pretty much what I expected."

As Kimberly walks to her car to join her daughter and grandson, I know I've just avoided revealing how my pilgrimage experience hasn't been anything at all like what I anticipated. I kept this detail to myself purposefully, because confiding it to a stranger could so easily make me out to be a bit of an egotist. And, while I chose not to share this with Nico's grandmother, I will here…

WHEN I FIRST started thinking about going on a very long walk to make a statement, I hoped, as my journey progressed, to gain a certain degree of renown — not so much due to blatant, shameless self-promotion, but more in a grass-roots, folk-heroic, Pied-Piper-ish kind of way. That hasn't happened. Instead, aside from my modest-but-loyal Facebook following, and the folks I've encountered personally, my journey has taken place almost entirely in anonymity. And that, ironically and remarkably, has only added to the richness of the experience.

I'M NO LONGER doing this to change any other person's mind, or to enhance someone else's life, or with any hope of garnering fame. I'm doing this first and foremost to prove to myself that I can do it, to fully immerse myself in whatever happens, and to be totally present for every moment. My intention is to interact directly and fully with whomever I meet, without any ulterior motive. So, no, Kimberly... it's not anything like what I expected. And, to my own surprise, I'm not the least bit disappointed.

☮ ☮ ☮ ☮ ☮

I'm pushing the Pilgrimmobile up a rough, rutted, winding incline when a helmeted man whizzes past me on a recumbent bicycle. Today's journey commenced with a kind-hearted "May God be with you" from a gracious octogenarian named George who, unlike Yours Truly, seems to have surrendered to the all-too-swift passage of time. Miraculously, since receiving George's blessing, I've felt safe and protected, as if surrounded by an aura of holy light. The walk, although 16 miles long, has been beautiful, and the day has been perfect — warm, and clear. At one point, I came to a bridge under construction, where a pair of flagmen were taking turns stopping traffic. "Be safe, my man," the second flagman called out, with a smile and a wave. "God bless ya!"

Yes, God must have been with me today. During one stretch, the highway narrowed into dark shadows. Bordered on one side by steep cliffs, the shoulder-less road snaked around blind, hairpin curves. Every time I'd get to a spot where I could easily have been crushed between a landslide and a log truck, I had free passage, with no traffic whatsoever. George had encircled me in a halo of safety, I'm quite certain of it.

I arrive at the entrance to the campground to find the helmeted recumbent cyclist now upright, standing at the self-pay kiosk. Dressed in a loud, multi-colored spandex top, his distended belly hanging over hip-hugging bike shorts, the large, white-haired man appears to be improvising a stand-up comedy routine. In a booming baritone voice, he spouts one-liners on a theme — his inability to figure out how to insert his registration form and five-dollar fee into the confounding contraption. Meanwhile, I — along with every camper and woodland creature in the park — learn that the boisterous fellow's name is Harold. He's 76. And, ironically, considering his manual ineptitude in sliding an envelope into a slot, he's a slight-of-hand magician who performs at children's birthday parties.

As I begin making camp, two couples return to the site across the pathway, clad in bathing suits, and bantering away in rapid-fire *Français*. A few minutes later, bounding from out of nowhere, still helmeted, his basketball belly bouncing over the waistband of his bike shorts, Mesdames et Messieurs, I give you Harold le Magnifique! — now armed with a deck of cards. Without asking permission, he foists himself upon the Francophile quartet, launches into some snappy, well-rehearsed magician patter, while performing a series of close-up card tricks. I'm not certain he's even aware that his captive audience can't comprehend even half of what he is saying.

After concluding the first show of the evening, Harold fulfills my most immediate fear by pogoing over to pay me a visit. Although I'm certainly impressed by the elderly gent's exuberance, I can't help but resent his evident presumption that every camper at Humbug Mountain State Park is in the mood for card tricks. After picking up on my *I'd rather be left alone* vibe, Harold mercifully spares me from a reprise of his act, bids me good night, and skulks off, his shoulders somewhat more stooped than they'd been only a few minutes earlier.

Suddenly, the evening seems very quiet. As I sit down to do some writing, I feel a pang of guilt for having disregarded the poor fellow's desperate need to transform the campground into another children's birthday party, where he can return to his comfort zone as the star attraction. But, honestly, I would be far more receptive to having a heart-to-heart conversation with Harold the person, rather than being forced to endure an in-your-face exhibition by Harold the entertainer.

Maybe all that's left for Harold at the end of the day is a recumbent bicycle, a deck of playing cards, and some snappy patter. But at least the old guy's out here pumping up his endorphins, seeing the sights, finding new audiences, and doing his thing — which beats the crap outta wasting away, waiting on the Grim Reaper to assist him in his closing trick.

CHAPTER 30

Whodunit? Who Cares?

JULY 8 · DAY SIXTY-NINE

For the first time since Southern California, I'm met with brawny, bracing wind. Some gusts hit me head-on with such force that forward progress is temporarily stalled. As I enter Port Orford, the westernmost incorporated community in the contiguous United States, one guerilla blast broadsides me from one direction, only to sneak attack a minute later from another.

I've been instructed to look for a royal-blue house with fuchsia trim. The vividly colored structure, neatly situated between a wetland area and a fresh-water lake, looks like a hand-painted picture postcard. A woman with a sculpted, short haircut, blond on top, dark on the sides comes to the door. "You must be Rand, I presume," she says.

Bowing at the waist like an Elizabethan lord, I respond, "And you must be Jean." It's immediately evident that Jean has trepidations about inviting a strange man into her home. And, who could blame her? A single woman of advancing age, opening her door to an overly tan, grey-bearded, cart-pushing pilgrim in a straw cowboy hat? I'm a friend of friends, yes — Gary Lahman and Cynthia Jacobi — but a stranger still, *and* a man. However, as we sit chatting at her kitchen table, Jean's distrust begins melting away.

Retired from a career in nursing, my hostess appears both vibrant and content, continuing to express her passion for life through painting and photography. Even in her later years, she retains a certain demure, girlish charm, blushing and giggling at certain things I say with the innocence of a sheltered-but-curious child. Then, she asks… If she's able to procure an extra ticket, would I be interested in accompanying her to tonight's Mystery Whodunit Dinner at the Senior Center? *Honestly, I can think of nothing I'd rather do.*

As I escort Jean into the event, she introduces me to one chipper, affable senior citizen after another. "This is Rand," she says. "He's passing through on a peace pilgrimage." Then, to draw me into the conversation, she queries, "How far have you walked so far, Rand?"

My answer, *about 680 miles,* is a natural source of intrigue to these fellow baby boomers. One particular reaction, however, stands out in stark contrast — coming from the one person in attendance who seems intent on throwing a wet blanket over the proceedings.

A petite, neatly dressed woman, with tidy, short-cropped hair, Gladys would probably be attractive if it weren't for the stream of negativity hissing from her tightly pursed lips. She's not happy about anything and has no qualms about voicing her discontent. In particular, she hasn't any attention to spare for a visiting peace pilgrim who she is appalled to learn has trekked nearly 700 miles on foot.

"Why the hell would you wanna do a thing like that?" Gladys snorts.

With one caustic question, this haughty sourpuss has expressed overt disrespect, ridiculed my mission, and made light of the pain and sacrifice I've endured for the last 69 days. If there were ever a perfect time to follow the old "if you can't say anything nice, don't say anything at all rule," this would be it. Then again, I recall a certain axiom about catching more flies with honey which, although it seems perfectly logical, has always left me puzzled as to why anyone would want to catch flies in the first place — let alone *more* flies.

Somehow, I know precisely what to say. Allowing a warm smile to spread across my face, while looking directly into the unhappy, discourteous woman's eyes, I answer, with all the sincerity I can muster, "So I can meet nice people like you." Disarmed, Gladys simply stands there, staring back at me, blushing, mouth agape.

"Nice line, Bud." This pithy, five-star review comes from a fellow at the adjacent table. His sly-eyed wink tells me he's more than delighted to see the cantankerous old bat getting her well-deserved come-uppance. I excuse myself politely, step away, and take my seat.

Once in a while, it's healthy to forget about the problems of the world and indulge in some pure, mindless escapism. Although the lasagna is bland and barely warm, the salad is limp, and the garlic bread is stale, the game is a hoot. In no time, a hall full of senior citizens is absorbed in a soap-opera world populated by comically ridiculous characters, everyone keenly focused on the race to solve a crime that never took place in a town that doesn't exist.

JULY 11 · DAY SEVENTY-TWO

The shrill, dissonant chorus of feathered creatures outside is making an unholy racket. Suddenly, the cacophony abates. And, now, two housekeepers, one male, one female, are engaging in boisterous, profanity-peppered banter right outside my door, loud enough that every guest in this end of the Shooting Star Motel surely must be able to overhear every indiscrete detail.

I'm beginning to feel as though I'm playing my own version of Bill Murray in *Groundhog Day,* walking the same pavement, repeating the same conversation. Folks are fully absorbed in their own day-to-day lives and, while they're invariably nice about it, they don't really want to get involved.

Adding to my emotional malaise is the undeniable fact that my body is wearing down. Every single step is excruciating for my right foot, my left heal is tender, and my lower legs, knees-to-ankles, are growing weak and wobbly. The impact of the pavement, the ups and downs, the compensating for the side-to-side slant and roughness of the road, the wind, and the parade of vehicles blasting by, mile-after-mile, have grown tiresome, wearying. Hours of solitude, absorbed in my own private contemplations, leave me feeling small, insignificant, and isolated. With only eighteen more days, just two and a half weeks to go, I find myself gasping for a seventy-third, second wind.

Sometimes, even the most basic and banal discovery can provide that desperately needed spark of hope. I'm browsing the Bandon Old Town Mercantile Store when I spy a rack of socks especially designed for hikers and runners. In preparation for this very long walk, I dedicated multiple hours to sock shopping — in retail stores and online — searching for a product that would support and, at the same time, protect my fragile underpinnings. I've invested a small fortune on the half-dozen pair I tote with me. However, regardless of whether they are spun from the priciest merino wool, woven out of cotton, spandex, nylon, or some secret blend of any or all of the above, no sock has been capable of providing the comfort and relief these two abused feet have been crying out for.

But, after 72 straight days of steadily increasing inflammation, maybe, just maybe I now hold the answer to my tootsie's prayers in my trembling hands: Thorlos, with Thor*lon® and Lycra fiber, 84N Runner, Foot Protection — FOR FEET THAT HURT DURING OR AFTER ACTIVITY! Padding clinically shown to: REDUCE BLISTERS, REDUCE PAIN. "Your feet will feel better or your money back!" $14.95. *What,* I ask myself, *has a pilgrim got to lose?*

I can't wait to try these suckers on. Outside the store, on the sidewalk, I find a bench. In defiance of the frigid, unforgiving, north wind, I sit down, kick off my shoes and socks, rip open the packaging, pull the brand-new Thorlos over my sore feet, slip back into my sneakers, and lace 'em up tight. I take a step, then another. It's unbelievable. It's not as though the pain is gone altogether. But there's certainly less of it, and what remains seems far more bearable. I bounce the mile and a half back to the Shooting Star with a fresh, new outlook. It's not as though I'm looking forward to tomorrow's trek — the forecast calls for yet more stiff, steady wind — but I'm no longer dreading it. Amazing that something as simple as a new pair of socks can chase away a cruel case of the blues.

JULY 13 · DAY SEVENTY-FOUR

Well, it was bound to happen sooner or later. And, while I'm glad it didn't happen sooner, I would have preferred to wait until even later. But this, after all, is the Oregon Coast. Rain is inevitable — many would even say probable. However, there was no precipitation in the forecast for this entire week. So, I wasn't prepared for this.

Pop! A sudden, intense drop of liquid on the tent roof startles me awake. *I hope that's not what I think it is.* Another loud pop-drop, then another. I try to go back to sleep. *If it's raining,* I reason, *there's nothing much I can do about it. Besides, it's not raining very hard. Just a few scattered drops. It'll be okay.* Then, it occurs to me… I'd better grab the large, waterproof bag my nephew Kelly gave me for keeping stuff dry. I've been using the dry bag as a welcome mat of sorts, to kneel on as I crawl through the triangular doorway of this tiny, one-person shelter. I unzip the tent screen and reach out. *Damn!* The dry bag is not remotely dry. In fact, it's now a sopping-wet bag. This has me worried. And, it turns out there's very good reason for my concern.

At about 5:30 AM, there's a hint of light. I reach for the wool beanie cap in which I always roll up my iPhone, my glasses, and my Chapstick. It's wet. I roll over. My self-inflating mattress is wet around the edges. I lift up one corner. *Damn again!* The thin mattress is the only thing keeping me and my sleeping bag from sinking into the inch of rainwater flooding the bivy floor.

I begin brainstorming a strategy. *In what order should I do what?* Slowly, deliberately, I start taking action, first by putting everything within reach into the vinyl Trader Joes food bags, which, fortunately, have yet to take on water. I pick up my mesh toiletry bag. It's saturated. So, I toss it out of the tent first.

Somehow, I manage to squeeze my sleeping bag and pillows into their stuff sacks, while balancing precariously on the mattress/life raft. I hoist the heavy food bags outside, and scramble my bare feet out behind them to survey the situation. There, in the morning twilight, I gaze at my pathetically sad bivy, drooping under the weight of the accumulated rain. The tent may be extremely wet on the outside. Inside, however, I've got myself a kiddy swimming pool. Had I any inkling that precipitation was on its way, I would surely have used the tarp as it was meant to be used, as a water-proof shield *over the tent*, instead of making it a water receptacle *beneath the tent*.

Weather forecasts change. I get that. An updated prediction on my iPhone Weather Channel App gives a 10% chance of rain. Peace Pilgrim 2017? Not today. Call me Joe Btfsplk — look him up; I had to — because this Joe just got deluged with 100% of the 10%.

The dry bag is now a wet bag for the soaked tarp and the soggy tent. I sit on the rolled-up mattress, between drooping clumps of grass and sagging fronds of water-logged weeds, to eat breakfast: an apple, a mangled Kind bar, and a Lara Bar, washed down with the dregs of an Odwalla strawberry smoothie. I strap the stuffed, wet bag onto the top of the fiberglass box, plow the Pilgrimmobile through muddy ruts, between sticker patches, onto the gravel, and to the highway. I dry my feet as best I can, pull on my new Thorlos socks, and lace up my sneakers.

As the road descends out of the Coos County forest, the bike lane disappears. Hours pass with no place to stop for lunch. Trucks and RVs scream by, leaving me rocked, awash in powerful waves of tailwind. According to Google maps, Coos Bay Christian Fellowship is about a half mile away. Surely, I'll find a place there to stop. It's been five hours since I've taken any sustenance, and the breakfast I managed to scrounge in the early morning bog didn't provide near enough fuel.

Yes! The church property sits up above the highway, surrounded by newly mown lawn. I push my cart up the steep, pot-holed, gravel driveway and park it next to a tall flagpole. A cherry-red Mustang sits parked in the lot, its driver-side door standing open. As I approach the idling vehicle, a man emerges from the church building. Sporting white hair and beard, he resembles ex-Doobie Brother Michael McDonald. I inform him that I'm on a peace pilgrimage and ask permission to sit down in the churchyard to eat a sandwich.

"Yeah," he says, "go ahead and crash out on the lawn." He slips behind the wheel of his Mustang and scoots down the drive and onto the highway. I remove my sopping tent and tarp from the sack, drape them over the light standards next to the church sign and allow them to waft in the breeze like sheets on a clothesline. Then, I roll out the camping pad on the grass and sit down to eat and to read my book. A half hour and a chapter later, the red Mustang darts back up the gravel incline. Noticing my tent and tarp flapping in the breeze, the Michael McDonald lookalike pauses, furrows his brow disapprovingly, but refrains from making comment. He pulls his shiny wheels into the lot, parks, and re-enters the church. I'm thinking the guy must be the minister. This being Thursday, he's probably composing his sermon for this coming Sunday service.

By the time I've read another chapter, the tent and tarp are relatively dry. But, before I go, I should thank the gentleman. I knock on the church door. After a minute, he answers. I extend my postcard to him. "This is about who I am and what I'm up to." He accepts the card, giving it no more than a cursory glance. "My name is Rand."

"Jim," he responds as we shake hands. "Do you need to use the bathroom?"

As I enter the church, I ask him if he's the pastor here. He confirms my guess. "Well," I say, "thank you for your Christian generosity."

I use the facilities, wash up, thank Jim again, and head for the door. "Be careful on that highway," he advises.

That Pastor Jim doesn't ask a single question about my trek baffles me. A man shows up at his church out of nowhere on a Thursday afternoon claiming to be on a pilgrimage and he's not the least bit curious? You'd think a minister, of all people, would want to find out more. But, surprisingly, I'm discovering that disinterest is not uncommon here in my home state. And, when fellow Oregonians do have questions, they usually don't ask why I've embarked upon this journey, they want to know where I sleep or if it's scary to walk the highway. I receive the occasional, "Thank you for what you're doing." But, most of the time, that's about as far as it goes.

CHAPTER 31

Bridge Crossing

JULY 14 · DAY SEVENTY-FIVE

"I was thinking… maybe I've got a peace pilgrim on my hands." The raspy voice is jovial and friendly. And, the man's introductory statement, referring to the banner on the Pilgrimmobile parked nearby, is undeniably glib.

I'm sitting on a bench at the Coos Bay Tug Boat Pavilion, reading my paperback, and finishing the remainder of a two-day-old sandwich. A grinning character is peering over my shoulder. "Well," I reply, "I guess you're right."

"Mind if I sit down?" he asks, not waiting for an answer. Jesse is in his late forties, fifties at most. He has a sharp, pointed nose and a pair of pale-blue, Paul-Newman-neon eyes. A navy-blue stocking cap is pulled down over his sandy, medium-length shag, and his ginger beard has, recently it appears, received the worst weed-whacking in the history of mankind.

"I thought maybe you were fishing for swordfish," he quips. I'm pretty sure that's what he said. His words are extremely slurred. So, it's difficult to be exact. The smile, now spreading across his rutted face, is more maniacal than impish.

"No, actually," I tell him, suddenly feeling slightly uneasy about this imposition, "I'm just reading my book."

"I'm taking a break," he announces.

"From what?"

"Life," he clarifies.

"Well, this is life," I remind him, gesturing out to the expanse of water in front of us, glittering in the early afternoon sunshine.

"Who's got all the money?" Jesse demands, as if I must have the answer. "Everybody's got more money than us."

"Is that true?" I respond. I don't want to argue with the guy. So, I think it best to reply with a question. It's clear he's made the assumption that, like him, I must be homeless. Exhibits "A" through "E": I'm sitting on a bench in a public place in the middle of the day, next to the cart I push, reading a tattered paperback book, eating a sandwich that looks like it might have been retrieved from a dumpster.

"I don't have any money. Who's got all the money?" Jesse seems intent on sticking to this theme. "That seven hundred I get every month? Don't go very far... *Wooo!* A few days later, it's gone. I just want my next beer. Where does it go? I have some friends. They need something, I give it to 'em. How much do I end up with? Twenty, thirty bucks, maybe." Jesse laughs. "I just want my next beer." He pauses, draws in a breath, exhales, and shakes his head at what he believes is the sad, unfair truth: "Everybody's out to beat the other guy."

Now I have to disagree. "That," I tell him, "hasn't been my experience."

"Oh, yeah," Jesse insists. "It's true. Everybody's out to beat the other guy." He abruptly jolts to his feet. "Well, thanks for the visit," he says, and careens away at a forward-leaning pitch.

I haven't quite finished reading another paragraph when Jesse plops back down. "Yeah, there's life going on out there," he observes, now gazing out over the rippling harbor. A pelican tucks its wings and plunges 40 feet out of the sky into the water. "We're just sitting here watching life go by." After a chuckle, he repeats the same statement, this time quieter, as if he's relishing his own wizened observation. "We're just sitting here watching life go by." After a lengthy pause, he wants to know, "You smoke weed?"

"Nope," I answer.

"Oh, well, that's just about all I got for ya. I'm just trying to get my next beer."

Having determined there is no mutually beneficial barter to

be struck here, Jesse makes his second and final exit, presumably to "take a break" somewhere else and continue his quest for that elusive next beer.

A few minutes later, a pair of police officers stroll down the boardwalk, eyes peeled for some well-known local character who, one informs the other, was last seen rummaging through a trash can near this location. Key words overheard from their interchange suggest that the person of interest might be challenged with mental-health issues. I wonder if they might be talking about a fellow named Jesse, with whom I just had an undeniably odd conversation.

I've stopped to take a photo of the sign in the window of a local business: *Guns, Guitars, and Jewelry.* I'm amused, thinking this could make an ideal title for an autobiography authored by any number of rock 'n' rollers or country-music renegades. A motorized wheelchair whizzes past on the sidewalk. I pocket my iPhone and follow, catching up at the next intersection. Gunning his electric motor, Wheelchair Man zips out into the crosswalk. However, a car darts out of nowhere, directly in front of his speeding chair. Alertly, Wheelchair Man quickly slams on his brake. *Close call!*

"Unbelievable!" I observe out loud. Without acknowledging my comment, Wheelchair Man rockets ahead, up the handicapped ramp, and down the sidewalk. With amused admiration, I observe him weaving his serpentine path, skillfully avoiding ruts and patches of gravel. It's clear this fellow is more than familiar with every potential pitfall along this route. After trekking several more blocks, I spy another wheelchair — this one not motorized — pulling out onto the sidewalk next to a smoke shop, across the highway from a small, funky, food market.

The man in this wheelchair is compact and wiry. Sporting a white, neatly trimmed beard, he wears a U.S. Navy Veteran ball cap, a down vest, and jeans. It doesn't escape my attention that his bare chest and flat belly are perfectly bronzed by the sun. I toss him a quick, "How's it goin'?"

"Just workin' on my tan," he says with a contented grin.
"Lookin' good," I respond, and march on.

Last night, I discovered that the North Bend July Jubilee takes place this weekend — for the 114th consecutive summer. *How, I asked myself, could I possibly depart on the eve of a wholesome, community tradition, more than a century in the making?* I pictured myself joining the "Five-K Jaunt," pushing the Pilgrimmobile, marching alongside the locals, slapping high-fives, initiating chants and leading sing-alongs, making new friends, and inspiring an uplifting Saturday of civil, constructive dialogue.

I made tonight's reservation at the Bay Bridge Motel based purely on its inexpensive price tag. The exact whereabouts of these bargain-basement accommodations, however, might prove to be less than ideal. The nice woman at the visitor center informs me that, no, there are no markets or restaurants within reasonable walking distance of the motel. So, if I plan on arriving at the isolated hostelry with adequate supplies, I'll need to double back to the small, funky, food market I passed 10 blocks ago, across the highway from that grinning Navy Vet, sunning himself in the wheelchair.

After picking up some essentials at the market, I find myself approaching the tanned, wheelchair-bound man for the third time. Having observed me entering the market and subsequently emerging with supplies, he's come to the logical conclusion that, although I'm pushing a cart, I must possess some resources. "You got a dollar and twenty cents?" he asks. I rarely give handouts to street people. However, I find the specificity of this man's request unusual and therefore intriguing.

"I think I might," I respond, fishing into my pocket and counting out a buck twenty.

"I didn't ask before," he explains, "because, you know…"

"I get it," I interrupt. "It's quite all right."

John Carpenter speaks in a certain *Big Lebowski,* Dude-ish

vocal cadence. As I stand here on the sidewalk, he launches into a litany of injuries he's suffered, shows me scars on his badly dislocated shoulder, from taking a header on his mountain bike. He laughs about wobbling that two-wheeler home over the bridge after a night of hard partying. He recounts mishaps on day jobs and accidents during trips up and down the coast. Then, there's the Airstream trailer he bought at auction for $2,500 back when he had credit cards, the one he and his buddies towed to the fishing port of Charleston, just south of Coos Bay. He recounts getting arrested in Pueblo, Colorado — they accused him of stealing his own car — and spending 120 days in jail before a judge finally dismissed the charges. Catholic Charities provided him with clothes, a haircut, and transportation back home to North Bend — his home for 40 years, except for the time he was in the Navy, or behind bars in Pueblo.

It's getting late. I tell him I'll probably see him tomorrow and trek onward toward my motel, having absolutely no clue what waits for me a half-mile up the road.

The Conde B. McCullough Memorial Bridge is listed on the National Register of Historic Places in recognition of its design, cultural significance, and economic importance. Constructed between 1934 and 1936 under the Works Progress Administration, this cantilevered marvel is just shy of a mile in length and clears the dark, deep, churning waters of Coos Bay by 145 feet. A drive across McCullough Memorial — even today, in its ninth decade of existence — is an awe-inspiring experience. Evidence of this is that every other vehicle traversing these snug, 13-foot-wide lanes seems to contain at least one passenger pointing a camera phone up at its 280-foot towers and sweeping, gothic arches. The awe struck into the heart of a pedestrian traveling the span, however, is less inspirational and, at this moment, more rooted in pure, intense fear.

Even without a 90-pound pushcart on the calmest day, crossing the McCullough span by foot is not for the faint of heart. This particular evening, with the coast wind swirling in gusts approaching 50 miles per hour, 5,305 feet of slender, elevated sidewalk is as filled with potential peril as a tightrope walk across the Grand Canyon. Squeezed between a constant stream of cars, SUVs, pick-ups, oversized travel trailers, semis, and log trucks rushing by a foot away from my right shoulder, and a 14-story drop to the frigid bay to my left, I take one tentative step at a time, struggling against the buffeting wind to keep the stroller wheels rolling straight ahead. It takes every bit of my strength and concentration to prevent the top-heavy load from catching a gust, blowing off of the high curb, and tumbling onto the roadway. This would result not only in the box and everything in it getting crushed, it would also most certainly cause a multi-vehicle pileup, very possibly counting a peace pilgrim as one of its victims.

The blurry vision I see ahead through wind-whipped tears is like a punch to the gut. For 100 feet or more, the sidewalk actually narrows — and, not just by a few inches, but by nearly a foot. It appears that, after trekking for 75 days and well over 700 miles, I've pushed the Pilgrimmobile a bridge too far. But this passageway is the only conduit, not just from here to the Bay Bridge Motel, but from here to the completion of my trek. There is no turning back. One apparent and irrefutable fact: with my over-stuffed supply bags dangling from both sides of the Pilgrimmobile, squeezing past this impediment will be impossible. Still, even without the bags, it seems doubtful that the reduced width of the sidewalk will accommodate the wheelbase of the stroller.

Summoning a newfound belief in miracles, I swing both bags up on top of the box, lay my outstretched left arm over the bags to hold them in place, and lean my body weight into the stroller handle to move the wheels ever-so-slowly forward, while steering with my right hand and forearm. With my eye fixed on the rear, right stroller wheel, teetering on the very edge of the elevated curb, while traffic continues to whiz past, now only inches away from my right ear, and the brutal wind pummeling and buffeting the cart from the west, I push ahead, one hazardous millimeter at a time. Somehow, astonishingly, this gambit works and, ever-so-slowly, I manage to slip the Pilgrimmobile through the narrowed section of sidewalk.

I cover an average highway mile in approximately 20 to 30 minutes. It was approaching 5PM when I mounted the southern ramp onto the mile-long span. With the north end of the bridge now in sight, it's closing in on seven. The physical and psychic trauma of the McCullough crossing has taken its toll. To say I'm spent would be a gross understatement. Still, I've done it. At the expense of some extremely frazzled nerves and an utterly exhausted body, I've crossed the Grand Canyon via tightrope.

JULY 15 · DAY SEVENTY-SIX

They say the definition of insanity is doing the same thing over and over and expecting different results. Pushing the Pilgrimmobile across the McCullough Memorial Bridge yesterday was crazy. Although the stunt did yield optimum results, I have no desire to perform a reprise this morning, only to cap off a day at the 114th North Bend July Jubilee by risking a third crossing in a 24-hour period. Without question, *that* would be the definition of insanity.

This decision, however, presents a challenge. The vinyl banner wrapped around the Pilgrimmobile announces who I am — *Peace Pilgrim 2017* — and advertises my mission. Sans Pilgrimmobile, I'll be just another anonymous, grey-bearded fellow striding along the Five-K Jaunt. It's less that I want to draw attention to myself than a desire to make my spontaneous North Bend layover more meaningful through maximum interaction with the locals. With that in mind, I fashion a rather silly-looking alternative by wrapping the banner around my torso and hanging it from my shoulders via bungee-cable suspenders. I resemble a hybrid character from the Wizard of Oz. The rolled-up, tube-like, vinyl banner from armpit to thigh offers a fresh twist on the Tin Man, if he were constructed out of PVC-pipe, while my straw cowboy hat adds a rather Scarecrow-ish topping.

At the southern end of the McCullough span, I encounter a stream of human bipeds, power-walking alongside the road, all wearing numbered bibs on their chests. The listing in the local paper had the Five-K Jaunt commencing at 9:45. *But, no! It actually kicked off at nine.* These walkers have already covered the first two kilometers of five.

Too late to register officially, I merge into the foot parade, only to discover that I'm among the last dozen stragglers. The walkers move along in pairs and clusters, couples shepherding their own kids, friends chatting up friends. There is little interaction between one tight group and the next that might give the walk any tangible sense of community. Other than getting out for a vigorous, aerobic stroll — something one could do on any pleasant Saturday morning — there seems to be no special meaning or purpose to the event. As the only solo jaunt-ee, I attempt to engage other walkers with some *How's it goin's* and *Beautiful days.* Responses, although not exactly unfriendly, are terse. No one seems the least bit interested in taking discourse beyond the cordial-but-cursory level. And, curiously, not a single soul even acknowledges the elephant on the path: the white, vinyl banner wrapped around my torso advertising *Peace Pilgrim 2017 YouTube.com.*

At the public square, the North Bend Fire Brigade and their extremely cheerful wives are serving up free hotdogs and miniature cupcakes. A pilgrim makes it a policy to never pass up free food (assuming the free food appears edible). And, after all, a small-town, all-American July-Jubilee experience would seem incomplete without indulging in a hotdog or two. As I make my way across the red-brick plaza to take my place in the food line, I notice a man wearing an Army Veteran cap, sitting by himself. The snarl directed my way gives me the impression he's not all that pleased with my peace-pilgrim banner. I decide this fellow would be the perfect person to join for lunch. By the time I return with my plate, the snarling fellow has already been joined — by a woman, also wearing a cap, hers emblazoned with a University of Oregon "O." As I, too, am a UO Duck fan, this will automatically give me a perfect ice-breaker…

"Mind if I join you?"

The glowering man mutters something that resembles *go ahead*.
"At least you're rooting for the right team," I jibe.

"Yeah," the woman snorts, "Beavers suck!" (A reference to in-state rival Oregon State.)

A few strategically asked questions get Grouchy Gary opened up enough to reveal that he spent 23 years as a drill sergeant in the Army, but only after serving four years in the Marines. Duck-Cap Debby rasps, "I'm a veteran-*ee!*" Chortling at her own joke, she over explains, "I married a veteran, didn't I?" A boyish woman, Debby appears to be decades younger than her husband. At first, I thought she might be his daughter. As I scarf down my dogs, she keeps glaring at me across the red-white-and-blue tablecloth through squinted eyes, as though she's letting me know, in silent, but no uncertain terms, that she doesn't trust me — not even for a nanosecond.

I ask her if she has any concerns about the direction of our country.

"No," she snaps, abruptly slamming the door shut on that subject. "I don't say much," she further informs me, "especially to strangers."

There is no doubt who the stranger is in this playlet. As I indulge in my first, tiny cupcake, Debby finds it necessary to repeat this statement two more times. Oddly, pretty much all she has to say to a stranger is that she doesn't say much — especially to strangers.

"Whoa!" I exclaim, tasting my second bite-sized confection, "this is red velvet cake! I thought it was chocolate."

"Well, duh!" says Debby, using two, succinct syllables to declare the interloper across the table to be a total ignoramus. At this juncture, a short, stocky man in an NRA cap stops by the table to chat with Gary. After the fellow moves on, Gary fills me in: We've just had a visit from North Bend's mayor. *Good to know.*

It should be noted that over the course of the more than two days I've been in Coos County, not a single person has expressed an iota of interest in me or my pilgrimage. Those who do engage — Grouchy Gary, for instance — seem willing, sometimes even eager, to talk about themselves. Then, of course, there's

Debby, who talks a lot about not talking much. As this conversation is feeling more and more like a heavy lift, I thank Gary and Debby for their company and excuse myself.

Almost immediately, I come face to face with the mayor. I introduce myself. We shake hands. This guy is 100% politician. He listens to me with well-practiced, Bill-Clinton-like intensity as I quickly explain the reason for my 90-day trek. Then, he jumps right on my peace train, agreeing that we most definitely need more civil, constructive dialogue. And, in his line of work, he shares, that's not always the easiest goal to achieve, especially when constituents arrive with competing agendas. "I'm proud of what you're doing," he concludes. "Here, let me give you my card."

"And," I quickly respond, reaching into my pocket, "I'll give you mine."

"That's the way it works, isn't it," the mayor quips. He slips my postcard into the back pocket of his Wranglers, gives me a warm, parting handshake, and says, "Let the peace of Christ rule in your heart." This, I'm thinking, is actually a very nice statement. Maybe not exactly appropriate coming from an elected official. But, if a person feels inspired to play the Jesus card, I'd rather have it be in reference to peace than a not-so-subtly veiled suggestion that I'd best get my immortal soul saved before it's doomed to eternal damnation.

☮   ☮   ☮   ☮   ☮

"What's that say?" the woman inquires. She's squinting, trying to make out the lettering on my banner. "Oh," she figures out, "Peace Pilgrim." Then she looks me in the eye and murmurs, "Thank you." As she collects a free ice cream bar from the back of the Umpqua Bank van, the woman sends yet another glance in my direction. Petite and low-to-the-ground, she is definitely well into senior-citizenship. Still, there is a vibrant cuteness about her. She wears a purple satin scarf around her head, flowered capris pants, and is toting a blue souvenir backpack embroidered with palm trees waving between letters that spell out *Aruba*.

The woman makes her way to a table directly in front of a local, instrumental combo, its three-piece horn section stabbing vainly at the melodies of classic hits. Once again, her gaze meanders my way. I take her cue. "You're curious about me, aren't you," I say, pulling up a chair. She admits that she is. I inform her that it's my second day in North Bend and she's the first person to exhibit the slightest interest.

"I think they're scared," she muses. "Everything is changing so fast, people can't keep up. I have a theory…" The sincere curiosity on my face encourages her to continue… "There are three kinds of people. People who take action; people who want to take action but, for some reason, just don't; and people who actually decide not to. You know why?"

"Tell me," I respond.

"Because," she opines, "they've decided not to know. If they became aware of certain things, they might have to do something. So, instead, they get really good at turning a blind eye."

Anna-Marie, I soon find out, is originally from Alaska, where she mothered seven children and adopted two more. She joined the Church of Jesus Christ of the Latter-day Saints because the Mormon doctrine resonated with her spirit. Adamantly pro-life, she was once arrested for linking arms with other demonstrators to prevent entrance to a family-planning clinic. She feels conflicted about her strong anti-war sentiments because her youngest daughter is presently serving in the Middle East as a tank gunner.

☮ ☮ ☮ ☮ ☮

"I'm in temporary housing," Anna-Marie suddenly blurts. We're standing on the sidewalk, amongst a cheering crowd of July Jubilee celebrants, as antique fire trucks, trained dogs, and beaming teenage baton twirlers parade past. "So, basically," she explains, "I'm homeless."

It's a story I've heard too many times over the course of my trek. A partner-less person, beyond retirement age and struggling to get by on a fixed income, finds herself priced out of the rental market. Anna-Marie raised a family. She contributed to society all her life. Ironically, she's worked tirelessly on behalf of the homeless. She volunteers at the library and was even awarded a citation from the city for her community service work. Now, she's unable to afford a place to live. "We don't make a living wage anymore," Anna-Marie says. "It takes two, maybe three people in a household working to make ends meet."

The local swing band takes the stage. A teenage crooner, barely capable of growing a faint dusting of mustache, does his thrift-store-tuxedo Frank Sinatra, rendering classic compositions from the Great American Songbook. This act is followed by horses dancing to the accompaniment of a Mexican horn band. The hooved routine is novel, but goes on far too long. Every piece of music is the same tempo, in the same key, and more than a little bit out of tune. Folks lose interest and start wandering off. Meanwhile, Anna-Marie shares the following story...

A Coos Bay community group raised enough money to buy 250 camping kits for the local homeless population — tents, sleeping bags, cooking essentials, etc. The idea was to provide them a layer of protection from the elements, which, logically, would prevent illness, and keep them from having to seek emergency-room treatment. After the kits were distributed, a tent community naturally sprung up, provoking complaints about this unsightly civic embarrassment. Succumbing to public pressure, the city council ordered the city manager to run the tent dwellers out of town. However, instead of allowing them to take their donated camping gear, authorities bulldozed the tents and threw everything in dumpsters. Now, the homeless are once again reduced to sleeping in alleyways and forested areas. With the return of damp-autumn and frigid-winter weather, many of them will be emerging from the shadows and showing up in the E.R. due to exposure.

I ask Anna-Marie how she plans to get "home." She sticks out her thumb, miming a hitchhiking gesture. There is something profoundly wrong that a 70-year-old woman should have to stand by the highway and hitch a ride to her temporary housing. "Hey, it's a nice day," she says, with a smile. "It could be much worse."

I have to admire this lady's pluck.

"Oh, I almost forgot," she says. "I wanted to show you some-thing. My bracelet." She rolls up her sleeve to reveal a chartreuse rubber wristband. Basic-black letters print out four words: *Love More—Judge Less.*

☮   ☮   ☮   ☮   ☮

Like yesterday — and, most likely, the day before — John Car-penter sits outside the smoke shop on Highway 101, sunning him-self in his wheelchair. As I approach, a wry smile weaves wrinkled spider webs around his eyes. Spying the guitar case slung over my shoulder, he asks, "You gonna play me a song?"

"I can do that," I respond. What song to perform for this man is the question. My heart gives me a prompt answer. Sitting on the cement divide between the tobacco-store parking lot and the sidewalk, while cars and trucks streak past, I begin plucking the church-like, chordal intro to the softest, most-intimate song in my repertoire.

"Beat down, weary," I sing, *"beast of a day. Everything aches, I'm a balled-up tangle of pain."*

John leans down from his chair, bringing his head within inches of mine. His eyes are gripped closed as if he's putting every bit of his sensory energy into optimizing his capacity to listen.

"Sunset fadin' over the hill. Turn on the porch light, I'm runnin' on nothin' but will. I'm gonna need some healin' time…"

John takes hold of the ivory cross hanging over his tanned chest.

"So, keep on throwin' me that line."

He pulls the cross to his lips and kisses it.

"I know it's gonna be all right, long as you give me some healin' time."

As I fingerpick the instrumental turnaround figure between verses, John murmurs, "I *love* my Lord."

My very first vocal performance was rendered in front of my kindergarten class at Lake Grove Elementary School. The song was "Davy Crockett (King of the Wild Frontier)." I wore a faux-fur coonskin cap on my brush-cut, blond head. I've been a professional in the music business for nearly 50 years. In all of my thousands of performances, over the course of those five decades, I've never had a more attentive, rapt, emotionally invested audience than John Carpenter. As I complete the song, tears stream down his white-whiskered cheeks.

Again, he declares his faith. "I *love* my Lord."

CHAPTER 32

Stubbed Toes on Stardust

JULY 16 · DAY SEVENTY-SEVEN

I hear a *ding* sound, like the bell on a hotel lobby desk. My iPhone screen is dark; this is not some message notification. A second *ding* — this one considerably louder.

Out of nowhere, a bicycle pulls up next to me on my left. Admittedly, I'm startled. Probably close to 40 years old, well over six-feet tall, with a Jay-Leno, lantern jaw, Michael says he noticed the banner on my cart and simply had to hang a U-turn to meet me. He then proceeds to point out the decals plastered all over his bike frame. The one on his crossbar reads, *When the power of love overcomes the love of power, the world will know peace.*

"Jimi Hendrix, right?" I ask.

He's not sure. However, he does remember putting a peace-sign sticker on his bike in 2003, on the fateful day the U.S. re-invaded Iraq. "I commend you for what you're doing," he says. Michael is riding in honor of his brother, taken tragically by suicide. To that purpose, he is re-tracing the same cycling route he took with his late sibling some years back — from his British Columbia home, to San Francisco.

My heart is immediately flooded with compassion and empathy. I, too, have suffered from clinical depression. I, too, lost my dear brother, suddenly, unexpectedly, tragically.

"Suicide is the leading killer of teenagers," Michael says.

I tell him that, only a few weeks ago, my niece was delivered home in an ambulance, after calling the suicide prevention hot line. "It's all about communication," I remark.

"Absolutely," Michael agrees. "We have to let teens know we're listening, that they have permission to share their pain." At this, he becomes more pensive. "I've been thinking about suicide as a metaphor. Maybe it's like a psychic cancer caused by a failure in the 'cognitive immune system.'"

It's an intriguing idea — poetic, yet holistic at the same time. To emerge from underneath this passing shadow, we take smiling selfies together before saying goodbye.

JULY 17 · DAY SEVENTY-EIGHT

This settlement's founders missed the boat. They should have christened it Dorothyville. It looks as though an entire town from the Kansas prairie was swept up in a tornado and plopped down 2,000 miles west. The strength of today's wind has, at times, approached Wizard-of-Oz intensity. Long, remote stretches of two-lane highway climbed steep grades, curved past thousands of acres of deep forest, then swooped down past amoeba-shaped freshwater lakes. The vista opened up on the final descent into this community by the sea to reveal the shops and businesses of "Dorothyville" stringing out along Winchester Boulevard like cheap, dime-store pearls.

At least one-third of Reedsport's commercial properties are vacant, for sale or lease. I'm traipsing along a sidewalk bereft of any distinguishing character when I come face-to-face with a young man. His greasy, tousled hair is tucked under a cap sporting a marijuana leaf appliqué, and he totes a beat-up skateboard under his arm. Smiling through brown, badly stained teeth, he points to my cart and asks what this peace pilgrim thing is all about. He thinks it's cool.

"So, you live here?" I ask.

"For now, yeah," the young man replies. "But, I'm gettin' ready to hit the road. A lot of people are doin' that these days."

"I know," I tell him. "I've met a bunch of them."

"Me an' some friends," he says, pointing to the trio of teenage ragamuffins shooting the bull on the opposite sidewalk, "those guys over there… We're probably goin' south."

"Well, I guess we're headed in opposite directions," I reply.

"Yeah," he says, cheerfully. "Well, good travels." As he lopes across the highway after his comrades, I can't help but wonder what will become of this lad and his carefree posse. What kind of future could possibly await them out there in this *Land of the Lost*?

JULY 18 · DAY SEVENTY-NINE

Trekking toward the north end of Reedsport, I'm receiving a number of peace signs, smiles, and waves from passing travelers. Ahead, in the right lane of the highway, a stationary line of vehicles waits to cross the historic WPA bridge spanning the Umpqua River. A flagger holding a stop sign flips it around, and waves northbound traffic through. As I approach, it becomes evident that repair work is underway. I call out to the flagger: "How should I cross the bridge?"

With a friendly wave, she shouts out over the traffic and construction noise, "The left lane should be clear for you. Just go around the cones."

A strapping young worker in a hardhat and yellow vest sees me coming and scurries to make a lane for me on the bridge's cluttered sidewalk. I find it amazing that any laborer is this thoughtful. Still, I can't resist teasing, "You guys are in my way."

"I'm trying to clear a path for you," the considerate young man explains.

"What's that all about?" The voice is gruff, but friendly in tone. I turn to the source of the query: a beefy, hard-hatted fellow, 45-ish, peeking out from his perch, suspended from the outside of the concrete bridge wall.

My answer: "Well, I've been walking for more than seven hundred miles, to see if I could get people to be nice to each other. I think folks have been real mean lately, don't you?"

"Oh, yeah," the man says, "especially Mike," getting a dig in at Mr. Considerate. "That guy's meaner than hell!" The irony of this jibe is obvious.

"Being nice?" the considerate young laborer now identified as Mike effuses, "I'm all about that!" He's suddenly taken on the personality of a big, slobbering Labrador retriever. If he had a tail, it would be wagging. The smile on his boyish face is charmingly goofy and uninhibited. If I had a ball right now, I could throw it and Mike the yellow-vested Labrador boy would surely play fetch with delight. He galumphs over and extends his hand for me to shake. His grip is strong and sincere as he works my forearm like a pump handle. "I support your cause, Brother!" he exclaims.

There is nothing more beautiful and mesmerizing than light reflecting off water. Depending on the time of day, the relative clarity of the sky, the angle of the sun, or the fullness of the moon, whether the air is still, breezy, or blustery, the very same liquid surface will take on new and ever-changing character. Gazing out over any expanse of water, I invariable feel a calming awe, knowing that, over the eons of time, every split second presents its own unique, natural spectacle of mirrored light, a sparkling, kaleidoscopic vision, one that I alone witness from my own unique viewpoint, a sight never to be repeated in its exactness for all eternity.

I'm standing at the end of a long, creaky, wooden dock, transfixed by a July sunset dancing off the ripples of Lake Tehkenitch. My meditation on light and water is abbreviated, as a pickup pulls in and begins backing down the launch ramp parallel to the dock, aiming its boat trailer into the ripples at the lake's edge. After steering slightly off-angle, truck and trailer pull ahead to straighten out, and the driver sets the brake. A slender man in his mid-to-late-thirties pops out from the driver's side, while an older gent, 70 or more, jogs around the vehicle, climbs behind the wheel, and resumes backing up. "A little to the right, Dad," the younger man calls out. "That's it." With the son's coaching, the white-haired elder manages to slip the boat and trailer cleanly into the lake.

Another voice is heard, high-pitched, excited. "Great job,

Grandpa!" A boy of 11 or 12 appears from behind the truck, skips down the slope to the lakeside, picks up a stick and begins poking it down into the silt.

The boat, now bobbing in the lapping water, couldn't be more basic: a simple, unpainted, aluminum hull with a 10-horsepower trolling motor bolted to its stern. The younger man begins gathering fishing gear — poles, tackle box, landing net, etc. — from the truck bed. "You gonna gimme a hand, son?" The boy winds up and hurls his stick like a boomerang out onto the lake. "Be careful," his dad chastises. "You might have hit the man."

"The man" to which he's referring is me. Suddenly, I realize I've been standing here in the last light of day, gaping at this wholesome scene as if I were in my own living room watching a television reality show.

"I'm fine," I reassure the boy's dad. This tableau, I'm thinking, would make for a reality show of genuine substance. My heart is warmed to observe a father teaching his son the same lessons his father once taught him, watching adult and child sharing a timeless bonding experience, one the youngster will likely remember for the rest of his life, and a tradition he might someday pass along to his own offspring. Who knows how many generations of this family have enjoyed this same rite of passage? At least three.

As the grandfather, his son, and his son's son putt-putt out across the steel-grey wavelets in the twilight, a vivid memory plays out in my head: My dad at 33, me at 11, drifting in a similar no-frills, aluminum boat, casting our lines out onto the sparkling surface of one of the thousand lakes of Eastern Washington State.

JULY 19 · DAY EIGHTY

Her name, she informs me, is Rapunzel. "You don't meet many of those," I jest.

"Oh, you'd be surprised," she responds, with a slightly flirtatious smile. "There are more of us than you may think." This woman's fairytale moniker is not her only unique feature. Wearing a plaid, flannel cowboy shirt, replete with metal-snap buttons, a paisley kerchief around her neck, her long, grey hair woven neatly into a French braid, and black, western-cut trousers with sky-blue piping down the outside seam of each leg, this Rapunzel looks to be striving for a senior-citizen Dale Evans-style statement.

Upon my entrance to this white, wood-framed cottage, a short, chunky woman poked her pie-shaped face out of an office. "Can I help you?" she inquired sweetly. This being the Visitor Information Center for Dunes City, Oregon, and me being a visitor in search of information, I responded that I sure hoped she could, which motivated her to rise from her office chair and lumber over to the counter.

"Where," I inquired, "might I find the nearest market or restaurant?"

A sheepish, somewhat apologetic expression came over the woman's ovular visage. "Well," she explained, "we're small." She extended the "a" and the "l's" in her elocution of the word small for emphasis. However, this detail had already become obvious. So far, this visitor had gleaned exactly zero worthwhile information. The hefty lady then proceeded to rattle off directions to Darling's Resort: "Go back to 101, to the next street, which is Clear Lake. Take a right. Then you come to a loop, which goes down to the lake...."

"How far is it?" I ask.

"Well, not so far by car," she figures. "But, if you're walking..." A grimace-like smile says she wouldn't be too enthused about making the schlep.

"Well, I've already walked seven hundred and fifty miles," I inform her. "I think I can make it."

This is when the woman soon to be identified as Rapunzel appears — from where, I know not. "It's at mile marker two-seven-en-six," the grey-haired cowgirl interjects, eyeing me with evident interest. "You'll like the people at Darling's," she says. "They're real nice. They've got a pub and a store and a restaurant, right there on the lake."

With my blood sugar crashing, this sounded ideal to me.

"You want some water?" the sweet, pie-faced woman asks eagerly, delighted to have thought of something tangible to offer me. "I can give you some water."

At first I decline — Say yes, I remind myself, always say *yes* — then changed my mind. The heavy-set woman bustles off and out of the room to fulfill her offer.

"So," the rodeo queen grills me, "what's all this seven-hundred-fifty miles of walking about?" I fill her in on my trek. She remarks dreamily, "You know, I've been thinking about doing something like that. But I haven't been able to set aside the time."

I've heard various versions of this from a handful of friends, expressing some level of envy that I've managed to rally my resources and carve out the months to tackle such an ambitious endeavor.

"After I told a few people," I confess, "I had to go through with it." At this point, I ask the woman her name. And, now, I'm standing here, intrigued by her Grimm-Brothers tag.

"Well, I admire you for your commitment," Rapunzel says sincerely, "and for stickin' to your guns. How far you plannin' to walk?"

The newly adjusted plan, I inform her, is to end my pilgrimage on its ninetieth day, a week from this Friday, on the final afternoon of Peace Village in Lincoln City.

Sweet, pie-faced woman re-enters, a cold bottle of water gripped in her stout fingers. I thank her. She shuffles off to resume whatever she'd been doing earlier in her office, leaving the peace pilgrim and the Dale Evans lookalike named Rapunzel to bid one another *happy trails.*

☮ ☮ ☮ ☮ ☮

The hike-and-bike campground at Jesse M. Honeyman Memorial State Park is unlike any I've visited thus far. All the campsites surround a common area, where two extra-long picnic tables have been pushed together end-to-end next to the industrial-sized, sunken, metal barrel that serves as a shared fire pit. I take an immediate liking to this wagon-wheel layout, as it should facilitate more communal interaction between campers. *Perhaps,* I'm hoping, *a hootenanny is in the offing.*

After setting up my site, I'm eager to cleanse my tainted skin of the residual bug spray necessitated by last night's mosquito attack at Tehkenitch Landing. I'm about to head for the showers, when a trio of hikers tromps noisily into the area. After stowing their gear at the site next door, they immediately break out chilled cans of Rolling Rock. Carol, from Snohomish, Washington, is on a family trek with her son Reece (25) and daughter Hailey (18). Reece is pretty enough to be a Calvin Klein model, yet rugged, with shoulder-length black hair. Under his overgrown, unkempt beard, a boyish face is affixed in a constant smile. Equally pretty, but beardless, with matching long, dark hair, Hailey appears to be more serious and introverted than her elder sibling. Not partaking in the beer, she's intent on reading her Jane Austin book. Mother Carol bears a distinct resemblance to the actress Francis McDormand, and her raspy voice projects well enough to be audible to every squirrel in a mile-wide radius.

While a shower was exactly what the doc ordered, I'm limping and wincing as I reenter the hike-and-bike. Carol sits at one of the long, communal picnic tables, blowing up an elaborate camping mattress. Panting and red-faced, she inquires, "How'd it go?"

"Great," I respond, "except for stubbing my toe on a (bleeping) root." Climbing the trail, my long-suffering right foot collided violently with a protruding tree root — for a second time! "And, it had to be the foot with the missing toe nail!"

"Well, that would be just about *all* of *my* toes," Carol laughs. After some commiseration about foot pain and remedies, I fetch my guitar and a Coors, sit atop the communal table and begin finger-picking some improvised blues. "Music at a hiker-biker," Carol remarks, cheerfully. "I *like* it!"

After drifting off for a while into my own musical trance, I open my eyes to discover someone else at the table. With long, thick, white hair flowing past his shoulders and a snowy, mountain-man beard, the dude bears a strong resemblance to Leon Russell — and, not when the famed musician was tickling the 88s with Mad Dogs and Englishmen; more like I imagine Russell must have looked lying in his coffin on the day of his funeral. He finishes hand-rolling a cigarette and offers it to me. When I decline, he fires it up himself. Noticing the large bandages on his forehead, I state the obvious: "You seem to have a head wound."

"Don't worry about it," he says. "It's healing." His name, he informs us is Sky. I ask Sky how long he's been here. With a Maharishi grin, he extends his arms out and forward in a gesture reminiscent of an operatic tenor building to a high B flat. "Forever," he announces.

"No," I say, as if I my original question needs clarification, "I mean, how long have you been at this campground?" Sky simply shrugs in mute condescension, as if to suggest that my query isn't worth the breath it would take to answer. Perhaps, I'm thinking, a different question might yield a more affable response. "How did you get here?"

"Oh, I just float from place to place," he says. A glance in Carol's direction suggests that she and I are sharing a mutual, unspoken skepticism about Sky's relationship with reality.

By this point, a cycling couple from Vancouver B.C. has begun busily setting up their campsite. Taking a quick census in my head, I quip, "So, we have five hikers, two bikers, and one floater." Carol finds this hilarious, and Sky, the floater, seems delighted to have been placed in his own category.

I begin vamping in 6/8 time on an open "G" chord, and segue into a slow-building, whisper-to-a-wail version of my ode to Sebra, "It All Goes Away." I finish off the song to the sound of two hands clapping (Carol's).

"Nice," Sky remarks. "Original?"

I affirm that, yes, I authored the piece.

He reaches out for my guitar. "May I?" he asks.

I begin to hand my little six-string to him. Then I remember something I learned years ago from legendary L.A. session guitarist/ hit producer Jay Graydon. "You just smoked a cigarette, right?" I ask. Sky nods. I withdraw the guitar. "Well, then, no. Your fingers will deaden the strings."

He puffs something about being able to wash his hands.

"The tar comes through your pores," I insist. "I don't wanna be an asshole, but these strings have gotta last at least two more weeks. And, this," I say, cradling my parlor-shaped Seagull acoustic, "is my baby."

"Well, I've got a baby of my own," Sky boasts haughtily.

While I'm relieved to hear this bit of information, I'm also curious as to what kind of far-out material we might be hearing from this odd fellow, should he deign to break out his "baby."

Meanwhile, the Canadian woman has begun blowing up an air mattress by stomping on a foot pump. "She's setting the rhythm," Carol observes.

"Well then, it's time for some mattress-pumping music," I say, kicking into a funk/blues riff in time with the lady's foot. This inspires Carol to flail into an uninhibited happy dance.

The Canadians, Bill and Jen share that they are taking this bike trip to celebrate their twentieth anniversary. Graciously, Jen tears open a bag of kettle chips and offers it to the table. We're crunching chips, sipping beer, and jabbering when another pair of bicyclists push their two-wheelers into the mix. The cycling couples quickly realize they've been traveling parallel southbound routes. There's a series of, "Didn't we see you guys at such and such a place..?" and, "Oh, that's right, you guys were the ones who..."

This collegial exchange naturally leads somebody to recall another shared experience — from earlier today. The bicyclists begin comparing hair-raising accounts of pedaling through a certain tunnel. Then, Reece one-ups them by recounting the trauma of passing through that same, long, dark, cement passageway with Mom and Sis on foot. Having traveled the stretch of 101 between Florence and Yachats many times, I'm familiar with the tunnel they describe — but only as a motorist. If surviving passage was this iffy for bike riders and backpackers, I can only imagine what kind of risk lies in store for a cart-pushing pilgrim. But, I'll save that worry for tomorrow. As the hike-and-bike population has reached 10, I'm thinking this shared evening would be substantially enhanced by a fire. I volunteer to head off in search of wood.

As the firewood shack is in the exact opposite corner of the 28-acre park, my errand turns out to be a great deal more strenuous than anticipated. I hoist two weighty, jagged-edged bundles onto my 67-year-old shoulders and tote them back to the hike-and-bike, in flip-flops, on sore feet and aching knees. The good news: I avoid a third toe-stubbing on my way up the path.

I'm getting the fire going. Sky plops down cross-legged in the dirt, guitar in lap, and begins strumming some surprisingly dulcet chords in an open tuning. "Come and join us," Carol invites the elfish musician. He insists he's quite all right where he is. "Are you connecting with the Earth?" Carol inquires.

"This isn't Earth," he corrects her, collecting a fistful of fine dirt and letting it run through his fingers. "This is stardust." He then begins crooning a meandering, raga-like melody on a subject he obviously knows a thing or two about… *sailing out into the galaxy.* Meanwhile, mosquitoes are sailing into *our* galaxy. Carol, Reece, and I gather around the fire pit, hoping the heat and light will keep the buzzing blood-suckers away.

Hailey peeks up momentarily from her book. I ask her what, as a recent high school grad now entering young adulthood, concerns her.

"Well, that's a big question," she ponders. "Of course, the environment."

I ask if her peers share those concerns.

"Well, some of them say, 'What can one person do?' But I say, lots! A person can tell another person about things. And, so on." Hailey says she doesn't hang out with anybody whose only goal is to make a lot of money any way they can. It's encouraging to observe that so many of today's youth are less materialistically motivated than previous generations, while expressing greater determination to do good and affect positive change. I only hope those values and that spirit survive when they're faced with the pragmatics of adulthood.

Carol pipes in. "You see, we come from a small town, with small-town values." I'm immediately intrigued as to what she means by small-town values. "Oh, you know," she explains, "neighbors helping neighbors, instead of depending on the government." Pretty conservative stance, I'm thinking. And, I'd tagged

Carol as a fellow progressive. Here is yet another reason to believe that Americans are more complex and nuanced than we may appear to be on the surface. Bob, my Trump-loving couch-surfing host in Brookings stays way out on the far right on most issues. Yet, he only eats organic food, advocates equal pay for women, and believes the U.S. should spend less on the military and more on infrastructure. Carol, who espouses a smaller, less intrusive government, champions protecting the environment and practices yoga.

CHAPTER 33
Tunnels, Truth, and Dragonflies

JULY 20 · DAY EIGHTY-ONE

Listening to last evening's campfire tales of *Terror in the Tunnel*, I did my Scarlett O'Hara bit, telling myself, *I'll think about that tomorrow.* Today, I'll take the *Gone-With-the-Wind* theme a step further, by accepting the kindness of a stranger. Stalwart, concerned friend that she is, Debbie Edwards has dispatched another friend to pick me up this afternoon in Florence to drive me over 25 miles of bad road and through the dreaded Cape Creek Tunnel.

I arrange to meet Debbie's friend in the parking lot of the Dollar Store. Robbie is affable, approximately my age and stature, with laughing eyes, and thinning hair pulled back in a scant pony-tail. His life's work has been primarily in equipping care facilities, especially for the disabled. While recapping his personal history, Robbie's compassion is evident, as is his enthusiasm for life.

I'm feeling enormously comforted to be riding in the passenger seat of this pickup. From where I sit, it's clear that pushing the Pilgrimmobile along this curly ribbon of road would have been unpleasant at best — not just for me, but for every passing, southbound motorist. In some spots, a pilgrim's mere presence might have caused catastrophe. Driving by Sea Lion Caves, I feel a twinge of nostalgia. My parents took me to this tourist attraction when I was a child. I continued that family tradition by returning here with my own daughter and son. I shudder to think, *could that really have been 30 years ago?*

We arrive at the place where, in 1931, a construction team

followed yet another Conde B. McCullough blueprint, drilling a massive hole through a steep, rocky, heavily forested outcropping, then lining the cavity with a sturdy archway of concrete. At more than 1,200 feet in length, it would take a cart-pushing pilgrim, at minimum, a full five minutes to pass through Cape Creek Tunnel. I don't even want to imagine the snarl of traffic and the snarls on the faces of the drivers, had I attempted passage on foot. The sustained honking now reverberating off the cement tube would not have been celebratory for me. I would surely have emerged from the tunnel's north end, not just with badly frazzled nerves, but having suffered substantial hearing loss to boot.

As we approach Heceta Head, Robbie fills me in on some local history. Yachats, he says, was originally envisioned as one of the first residential developments on the Central Oregon Coast. Gambling that the railroad's route from the Willamette Valley would end here, speculators purchased hundreds of acres of coastal land and portioned the property into lots. When the railroad settled on Toledo instead as its western terminus, those land grabbers were left high and dry.

> SUBSEQUENTLY, I LEARN that the land in question had previously been granted to local Native American tribes in a signed treaty. This part of the coast was deemed too remote and rugged for settlement, so white authorities figured "the savages" might as well keep it. As soon as whites thought the property might have some value, they tore up the agreement, laid claim to the land, and herded the natives onto inland reservations. Perhaps there was some heavy karma in the railroad's decision to make Toledo its terminus, instead of Yachats.

Before dropping me off, Robbie invites me to stay at his house tomorrow night in Seal Rock. This works out perfectly, as it will neatly divide the trek to Newport to visit my parents, my brother, and my dog, into two equal halves. After a parting hug, and some best wishes, kind-hearted Robbie leaves me by the side of the highway.

The little seaside town of Yachats is bustling with busy eateries and gift stores. However, while local merchants are enjoying the financial largess of the burgeoning tourist trade, and service jobs are plentiful, those who fill those positions find themselves challenged to find available, affordable places to live. Local scuttlebutt suggests the housing situation has gotten to such a crisis state, that a number of the servers and hotel housekeeping staffers are living in tents in the surrounding forests.

At the north end of town, I'm passing the entranceway to a private, gated, beachside community, when a small, compact car swings off the road, pulls into the driveway, and jerks to a stop. The woman at the wheel gestures emphatically, insistently. She wants to speak to me. Obediently, I park the Pilgrimmobile by the side of the highway, lock its wheels, and approach the idling car. The woman driver leans across the lap of the man in the passenger seat. "I met the original Peace Pilgrim," she exudes.

"Oh, my God!" I exclaim, one-upping her enthusiasm level. "You actually met her? She's my inspiration! That's amazing!"

"I gave her a ride," the woman says. This claim seems improbable. I'm immediately skeptical of its veracity. Peace Pilgrim almost never accepted rides. It was only in her later years, as her notoriety grew and she became an in-demand speaker that occasional automobile travel became necessary. After walking more than 30,000 miles on the roadways of North America, Mildred Lisette Norman, AKA Peace Pilgrim, was midway through her seventh cross-continental trek the day she met her sudden, unfortunate demise. A college student was giving her a lift to a scheduled engagement in Indiana when a drunk driver crossed over the center line. In a matter of minutes, a 28-year pilgrimage for peace was abruptly terminated. As the Fates prescribed it, this courageous, heroic woman perished — not while loping along the shoulder of some highway on threadbare sneakers, radiating that signature smile, but while riding passively in the passenger seat of a motor vehicle — from injuries suffered in a head-on collision.

As the driver of this compact car certainly can't be claiming to be the student who chauffeured Peace Pilgrim to her final reward,

I refrain from making a snide remark to that effect. Instead, I nod, maintain my smile, and continue listening. And, as she fills me in on the details, I am stunned. Providing backdrop to the tale, Karli informs me that she and her husband Steve — "Nice to meet you, Steve," I say, shaking the hand of the gentleman in the passenger seat — only recently moved to Yachats from Santa Cruz, California, where she once worked in production for a local television channel.

"Peace Pilgrim was at the station for an on-air interview," Karli recounts. "She said she needed to get to Los Gatos for her next appearance and I said, 'Well, it would be way too dangerous to walk on Highway Seventeen!' So, she let me give her a ride."

I'm standing here, jaw agape, knees wobbling, dumbstruck, astounded, flabbergasted. *This*, I'm thinking, *cannot be possible!*

"Oh! My! God!" I reiterate, this time in a stutter. "I was in Santa Cruz! In May. I needed to get to Sunnyvale. Everybody told me not to walk over Highway Seventeen! Fritz, my best friend from high school, gave me a ride!" Although Karli is already blown away by the serendipity of meeting a second Peace Pilgrim, I'm not sure she totally grasps how significant the information she's just shared is to the second Peace Pilgrim she just met. *I needed to hear this story!* The surprise revelation that, 40 years later, I had an almost identical experience as the woman who inspired my mission gives my pilgrimage even greater providence.

That I was walking this very stretch of highway on this very afternoon, pushing the Pilgrimmobile across the driveway of this gated community at the same moment Karli and Steve were pulling in can't merely be serendipity at work. Feeling certain that I've been scooped up into the hand of Destiny, my mind flashes back to the early morning of the twenty-second day of my trek…

Fritz Torp scoots his Honda Civic up the winding grade of Highway 17. I'm riding shotgun, keeping a tight grip on my dog's leash. The nervous beagle is curled up under my feet, trembling fearfully, droplets of hot saliva drooling from her panting tongue.

Millie has never been a particularly willing car traveler and the Mad-Max jogs of this road are making her natural anxiety that much more severe.

I am giving silent thanks that I've been spared from pushing the Pilgrimmobile up this incline. The pavement has no shoulder to speak of. It's 6:30 AM, not even rush hour, yet oncoming vehicles, one after another, careen around blind curves, as if sliding helter-skelter down some corkscrew flume ride. Brake lights suddenly ignite on the car ahead of us. Its rear wheels fishtail and the black smoke of burning rubber rises from skid marks on the asphalt. Rear-end collision narrowly avoided!

As I'd been warned, twice yesterday — first by a sales clerk in a Patagonia Outlet store, then by the man behind the wheel — the Highway 17 corridor offers more than enough risk for motor vehicles. A peace pilgrim trekking its shoulder would have been inviting disaster.

It seems incomprehensible that, four decades earlier, my namesake heeded an identical warning. She, too, rode shotgun in a motor vehicle — hers piloted by a young television production assistant named Karli — over that same perilous stretch of highway. And, if that wasn't mind-blowing enough, two months after being chauffeured to safety, I'm encountering that same production assistant, completely by chance, on the outskirts of Yachats, Oregon!

Karli fumbles several one-dollar-bills in my direction. "Here's a contribution to your cause," she says. I don't have a postcard handy, so I give her a CD instead.

I inhale deeply, exhale, allow an ear-to-ear smile to widen across my face, and watch Karli and Steve's little compact car pull away, down the driveway and into the gated neighborhood.

A brand-new pain has come for a visit. Could there be some symbolism here? I'm pushing my cart along the *left* shoulder of Highway 101 and *my* left shoulder goes into spasm. More likely, this is an old man's payback for last night's heroics — fetching two heavy, awkward bundles of firewood from the far corner of expansive Honeyman State Park to the hike-and-bike campground. Regardless of the source of this new irritation, it only compounds the fact that I'm growing weary, cranky, and simply want to get today's leg of the journey over and done with.

A lone bicycle appears over the horizon. Even from a distance, this cyclist doesn't look remotely typical — not long and lean, not tan, or exceptionally fit. He's swarthy, pale, with substantial love handles, and several day's growth of heavy, black, beard stubble. This rider looks less like Lance Armstrong and more like the guy you'd order a Rueben sandwich from at a Brooklyn delicatessen. By the furrow of his dark brow, and the squint of his eyes, it seems evident that he's straining to read the banner wrapped around my cart. He reaches out his right hand, offering a high five. I hold my right hand up, prepared to meet his. Our palms meet. Then, as he rides on, I hear him say, emphatically, "THANK YOU." In two succinct, sincere syllables, I'm hearing him express both appreciation and relief that, amid the constant sturm and drang, somebody is doing *something* to promote peace.

This simple expression of gratitude from a complete stranger hits me square in the heart. Perhaps it's because I'm coming so close to the end of my long, continually challenging, yet always amazing trek. Maybe it's the pain in my feet, or an accumulation of short and long term fatigue. Regardless, I'm vulnerable, unguarded, emotionally naked. Suddenly, spontaneously, I burst into tears. In seconds, I'm sobbing, blubbering, bawling — shoulders heaving, tears streaming down my face, nose running, vision bleary. I can feel my facial muscles involuntarily stretching and contorting. Here I am, a 67-year-old, grey-bearded puddle of goo in a bright-red T-shirt and a straw cowboy hat, pushing a cart on the shoulder of the highway in the light of day, very obviously weeping like a lost child.

I don't recognize these tears. Are they tears of grief or tears of joy? No, I realize these come from another wellspring altogether. These are tears of connection. In the split-second slap of one palm against another, this swarthy solo bicyclist has just acknowledged the sacrifice I've made during these 81 days. In the uttering of two short, snappy, earnest words, he has honored my ongoing efforts to encourage folks to lay down their defenses and communicate with respect and civility. A number of people — friends and strangers alike — have expressed their gratitude to me for taking on this quest. Until now, however, I hadn't quite been ready to fully accept their thanks. It took an anonymous stranger to get the message across. It's so rare when everything makes sense. Massaged by the heaving, and lubricated by the sobbing, the spasm in my shoulder has vanished.

JULY 21 · DAY EIGHTY-TWO

Hosting a strange man at her home is a genuine act of bravery for Robyn. "Everybody's chastising me for it," she confided last evening as I draped my still-damp tarp in her yard to dry. Although I understood the apprehension Robyn's girlfriends expressed about inviting an itinerate fellow to stay, it stung to think that I could possibly be the source of fear for any woman. "They say, 'You don't even know the man,'" she shared. "So, I told them, 'It looks like he's walking for a pretty good reason, so...'" No need to finish her statement — especially for me, of all people.

But, while Robyn recognized that this man has good reason for his 90-day pilgrimage, she, too, has good reason for distrusting all men. Newly divorced, she is still working to recover from trauma caused by years of abuse. As she confided her story, I realized that this stopover was not merely about a roof, four walls, and a bed. This visit held far more significance than that.

Had Robyn put 100 applicants through a stringent screening process, it would be difficult to believe she could have invited a more empathetic, compassionate person to be her first, post-divorce male houseguest. The longer I visited with Robyn, the more

I recognized the same festering, residual PTSD my beloved Sebra has been battling since long before she and I met three years ago.

Robyn's modest house hides behind a tall, wooden fence a mile's climb above Wakonda Beach. As she showed me inside, she immediately apologized for the still, stale, heavy atmosphere. Her fear of spiders, she explained, prevents her from opening windows. I was moved that my hostess felt compelled to set the dining room table formally. Over a hot, home-made, sit-down meal, Robyn tells me she's been focusing her energy on authoring a self-help book — subject: marriage — cleverly titled *I Do, But Why?* When I asked if she was planning to go out on a book tour to speak and read, her face went grey. It was clear she felt extreme trepidation over the idea of speaking in public. "That's your hook," I suggested. "Get up there and tell them just how frightened you are." Robyn smiled, amused by the irony of using her painful timidity as a marketing tool.

This morning, sitting in the kitchen, sipping tea, Robyn says she's deeply concerned about the truth — how rare it's become and how too few in this country seem genuinely interested in seeking it. I know exactly what she's saying. And yet, "truth" has always been a relative, subjective concept. That's why our language so frequently refers to truth in those terms. I wrote a song about it. I unpack my guitar and share it with her on the spot...

> *It's ugly and it's beautiful and it's awful*
> *It's cold, hard, naked, bitter, even gospel*
> *It's shocking, seldom kind, stranger than fiction*
> *It never changes, yet it's fraught with contradiction*
>
> *We hide from it, hunger for it, and pursue it*
> *Dance around it, reinvent it, wake up to it*
> *Lose sight of it, stretch it, skirt it, sugarcoat it*
> *Then admit it, face it, even claim to know it*
> *And that's the truth, that's the truth*
>
> *It's doled out in single grains and tiny kernels,*
> *Scribbled privately in diaries and journals*

How can something universal and conclusive
Be rare, concealed, subjective, and elusive
But, that's the truth, yes, that's the truth

Truth is no one ever really wants to hear it
Most will do most anything to not go near it
Then, of course, some crazy fool dares to announce it
Tells it, yells it, shouts about it, spouts it, outs it
That's when fan blades tend to hit the feces
And some people put their faith in Maharishis
Gurus, psychic readings, tea leaves, cryptic scriptures
Mediums and mushrooms, pills, and strange elixirs
In our endless quest to reach the summit
It seems we just keep getting further from the truth

The whole truth and nothing but, you gotta love it
When every gut is making up its version of it
They say you'll recognize it when you see it
Yet, sometimes, all we wanna do is flee it
And that's the truth, that's the truth
Truth is no one ever really wants to hear it
And that's the truth

— RAND BISHOP, © 2016
WEIGHTLESS CARGO MUSIC, BMI

It's hard to describe how gratifying it is for a songwriter when the listener really gets it, as Robyn so obviously does.

We hear voices tittering outside, followed by a brisk tapping on the sliding glass door. Two women are peering in through the glass. "Oh, those are my friends," Robyn explains. "I was planning to go on a hike with them this morning. But, since you're here…"

"Oh, you should go!" I protest. "I wish you'd just told me. I'd be on my way by now."

"No, no," she says, scooting across the den to open the door, "I really wanted to talk." As Robyn introduces her gal pals, they leer at me suspiciously as if I'm the three-legged man at the circus.

After finally coming to the conclusion that the wandering stranger poses no threat to their all-too-vulnerable friend, the two women sheepishly slip out into the fresh air to resume their hike.

This reminds me that the morning is quickly disappearing and I, too, need to start putting one foot in front of the other.

As I begin making myself at home, my host is poised at the top of a ladder, fussily re-positioning a dragonfly-shaped kite and the light bulb he's mounted behind its colorful, translucent-paper body. This inventive, makeshift lamp, suspended high in a corner, is to be my nightlight in this outdoor, pyramid-roofed, back-patio guest room. Everything in the backyard of the two-story house Robbie shares with his wife Barbara seems to be some sort of functional sculpture, from the furniture to the impressive, glass-enclosed fire pit. Robbie takes extra pride in one particular area he calls "the clamshell," an amphitheater-shaped mosaic wall, on which a long-tailed Chinese dragon, miscellaneous sea creatures, and symbols of peace and brotherhood are depicted in brightly colored tile.

"You might be wondering about the dragonflies," Robbie suggests. By now, we're sitting at a patio table, sipping beers. Robbie puts a flame to the bowl of a clay pipe and draws a deep toke into his lungs. A sharper perusal of the environs reveals that, sure enough, the nightlight in my room has plenty of pals. Every other object on the patio is in the shape of a dragonfly: an ashtray, a table-top lamp, a twisted-metal figurine mounted on a four-by-four support beam. "There's a story," Robbie confides, exhaling a lungful…

Earlier in their relationship, Robbie and Barbara lived in Northern California. One Saturday, after spending a glorious afternoon bobbing around in a remote eddy on the Klamath River, Robbie's car keys went missing. They were retracing their every movement, looking everywhere and finding nothing, when Barbara noticed a swarm of dragonflies hovering over the river at the very spot where, hours earlier, they had jumped onto their air mattresses. She pointed this out to Robbie. Thinking anything was worth a shot, he waded out chest deep to the dragonfly swarm and dove under. Amazingly, he came to the surface holding the keys in his hand.

Since that memorable day, the couple has felt a strong spiritual connection with these colorful, lace-winged insects. So, here we are, two guys drinking beer, sharing stories, surrounded by replicas of this spookily beautiful, blazingly swift, flying creature. Suddenly, I, too, feel the connection. The dragonfly symbolizes change and self-realization. And, as my pilgrimage nears its culmination, I know that my life and perspective will be forever altered. And, surely, I've gained deeper insight into who I am, what I'm capable of, and why I'm here.

Robbie's recollections, although fascinating, tend to be cryptic. His narrative bobs and weaves like a boxer who's taken too many punches. I wonder if it's the cannabis that sets his stream of consciousness meandering, or if he might have a touch of attention deficit. I notice a subtle tic as he speaks, a slight head-jerk accompanied by a quick, double blink of his dark brown eyes.

In the downstairs bathroom, I notice the special shower fixtures and an elaborate, high-tech toilet. An elevator chair has been installed on the staircase. I'm wondering if an infirm parent pays the occasional extended visit. Perhaps Robbie's wife, who is away on business, is disabled and requires these aids. I decide not to impose by asking.

Robbie begs off to watch TV, leaving me alone on the patio. I take my acoustic into the "clamshell" to indulge in some instrumental improvisation. The tile-lined mini-amphitheater augments and reverberates every delicate pluck and strum of the strings, super-powering the small-bodied guitar into a massive, vibrant, Earth-shaking instrument of the Gods.

CHAPTER 34

Rites of Passage

Building and adapting facilities for the disabled has been Robbie's life's work. So, if there were someone in his immediate sphere with special physical needs, it makes perfect sense that he would do everything within his power and expertise to make certain those needs were met. However, as I'm discovering, Robbie has not installed the stairlift, the handicapped shower stall, and the futuristic toilet in this house for a loved one. Robbie has done all of this for himself. As I sip my host's special-blend, super-food smoothie, Barbara reveals something about her beloved: Robbie is in the early stages of Parkinson's Disease.

Barbara, who evidently arrived home last night while I was slumbering under the patio pyramid, is among the warmest, most welcoming people I've ever met. And, it's clear that she and Robbie adore one another with unconditional devotion. The couple sees their future together through clear eyes. The house is paid for and they've set aside enough to supplement Social Security, allowing for a modest but adequate lifestyle into their waning years. That this couple has planned and prepared for their old age and Robbie's infirmity so thoughtfully and thoroughly is laudable. They are a living example from whom other American baby boomers, including Yours Truly, could learn much.

I'm wheeling the Pilgrimmobile, step-by-cautious-step, down the steep, gravel driveway. Robbie feels compelled to relay one final story before I depart. He describes officiating a Native American sage-burning ritual at the Oregon Country Fair. After the ceremony, an observer approached Robbie, remarking, "Man, I don't know what you did there, but it totally changed the energy."

As the intent of a sage ritual is to clear away old lingering negativity to make room for something new, something better to happen, Robbie felt satisfied that his smudging had been a success. Then, this guy, who Robbie had never met until that very moment, asked, "Will you come and do that for my wedding?" Amazingly, the fellow made good on his invitation, and flew Robbie from Oregon to Austin, Texas to repeat the smoky blessing prior to the nuptials.

With its series of graceful arches, the Yaquina Bay Bridge has been dubbed an Oregon architectural icon. Yet another depression-era Conde B. McCullough design, the structure extends 3,260 feet across the estuary of the Yaquina River at a peak height of 246 feet. The sidewalk is plenty wide enough to accommodate the Pilgrimmobile and, unlike so many prior spans, this one is not presently undergoing renovation or repair. The wind, however, is extremely stout, and its strength and velocity only increases as I climb higher and higher over the bay below.

By the time I reach the north end of the bridge, the brim of my straw cowboy hat is flapping against my forehead like a battlefield flag. But I'm smiling. For the first time since April 23rd , the day Millie and I drove out of this town, I'm home — if only for a day or two. I hang a hairpin left turn, pushing the Pilgrimmobile past a line of vehicles waiting to enter the highway. One car displays what, to a peace pilgrim, seems a fantastically creative and highly appropriate bumper sticker: the word "Out," but the "O" is a peace symbol. The *Peace-Out* driver and I acknowledge one another with a wave and a smile. "Hey!" he shouts. He's extending something in my direction, a contribution to my cause. A closer look reveals the gift in his hand is, of all things, a package of raw hamburger.

"No. No, thanks," I say, with a grateful but bemused smile.

"Really." He shrugs and withdraws his offering. Over the last 83 days, gracious, good-hearted, kind people have offered me cash, water, crackers, canned tuna, popsicles, pet food, fire starter, and essential oils. One friendly fellow attempted to foist a corn dog on me. Raw meat, however, is a first.

Mounting the front porch of my parents' duplex, I call out a shrill, falsetto, "Milleeeee... Millie-Mill!" I push the door open. There's my dog, all wiggle and wag. The unrestrained howling song of an overly excited beagle begins.

"You're no kid of mine," my father jokes. "You're too skinny!" I hug him. It's evident how genuinely relieved my chronically worried dad is to behold his firstborn son in the flesh, thinner to be sure, somewhat hobbled of foot, but otherwise in good health. Mom rises unsteadily from the couch. I take her shrinking body in my arms for a soft embrace. Then my heroic youngest brother Jayson gets a monster hug and a kiss on the lips. For the third consecutive year, my gifted, loving, truly Christian sibling, 13 years my junior, has sacrificed two months of his summer to cook and clean and look after Mom and Dad — and, this time around, he's had the extra responsibility of dealing with his big bro's rather ornery beagle.

Although I'm happy to be in the loving presence of family, I'm already feeling a hint of melancholy. I'm impatient, short-tempered with my parents and my dog. I've been concerned that depression might set in when my journey reached its conclusion. The simple, unfettered process of setting a daily goal, trekking from point A to point B, taking sustenance along the way, and bedding down at day's end has been the entirety of my life for long enough that my metabolism has gotten rewired. At the end of the trail, when I'm home again, ensconced in my comfy apartment, I wonder if I'll feel the same sense of purpose. If I'm not walking and pushing a cart hour after hour, day after day, where then will I find exhilaration?

JULY 24 · DAY EIGHTY-FIVE

Entering the community room at St. Stephens Episcopal Church, I'm greeted with broad smiles, exultations, and big hugs. These are some of my favorite people. The Peace Village Newport steering committee is made up of selfless volunteers who care enough to donate their valuable time, energy, and multiple talents year-round to planning an annual, week-long day camp — five days of teaching children the ways of non-violence, walking softly on Mother Earth, and the awareness to navigate this media-obsessed world. Our white-bearded treasurer, Earnie Bell, a soft-spoken, stoop-shouldered octogenarian with twinkling eyes, asks me how it feels to be home. I remind him that I still have four more days to go. Certainly, I've been looking forward to the culmination of my 90-day trek, being under my own roof, cooking in my own kitchen, and sleeping in my own bed. Still, with complete candor, I confess, "Honestly, Earnie, I wonder how I'm going to handle the mundanity."

I've noticed that, if I remain indoors for any length of time, I tend to become unsettled and edgy. Surrounded by walls, with a roof over head, I feel confined, trapped, suffocated. Two nights ago, I was much happier sitting in Robbie and Barbara's backyard patio than inside the house. Upon hearing me say this, our camp director Joyce remarks, "That's pretty common with the homeless." *Interesting.* And, it makes sense. If a person becomes accustomed to breathing cool, moving, fresh air and having nothing overhead but the infinite sky, a 12-by-12 room with a cottage-cheese ceiling feels like a jail cell, even if it does provide protection from the elements.

JULY 25 · DAY EIGHTY-SIX

As I push the Pilgrimmobile out of Depoe Bay, I feel that familiar charge of morning excitement and optimism coursing through my veins. This exultation, however, turns out to be short-lived. Across the highway, I spy something that immediately throws a pall over my spirits. Inside the window of a large, grey-shingled house, displayed strategically for all northbound traffic to see, is draped a large, cloth, flag — the Confederate banner under which soldiers from 13 colonies fought in their ultimately futile effort to separate from the Union. The bloody rebellion's purpose was to preserve southern states rights. And, the specific right they were most concerned about preserving was a white man's right to own and enslave human beings imported from Africa. Therefore, to this day, the Southern Cross remains a symbol, not only of a defiant, fiercely independent spirit, but of white dominion and superiority over people of color.

Oregon achieved statehood in 1859, two years before the Civil War began. Although the state constitution banned slavery, it is every Oregonian's shameful legacy that we are the only one of these United States ever to declare itself from the outset as "whites-only." Some 15 years before being officially accepted into the Union, all persons of African descent were ordered out of what was then called Oregon Country. Refusing to comply subjected the law-breaker to a lashing of "no less than twenty, and no more than thirty-nine stripes," to be repeated every six months until he or she vacated the territory. It was a crime in Oregon to be Negro or mulatto. Blacks were forbidden from owning land or businesses. Astoundingly, shamefully, these statutes were not removed from state law until 1922. Oregon also declined to ratify the 14th and 15th Amendments to the U.S. Constitution.

Although today, my home state prides itself as a bastion of liberalism, espousing inclusionary attitudes and policies, the lingering perception that this is a lily-white part of the country provides fertile ground for continued intolerance. Thus, the scourge of white supremacy pervades, evidenced by the flag I see in that window.

Coyote Rock RV Resort and Marina sits nestled in a magical nook on the north bank of the Siletz River. My lady and I have been enjoying a blissful reunion at the tent site I selected for its privacy. If not for the 80's rock blaring incessantly from a group of partying campers on the far side of the trees, Sebra and I wouldn't know there were any other human beings around. Still, we haven't let the bombastic imposition bother us. Instead, we laugh about it, join right in, and sing along. For me, enduring a double dose of Poison and Guns and Roses is small sacrifice to be alone under a canopy of evergreens with the woman I love.

It's after 10 PM, late in campground time. Sebra wants to take a shower. I decide it's best that I chaperone her. On the way, we trod across an unlit playground, no doubt constructed in the long-ago days of my own childhood. My flip-flop meets a metal horseshoe stake, sending me tumbling to the ground, my foot throbbing in pain. Even this potentially disastrous mishap becomes fodder for laughter. "This place is one booby-trap after another!" I joke, as I gather myself up from the ground to gimp on.

I'm escorting my now-squeaky-clean lady back to our wooded campsite. Ambling along, hand-in-hand, my eyes are once again assaulted by ugliness. The Confederate flag hanging in that Depoe Bay house had rubbed me wrong. This banner, in the window of a parked travel trailer, makes an even more deplorable statement. Glaring from the center of this Southern Cross is a skull, with daggers for eyes, its expression fixed in a maniacal, threatening smirk.

An extremely cynical remark slips out of my mouth, one, as an entitled white male, I have no right to utter, but can't mute: "*That* oughtta keep the (plural "n" word) away!" I expect Sebra to take offense. Instead, she gives my hand a jocular squeeze.

"It doesn't mean they're *all* bad," she remarks.

Certainly, the First Amendment protects this citizen's right to display the stars and bars with a glowering skull. And, admittedly, Sebra is absolutely correct. I have no justification for assuming that someone who would display such a symbol is "all bad." In my defense, I didn't, nor would I ever make that claim. I blurted the remark because of what this hideous flag announces to the world and the hate-filled warning it conveys: *Don't come around here, boy, or there's bound to be trouble. We don't want your kind around us, especially around our kids.*

Speaking of kids. There are several children's bicycles parked outside this trailer. Whomever so boldly displays this obscene banner evidently has no qualms about teaching the next generation that expressing blind hatred is not merely acceptable, it's the proper and moral way for all good, white, Christian Americans to behave. Had it not been for generations of fathers and mothers like these, teaching their sons and daughters to look down upon those who happen to have been born with different skin color, racism would no longer exist. And, while we so often commend ourselves for the positive progress we've made in race relations, inclusion, and equality, seeing this emblem of bigotry on display reminds me that we still have a very long way to go.

What that flag stands for *is* "all bad." And it offends me to my core. I can only imagine how deeply it must offend any person of color who has the misfortune of laying eyes upon it.

JULY 27 · DAY EIGHTY-EIGHT

As I guide the Pilgrimmobile down the steep, sloped drive-way, I'm beckoned by a pair of women sitting in a parked Honda SUV. The question, "How far are you walking?" has been asked of me countless times over the last 88 days. However, I'm relatively certain that the woman giving voice to this common query is the first person I've ever met named Turquoise. Her striking visage reveals that, in her younger days, she was spectacularly beautiful. And, even in advancing age, her innate beauty shines through. She nods as I fill her in on the details of my journey. Then, adopting the smile of a goddess, she places her hands together in prayer position and bows her head reverently.

"It's so important what you're doing," Turquoise opines. "It's us, the older generation, who are paying attention." She mimes poking at an invisible smart phone in her hand. "The younger ones are all focused on this."

"If you met our Peace Village kids," I advise her, "you'd have a lot more hope."

I'm here at the Devil's Lake Campground to join Sebra and several other dear friends — the core crew that has facilitated the Lincoln City Peace Village camp every summer for nearly two decades. Peace Village was the inspiration of Reverend Charles Busch. Alarmed about a serious bullying incident at the local junior high school, Charles assembled a confab of faith leaders, representatives from the Peace Studies Department of Pacific University, and the Native Youth Council of the Siletz Nation. Together, they brainstormed to design a curriculum to equip children with the tools of non-violent conflict resolution. Their inaugural weeklong day camp took place on the campus of the Congregational Church of Lincoln City in 1995. This week's camp marks PVLC's 22nd consecutive year at the same location.

Over the interim, the Peace Village program has been expanded to include environmental and media studies, mindful movement, and exercises in empathy. In addition to the Lincoln City flagship, 20 other camps — including Peace Village Newport, where I lead music and teach a class in media literacy — will ultimately take place over the course of this summer. I limited my pilgrimage to 90 days purposefully, so that I could meet my annual commitment to the Newport camp. In addition to my camp and steering committee volunteer work, I was privileged to serve on the board of directors of the non-profit corporation for three years. PVLC brought me together with my lady, Sebra, who has been leading the Lincoln City campers in song for more than 15 years.

"You're an angel," Turquoise flatters me, referring to my pilgrimage.

"No, no," I contend, "not even close. I just couldn't sit by while this country turned into something I didn't recognize." This gorgeous, wizened woman understands completely.

Elaine, the quieter one in the driver's seat finally speaks, revealing that both she and her friend Turquoise are in their eighties. "Well," I respond, "you look fantastic!" This compliment comes effortlessly and with absolute sincerity.

Turquoise beams her goddess smile, points to the sky, and affirms, "We're in touch with the light." *There is no question about that.*

JULY 28 · DAY EIGHTY-NINE

In almost every campground, the first bustlings of awakeness are similar: kindling crackling in a newly lit fire, the spout of an empty tea kettle bumping against the spigot of a water faucet, footsteps treading across dirt and gravel, coughs, yawns, clearing throats, and the low murmurings of conversation. It's early, just past 6AM. Sebra and I crawl out from our bed in the rear hatch of her Toyota Highlander into a fresh new day.

The women who make Lincoln City Peace Village run have been erecting their own temporary village here at Devil's Lake State Park for years. Thus, they've got the gears of their morning routine humming like a fine-tuned machine. Elizabeth "Lizzie" Wilson shares her tent, large enough for an Arabian prince, with her two, talented, smart, beautiful teenage daughters. Directly across the dirt lane, Lizzie's co-camp-director Wintry Whitt-Smith, is lodged with her two daughters, both a decade younger than Lizzie's, but equally as sharp and lovely. The kitchen boss is Stacy Renfro. She and her sister Christy are at the grill, taking breakfast orders with the proficiency of two gum-smacking career Waffle House waitresses. As the kids consume their morning fuel, I contribute a soundtrack to the organized mayhem with some improvisational finger picking on my acoustic.

As suddenly as it began, this squall of activity has passed. The dust has settled and the ruckus has faded. The kids and their moms are all off to camp. I fix a bowl of cereal for myself and contemplate the day ahead.

As far as I know, Lincoln City is the only Peace Village camp that offers rites of passage for its 12- and 13-year-old campers. For the last three summers, I have guided the boys through this life-changing experience. Tonight's rites, however, will be officiated by the man who conceived this tradition 15 years ago, custom-crafted its content, and conducted the ritual every summer until, due to his desire to move on to other pursuits, passed the awesome responsibility to me.

Darren Reilly was one of the early architects of the Peace Village curriculum and served as unpaid Executive Director during the burgeoning not-for-profit's formative years. I have enormous respect and affection for Darren. In turn, Darren seems to appreciate my often-edgy sense of humor and refusal to indulge in pretense or artifice. I think Darren likes me, too. And, let's face it, we tend to like people who like us. As my witty third ex-wife Stacey used to say, "The thing I like most about you is how much you like me."

I very much look forward to observing the formidable Mr. Reilly at work as he shepherds the boys through an all-night test of will and stamina.

A rite of passage is the symbolic gateway through which a person leaves one stage of life to enter another. It's also a community's way of acknowledging a significant change in that person's status. One of the most universally recognized rites of passage involves a child's transition to adulthood. I experienced a genuine rite of passage when, at 11, I took catechism classes toward having my relationship with the Holy Spirit confirmed by the Bishop of Eastern Washington State. My Episcopalian confirmation didn't come with the cultural import of a Jewish bar or bat mitzvah. Still, it did require months of significant study, culminating in a public ceremony. And, it changed my status in a very real way. I was, after all, henceforth permitted to kneel at the communion rail and partake of "the body and blood of Christ." This change in status made me feel very grown-up indeed. Especially since, the "blood" in the chalice at Spokane's St. John's Cathedral was real, thick, sour, red wine.

Aboriginal cultures all over the globe developed initiations to usher their progenies into adulthood. Many of these native rites required initiates to endure extreme pain and suffering. Darren Reilly's thumbnail prescription for an American child's coming of age is basically a condensed, hybrid version of the Native American vision quest. The vision quest is based upon a belief that every human being is placed on Earth for a specific spiritual purpose. Unless we are absolutely certain of our purpose, we cannot proceed through life with clear intent toward fulfilling our highest destinies. This makes the juncture between childhood and adulthood an ideal time for a person to discover their own identity and purpose, so they can proceed to make their own special contribution to the world. To gain this clarity, a young Native American is expected to sit naked in the wilderness, in silence, fasting, and meditating for four consecutive days and nights.

In vision-quest tradition, the Peace Village rites are led by elders at a remote place of the elders' choosing. And, the youthful participants are also expected to make significant, personal sacrifices. Over one single night, they remain alone, in or outside their tent, separate from their peers, refraining from speaking, eating, or drinking, and attempting to remain awake until sunrise. They pledge not to kill any living creature, even a mosquito, to pay close attention to anything they see, real or imagined, and to listen for any messages that might inform them of their life's purpose and/or identity. In the morning, when the silence is broken, these visions and messages can be shared. However, nothing revealed or observed during or after this long night's journey into day is to be repeated outside of this deeply bonded, fraternal circle.

From my first involvement, I've held this night to be sacrosanct. As Darren first described it to me, guiding these rites of passage presents an awesome opportunity to help boys on the cusp of maturation as they formulate their visions of what kind of men they intend to be. Under our tutelage, this night offers the boys a chance to meditate on how they plan to conduct their lives, how they see themselves treating one another — *especially* the females in their future — and how they imagine interacting with all of their relations, their communities, and this fragile planet.

When the initiates arrive at the ceremony site along the banks of the Salmon River, I will already have my bivy pitched. One final pilgrimage day awaits me tomorrow. I will need to have some energy left at the trail's end. So, I'm hoping tonight will not be as grueling, chilling, exhausting, or emotionally draining as previous years have been. I plan to get some sleep and keep warm. Not having to be the head honcho for tonight's goings-on reduces my stress level, especially when it's the man himself, Darren Reilly, taking charge.

☮ ☮ ☮ ☮ ☮

I find it curious, even a bit disingenuous, when a person born into one ethnic tradition assumes the trappings of another. Through the years, I've met several individuals, mostly white, who have totally immersed themselves in Native American culture. When a 60-year-old Caucasian woman, with feathers woven into her hair, introduces herself as Laughing Elk, I can't help but be somewhat amused — especially since, when I met her five years ago, she was Shirley, or Martha. If someone feels compelled to attend a sweat lodge, join a drum circle, or study shamanism, more power to them. Adopting indigenous culture, without having a drop of native blood, seems dubious.

Darren Reilly doesn't don the raiment, put on airs, or pretend to be someone he's not. Darren is still the white guy from a tough neighborhood in Arizona. However, he demonstrates substantial knowledge of, and reverence for, the sacred vision-quest tradition. With all the proper paraphernalia laid out on a teetering, make-shift altar — feathers, sage, cedar, tobacco, each item carrying its own symbolic import — Darren makes the experience absolutely wondrous for the boys. After weaving a hypnotic spell, he segues, quietly, in a near whisper, into a very personal confession, recalling his own youthful journey to tame an aggressive nature; how he grew into manhood, gradually learning that masculinity is not about physical strength, as much as strength of character.

When a boy has something personal to add, he takes a pinch of tobacco and sprinkles it into the flames, sending his expression into spirit. It's clear that the "young men," as Darren has begun to call them, understand how profound tonight's transformation can be — if they approach this trial with the proper seriousness. Darren has laid the table for a life-changing overnight these privileged lads will never forget. Before Darren sends them off to their tents, I ask for permission to say a few words, to share something I've emphasized to my initiates, year after year…

"This," I inform them, "is an experience not very many American kids get to have. Having these teachers, who care enough to give up a night of their lives; elders willing to suffer and sacrifice along with you, sharing wisdom they've gathered over the course of their lifetimes… it's a very special privilege. You will carry tonight with you for the rest of your lives. I really hope you appreciate that."

After responding to a few last questions, Darren gives final instructions to his charges. "Okay. It's time. From now on, until dawn, no more talking. No eating. No drinking. No killing of any living thing. Go!" Dogged by apprehension, yet stoked with excitement, filled with self-doubt, but as prepared for a vision quest as a soft, spoiled American 12-year-old could possibly be, six boys trundle off across the dewy grass, taking their first, symbolic steps toward manhood.

☮   ☮   ☮   ☮   ☮

"How can you say he's intelligent," Darren challenges me, "when he believes all that garbage?" At Darren's request, I've been sharing stories and reflections from my pilgrimage. Since the subject shifted to any- and everyone who voted for the current president, the tenor of the conversation has turned sour. Like so many of my hard-left-leaning friends, Darren believes that all Trump supporters must be mentally deficient. I'm trying to open his mind a little, by citing my interaction with Bob in Brookings.

"Well," I explain, "he attended an excellent college. Rutgers. He was accepted at M.I.T."

"But he doesn't believe in evolution!" Darren argues, making a solid point.

"True," I admit. "But just because a guy votes a certain way or believes some whacked-out crap, doesn't necessarily mean he's an idiot."

I hear some murmuring among the teen leaders.

"Well, why don't you ask him?" Ben whispers.

"Because, I'm embarrassed," Matt responds.

Two years ago, as a 13-year-old camper, Matt had been the only boy to successfully stay awake the entire night. He was an earnest kid then, and remains an earnest young man now. Ben, at 20, is married, and the most confident and mature of tonight's mentors.

"Matt wants to know if you'll play the guitar," says Ben.

As I sit here by the fire, guitar in lap, taking requests, I am reminded that every one of us has been blessed with a unique set of talents. Each individual has his or her own purpose in life. By acknowledging those innate skills, by nurturing and honing them, and passing our gifts forward, sharing them generously with the world, we honor the awesome, unfathomable, creative energy of the universe, each individual contributing a miniscule, yet critically important part to the grand, dynamic symphony of life.

CHAPTER 35

And So It Is

JULY 29 · DAY NINETY

Singing in unison and pounding drums, "the men" march across the meadow to join "the women" at their riverside encampment. The dawn fire circle reunites masculine with feminine for the first time since these young campers officially entered their ritualistic passage to adulthood. Lisa, lead elder in the female rites, asks the young men to look across the circle at the young women, to truly see their beauty and their strength. (At this very moment, a pretty young lady is simultaneously scratching her crotch and pulling her sweat pants out of her butt crack. *Ah, the awkwardness of adolescence!*)

Earlier in the week, in preparation for their rites of passage, each camper made his or her own prayer tie. In Native American spiritual tradition, a bundle of tobacco tied in yarn represents a person's loftiest intentions and, equally as important, everything they are grateful for. One-by-one, the young men and women approach the fire to drop their prayer tie into the flame. Dreams for the future combust, changing from solid form to vapor, drifting heavenward, and becoming one with all spirit.

Minutes always seem to travel at a glacial pace over a rites-of-passage night. The blanket of stars above may be wondrous and awe inspiring, but it provides no warmth. Yes, it's mid-summer. But this is the Oregon Coast, where the night air becomes saturated with a chilled dampness that permeates clothing and seeps into your bone marrow. Remaining awake takes every bit of self-discipline a person can muster. In past years, by the long-awaited arrival of dawn, I have begun post-rites Friday mornings feeling as vulnerable as a father beholding his newborn child for the first time. This fragility sneaks up on me and brings my rawest emotions bubbling to the surface, uncontained. A deep, emotional bond with these tender-yet-courageous boys combines with exhaustion and relief that a merciful dawn has brought the ordeal to an end. Perhaps because I've actually had some sleep, or because last night I was less teacher than auditor, or maybe because I've endured so many nights on hard, cold ground over the last three months, this morning, I feel far more composed. With some thoughts to share, I request permission to address the group…

"We live in a country that rewards its children for simply showing up," I begin, "by giving them 'participation trophies.' Quite honestly, this practice really rubs me the wrong way. I think children should learn what it's like to work hard, to make sacrifices in order to achieve excellence. They should know how it feels to fall short, to suffer defeat, because that's what the real world is all about. Children who are rewarded for simply participating, and who only engage in non-competitive games where no one wins and no one loses, those kids will not be prepared to enter the adult world, where competition is real and sometimes cutthroat.

"In this case, however, every one of you deserves commendation for showing up, for participating. There are no losers here this morning. You are *all* winners. Because, to willingly volunteer to face discomfort, to challenge yourselves to stay awake all night, to go without nourishment, while contemplating and visualizing your future? Well, that's something few people would choose to do. So, congratulations. I don't have trophies for you. If I did, every one of you would get one."

I feel as though my words must be flowing from some higher source. "This," I conclude, "is a country that seems to value greed and consumerism over love and gratitude. So, remember this, always… If you live in greed, always striving to acquire more things, you will never be fulfilled. If you live in gratitude for what you already have and for your every experience, you will always be fulfilled."

☮   ☮   ☮   ☮   ☮

The campers have departed to enjoy a very real reward: a well-earned pancake breakfast. I remain to break down my own camp and imbibe a little something to fuel my final day's walk: eight miles from here to the Congregational Church in Lincoln City. As I emerge from my parting stop at the porta-potty, there's Ron, the kind gentleman who has, for three consecutive summers, graciously donated this land on one Thursday night in July to facilitate rites of passage for the youth of Peace Village. He'd seen me arrive yesterday afternoon in advance of the campers. He wants to know what this Pilgrimmobile is all about. After filling him in on my pilgrimage, I say, "Basically, I just wanted to know if there were still nice people in the world."

"I'll bet you didn't find very many," he remarks. I immediately feel remorse for this elderly fellow, so pessimistic, so downbeat about the state of this nation. Yet, I recall that, last November, as the level of national rancor was reaching its apex, I could easily have leapt to a similar assumption.

Ron seems both surprised and pleased when I report, "No, my experience was quite the opposite." Then, I feel I need to qualify my report. "Not a hundred percent mind you. I'm not claiming I didn't encounter a few rotten apples along the way."

When I tell Ron about getting coal-rolled on the Smith River Bridge, he nods his head, knowingly. As a retired trucker, he knows exactly what I'm talking about. He expresses amazement that this hadn't happened to me more than once.

☮   ☮   ☮   ☮   ☮

The highway from Otis to Lincoln City poses some real challenges for a pedestrian, especially a pedestrian pushing a cart. Some blind corners have no shoulder or bike lane. As always, I'm confronted with oncoming cars, SUVs, dump trucks, semis, log trucks, massive RVs, and pickups pulling fifth-wheel travel trailers. Most take a wide swath around me. A few distracted motorists, however, meander across the white line onto the shoulder. When this happens, I halt in my tracks, as if a few extra steps would actually make the difference between close call and fatality. As an unaware driver swerves around me, I shake my head, emit another enormous sigh, and imagine the ironic headline: *Newport Man Meets Demise on Final Day of 90-Day Pilgrimage.*

As I've come ever closer to the end of the trail, my level of apprehension has spiked. It feels as though every day is one more toss of the dice and the likelihood they'll come up snake eyes increases with every roll. I'm relieved when I reach West Devils Lake Road, where I can steer away from hurried drivers racing frantically to get from place to place. I stop to eat my BLT, purchased yesterday at the Otis Café. Sitting on a stump, I contemplate. This is my last supper, my final meal by the side of the road. Feeling time pressure, I finish half of the sandwich, pack up, and get back on the road.

If my calculations are correct, I should have 10, maybe 15 minutes to rest before the ceremony begins.

I'm sitting on the curb on Oar Street, next to the parked Pilgrimmobile, checking email and Facebook on my iPhone. I receive a text from Sebra: *We are ready.* I take a deep breath, steady my wobbly legs under me, and begin pushing my cart up the paved driveway. As I make my way across the blacktop, I see 50-some children, all clad in their blue T-shirts embossed with the words, *Teach Peace.* Sebra and Gabe Busch are playing guitars. Campers, from six to 13, teen counselors, and teachers are singing in unison. Closer proximity allows me to make out the tune. Two summers back, I was inspired to compose a special song for the rites-of-passage initiates to sing following their long night's trial, on a day very much like today…

I am powerful enough to make a choice
I will always listen to my inner voice

And, with every choice I make, I'll be giving my life shape
I am powerful enough to choose empathy and love
I am power enough to make a choice

I am powerful enough to take a stand
I will never be untrue to who I am
And, with every passing day, my true
heart will lead the way
I am powerful enough to stand up for peace and love
I am powerful enough to take a stand

— RAND BISHOP, © 2015
WEIGHTLESS CARGO MUSIC, BMI

I wrote "Powerful Enough" as an affirmation in song, a hymn, not in supplication to an unseen God, but to summon up the God Force within. To hear a group of children sing this song, *my* song, with conviction, declaring their strength and resolve loudly and clearly always warms my heart. Every time a child sings about taking responsibility for the decisions he or she makes and the values he or she intends to stand for, the more resonant those truths become, and the more likely those truths will manifest throughout that child's life.

This rendition, at this time and place, however, takes on even greater meaning. Ninety days ago, I claimed my power and, for every day since, I've put that claim into action. I made my choice to embrace empathy and love, to stand up and walk for the possibility that humans can co-exist in peace. On May Day, with a smile on my face and a wide-open heart, I began putting one foot in front of the other, casting my fate to the wind, trusting that *my* choice, as foolhardy and illogical as it seemed to some, was the right one, and that it would ultimately result in something positive. I wrote this song for the children of Peace Village in declaration of their own self-empowerment. Here they are singing it to me in acknowledgement of mine. *How beautiful, how right, how very perfect is this?*

I am presented with a gift. In 1995, a bullying incident in a Lincoln City school inspired Charles Busch to convene the first weeklong Peace Village day camp at this location. In the intervening years, the children who attended that maiden camp have passed into adulthood. Eli is the son of one such young woman, who attended that first camp 22 years ago. The irresistibly adorable four-year-old emerges from the group, holding an elaborate, handmade token, woven out of yarn, feathers, and shiny beads. As I accept the honor, little Eli hugs me around my legs, inspiring a spontaneous, unison "*Awwwww!*"

"Does it fit?" Sebra shouts.

"Around my neck?" I ask. I'm not absolutely certain what I've just been given. She confirms that, yes, it goes around my neck. The trophy necklace hangs across my chest perfectly, which inspires more cheers and applause. I'm thinking, perhaps it's time for me to make some remarks…

"Well," I begin, haltingly, "I can't think of a more perfect way to end my ninety-day peace pilgrimage, than here in Lincoln City, on the last day of Peace Village."

A strawberry-blond-braided teen counselor shouts out, "Thank you for the work you do!"

"How does everybody feel about going inside and singing some songs?" I ask. The response is 100% enthusiasm. Counselors and teachers herd the campers into the church building.

☮   ☮   ☮   ☮   ☮

I'm standing, guitar strap slung over my shoulder, in front of a sea of faces: children sitting on the floor among teen counselors, teachers, teachers' kids, volunteers, and staff. I've kicked into autopilot, muscle memory from decades of performances.

"I'd like to start by showing you a song I've sung for children all up and down the west coast." I divide the room into four equal groups, teaching the "squirrels" to *chatter*, the "sparrows" to *chirp*, the "mice" to *squeak*, and the "bees" to *bzzzz*. When I point to a group, they make their animal sound, loudly, clearly, enthusiastically. For weeks, I've been imagining doing "Wild, Wild Party in the Loquat Tree" as a group participation number. It works exactly as I pictured… a big hit, a rousing success.

Next is a boisterous reprise of "Powerful Enough," followed by a sing-along on my medley arrangement of Bob Marley's "One Love" and Curtis Mayfield's "People Get Ready;" then, a break for Q&A…

"Did your feet hurt?" one little girl asks.

"Where did you sleep?" queries another.

One particularly pragmatic lad wants to know, "Where did the money come from so you could eat?" With questions asked and answered, we have 10 minutes to spare before the camp graduation ceremony is scheduled to begin.

"You wanna hear a song about sore feet?" I ask them. Of course, they do. "This is a very soft song," I say. "So, you'll have to stay very still while I sing it." As I pluck the placid intro to "Healin' Time," the room grows pin-drop quiet. I sing this tender, gospel-tinged original for 50 children, ages six to 13. Not a single one of them has ever heard it before. This is the fifth and final afternoon of Peace Village. Surely, these kids must be tired and restless. Still, they sit rapt, hardly making a peep. Only a couple of bodies even shift position. I am amazed that they would respond this way to such a slow-paced, sentimental, grown-up song.

For a finale, I launch into Lester Harrison's grinding, bluesy "Let's Work Together," inviting the kids to stand up, dance, and clap in time. By the song's end, the entire room is joining in on the refrain: "Together we will stand, every boy, girl, woman and man."

I sit in the vestibule with Sebra and the other musicians. Smiles abound from the shoulder-to-shoulder crowd in this packed chapel. Peace Village, we all know, is not just an ordinary day camp, meant to give little ones an active, healthy, energetic experience and, ultimately, wear them out physically. As Darren and Lisa acknowledge the teen leaders and the "young men and women" who bravely endured their rites of passage, parents in the pews seem fully aware how wise their decision was, to entrust their children to such enlightened mentors. Their kids have been given a rare opportunity to learn something about making peace in a very frightening, chaotic world.

Darren relays a truth that not only testifies to the value and importance of Peace Village, but resonates profoundly with my peace-pilgrimage experience as well: "We are living in a country where children often don't learn how to be adults, and where adults act childish. There is a big difference between acting childish and being childlike. A childlike nature is a good thing. It's about maintaining your innocence, being playful and light hearted. Childish people, on the other hand, only think about themselves. And, if they don't get their way, they pick fights. They drop bombs. Manliness, machismo is not what causes wars. Childishness causes wars."

No song emblemizes the Peace Village philosophy more succinctly than John Lennon's "Imagine." There are few dry eyes in the chapel as we all hold hands, sway to and fro, and sing the late Beatle's contemporary hymn, visualizing a future for our children of peace, justice, and equality.

Graduation is over, as is my pilgrimage. I'm circulating among the campers, their relatives, counselors, teachers, and staff. The atmosphere is ebullient, festive, and emotional. New friends and old friends trade compliments, expressions of thanks, and affectionate hugs. More tears flow.

Here is the manifestation of a bonding experience, the feeling of family and community that invariably results when a group of dedicated human beings has accomplished something as a team, at the completion of working together toward a common goal. This same phenomenon happens with the cast and crew on closing night of a play, or among athletes and coaches as another sport season comes to an end. I'm selling CDs on a whatever-you-can-afford basis, all of the proceeds going to Peace Village.

Lisa approaches me. Tearfully, she takes me by both hands and looks into my eyes. "When I saw you performing for the children," she says, "when I observed your joy, it moved me so deeply."

"Thank you, Lisa," I respond. "It's very kind of you to say that. It means a lot to me. Coming from you, especially."

But Lisa is not finished. She goes on to convey her absolute certainty that my pilgrimage has brought me to this perfect point in time, this important crux in my life, to share my talents, and to make the world a better, more peaceful place.

I will accept those sincerely, spontaneously expressed words graciously and humbly. I choose to believe she has spoken the truth. And, so it is.

THE END

Epilogue

☮ ☮ ☮

My landing was not a soft one. Battling insomnia and claustrophobia, feeling caged and stifled by the roof over my head, I was suffering a kind of cold-turkey withdrawal. Pushing my body to its limit day after day with hours of pounding, aerobic exertion had rendered me dependent upon a constant rush of the natural, stress-reducing chemical secretions that ward off anxiety and depression, boost self-esteem, and deepen sleep. I was an endorphin junkie, craving my daily fix, and I had no way of tapering my dose to ease the crash.

I came home with a story to tell — *this* story. I immediately delved into writing a book — *this* book — which meant sitting in a chair at the computer keyboard for hours every morning, seven days a week, before taking Millie on our jaunt on Nye Beach. These afternoon dog walks failed to substitute for the high to which I'd become addicted on those consecutive 12-, 15-, sometimes 18-mile days, pushing a weighty cart up grades and down, anticipating the unknown waiting around every next corner. And, my feet were still suffering debilitating physical trauma. So, there I was, in emotional and physical freefall, trying to remain productive and make progress on a memoir, while struggling to keep the toxic dogs of depression at bay.

It must have been difficult for Sebra. She had waited so patiently and faithfully for my return, for our life partnership to resume some rhythm of normalcy. Yet, I could only be partially present, and then only for brief periods of time. Instead of reuniting with her, heart-and-soul, I was often distant, unable to keep my mind from returning to solitary places. And worse, I failed to fully acknowledge the sacrifice she had made in giving me full permission to do something that not only left her alone, but caused her understandable angst. The magnificent reception I received at Lincoln City Peace Village was almost entirely due to Sebra's efforts. It was only months later that I fully recognized those efforts and got around to properly thanking my lady for making the culmination of my pilgrimage so very meaningful.

When I was finally able to sleep, I experienced "walking dreams." Always traveling solo, I'd be pushing my cart through a remote, wooded pathway, over a hillside, or through a small town. I don't know the exact significance of this continuing journey of the subconscious. Perhaps I left a piece of my soul out there, still searching for some, still-elusive, extended family circle where I fit in, where I matter and can make my most meaningful contribution.

With the season not yet halfway passed, the summer of 2017 had already made history for the severity of Oregon wildfires. By August twenty-first, smoke from the Chetco Bar blaze was blanketing the southwest corner of the state. As planned, Bob (the evolution-skeptic couch-surfing host) was visiting me in Newport to witness the total eclipse of the sun. Soon after experiencing this awesome, once-in-a-lifetime, celestial phenomenon, Bob jumped into his litter-filled Honda Civic, adorned with anti-abortion bumper stickers, and hurried southward on Highway 101 toward his home at the edge of a forest, just north of Brookings. Four days later, Oregon Governor Kate Brown was paying Bob's panicked community a visit. By then, the fire-breathing dragon from Chetco Bar had charred more than 100,000 acres and was coming dangerously close to the couch in that unfinished living room, where this peace pilgrim rested only seven weeks earlier. This massive, destructive burn began with a stroke of lightning in mid-July. The blaze, which ultimately engorged 190,000 acres, was not officially declared contained until the first week of November. Mercifully, Bob's neighborhood, his house, and that couch were spared.

Tragically, the same can't be said for the stately home in Santa

Rosa where I enjoyed such a meaningful reunion with Ardythe Brandon. Unlike the slow burn of the Chetco Bar blaze, the North Bay wildfires did their catastrophic work with haste. October eighth and ninth amounted to 48 hours of Hell on Earth for wide swaths of Napa and Sonoma Counties, as four massive, raging infernos roared in with the efficiency of a quadruple carpet bombing. Fortunately for the Brandons, they had sold their house in July. Still, I can only imagine the grief Ardythe and Tom must feel, knowing that 25 years of family memories went up in smoke.

Not a single building I passed along Old Redwood Highway through Wikiup and Larkfield were left standing after the Tubbs fire torched 5,500 homes and businesses, while wasting 22 human lives. In the wake of that horrific devastation, Sebra's sister Alice Bailey demonstrated the purest form of Christian charity, by volunteering countless hours to the suffocating, backbreaking labor of sifting ashes in the decimated neighborhood of Coffey Park.

As the year drew to a close, it seemed as if one blaze after another was spookily reenacting my pilgrimage in reverse. By December tenth, whipped by ruthless, bone-dry Santa Ana winds, the monstrous Thomas Fire was pushing toward the very roads I traipsed through Carpenteria, Montecito, and Santa Barbara. Ultimately, this gargantuan conflagration consumed more than 280,000 acres and left 1,100 buildings destroyed.

But, even after it had been quelled, the Thomas Fire had yet more damage to do. On January 9, 2018, after days of torrential rain, the stripped Earth gave way, causing debris flows in several parts of Santa Barbara and Los Angeles counties. Worst hit was Montecito. I winced, listening to a woman's account on NPR of how, while surveying the devastation the morning after, she came upon her neighbor's lifeless arm protruding from a glacier of mud. I was stunned to see a live, network television news report, broadcast from the cobblestones over which Millie and I trekked on that first week in May. The very gas station parking lot where I purchased a box of sweet cherries from a farm stand was buried in a thick layer of heavy, wet, dark-brown muck. Twenty-two more lives were lost in this tragedy.

I was merely a pilgrim, a vagabond. Still, I can't help but feel a powerful affinity with the residents of those stricken communities, having paid their towns a brief, transient visit before my picture-postcard memories were reduced to ashes and mud.

In truth, the atmosphere of this entire nation is incendiary and the destruction immeasurable. However, in this metaphorical wildfire, we can't claim to be victims of natural disaster. We are in the throes of a cataclysm of our own making. The structures being threatened by this raging blaze of vitriol are the fundamental institutions of democracy. The United States of America is faced with a litany of very real, extremely urgent problems. Our Constitution grants us the freedom to participate in the solving of those problems as we see fit. Exercising that freedom constructively, respectfully is difficult. It demands patience and humility and requires us to pay attention to those with whom we disagree. Conversely, bunkering down with those of like mind doesn't ask us to listen, or consider alternative ideas, or even to think. Lobbing word grenades at our perceived enemies rewards us with an immediate payback, a delicious, cathartic, sugar rush. Forget about solving problems. Playing the blame game abrogates our responsibility as citizens, by kicking the can down the road, allowing all those very real, extremely urgent problems to fester and worsen, while we the people grow more entrenched and even more divided.

Those who reap the greatest benefit from the resulting paralysis — party leaders, greedy billionaires, lobbyists, and self-serving, egomaniacal, media personalities — continue to fan the flames. Keeping the tribes at war enables them to hold power, maintain control, and carve off ever-larger slices of the pie for themselves. Hostile foreign governments pitch in, too, stoking the coals, surreptitiously seeding distrust in our democratic institutions, while further egging Americans on against Americans. If they can keep us bickering among ourselves, they know we'll be too weak to face our common adversaries. Sadly, we make it so easy for them.

I am reminded of that banner hanging outside a Ukiah, California, elementary school — the one that spelled out a once-treasured axiom: *Character Always Counts*. If winning at any cost is our only goal, how does character factor into the equation? Today, victory is too often achieved by defining one's opponent and everyone who would support him as the enemy, and staying on the attack, not with any plan to improve people's lives, but with every intent of smearing, defaming, and ultimately crushing the evil opposition. While every election is hyped as "white hat vs. black hat," the contenders are often so caked in mud by the time the votes are tallied, you can't tell one from the other. As long as the tribal creed is *Us-Good! Them-Bad!* this nationwide maelstrom will rage on, and the quaint concept of character will count less and less. Even if we somehow manage to extinguish the blaze, if and when the rains come, and if any common ground remains, it may be too unstable to hold.

On the precipice of civil war, President Lincoln sagely warned, "A house divided against itself cannot stand." Our house is not just divided. It's on fire. Too many of us, I'm afraid, are turning to the arsonists to save the day, when we should be joining the bucket brigade.

Yet, I haven't abandoned all hope. Or, perhaps, hope hasn't abandoned me. If there is any upside in the current crisis, it's that so many heretofore passive, apathetic Americans have awakened to activism. We inherited a precious gift from the founding fathers. It's called democracy. At its inception, this inspired design was first a blueprint, then a test model and, finally, a working prototype. Now, with more than two centuries of rough, stormy seas under its hull, this aging galleon requires constant maintenance to keep it seaworthy and skirting past the icebergs.

However, beware. There's real danger in assuming that protest is enough. Protest is about what we don't want, what we can't live with, the policies and attitudes we want to put an end to. But, with our protestations, we're also placing all the blame for what we object to on someone else. I don't recall ever seeing a march with folks waving signs about how we all need to take more responsibility for this awful mess we're in. (That might make for a humorous cartoon.)

So, in addition to decrying what we don't want, we also need to be equally clear about what we do want, what we're willing to stand up for and work to achieve. We'll need to agree on the change we want, and decide together how to go about making that change happen. Yes, it's exhilarating to link arms with one's sisters and brothers in a mass display of resolve and solidarity. But, while everybody always walks away all revved up, unless there's a plan in place to direct that energy into constructive action, all that positive inspiration could very quickly and easily dissipate, leaving even more widespread, deeper disillusionment in its aftermath.

It's possible that true and lasting change doesn't only take root in the streets or ballot boxes, but also over backyard fences, on front porches, at church socials, and PTA meetings, places and circumstances where people have an opportunity to relate to one another, not as members of political parties or as advocates for a cause, but as concerned parents, neighbors, and community members.

☮ ☮ ☮ ☮ ☮

Since childhood, I've imagined myself achieving greatness, accomplishing something significant and meaningful. Early on, I was primarily driven by a lust for fame and fortune. Now, however, this undying urge is no longer all about ego or ambition. It's more about answering the call, using my unique gifts to make a positive difference in the world. Too, it's about making up for all the years I squandered, struggling to draw attention to myself for all the wrong reasons.

When people ask, as they often do, if I'll ever do it again, my response is always a quick and decisive "No!" Once I decided to take on my trek, I had to see it through. Backing out, or giving up prematurely would have left me feeling woefully unfulfilled and disingenuous. Blind trust that, at 67, I was capable of walking from Southern California to the Central Oregon Coast in 90 days put my feet in motion. Watching the miles melt away, realizing measurable forward progress at the end of each day kept me going.

Considering my age, I returned home relatively unscathed.

Thanks to my stalwart posse of angels, I managed to escape serious accident, injury, or exposure. Mercifully, I never got myself hopelessly lost, nor did I experience unbearable fear. At trek's end, I was in the best physical condition of my entire life. But the wear and tear on my body was real and substantial. So, no, I'll not take on another 90-day, 900-mile trek.

On the other hand, do I harbor a single pang of regret? Once again, a quick, unequivocal, "No!" To which, I'll add, "Never! Not even for a split second!" My pilgrimage turned out to be an adventure of a lifetime. Following through with this impulsive, risky, seemingly illogical scheme forced me to drill down deep for untapped strength and resilience. For those reasons alone, I will always look back at this accomplishment with a certain measure of pride.

Still, by far, the greatest fulfillment from trekking those 900 miles came with the extraordinary opportunity to connect with a thousand decent Americans. In fleeting moments, over the course of hours, or across the expanse of days, those encounters rekindled my faith, not in the power and glory of some invisible God, but in the innate goodness of humankind. The nice, kind, sometimes exceedingly generous people I met along my pilgrimage path replenished the hope I'd lost and so desperately needed to find and feel again. And, without that hope, I don't know if I would still be capable of rising and shining every morning.

No, my friends, I wouldn't do it again. But, I'm sure glad I did it once.

Acknowledgements

☮   ☮   ☮

I could not have accomplished this quest without the aid and encouragement of the following friends. For their demonstrations of support, I will be grateful till I take my very last breath.

Angels First Class: *Theo and Kelly Bishop, Gary Lahman and Cynthia Jacobi, Karl Hoffheinz and Monica Rizzo Lopez, Wendy Hunter, Debbie Edwards, Brian and Carol Barnes, Melanie and James Weber, Alice and Tom Bailey, Ardythe and Tom Brandon, Kristi Humphrey Ryder, Jayson Bishop, and of course, Sebra Oden.*

Angels Above and Beyond: *Daniel DeMento, Jean Shank, Dana Worsnop, Franki-Trujillo Dalbey, Bill Dalbey, Steve Love, Paula Williams, Loren Cannon, Robyn Annala, Robbie Alvord, Duane DeVries, Dove Joans, Dede Amescua, Marty Harris, Mike Kloeck, J.P. at UUSSB.*

Angel Financial Supporters: *Daniel Davis, Jim Wilson, Tamara Berg, Emily Sudd, Daniel Portis-Cathers, Wintry Whitt-Smith, Nolle Rainbow, Charles Busch, Rhonda Harmon, Jeanne St. John, Elizabeth Jones, Karen Schmidt, Gerald Dewan, Sandi Hanna, Greg Lindsey, Corey Becker, Janet Johnson, Tony Goiburn, Bruce Venezia, Jane Leher, Earnie Bell, Sharon and Larry, Connie and John Kiger, Dave Isaacs, Dana Heald, Graham Bishop, David Goggin, Amanda McBroom and George Ball, Danny Simon, Tim Stull, David Black, Lisa-Catherine Cohen, Paddy O'Brien, Joseph Visaggi, Lin Schubert, Vann Slater, Jeffrey Cohen, Corinne Broskette, Marty Cranswick, Sandy Berg, Audrey Wells, Trish Steel, CM Hall, Dan Mahoney, American Songwriter Magazine, Annie Bishop, Carlie Schmidt, Marsha Stewart, Evans Longshore, Therese Price.*